CW01237421

365 days with **Spurgeon**

Volume 6

A further collection of daily
readings from sermons preached by
Charles Haddon Spurgeon
from his Metropolitan Tabernacle Pulpit

Selected and arranged by
Terence Peter Crosby

Day One

© Day One Publications 2011
First printed 2011

ISBN 978-1-84625-278-5

Unless otherwise stated, all Scripture quotations are from
the Authorised Version Crown Copyright

British Library Cataloguing in Publication Data available

Published by Day One Publications
Ryelands Road, Leominster, HR6 8NZ
☎ 01568 613 740 FAX 01568 611 473
email—sales@dayone.co.uk
web site—www.dayone.co.uk
North American—e-mail—sales@dayonebookstore.com
North American web site—www.dayonebookstore.com

All rights reserved
No part of this publication may be reproduced, or stored in a retrieval system, or transmitted, in any form or by any means, mechanical, electronic, photocopying, recording or otherwise, without the prior permission of Day One Publications.

Chief Sub-Editor: Mrs Trudy Kinloch
Designed by Steve Devane and printed by ScandBook AB

Dedication

To Pastor Alan Stephens,

former minister of

East Hill Baptist Church, Wandsworth,

the very first of the many 'Baptist causes'

Spurgeon was instrumental in starting

INTRODUCTION

Commencing on the very first day of 1885, this sixth and final volume of *365 Days with Spurgeon* covers the sermons published during the last six and a half years of his ministry. This turned out to be one of the most distressing and difficult periods of his whole life.

Illness was never very far away. After preaching on New Year's Day and the following Sunday morning, Spurgeon was absent from his pulpit until 12 April 1885, the greater part of that time being spent at Mentone, his annual retreat in the South of France. In the meantime many of his evening sermons from 1884 (already featured in volume 5 of this series) were published in the absence of new sermons.

Spurgeon continued to winter at Mentone each year either due to sickness or in an attempt to avoid it. A multitude of sick notes are appended to the sermons published during these years (nos. 1875–6, 1881, 1900, 1931–2, 1937–40, 1942, 1987, 1991–4, 1997–8, 2052–3, 2055–8, 2061–4, 2067–71, 2117–20, 2122, 2125, 2127, 2174–8, 2182–4, 2186–7, 2207). One of these, written on 3 January 1889, reported a fall down a marble staircase at Mentone resulting in the loss of two teeth and a bruised knee.

After 1884 Spurgeon never again preached at the Metropolitan Tabernacle during the month of December, with the result that the last month of this volume (including the end-of-year sequence) consists entirely of undated sermons apart from a short Christmas series constructed from surplus sermons preached in September on texts appropriate to Christmas. In contrast, from 1886 to 1891 Spurgeon always made a point of preaching a specific Easter Sunday morning sermon on the theme of the resurrection, something which he had rarely done during the 1870s. In 1891 he preached what appears to be his only sermon specifically related to Palm Sunday (no. 2196).

These years were difficult for other reasons. Spurgeon and his faithful

Charles Haddon Spurgeon
in 1890

stand for Biblical truth were shamefully vilified in what became known as the Downgrade Controversy. Then in September 1890, some sixteen months before his own death, the Spurgeons were grieving over the death of a baby grandson. The last few weeks of his ministry were particularly trying. No. 2203, the sermon intended for the evening of 26 April 1891, had to be postponed until the following Sunday morning due to Spurgeon being forced out of the pulpit by an attack of overpowering nervousness. On 17 May he was again too sick to preach in the evening and was then absent until the morning of 7 June when he preached what was to be his final sermon in London (no. 2208).

Thereafter reports of the progress of his long, final illness were appended to nos. 2211–40. Spurgeon was moved to France in October and enjoyed some measure of recovery at Mentone where he gave two brief addresses on New Year's Eve 1891 and New Year's Day 1892 (both published in *The Sword and the Trowel* in February 1892 under the title 'Breaking the long silence'). His sudden final relapse and consequent death on 31 January 1892 was announced in no. 2242 and on 11 February 1892 he was buried at Norwood Cemetery amidst an enormous throng of mourners. The first sermon for circulation in 1892 (no. 2237) had been specially selected and prepared by Spurgeon; the first part of its text, 'I shall not die, but live, and declare the works of the LORD' (Psalm 118:17) was fulfilled not literally but, more in keeping with Hebrews 11:4, by the continued weekly publication of his sermons for another quarter of a century.

Those familiar with previous volumes of *365 Days with Spurgeon* will be familiar with the ground rules adopted for this series, which are as follows. The majority of the readings have been allocated to coincide with the actual dates on which the sermons were preached. Each reading indicates Spurgeon's own title and text; where necessary long texts have been abbreviated but listed in full in the Scripture index. The reader's attention is drawn to contemporary topics of personal, national and international interest to which Spurgeon sometimes referred. There has been a minimum of sympathetic updating of the original material to remove antiquated language and terminology; occasionally Spurgeon's Scripture quotations (probably from memory) have been corrected to remove inaccuracies. Part or the whole of Spurgeon's own Scripture readings have been selected for the further suggested reading on 34 days where they were particularly relevant to the chosen sermon extract; otherwise the readings have been selected by the compiler. The footnotes for meditation have been added by the compiler, though two-thirds of the readings conclude with a suitable verse from one of the hymns indicated as having been sung on each particular occasion. The importance Spurgeon attached to the choice of hymns can be seen from a passage from *The New York Examiner and Chronicle* which he had quoted approvingly in *The Sword and the Trowel* in 1881—'The preacher who does not select his hymns with special reference to their appropriateness to the subject of his sermon loses at least half of their effect upon the congregation ... a careless, shiftless selection of the hymns to be sung is utterly inexcusable in any pastor.'

In addition to the usual subject, Scripture and location indices, further indices have been included to cover all 63 volumes of the *New Park Street* and *Metropolitan Tabernacle Pulpit*. These deal with sermon locations, special sermons preached on behalf of societies etc., the number of published sermons for each year of Spurgeon's ministry, and those preached to mark particular seasons in the church calendar.

Thanks are due once again to all at Day One, especially to John Roberts and Jim Holmes for their support and encouragement throughout the publication of this series, also to Digby James for all he has achieved on his computer to prepare these daily readings for printing, and to Mrs Trudy Kinloch for her detailed editorial skills. But it is fitting to conclude this final introduction with the ascription of praise to God which graced the annual volumes of Spurgeon's sermons:

Charles Haddon Spurgeon in his study (1890)

Charles Haddon Spurgeon at Mentone

'To the one God of heaven and earth, in the Trinity of his sacred persons, be all honour and glory, world without end, amen. To the glorious Father, as the covenant God of Israel; to the gracious Son, the redeemer of his people; to the

Holy Ghost, the author of sanctification, be everlasting praise for that gospel of the free grace of God herein proclaimed unto men.'

Terence Peter Crosby
Wandsworth, London

One of the last photographs of
Charles Haddon Spurgeon
Photograph taken from
Photograph taken from *C.H. Spurgeon Autobiography: 2 The Full Harvest*
(Edinburgh: The Banner of Truth Trust, 1973), plate 32.

1 JANUARY (1885)

Sermon for New Year's Day

'And he that sat upon the throne said, Behold, I make all things new.'
Revelation 21:5
SUGGESTED FURTHER READING (Spurgeon): Psalm 103:1–22

There has been so much evil about ourselves and our old nature, so much sin about our life and the old past, so much mischief about our surroundings and the old temptations, that we are not distressed by the belief that old things are passing away. Hope springs up at the first sound of such words as these from the lips of our risen and reigning Lord: 'Behold, I make all things new.' It is fit that things so outworn and defiled should be laid aside, and better things fill their places. This is the first day of a new year, and therefore a solemnly joyous day. Though there is no real difference between it and any other day, yet in our mind and thought it is a marked period, which we regard as one of the milestones set up on the highway of our life. It is only in imagination that there is any close of one year and beginning of another; and yet it has most fitly all the force of a great fact. When men 'cross the line,' they find no visible mark: the sea bears no trace of an equatorial belt; and yet mariners know whereabouts they are, and they take notice thereof, so that a man can hardly cross the line for the first time without remembering it to the day of his death. We are crossing the line now. We have sailed into the year of grace 1885; therefore, let us keep a feast unto the Lord. If Jesus has not made us new already, let the new year cause us to think about the great and needful change of conversion; and if our Lord has begun to make us new, and we have somewhat entered into the new world 'wherein dwelleth righteousness', let us be persuaded by the season to press forward into the centre of his new creation, that we may feel to the full all the power of his grace.

FOR MEDITATION: (*Our Own Hymn Book*, no. 208 v.5—John Ryland, 1777)
    'Times the tempter's power to prove;
    Times to taste a Saviour's love:
    All must come, and last, and end,
    As shall please my heavenly Friend.'

SERMON NO. 1816

2 JANUARY (UNDATED SERMON)

Jehovah-shammah: a glorious name for the New Year

'The name of the city from that day shall be, The LORD *is there [or in the Hebrew "Jehovah-shammah"].'* Ezekiel 48:35
SUGGESTED FURTHER READING: Psalm 16:1–11

These words may be used as a test as well as a text. They may serve for examination as well as consolation, and at the beginning of a year they may fulfil this useful double purpose. In any case they are full of marrow and fatness to those whose spiritual taste is purified. It is esteemed by the prophet to be the highest blessing that could come upon a city that its name should be, 'JEHOVAH-SHAMMAH, The Lord is there.' Even Jerusalem, in its best estate, would have this for its crowning blessing: nothing could exceed this. Do *we* reckon the presence of the Lord to be the greatest of blessings? If in any gathering, even of the humblest people, the Lord God is known to be present in a peculiarly gracious manner, should *we* make a point of being there? Very much depends upon our answer to these queries. Doubtless many would be greatly pleased if there were no God at all; for in their hearts they say, 'No God.' God is not to them a father, a friend, a trust, a treasure. If they were to speak from their hearts, and could hope for a satisfactory answer, they would ask, 'Whither can I flee from his presence?' If a spot could be found wherein there would be no God, what a fine building speculation might be made there! Millions would emigrate to 'No God's land,' and would feel at ease as soon as they trod its godless shore. There they could do just as they liked, without fear of future reckoning. Now, friend, if you would escape from the presence of God, your state is clearly revealed by that fact. There can be no heaven for you, for heaven is where the Lord's presence is fullness of joy. If you could be happy to be far off from God, I must tell you what your fate will be. You are now going away from God in your heart and desire, and at last the great Judge of all will say to you, 'Depart from me, ye cursed,' and you will then be driven 'from the presence of the Lord, and from the glory of his power'.

FOR MEDITATION: (*Our Own Hymn Book*, no. 847 v.1—Charlotte Elliott, 1836)

'Let me be with Thee where Thou art, my Saviour, my eternal rest!
Then only will this longing heart be fully and for ever blest.'

SERMON NO. 2182

3 JANUARY (PREACHED 29 MARCH 1888)

Shoes of iron, and strength sufficient: a New Year's promise

'And of Asher he said, Let Asher be blessed with children; let him be acceptable to his brethren, and let him dip his foot in oil. Thy shoes shall be iron and brass; and as thy days, so shall thy strength be.'
Deuteronomy 33:24–25
SUGGESTED FURTHER READING (Spurgeon): Psalm 37:18–29

The Saviour has said 'without me ye can do nothing', and that is the full extent of what you can do. The Lord promises you strength, which he would have no need to promise you if you had it naturally apart from him. But he promises to give it, and therein he assures you that you need it. Come down from your self-esteem: stoop from the notion of your own natural ability: divest yourself of the foolish idea that you can do anything in and of yourself, come down to the strong for strength, and ask your Lord to fulfil this promise in your experience, 'as thy days, so shall thy strength be.' The strength which is here promised is to abide through days. 'As thy days, so shall thy strength be', not for today only, but for tomorrow, and for every day as every day shall come. The longest and the shortest day, the brightest and the darkest day, the wedding and the funeral day, shall each have its strength measured out, till there shall be no more days. The Lord will portion out to his saints their support even as their days follow each other.

> 'Days of trial, days of grief, in succession thou may'st see;
> This is still thy sweet relief, "as thy day, thy strength shall be."'

This strength is to be given daily, never two days' at a time.

> 'Day by day the manna fell: oh, to learn this lesson well,
> "Day by day" the promise reads: daily strength for daily needs!'

FOR MEDITATION: (*Our Own Hymn Book*, no. 46 version 1 v.5—Isaac Watts, 1719)
> 'That sacred stream, Thine holy Word,
> That all our raging fears controls:
> Sweet peace Thy promises afford,
> And give new strength to fainting souls.'

SERMON NO. 2062

4 JANUARY (1885)

The song of a city, and the pearl of peace

'Thou wilt keep him in perfect peace, whose mind is stayed on thee: because he trusteth in thee.' Isaiah 26:3
SUGGESTED FURTHER READING: Romans 5:1–11

God himself, at one time, seemed to be against us: the ten great cannon of his Law were turned against our walls; all heaven and earth mustered for battle; God himself was against us, at least, so conscience reported from her look-out. But, now, at this moment, having believed in Jesus Christ, we have entered into rest, and we have perfect peace as to our former sins. Who is he that can harm you that are reconciled to God? 'If God be for us, who can be against us?' 'Who shall lay anything to the charge of God's elect?' We have by faith arrived at a state of perfect reconciliation with God. The divine Fatherhood has covered us. We inherit the spirit of children, the spirit of love and of unquestioning confidence. Everything is quiet, for we dwell in our Father's house. Look upward, and you will perceive no seat of fiery wrath to shoot devouring flame. Look downward, and you discover no hell, for there is 'no condemnation to them which are in Christ Jesus'. Look back, and sin is blotted out. Look around, and 'all things work together for good to them that love God'. Look beyond, and glory shines through the veil of the future, like the sun through a morning's mist. Look outward, and 'the stones of the field', 'and the beasts of the field shall be at peace with thee.' Look inward, and 'the peace of God, which passeth all understanding, shall keep your hearts and minds through Christ Jesus.' The Lord leads us by still waters at such happy times, along that road of which we read, 'No lion shall be there'. If you who are believers in Jesus do not usually enjoy this peace, the blame must be laid to your own door: you make your own disquietude, for God says to you, 'Peace, peace,' and he will keep you there if your mind is stayed on him.

FOR MEDITATION: (*Our Own Hymn Book*, no. 738 v.1—Augustus M. Toplady, 1771)
   'A debtor to mercy alone, of covenant mercy I sing;
   Nor fear, with Thy righteousness on, my person and offering to bring:
   The terrors of law, and of God, with me can have nothing to do;
   My Saviour's obedience and blood hide all my transgressions from view.'

SERMON NO. 1818

5 JANUARY (PREACHED 7 MARCH 1889)

The keynote of the year

'Bless the LORD, *O my soul: and all that is within me, bless his holy name.'* Psalm 103:1
SUGGESTED FURTHER READING: Psalm 104:1–35

That mode of blessing God to which we are called is very spiritual—a matter of soul and spirit. I am not to bless God with my voice only, nor merely with the help of a fine organ, or a trained choir; but I am to do it after a far more difficult manner. 'Bless the LORD, O my soul'. Soul music is the soul of music. The music of the soul is that which pleases the ear of God: the great Spirit is delighted with that which comes from our spirit. Why! you do not think that even the music of the best orchestra, majestic though it be, affords pleasure to God, in the sense in which sweet sounds are pleasing to us. As for all human melody, it must seem so imperfect to the All-glorious One, that it is no more to him than the grating of an old saw to Mozart or Beethoven. His idea of music is framed on a far higher and nobler platform of taste than ever can be reached by mortal man. The songs of cherubim and seraphim infinitely exceed all that we can ever raise, so far as mere sound is concerned; and mere sound is as nothing to God. He could set the winds to music, tune the roaring of the sea, and harmonize the crash of tempests. If he needed music, he would not ask of human lips and mouths. A heart that loves him makes music to him. A heart that praises him has within itself all the harmonies that he delights in. The sigh of love is to him a lyric, the sob of repentance is melody, the inward cries of his own children are an oratorio, and their heart-songs are true hallelujahs. 'Bless the LORD, O my soul'. The unheard of man is often best heard of God. Speechless praise: the heart's deep meaning—this is what he loves.

FOR MEDITATION: (*Our Own Hymn Book,* no. 146 version 1 v.1—Isaac Watts, 1719)
   'Praise ye the Lord; my heart shall join
   In work so pleasant, so divine;
   Now, while the flesh is mine abode,
   And when my soul ascends to God.'

SERMON NO. 2121

6 JANUARY (UNDATED SERMON)

'A little sanctuary'

'Therefore say, Thus saith the Lord GOD; *Although I have cast them far off among the heathen, and although I have scattered them among the countries, yet will I be to them as a little sanctuary in the countries where they shall come.'* Ezekiel 11:16
SUGGESTED FURTHER READING: Genesis 28:10–22

What is a place of worship? I hope that our bedchambers are constantly places of worship. Place of worship? Why, it is one's garden where he walks and meditates. A place of worship? It is the field, the barn, the street, when one has the heart to pray. God will meet us by a well, a stone, a bush, a brook, a tree. He has a great range of trysting-places when men's hearts are right. *'Where'er we seek him he is found, and every place is hallowed ground.'* When a man lives near to God, and abides in him, he should shake off the folly of superstition, and talk no more of holy places. God himself, his own presence, makes a place of worship. Do you not catch the fullness of the thought? Yonder is Jacob. He lies down to sleep in a desert place with a stone for his pillow. No bishop had ever been upon the spot to consecrate it, no service had been held in the place by way of dedication, and yet when he awoke in the morning, he said, 'How dreadful is this place! this is none other but the house of God, and this is the gate of heaven.' God had been to his servant 'a little sanctuary' in that instance, as he has often been since. Whenever you go to sea, God in your cabin shall be to you 'a little sanctuary'. When you travel by railway, the carriage shall, through the Lord's presence, be 'a little sanctuary'. God's presence, seen in a bit of moss, made in the desert for Mungo Park 'a little sanctuary'. How often have the streets of London been to some of us as the golden pavements of the New Jerusalem, for God has been there! The Lord himself is the temple of saints in heaven, and he is their temple on earth. When God draws near to us, we worship and rejoice. Whenever we are abroad, and cannot come to the visible sanctuary where multitudes worship, let us ask the Lord to be to us 'as a little sanctuary'.

FOR MEDITATION: (*Our Own Hymn Book,* no. 708 v.3—Anna Lætitia Waring, 1850)
'I thirst for springs of heavenly life, and here all day they rise;
I seek the treasure of Thy love, and close at hand it lies.'

7 JANUARY (UNDATED COMMUNION SERMON)

'On his breast'

'Now there was leaning on Jesus' bosom one of his disciples, whom Jesus loved. Simon Peter therefore beckoned to him, that he should ask who it should be of whom he spake. He then lying on Jesus' breast saith unto him, Lord, who is it?' John 13:23–25
SUGGESTED FURTHER READING: John 11:1–36

It is clear, as a matter of fact, that the divine love is manifested to some more clearly than to others. My beloved brethren, you must know this to be the case; for there are those among us who walk with God, who enjoy the light of Jehovah's countenance at all times, who, if depressed, have the art of rolling their burden upon the Lord, and soon are delivered from it. You know them; they are the brethren who feel like singing all the while, for Jesus is their friend, and they rejoice in him. There was one in the Old Testament who was called 'a man greatly beloved,' and there are Daniels on earth even now. Christ has among women still his Marys, whom he loves. He loved Martha, too; but still there was a special place for Mary. Jesus has still his Johns, whom he peculiarly loves. He loves Peter, Nicodemus, Nathanael and all of them, but still there are some who know his love more than others, live in it more than others, drink into it more than others, reflect it more than others, and become more conformed to it, saturated with it and perfumed with it than others are. There are first as well as last. All may be of Israel, but all the tribes are not Judah, and in Judah all the men are not Davids. Who shall deny that there are degrees in grace? Have we not among us babes, and young men, and fathers? Have we not 'first the blade, then the ear, after that the full corn in the ear'? It is so, for we see it with our eyes, that there are degrees of grace, and especially degrees in the enjoyment of the love of Jesus. Amongst those who do really love their Lord, and are really loved by him, 'one star differeth from another star' in the glory of that love.

FOR MEDITATION: (*Our Own Hymn Book*, no. 778 v.2—Jeanne Marie Guyon, 1722; tr. by William Cowper, 1801)
    'All scenes alike engaging prove
    To souls impressed with sacred love!
    Where'er they dwell, they dwell in Thee!
    In heaven, in earth, or on the sea.'

SERMON NO. 2052

8 JANUARY (1888)

The secret of power in prayer

'If ye abide in me, and my words abide in you, ye shall ask what ye will, and it shall be done unto you.' John 15:7
SUGGESTED FURTHER READING: Matthew 6:7–13

Suppose a man of God is in prayer, and he thinks that such and such a thing is desirable, yet he remembers that he is nothing but a babe in the presence of his all-wise Father, and so he bows his will, and asks as a favour to be taught what to will. Though God bids him ask what he wills, he shrinks and cries, 'My Lord, here is a request which I am not quite clear about. As far as I can judge, it is a desirable thing, and I will it; but, Lord, I am not fit to judge for myself, and therefore I pray thee, give not as I will, but as thou wilt.' Do you not see that, when we are in such a condition as this, our real will is God's will? Deep down in our hearts we will only that which the Lord himself wills; and what is this but to ask what we will, and it be done unto us? It becomes safe for God to say to the sanctified soul, 'ask what thou wilt, and it shall be done unto thee.' The heavenly instincts of that man lead him right; the grace that is within his soul thrusts down all covetous lustings and foul desires, and his will is the actual shadow of God's will. The spiritual life is master in him, and so his aspirations are holy, heavenly, Godlike. He has been made a partaker of the divine nature; and as a son is like his father, so now in desire and will he is one with his God. As the echo answers to the voice, so does the renewed heart echo the mind of the Lord. Our desires are reflected beams of the divine will: you shall ask what you will, and it shall be even so.

FOR MEDITATION: We cannot expect to know God's will unless we admit our ignorance of it (Romans 8:26–27), ask for instruction about it (Psalm 143:10), affirm our intentions regarding it (John 7:17) and accept his influences towards it (Romans 12:1–2).

SERMON NO. 2002

9 JANUARY (UNDATED SERMON)

To those who are angry with their godly friends

'And the LORD said unto Cain, Why art thou wroth? and why is thy countenance fallen?' Genesis 4:6
SUGGESTED FURTHER READING: 1 Peter 2:11–17

In the early days of Christianity, multitudes of Christians were tormented to death because of their faith in Jesus. There was no excuse for it, for they had done no harm to the State. Christianity does not come into a nation to break up its arrangements, or to break down its fabric. All that is good in human society it preserves and establishes. It snaps no ties of the family; it dislocates no bonds of the body politic. There are theories of socialism and the like which lead to anarchy and riot, but it is not so with the mild and gentle teaching of Jesus Christ, whose every word is love and patience. He says, 'resist not evil: but whosoever shall smite thee on thy right cheek, turn to him the other also.' His apostle says, 'Wives, submit yourselves unto your own husbands'. 'Husbands, love your wives'. 'Children, obey your parents in all things'. 'Servants, obey in all things your masters...not with eyeservice, as menpleasers'. 'Masters, give unto your servants that which is just and equal; knowing that ye also have a Master in heaven.' Such precepts as these are no injury to government. Paul was no leader of sedition, no destroyer of the rights of property. Caesar needed not to fear Christ. Jesus did not covet Caesar's purple or Caesar's throne. Even Herod needed not to tremble for his princedom, for the child that was born at Bethlehem would not have hunted that fox or disturbed his den. 'My kingdom is not of this world', said our Lord Jesus, else 'would my servants fight, that I should not be delivered to the Jews'. Now, inasmuch as the religion of Jesus Christ does no hurt to social order, teaches no one to be rebellious, takes away from no man his rights, but guards the rights of all from the meanest to the greatest, all excuse is taken away from any government that dares to put out its hand to touch the church of God. As to each disciple of Jesus, the government may be satisfied that he is loyal.

FOR MEDITATION: The government's God-given duty is to encourage good behaviour and oppose evil (Romans 13:1–4), but Christians have always expected to suffer for doing right (1 Peter 2:12,19–20; 3:13–14,17; 4:14–16). 'Woe unto them that call evil good, and good evil' (Isaiah 5:20).

SERMON NO. 1929

10 JANUARY (UNDATED SERMON)

Our expectation

'He shall see his seed.' Isaiah 53:10
SUGGESTED FURTHER READING: Acts 12:1-24

If it had been possible to destroy the church of God on earth, it would have been destroyed long ago. The malice of hell has done all that it could do to destroy the seed of Christ that sprang from his death. Standing in the Colosseum at Rome, I could not, as I looked around on the ruins of that vast house of sin, but praise God that the church of God existed, though the Colosseum is in ruins. Anyone standing there, when thousands upon thousands gloated their eyes with the sufferings of Christians, would have said, 'Christianity will die out, but the Colosseum, so firmly built, will stand to the end of time;' but the Colosseum is a ruin, and the church of God more firm, more strong, more glorious than ever! Only read the story of the persecutions under Nero, and under Diocletian, in the olden times, and you will wonder that Christianity survived the cruel blows. Every form of torture which devils could invent was inflicted upon Christian men and women. Not here and there, but everywhere, they were hunted down and persecuted. It makes one thrill with horror as he reads of women tossed on the horns of bulls, or set in red-hot iron chairs, and men smeared with honey to be stung to death by wasps, or dragged at the heels of wild horses, or exposed to savage beasts in the amphitheatre. But I will say no more about it. The gallant vessel of the church ploughed the red waves of a crimson sea, her prow scarlet with gore, but the ship itself was the better for its washing, and sailed all the more gallantly because of boisterous winds. As to our own country, read the story of persecutions here. You will have enough if you only read Foxe's *Book of Martyrs*. I wish that every house had in it a large-typed copy of the *Book of Martyrs*. Well do I recollect, as a child, how many hours, how many days, I spent looking at the pictures in an old-fashioned *Book of Martyrs*, and wondering how the men of God suffered, as they did, so bravely.

FOR MEDITATION: (*Our Own Hymn Book,* no. 325 v.1—Augustus M. Toplady, 1771)
  'Awake, sweet gratitude, and sing th'ascended Saviour's love;
  Tell how He lives to carry on His people's cause above.'

SERMON NO. 2186

11 JANUARY (UNDATED SERMON)

Christ's connection with sinners the source of his glory

'Therefore will I divide him a portion with the great, and he shall divide the spoil with the strong; because he hath poured out his soul unto death: and he was numbered with the transgressors; and he bare the sin of many, and made intercession for the transgressors.' Isaiah 53:12

SUGGESTED FURTHER READING: 1 John 4:7–12

'Jesus Christ died as an exhibition of divine love.' This is true in a certain sense, but from another point of view, of all the things I have ever heard, this does seem to me to be the most monstrous statement that could be made. That Jesus Christ, dying because of our sins, is a wonderful example of divine love, I do know, admit, and glory in, but that Christ's dying was an instance of divine love, if he did not die because he bare our sins, I entirely deny. There is no exhibition of divine love in the death of Christ if it be not for our sins, but an exhibition of a very different sort. The death of the perfect Son of God, per se, and without its great object, does not exhibit love, but the reverse. What? Does God put to death his only begotten Son, the perfectly pure and holy being? Is this the finale of a life of obedience? Well, then, I see no love in God at all. It seems to me to be the reverse of love that it should be so. Apart from sin-bearing the statement that Jesus must die the death of the cross to show us that his Father is full of love is sheer nonsense; but if he died in our room and stead, then the gift of Jesus Christ by the Father is undoubtedly a glorious instance of divine love. Behold, and wonder, that 'God so loved the world, that he gave his only begotten Son, that whosoever believeth in him should not perish, but have everlasting life.' This is love, if you please, but not the mere fact that the Son of God should be put to death. That would be a thing altogether unaccountable, not to be justified, but to be looked upon as a horrible mystery never to be explained, that the blessed Son of God should die, if we did not receive this full and complete explanation, 'he bare the sin of many'.

FOR MEDITATION: (*Our Own Hymn Book*, no. 288 v.1—William Cowper, 1779)
   'There is a fountain filled with blood, drawn from Immanuel's veins;
   And sinners, plunged beneath that flood, lose all their guilty stains.'

SERMON NO. 2070

12 JANUARY (UNDATED SERMON)

Help for your sickness

'They brought unto him many that were possessed with devils: and he cast out the spirits with his word, and healed all that were sick: that it might be fulfilled which was spoken by Esaias the prophet, saying, Himself took our infirmities, and bare our sicknesses.' Matthew 8:16–17
SUGGESTED FURTHER READING (Spurgeon): Isaiah 53:1–12

If you trust Christ, you may be sure that you are among the number of those whose sins were laid on Christ. He was punished in your room, place and stead. Now, it is not just that, if another was punished in your stead, you should be punished too; and therefore the very justice of God requires that, if Christ suffered in your stead, you should not suffer. Do you see that? 'But did he suffer in my stead?' I must answer this question by another. 'Do you believe that Jesus is the Christ? Will you trust your soul with him?' Well, if you do, your transgressions are not yours, for they were laid on him. They are not on you, for, like everything else, they cannot be in two places at one time; and if they were laid on Christ, they are not laid on you. But what did Jesus do with the sins that were laid on him? Can they not come back to us? No, never; for he took them to the sepulchre, and there he buried them for ever. And now, what says the Scripture? 'In those days, and in that time, saith the LORD, the iniquity of Israel shall be sought for, and there shall be none; and the sins of Judah, and they shall not be found.' 'I have blotted out, as a thick cloud, thy transgressions, and, as a cloud, thy sins'. 'Thou wilt cast all their sins into the depths of the sea.' Our sins are gone. Christ has carried them away. 'As far as the east is from the west, so far hath he removed our transgressions from us.' Believers are the seed for whom the victory has been gained. They are the seed to whom the promise is sure. It is not to those who are of works, but to those who are of faith. Those that are born again, of the Spirit of God, through faith which is in Christ Jesus, these are 'redeemed from among men.'

FOR MEDITATION: (*Our Own Hymn Book,* no. 410 v.2—Isaac Watts, 1709)

'"Twas He that cleansed our foulest sins,
And washed us in His richest blood:
'Tis He that makes us priests and kings,
And brings us rebels near to God.'

SERMON NO. 2124

13 JANUARY (UNDATED SERMON)

Redemption through blood, the gracious forgiveness of sins

'In whom we have redemption through his blood, the forgiveness of sins, according to the riches of his grace.' Ephesians 1:7
SUGGESTED FURTHER READING: Titus 2:11–3:7

Suppose that somebody has offended you, and you say, 'Think no more of it; it is all forgiven.' Very well: that is kind of you, and commendable. It shows the graciousness of your character. But suppose, on the other hand, you were in office as a judge, and felt compelled to say, 'I am willing to forgive you, but your offence has resulted in such and such great mischiefs, and all these things have to be cleared away. I will tell you what I will do. I will clear them away myself. I will bear the result of your sin in order that my pardon may be seen to be most sure and full. I will pay the debt in which you have involved yourself. I will go to the prison to which you ought to go, as the consequence of what you have done. I will suffer the effect of your wrongdoing instead of condemning you to suffer it.' Well, now, the forgiveness that cost you so much would manifest your graciousness much more than that which costs you nothing beyond a kind will and a tender heart. Oh, if it be so, that God, the Divine Ruler, the Judge of all the earth, says to guilty man, 'I will pardon you, but it is imperative that my law be carried out; and this cannot be done except by the death of my dear Son, who is one with me, who is very God of very God, who himself wills to stand in your stead, and vindicate my justice, by suffering the penalty due to you'—then I say that the grace of God is a thousand-fold more clearly shown than by the free forgiveness which 'modern thought' pleads for! Pardon which has cost God more than it cost him to make all worlds, which has cost him more than to manage all the empires of his providence, which has cost him his Only-begotten Son, and has cost that Only-begotten Son a life of sorrow and a death of unutterable and immeasurable anguish, I say that this pardon is pre-eminently gracious.

FOR MEDITATION: (*Our Own Hymn Book*, no. 289 v.3—Isaac Watts, 1709)
  'Here I behold His inmost heart,
  Where grace and vengeance strangely join,
  Piercing His Son with sharpest smart,
  To make the purchased pleasures mine.'

SERMON NO. 2207

14 JANUARY (UNDATED SERMON)

The Lord no more wroth with his people

'For this is as the waters of Noah unto me: for as I have sworn that the waters of Noah should no more go over the earth; so have I sworn that I would not be wroth with thee, nor rebuke thee.' Isaiah 54:9
SUGGESTED FURTHER READING: Isaiah 12:1–6

If it be so, that God has sworn that he will not be wroth with us, then, first, *believe it*. The inference is clear: Jehovah swears—shall not his children believe? For any man to doubt me is to dishonour me, but for my child to mistrust my oath would be the unkindest cut of all. Believe without hesitation. That is one word. The next is, *rejoice*. If he will not be wroth with you, nor rebuke you, then be glad. Here is constant theme for song. The nightingale sings in the dark, and so may you. Midst darkest shades with such a word as this your dawning has begun. Rejoice evermore. The third word is, *be resigned*. If the Lord will not be wroth with you, meekly bear without repining whatever his will ordains. You see the cup is sweetened with love; why do you make wry faces over it? Will you not accept what perfect love proffers? Oh, do not kick against a God so gracious! Lastly, *impart*. If you have learned this love in your own heart, then tell it out to others. If indeed it be glad tidings to you, tell out the happy message, and say to every sinner you meet with, 'Believe on the Lord Jesus Christ, and thou shalt be saved'; 'Ho, every one that thirsteth, come ye to the waters'; 'whosoever will, let him take the water of life freely.' You can prove your knowing this for yourselves, by your desire to make it known to others; and you need to doubt whether you truly understand the salvation of the Lord in your own soul, if you feel no inward impulse to make others know the glorious promise of your Lord. May God bless you, dear friends, by putting this text right into your souls!

FOR MEDITATION: (*Our Own Hymn Book*, no. 748 v.3—John Kent, 1803)
 'To His church, His joy, and treasure,
 Every trial works for good:
 They are dealt in weight and measure,
 Yet how little understood;
 Not in anger,
 But from His dear covenant love.'

SERMON NO. 2176

15 JANUARY (1888)

Young man, is this for you?

'And he said, Young man, I say unto thee, Arise. And he that was dead sat up, and began to speak. And he delivered him to his mother. And there came a fear on all: and they glorified God.' Luke 7:14–16
SUGGESTED FURTHER READING: Ephesians 2:1–7

Our Lord, when he puts the new life into young men, does not want to take them away with him from the home where their first duty lies. Here and there one is called away to be an apostle or a missionary, but usually he wants them to go home to their friends, bless their parents and make their families happy and holy. He does not present the young man to the priest, but he delivers him to his mother. Do not say, 'I am converted, and therefore I cannot go to business any more, or try to support my mother by my trade.' That would prove that you were not converted at all. You may go for a missionary in a year or two's time if you are fitted for it, but you must not make a dash at a matter for which you are not prepared. For the present go home to your mother, make your home happy, charm your father's heart, be a blessing to your brothers and sisters, and let them rejoice because one 'was dead, and is alive again; and was lost, and is found.' What was the next result? Well, all the neighbours feared and glorified God. If that young man, who last night was at the music-hall, and a few nights ago came home very nearly drunk, is born again, all around him will wonder at it. If that young man, who has got himself out of a situation by gambling, or some other wrong-doing, is saved, we shall all feel that God is very near us. If that young man who has begun to associate with evil women, and to fall into other evils, is brought to be pure-minded and gracious, it will strike awe into those round about him. He has led many others astray, and if the Lord now leads him back, it will make a great hubbub, and men will enquire as to the reason of the change and will see that there is a power in religion after all. Conversions are miracles which never cease.

FOR MEDITATION: Though the people feared and God was glorified when Jesus raised this young man from the dead, responses ranged from faith to hostility when he did the same for Lazarus (John 11:45–46; 12:9–11). Likewise the parable of the prodigal son teaches us that conversion causes some onlookers to rejoice and others to criticise (Luke 15:24–30).

SERMON NO. 2003

16 JANUARY (UNDATED SERMON)

Love's competition

'Tell me therefore, which of them will love him most? Simon answered and said, I suppose that he, to whom he forgave most. And he said unto him, Thou hast rightly judged.' Luke 7:42–43

SUGGESTED FURTHER READING: Psalm 100:1–5

Do your choicest and best for Jesus, for Jesus personally. *Try to do it most humbly.* Stand behind him. Do not ask anybody to look at you. Do it very quietly, feeling that it is a great honour to be permitted to do the least service for Jesus. Do not dream of saying, 'I am somebody. I am doing great things. I do more even than Simon, the Pharisee. Come see my zeal for the Lord of hosts.' Jehu talked in that fashion; but he was good for nothing. Do your personal part without seeking to be seen of men. *Do it self-sacrificingly.* Bring your best ointment. Pinch yourself for Christ. Make sacrifices; go without this and that to have something wherewith you can do him honour. *Do it very penitently.* When you serve him best, still let the tears fall on his feet, mingling with the costly ointment. The tears and the ointment go well together. Mourn your guilt, while you rejoice in his grace. *Do it continuously*: 'this woman,' said Christ, 'since the time I came in hath not ceased to kiss my feet.' Do not leave off loving him and serving him. Do it on, and on, and on, however much the flesh may ask for respite from service. *Do it enthusiastically.* See how she kissed his feet; nothing less than this would express her love. Stoop down, and kiss and kiss again those blessed feet which travelled so far in love for you. Throw your whole soul into your deed of love. 'Why,' they will say, 'Mrs So-and-so is enthusiastic. She is quite carried away by her zeal.' Let it be true, more and more. Never mind what the cold-hearted think, for they cannot understand you. They will say, 'Ah! that young person is too fast by half.' Never mind. Be faster still. Wise people cry out, 'He has too many irons in the fire.' But I say to you, blow up the fire; get all the irons red hot and hammer away with all your might. With all your strength and energy plunge into the service of your Master.

FOR MEDITATION: 'Serving the Lord with all humility of mind' (Acts 20:19) should preserve us from complaining about the terms (Matthew 20:10–13), the loneliness (Luke 10:40) or the length (Luke 15:29) of our service for him.

SERMON NO. 2127

17 JANUARY (UNDATED SERMON)

A gracious dismissal

'He said to the woman, Thy faith hath saved thee; go in peace.' Luke 7:50
SUGGESTED FURTHER READING: Romans 16:17–20

The child of God would find it to be his greatest wisdom, whenever he is in company that begins to assail his Lord or to denounce his faith, just to go about his business and let the scoffers have their scoffing to themselves. Some of us have thought it our miserable duty to read certain books that have been brought out against the truth, that we might be able to answer them, but it is a perilous calling. The Lord have mercy upon us when we have to go down into these sewers, for the process is not healthy! 'Oh,' says a man, 'but you must prove all things!' Yes, but if one should set a joint of meat on his table and it smelt rather high, I would cut a slice and if I put one bit of it in my mouth and found it far gone, I should not feel it necessary to eat the whole round of beef to test its sweetness. Some people seem to think that they must read a bad book through; they must hear a bad preacher often before they can be sure of his quality. Why, you can judge many teachings in five minutes! You say to yourself, 'This is good meat—for dogs. Let them have it, but it is not good meat for me, and I do not intend to poison myself with it.' The Saviour does not tell the woman, 'Stop and hear what Simon has got to say. You have been washing my feet with tears, and here is a highly intelligent gentleman, a Pharisee, who has a very learned lecture to deliver; give him a fair hearing. You have to prove all things; therefore, stop and hear him. And here are more gentlemen who object to my pardoning your sins; their objections are fetched from deep veins of thought. Listen to them, and then I will meet their questions, and quiet your mind.' No; the Saviour says, 'Go in peace. You have peace: do not stop till you lose it. You have your comfort and joy: refuse to be robbed of them.'

FOR MEDITATION: (*Our Own Hymn Book*, no. 726 vv.2&4—Horatius Bonar, 1856)
'Yes; keep me calm, though loud and rude the sounds my ear that greet;
Calm in the closet's solitude, calm in the bustling street;
Calm in the sufferance of wrong, like Him who bore my shame;
Calm 'mid the threatening, taunting throng, who hate Thy holy name.'

SERMON NO. 2183

18 JANUARY (UNDATED SERMON)

How to become fishers of men

'And [Jesus] saith unto them, Follow me, and I will make you fishers of men.' Matthew 4:19
SUGGESTED FURTHER READING: 2 Peter 2:1–3

To talk about the punishment of sin, to speak of eternal punishment, why, these are unfashionable doctrines. It may be that they are taught in the Word of God, but they do not suit the genius of the age. We must pare them down. Brothers in Christ, I will have no share in this. Will you? 'O my soul, come not thou into their secret'! Certain things not taught in the Bible our enlightened age has discovered. Evolution may be clean contrary to the teaching of Genesis, but that does not matter. We are not going to be believers of Scripture, but original thinkers. This is the vain-glorious ambition of the period. Mark you, in proportion as the modern theology is preached the vice of this generation increases. To a great degree I attribute the looseness of the age to the laxity of the doctrine preached by its teachers. From the pulpit they have taught the people that sin is a trifle. From the pulpit these traitors to God and to his Christ have taught the people that there is no hell to be feared. A little hell, perhaps, there may be, but just punishment for sin is made nothing of. The precious atoning sacrifice of Christ has been derided and misrepresented by those who were pledged to preach it. They have given the people the name of the gospel, but the gospel itself has evaporated in their hands. From hundreds of pulpits the gospel is as clean gone as the dodo from its old haunts; and still the preachers take the position and name of Christ's ministers. Well, and what comes of it? Why, their congregations grow thinner and thinner; and so it must be. Jesus says, 'Follow me, and I will make you fishers of men', but if you go in your own way with your own net, you will make nothing of it, and the Lord promises you no help in it. The Lord's directions make himself our leader and example. It is, 'Follow me. Preach my gospel. Preach what I preached. Teach what I taught, and keep to that.'

FOR MEDITATION: False teaching is not just another viewpoint. 2 Peter 2:17–22 illustrates the damage it can do. It can deceive even the elect (Matthew 24:4,24) and cause Christians to be drawn away (Acts 20:29–30), destabilised (2 Peter 3:16–17) and deprived of reward (2 John 7–8).

SERMON NO. 1906

19 JANUARY (UNDATED SERMON)

The burden of the word of the Lord

'The burden of the word of the Lord.*'* Malachi 1:1
SUGGESTED FURTHER READING: 1 Timothy 4:6–16

Do you think it an easy thing to stand before the people and deliver a message which you believe you have received from God? If you so imagine, I wish you would try it. He that finds it easy work to preach, will find it hard work to give an account of his preaching at the last great day. One has carefully to look around, and think while he is preaching, 'I must mind that I do not put this truth in such a way as to exaggerate it into a falsehood. I must not so encourage the weak that I dwarf the strong, nor so commend the strong as to grieve the weak. I must not so preach the grace of God as to give latitude to sin: I must not so denounce sin as to drive men to despair.' Our path is often narrow as a razor's edge, and we keep on crying in our spirit, while we are speaking, 'Lord, direct me! Lord, help me to deal wisely for thee with all these souls!' The anxieties which we feel in connection with our pulpit work are enough to make us old before our time. I have heard of one who thought he would give up his ministry because he had so small a chapel, into which he could not get more than two hundred people; but a good old man said to him, 'You will find it quite hard enough to give a good account of two hundred at the last great day.' It is an idle ambition to desire a large congregation, unless that desire is altogether for God's glory, for we only increase our responsibilities when we increase the area of our influence. Still, some are responsible for not having a large congregation. If their dullness keeps people from hearing, they do not thereby escape from responsibility. To speak aright God's Word beneath the divine influence is, in the speaking as well as in the getting of the message, the burden of the Lord.

FOR MEDITATION: (*Our Own Hymn Book,* no. 900 v.2—John Joseph Winkler, 1714; tr. by John Wesley, 1739)

> 'Awed by a mortal's frown, shall I
> Conceal the Word of God Most High?
> How then before Thee shall I dare
> To stand, or how Thy anger bear?'

SERMON NO. 2114

20 JANUARY (UNDATED SERMON)

A plain man's sermon

'It shall be perfect to be accepted; there shall be no blemish therein.'
Leviticus 22:21
SUGGESTED FURTHER READING: Matthew 5:17–30

It is a blessed thing to declare the gospel, but I do not believe that any man can preach the gospel who does not preach the law. The book of Leviticus and all the other typical books, are valuable as gospel-teaching to us, because there is always in them most clearly the law of God. The law is the needle, and you cannot draw the silken thread of the gospel through a man's heart, unless you first send the needle of the law through the centre thereof, to make way for it. If men do not understand the law, they will not feel that they are sinners, and if they are not consciously sinners, they will never value the sin-offering. If the Ten Commandments are never read in their hearing, they will not know wherein they are guilty and how shall they make confession? If they are not assured that the law is 'holy, and just, and good', and that God has never demanded of any man more than he has a right to demand, how shall they feel the filthiness of sin, or see the need of flying to Christ for cleansing? There is no healing a man till the law has wounded him, no making him alive till the law has slain him. I do pray, dear friends, that God, the Holy Spirit, may lay the law, like an axe, at the root of all our self-righteousness, for nothing else will ever hew down that upas tree. I pray that he may take the law, and use it as a looking-glass, that we may see ourselves in it, and discover our spots and blots, and all the foulness of our lives, for then we shall be driven to wash until we are clean in the sight of the Lord. The law is our pedagogue 'to bring us unto Christ,' and there is no coming to Christ unless the stern pedagogue shall lead us there, with many a stripe and many a tear.

FOR MEDITATION: Teachers who neglect the preaching of the law deprive themselves and their hearers of a tool which reveals sin (Romans 3:20; 7:7), condemns the sinner (Galatians 3:10) and points the sinner to the Lord Jesus Christ (Galatians 3:24). What a valuable resource it is!

SERMON NO. 1879

21 JANUARY (UNDATED SERMON)

Small rain for tender herbs

'As the small rain upon the tender herb.' Deuteronomy 32:2
SUGGESTED FURTHER READING: Psalm 119:97–104

Many miss the charming influences of heavenly truth because they do not think enough. How often does the word fail to enrich the heart because it is not thought over! The small rain does not get to the root of the tender herb, for time and opportunity are not allowed to it. O you that would profit by the ministry of the gospel, take this for your golden rule—hear once, meditate twice, and pray three times! I prescribe to you, as a composition and compound of excellent virtue, that there should be at least twice as much meditating as there should be hearing. Is it not strange that people should think sermons worth hearing, but not worth meditating upon? It is as foolish as if a man thought a joint of meat worth buying, but not worth cooking, for meditation is, as it were, a sort of holy cookery by which the truth is prepared to be food for the soul. Solomon says: 'The slothful man roasteth not that which he took in hunting', and there are many of that sort, who hunt after a sermon, and when they have found it they roast it not; they do not prepare it as truth should be prepared before it can be digested and become spiritual meat. Why get books if you never read, or clothes if you never dress, or carriages if you never ride? Yet any one of these things is more sensible than hearing sermons and never meditating upon them. Do not so, dear brethren, I pray you! We are not members of the Society of Friends, although I hope we are friends and members of a society, but we should try and do after service what they try to do during the service. Let us keep silence and let the truth sink into us. We should be all the better if occasionally we were famished of words, for too often we are smothered with them. It would be profitable to have the supply of words stopped, that we might get below the language and look inward at the hidden sense, that we might reach the bowels of truth and feel its energetic operation upon our heart and soul.

FOR MEDITATION: (*Our Own Hymn Book*, no. 403 v.1—Newman Hall, 1857)
  'Friend of sinners! Lord of glory! lowly, mighty! Brother, King!
  Musing o'er Thy wondrous story, fain would I Thy praises sing.'

SERMON NO. 1999

22 JANUARY (1888)

The lover of God's law filled with peace

'Great peace have they which love thy law: and nothing shall offend them.' Psalm 119:165
SUGGESTED FURTHER READING: Colossians 3:12–17

This love is productive of many good things. They that love God's Word will meditate on it and make it the man of their right hand. What a companion the Bible is! It talks with us by the way, it communes with us upon our beds: it knows us altogether and has a suitable word for every condition of life. Hence we cannot be long without listening to our Beloved's voice in this Book of books. I hope we realize the character described in the first Psalm: 'his delight is in the law of the LORD; and in his law doth he meditate day and night. And he shall be like a tree planted by the rivers of water'. Love to the Word of God creates great courage in the defence of it. It is wonderful how the most timid creatures will defend their young, how even a hen becomes a terrible bird when she has to take care of her chicks: even so, quiet men and women contend earnestly 'for the faith which was once delivered to the saints', and will not tamely submit to see the truth torn in pieces by the hounds of error and hypocrisy. The love of the law of God breeds penitence for having sinned against it, and perseverance in obedience to it. It also begets patience under suffering, for it leads the man to submit himself to the will of God whom he loves so much. He says, 'It is the LORD: let him do what seemeth him good.' The Word of God begets and fosters holiness. Jesus said, 'Sanctify them through thy truth: thy word is truth.' You cannot study the Scriptures diligently and love them heartily without having your thoughts and acts savoured and sweetened by them. A gentleness and kindness will be infused into your spirit by the very tone of the Word; a sacred delicacy and carefulness of conduct will surround your daily life in proportion as you steep your mind in Scripture.

FOR MEDITATION: Consider some of the other blessings the writer of Psalm 119 derived from his study of God's word—cleansing (v.9), strength (v.28), liberty (v.45), comfort (v.52), wisdom (v.98), illumination (v.105), orderliness (v.133) and joy (v.162). These are only a selection of the benefits to be enjoyed!

SERMON NO. 2004

23 JANUARY (UNDATED SERMON)

Pleading prayer

'Remember the word unto thy servant, upon which thou hast caused me to hope.' Psalm 119:49
SUGGESTED FURTHER READING: 1 John 5:13–15

Ungodly men cannot make out what prayer is. 'Do you suppose,' say they, 'that you can change the will of God?' We reply to them that we never supposed anything of the kind, but we suppose that our prayer is the shadow of a coming blessing. As 'coming events cast their shadows before them,' so, when God is about to bless us, he moves us to pray for that very blessing. If it were possible to shut out the man's shadow, we could not expect the man to enter; and if it were possible to shut out prayer from our soul, we should feel at the same time that we had shut out the blessing. Our Lord is pleased to duplicate his mercies. The blessing itself is great, but it is an equal blessing to be made to pray for it. It frequently does a child more good to get a favour from his father than the favour itself brings him. If the father sets him some little task to do, if he says, 'Now, my child, prove to me that this will be a good thing,' the mental exercise, the pleading, the asking, may be as useful in the child's education as the thing for which he asks. I say, again, our God doubles his blessings by making his servants pray for them. Prayer, then, is nothing more than this—my believingly remembering that God has promised a certain blessing, and then my reminding him that he has promised it. It is not supposable that he will forget, but he would have me act towards him as if he might forget, in order that by such an exercise I myself may come to value the blessing and may be stirred up to importunity and fervour. The prayer is a right one when we say, 'Remember the word unto thy servant': it is, in fact, what God always intends prayer to be, a reminding our heavenly Father of his promise.

FOR MEDITATION: If we remember God's works (Psalm 105:5) and his past faithful remembrance of his covenant, word and promises (Psalm 105:8–10,42), we will, like Nehemiah, be better prepared to plead with God, 'Remember ... the word' (Nehemiah 1:8).

SERMON NO. 1969

24 JANUARY (UNDATED SERMON)

My own personal holdfast

'*My God will hear me.*' Micah 7:7
SUGGESTED FURTHER READING: Nehemiah 1:1–11

We ought to have set times for private prayer; it is most healthful that we should; but I question whether our best prayers are not those which are quite irrespective of time and season. When a man does not pray because it is seven o'clock in the morning, but because he has a pressing need, when he does not pray because it is time to go to bed, but because he feels drawn to speak with God, then he prays indeed. When a man has a constant confidence in the prevalence of prayer, he slips away from a trying business to seek guidance and support. The confident pleader, when he walks the street groaning in spirit, makes known his desire to the Most High. Perhaps Cheapside has been a Bethel to some of you, and your shop has been a temple. The most living prayer bursts naturally from the swollen heart, and does not come because of time. I have heard of a minister who put in the margin of his manuscript sermons, 'Cry here' and in another place, 'Here lift up your eyes.' It must be very dreadful preaching when the emotion is made to order and the same is true of praying. The fear is that you should not really pray when the clock says, 'Now pray.' I do not think we can always keep the watch of the soul in exact time with the clock on the mantelpiece; therefore I think that the most living prayer is that which comes by the movement of the Spirit of God just at that time when it is most of all required. 'Let us pray' is, however, a voice which is never unseasonable. When would it be unfit for such an exhortation to be given? When would it not be profitable to pray? The Lord is always willing; therefore let us be always praying in one form or another. Let us pray, no matter what may be the trial, no matter what the joy, no matter what the company. 'Pray without ceasing.'

FOR MEDITATION: (*Our Own Hymn Book,* no. 980 v.1—John Newton, 1779)
'Come, my soul, thy suit prepare,
Jesus loves to answer prayer;
He Himself has bid thee pray,
Therefore will not say thee nay.'

SERMON NO. 2069

25 JANUARY (UNDATED SERMON)

The filling of empty vessels

'Even empty vessels; borrow not a few.' 2 Kings 4:3
SUGGESTED FURTHER READING: Genesis 18:22–33; 19:15–29

If our children are not converted, is it not, in some cases, the fact that we have not prayed for them as we should? We have not brought them before God in supplication, and if they remain unconverted and worldly, how can we wonder? Let us not leave the empty vessels unfilled. Come, friends, think of the unconverted at home. You have still some unsaved ones; mention them again and again in prayer by name, and cease not to pray, for Christ's grace ceases not to flow, and the efficacy of prayer is not stayed. Do not cease to pray till all the family is converted, till there is not another vessel left. Let us do the same with our neighbours. Are we sufficiently earnest before God with regard to them? Might we not expect to see a great change in London, if the districts wherein we dwell were oftener on our hearts in prayer? You have heard of the great revival which followed Jonathan Edwards' marvellous sermon upon 'Sinners in the hands of an angry God.' That sermon was marvellous in its effects. The power of that sermon may be traced to the fact that a number of Christian people had met together some days before and prayed that God would send a blessing with the minister who was to preach on that occasion. Their prayer put power into Jonathan Edwards' sermon, and so sinners were converted. If we were to take up villages, hamlets and towns, and pray for them with earnest, believing faith, God might prosper instrumentalities that are now unblessed, and ministers, who are now sowing seed that never springs up, might have to tell of a joyful harvest. They might not know the reason, but those who prevailed with God would be able to solve the riddle. Prayer to the Most High would be a quiet setting of the empty vessel under the running oil, and without noise it would be filled. Let us see what we can do in this matter.

FOR MEDITATION: If we can lose out by failing to pray for ourselves (James 4:2), others can likewise be deprived if we fail to pray for them (1 Samuel 12:19,23).

SERMON NO. 2063

26 JANUARY (UNDATED SERMON)

The sluggard's farm

'I went by the field of the slothful, and by the vineyard of the man void of understanding; and lo, it was all grown over with thorns, and nettles had covered the face thereof, and the stone wall thereof was broken down. Then I saw, and considered it well: I looked upon it, and received instruction.' Proverbs 24:30–32

SUGGESTED FURTHER READING: 1 Samuel 3:10–14

May I ask you to look into your own house and home? It is a dreadful thing when a man does not cultivate the field of his own family. I recollect in my early days a man who used to walk out with me into the villages when I was preaching. I was glad of his company till I found out certain facts, and then I shook him off, and I believe he hooked on to somebody else, for he had to be gadding abroad every evening of the week. He had many children and these grew up to be wicked young men and women, and the reason was that the father, while he would be at this meeting and that, never tried to bring his own children to the Saviour. What is the use of zeal abroad if there is neglect at home? How sad to say, 'mine own vineyard have I not kept.' Have you never heard of one who said he did not teach his children the ways of God because he thought they were so young that it was very wrong to prejudice them, and he had rather leave them to choose their own religion when they grew older? One of his boys broke his arm, and while the surgeon was setting it the boy was swearing all the time. 'Ah,' said the good doctor, 'I told you what would happen. You were afraid to prejudice your boy in the right way, but the devil had no such qualms; he has prejudiced him the other way, and pretty strongly too.' It is our duty to prejudice our field in favour of corn, or it will soon be covered with thistles. Cultivate a child's heart for good, or it will go wrong of itself, for it is already depraved by nature. O that we were wise enough to think of this, and leave no little one to become a prey to the destroyer.

FOR MEDITATION: 'A child is known by his doings' (Proverbs 20:11). Long-term benefits can be achieved by means of training (Proverbs 22:6) and correction (Proverbs 22:15; 23:13), 'but a child left to himself bringeth his mother to shame' (Proverbs 29:15).

SERMON NO. 2027

27 JANUARY (UNDATED SERMON)

The hedge of thorns and the plain way

'The way of the slothful man is as an hedge of thorns: but the way of the righteous is made plain.' Proverbs 15:19
SUGGESTED FURTHER READING: 2 Thessalonians 3:6–13

Every good thing withers in the drought of idleness. In fact, all kinds of vices are comprehended in the one vice of sloth and, if you tell me that a man is a sluggard, I have his whole character before me in the blackest of letters. His fallow fields are well adapted for evil seed and, no doubt, Satan will raise a fine crop of weeds in every corner of his life. What this world would have been if we had all been gentlemen, with nothing to do, I cannot tell. The millions that have to work are largely kept out of mischief by their toil and, although crimes are abundant enough in our great city as it is, what would they have been if there had not been daily tasks to keep men from excessive indulgence in drink and other forms of evil? Without labour the ale-houses would have been crammed every one of the twenty-four hours, folly would have held unbroken carnival and licentiousness would have burst all bounds. Amongst the sanitary and salutary regulations of the moral universe there is none much better than this—that men must work. He who does not work is not a righteous man, for he is out of accord with that which makes for righteousness. In some form or other, with either brain or hand, either by working or enduring, we share the common labours of the race appointed them by heaven and if we are not doing so, we are not righteous. I call to your remembrance the remarkable words of the Saviour, 'Thou wicked and slothful servant'. Those two adjectives are nearly related—'wicked and slothful'. Might not our Lord have said 'slothful' alone? He might, but he knew how much of wickedness goes with sloth and is inherent in it and, therefore, he branded it with the condemning word.

FOR MEDITATION: Work is a good thing. God was the first to work (Genesis 2:2–3) and from the first he put Adam to work (Genesis 2:15). Only after Adam sinned did work turn into toil and hard labour (Genesis 3:17–19). But even in a fallen world work is highly commended and encouraged (Ecclesiastes 5:18–20). Idleness has never received the seal of God's approval.

SERMON NO. 1948

28 JANUARY (UNDATED SERMON)

Something done for Jesus

'She hath wrought a good work upon me.' Matthew 26:10
SUGGESTED FURTHER READING: Colossians 3:18–4:1

The entire life of the Christian ought to be, in many respects, 'a good work' done unto Christ. Albeit that there must be in our life an eye to the good of our fellow-men, yet may we do it all unto the Lord. The same law which says, 'Thou shalt love the Lord thy God with all thy heart, and with all thy soul, and with all thy mind,' adds, 'Thou shalt love thy neighbour as thyself', which proves that it does not necessarily take away any part of our love from God when we act in love to our fellow-men. The duties of life, though they are to be done with a view to our neighbour as God's will requires, still ought, in the highest sense, to be performed mainly with an eye to the glory of Christ, and out of love to him. The servant is bidden to work, 'as to the Lord, and not unto men'. The master, also, ought to discharge his duties knowing that he has 'a Master in heaven', and the thought of that Master above should guide him in all he does. O Christian men and women, whatever your calling, discharge the duties of it with a view to glorifying him, whose name, as Christians, you bear! So let it be in every relation of life. Should not the child seek to honour Christ by being like the holy child Jesus? Should not the parent devote his child to Christ, earnestly praying that he may grow up in the fear of the Lord, and may serve the Lord? Every lawful relationship can be consecrated. In every condition of life we can glorify Jesus. In all the moral obligations of life, Jesus should be before us. We should be honest, not only for our reputation's sake, for that would be an unworthy motive, but for Christ's sake. Would we have Christ's disciples called 'thieves'? We should be sternly upright, never by any means under suspicion of untruth or double-dealing, because we serve the Lord Christ, who is faithful and true. Of us more is expected than of others, since we serve a better Master than all others.

FOR MEDITATION: (*Our Own Hymn Book*, no. 663 v.2—James George Deck, 1837)
  'I am Thine, and Thine alone, this I gladly, fully own;
  And, in all my works and ways, only now would seek Thy praise.'

SERMON NO. 2126

29 JANUARY (1888)

Knowing the Lord through pardoned sin

'And they shall teach no more every man his neighbour, and every man his brother, saying, Know the LORD: *for they shall all know me, from the least of them unto the greatest of them, saith the* LORD; *for I will forgive their iniquity, and I will remember their sin no more.'* Jeremiah 31:34
SUGGESTED FURTHER READING: 2 Chronicles 33:1–13

I venture to say that there is a clearer revelation of God to the individual in the forgiveness of his sin than can be found anywhere else. God is to be seen in *nature*. Who among us would wish to question it? Walk abroad, look around you and above you, and behold your God! But while men are under the dominion of sin, nature does not reveal God to them; their eyes are blinded and they will not perceive him. Some of the most eminent students of nature have remained without the discovery of God. The same is true of *providence*. God comes very close to many men by preserving their lives from imminent peril or by providing them with things necessary in the moment of great need, yet we have known men living in the centre of wondrous providences, who have only thought themselves lucky fellows or clever persons, and so have traced God's mercy to chance or self. And let me go a little further. The revelation which God has made in this *Holy Book*, though it is an eminently clear and heavenly revelation, does not bring the personal assurance to men which comes by pardon of sin. Many have read the book from their childhood and know large portions of it by heart, and yet they have never seen God in his own Word. But if you have ever felt the guilt and burden of sin, and God has come to you and brought you to the Saviour's feet, and you have looked up and seen the great Sacrifice and put your trust in him, and the Spirit has borne witness with your spirit that your sins and your iniquities have been forgiven you, then you know the Lord with emphasis and beyond all doubt. In such a discovery of the Godhead there is a joyful conviction, an absolute certainty, a more than mathematical demonstration.

FOR MEDITATION: Pharaoh was given ample opportunity to know about God through plagues (Exodus 7:17–18; 9:13–14) and providences (Exodus 8:9–11,22–23; 9:29; 11:5–7), but his insincerity in seeking forgiveness (Exodus 9:27,34; 10:16–20) left him no further forward than when he had said 'I know not the LORD' (Exodus 5:2).

SERMON NO. 2006

30 JANUARY (1887)

Christ's work no failure

'He shall not fail nor be discouraged, till he have set judgment in the earth: and the isles shall wait for his law.' Isaiah 42:4
SUGGESTED FURTHER READING: Luke 17:20–37

Our Lord has come to save his own elect and he will save every one of them. No soul for whom he stood as surety and substitute shall ever be cast away. The sheep shall pass again under the hand of him that counts them, and they shall all be there. 'He shall not fail nor be discouraged,' but 'He shall see of the travail of his soul, and shall be satisfied'. As for the Lord's second coming, we know not when it shall be. Shall the world grow darker and darker till he comes? It may be so. There are passages of Scripture and signs of the times which may be taken to indicate it. On the other hand, shall the age grow brighter and brighter till he appears to bring the perfect day? Through the preaching of the gospel shall there yet be periods in which multitudes shall be converted and whole nations shall be saved? I do not know: there are texts that seem to look that way, and many a brave worker hopes as much. There are brethren who can map out unfulfilled prophecy with great distinctness, but I confess my inability to do so. They get a box of mathematical instruments. They stick down one leg of the compasses and describe a circle here and a circle there, and they draw two or three lines, and there it is. Can you not see it, as plain as a pikestaff? I am sick of diagrams; I have seen enough of them to make another volume of Euclid. My impression is that very little is to be learned from the major part of these interpretations or speculations. I do not think that anybody can map out the future so as to be absolutely sure of anything definite except certain great clearly-stated facts. It is certain that the Lord will come, that he will come in such an hour as the most of men look not for him, and that his coming will be a surprise even to many of his own church.

FOR MEDITATION: (*Our Own Hymn Book,* no. 72 song 1 v.1—Isaac Watts, 1719)
   'Jesus shall reign where'er the sun
   Does His successive journeys run;
   His kingdom stretch from shore to shore,
   Till moons shall wax and wane no more.'

SERMON NO. 1945

31 JANUARY (UNDATED SERMON)

The love of God and the patience of Christ

'And the Lord direct your hearts into the love of God, and into the patient waiting for Christ.' 2 Thessalonians 3:5
SUGGESTED FURTHER READING: James 5:7–11

We shall want *the patience of working*, working on when nothing comes of it, pleading on with souls that are not converted, preaching when preaching seems to have no effect, teaching when the children do not care to learn. We need the patience of Christ, who set his face like a flint and would accomplish his work, cost what it may. He never turned aside from it for a moment. The Lord direct our hearts into patient working. Then there is *the patience of watching in prayer*, not giving it up because you have not received an answer. What? Did a friend say she had prayed for seventeen years for a certain mercy and now meant to ask it no more? Sister, make it eighteen years, and when you have got to the end of eighteen make it nineteen. May the Lord direct our hearts into the patience of Christ in prayer! We long kept him waiting: we need not complain if he makes us await his leisure. Still believe; still hope; still wrestle until the break of day. Pray for *the patience of waiting his will*, saying, 'let him do what seemeth him good.' Though it be for months, for years, wait on. Christ is glorified by our patience. Depend on it, the best way in which certain of us can extol him is by letting him have his way with us. Even though he plunges me into seven boiling caldrons one after the other, I will say, 'Let him do what he wills with his own, and I am his own. I am sure that he does not make the furnace one degree too hot. If he means to give his servant ten troubles, let his heavy hand fall even to the tenth, if so he pleases.' We want to be directed into patience towards Christ, and especially *patience in waiting for his coming*. That, no doubt, is very justly inferred and so it is put in our translation very prominently: 'patient waiting for Christ.' He will come, brothers; he will come, sisters.

FOR MEDITATION: (*Our Own Hymn Book*, no. 766 v.3—Thomas Shepherd, 1692)
    'When wilt Thou come unto me, Lord?
    Until Thou dost appear,
    I count each moment for a day,
    Each minute for a year.'

SERMON NO. 2028

1 FEBRUARY (PREACHED 12 APRIL 1885)

The man Christ Jesus

'Now consider how great this man was.' Hebrews 7:4
SUGGESTED FURTHER READING (Spurgeon): Psalm 110:1–7

'Consider how great this man was' as to the singularity of his person, 'Without father, without mother, without descent,' that is to say, we know nothing as to his birth, his origin, or his history. Even this explanation hardly answers to the words, especially when it is added, 'having neither beginning of days, nor end of life'. So mysterious is Melchizedek that many deeply-taught expositors think that he was veritably an appearance of our Lord Jesus Christ. They are inclined to believe that he was not a king of some city in Canaan, as most of us suppose, but that he was a manifestation of the Son of God, such as were the angels that appeared to Abraham on the plains of Mamre, that divine being who appeared to Joshua by Jericho, and to the three holy ones in the furnace. At any rate, you may well 'consider how great this man was' when you observe how veiled in cloud is everything about his coming and going, veiled because intended to impress us with the depth of the sacred meanings which were shadowed forth in him. How much more shall this be said of him of whom we ask, *'Thy generation who can tell, or count the number of thy years?'* 'Consider how great this man was' in the speciality of his office. He had no predecessor in his priesthood and he had no successor. He was not one who took a holy office and then laid it down, but as far as the historic page of Scripture is concerned we have no note of his quitting this mortal scene; he disappears, but we read nothing of his death any more than of his birth. His office was perpetual and passed not from sire to son, for he was the type of one 'Who is made, not after the law of a carnal commandment, but after the power of an endless life.'

FOR MEDITATION: (*Our Own Hymn Book,* no. 392 v.3—John Wingrove, 1785)
   'Hail, Melchizedek, divine;
   Great High Priest, Thou shalt be mine;
   All my powers before Thee fall;
   Take not tithe, but take them all.'

SERMON NO. 1835

2 FEBRUARY (1888)

The Spirit and the wind

'The wind bloweth where it listeth, and thou hearest the sound thereof, but canst not tell whence it cometh, and whither it goeth: so is every one that is born of the Spirit.' John 3:8

SUGGESTED FURTHER READING: John 16:1–15

I do not think you can tell, with regard to yourself, when the first gracious thought was sown in you, when first you lived towards God. You can tell when you first perceived that you believed in God, but there was an experience before that. You cannot put your finger upon such and such a place and say, 'Here the east wind began,' nor can you say, 'Here the Spirit of God began to work on me.' Neither can we always tell what was the first process. Does a man pray first or believe first? If he prays without faith he will not be heard. Which comes first, repentance or faith? A repentance that has no faith in it is no repentance; a faith that has no repentance with it is no faith. These gracious products are like the spokes of a wheel; they all move at the same time. When the wheel of spiritual life moves, we cannot tell which grace in it moves first. The processes of divine grace may, in your case, begin with a soul downcast, and in the case of another person they may begin with a lifting up of holy faith. We cannot 'tell whence it cometh'. Neither can we always tell the exact means of our receiving the Spirit. You say it was by this minister's preaching. Be grateful. But before that sermon an unknown person did a deal of ploughing within your heart. How would the one have sown had not the other ploughed? Many a man who thinks he has never done any good will find out at the last great day that he did much more than he fancied, and that he accomplished an essential part of the work though it remained hidden. You cannot 'tell whence it cometh'.

FOR MEDITATION: (*Our Own Hymn Book,* no. 448 v.3—Isaac Watts, 1709)

'The Spirit, like some heavenly wind,
Blows on the sons of flesh;
Creates a new—a heavenly mind,
And forms the man afresh.'

SERMON NO. 2067

3 FEBRUARY (PREACHED 2 FEBRUARY 1890)

Heaven above, and Heaven below

'They shall hunger no more, neither thirst any more; neither shall the sun light on them, nor any heat. For the Lamb which is in the midst of the throne shall feed them, and shall lead them unto living fountains of waters.' Revelation 7:16–17

'They shall not hunger nor thirst; neither shall the heat nor sun smite them: for he that hath mercy on them shall lead them, even by the springs of water shall he guide them.' Isaiah 49:10

SUGGESTED FURTHER READING: Colossians 2:20–3:4

I think I hear you saying, 'This is all about heaven, but we have not yet come to it. We are still wrestling here below.' Well, if we cannot go to heaven at once, heaven can come to us. The words which I will now read refer to the days of earth, when the sheep feed in the ways and come from the north and south at the call of the shepherd. 'They shall not hunger nor thirst; neither shall the heat nor sun smite them: for he that hath mercy on them shall lead them, even by the springs of water shall he guide them.' Look at the first passage and at this. The description is the same. When I noticed this parallel, I stood amazed. John, you are a great artist; paint me a picture of heaven! Isaiah, you have a great soul; draw me a picture of the life of the saintly ones on earth when their Lord is with them! I have both pictures. They are masterpieces. They are so much alike that I wonder if there is not some mistake. Surely they are depicting the same thing. The forms, the lights and shades, the touches and tones are not only alike, but identical. Amazed, I cry, 'Which is heaven and which is the heavenly life on earth?' The artists know their own work, and by their instruction I will be led. Isaiah painted our Lord's sheep in his presence on the way to heaven, and John drew the same flock in the glory with the Lamb; the fact that the pictures are so much alike is full of suggestive teaching. Here are the same ideas in the same words. May you and I as fully believe and enjoy the second passage, as we hope to realize and enjoy the first Scripture when we get home to heaven.

FOR MEDITATION: (*Our Own Hymn Book*, no. 859 v.1—Charles Wesley, 1759)
   'Come, let us join our friends above who have obtained the prize,
   And on the eagle wings of love to joy celestial rise.'

SERMON NO. 2128

4 FEBRUARY (PREACHED 6 FEBRUARY 1887)

Eternal life within present grasp

'Lay hold on eternal life ... Laying up in store for themselves a good foundation against the time to come, that they may lay hold on eternal life.' 1 Timothy 6:12,19

SUGGESTED FURTHER READING: Luke 12:13–31

There is a higher and a better life than that which is known to the most of men. There is an animal life which all possess; there is a mental life which lifts us up above the beasts: but there is another life as much above the mental life as the mental life is above the mere animal life. The bulk of men are not aware of this, and when they are told of it they do not believe the statement. Men whom they would believe upon any other subject, honest and true men, are, nevertheless, regarded like madmen when they begin to talk about a spiritual life. How should the carnal mind discern that which is spiritual? It can only be spiritually discerned. But there is such a life, as many of us know assuredly, and this is the life eternal, which we are bidden to lay hold upon. The life of heaven is none other than the divine life which God's grace imparts to believers here below, only it is developed and brought to perfection. There is no jerk to the believer in death: his line of life is unbroken. There is a change in his condition, for he drops this mortal body and those tendencies to sin which cling to it, but the same life is in him, in the body or out of it, unclothed or 'clothed upon with' his 'house which is from heaven'. His life is the same day, only here it is the dawn, and in glory it is full moon. His life is one and flows on like a river, widening and deepening until at last it swells into a sea of joyous, perfected life in heaven. Dream not that any of you will ever obtain eternal life hereafter unless you receive it in this life. Unless you are partakers of it now, tremble for the consequences. Where death finds you eternity will leave you.

FOR MEDITATION: (*Our Own Hymn Book,* no. 229 v.2—Thomas Olivers, 1772)

'The God of Abraham praise, at whose supreme command,
From earth I rise, and seek the joys at His right hand:
I all on earth forsake, its wisdom, fame, and power;
And Him my only portion make, my shield and tower.'

5 FEBRUARY (1888)

Holding fast the faith

'I know ... where thou dwellest, even where Satan's seat is: and thou holdest fast my name, and hast not denied my faith.' Revelation 2:13
SUGGESTED FURTHER READING: 2 Timothy 4:1–8

The faith I hold bears upon it marks of the blood of my ancestors. Shall I deny their faith, for which they left their native land to sojourn here? Shall we cast away the treasure which was handed to us through the bars of prisons, or came to us charred with the flames of Smithfield? When my bones have been tortured with rheumatism, I have remembered Job Spurgeon, who in Chelmsford Jail was allowed a chair because he could not lie down by reason of rheumatic pain. That Quaker's broad-brim overshadows my brow. Perhaps I inherit his rheumatism, but that I do not regret if I have his stubborn faith, which will not let me yield a syllable of the truth of God. When I think of how others have suffered for the faith, a little scorn or unkindness seems a mere trifle. An ancestry of lovers of the faith ought to be a great plea with us to abide by the Lord God of our fathers and the faith in which they lived. I must hold the old gospel: I can do no other. God helping me, I will endure the consequences of what men think obstinacy. If the Lord does not speedily appear, there will come future generations, which will all be tainted and injured if we are not faithful to God and to his truth today. We have come to a turning-point in the road. If we turn to the right, our children and their children may go that way, but if we turn to the left, generations yet unborn will curse our names for having been unfaithful to God and to his Word. I charge you, not only by your ancestry but by your posterity, that you seek to win the commendation of your Master, that though you dwell 'where Satan's seat is', you yet hold fast his name, and do not deny his faith.

FOR MEDITATION: (*Our Own Hymn Book*, no. 409 v.4—George W. Doane, 1826)
    'Thou art *the Way, the Truth, the Life*; grant us that Way to know,
    That Truth to keep, that Life to win, whose joys eternal flow.'

N.B. Spurgeon's pleas were made in the weeks before the climax of the Downgrade Controversy on 23 April 1888, when the Baptist Union overwhelmingly voted against the stand he had been taking.

SERMON NO. 2007

God forgiving sin

'He will abundantly pardon. For my thoughts are not your thoughts, neither are your ways my ways, saith the LORD. *For as the heavens are higher than the earth, so are my ways higher than your ways, and my thoughts than your thoughts.'* Isaiah 55:7–9
SUGGESTED FURTHER READING: Micah 7:18–20

You come to an end of your forgiveness before long. After being offended seven times, you do not go on to seventy times seven. If you did so, surely you would make a great wonder of it and think that you deserved great praise. But God goes on to seventy times seventy times, on and on and on, and never comes to the end of pardoning mercy so long as a soul cries to him for forgiveness. *Some things you find it hard to forgive.* You say, 'Well now, this is really very provoking. I am of a forgiving spirit and I have overlooked offences a great many times, but you do not expect me to endure such treatment as this? Surely, nobody can expect me to be always trodden on.' No, nobody does expect it of you, and if he did he would be disappointed. God does far more in the way of pardon than we ask or even think. Our offences may be great, but as soon as we cry to him for pardon, he answers with forgiveness. I am afraid I must say of some of you that *you forgive, but you do not forget.* Now, God promises to forget our iniquities. It is more than omniscience can do to forget and yet God declares that he does forget. 'Thou hast cast all my sins behind thy back.' 'Thou wilt cast all their sins into the depths of the sea.' They shall not be remembered. *We forgive, and yet feel some return of anger.* You forgive, and mean it, but there are times when you get chewing over the old offence, and you feel grieved again. The offence sticks in your throat, does it not? It floats up again, though you thought you had drowned it. But it is never so with God; there are no back reckonings with the All-merciful. 'I have blotted out,' says he, 'thy sins.' Once blotted out, they are done with for ever.

FOR MEDITATION: (*Our Own Hymn Book*, no. 202 v.3—Samuel Davies, 1769)
   'In wonder lost, with trembling joy we take the pardon of our God;
   Pardon for crimes of deepest dye; a pardon bought with Jesus' blood:
   Who is a pardoning God like Thee? Or who has grace so rich and free?'

7 FEBRUARY (1886)

The problem of the age

'And his disciples answered him, From whence can a man satisfy these men with bread here in the wilderness?' Mark 8:4

SUGGESTED FURTHER READING: Psalm 85:1–13

This era is a desert place: in pulpits and out of pulpits, in social morals and in politics, it is a dreary wilderness. 'From whence can a man satisfy these men with bread here in the wilderness?' The Lord has often suffered the multitude to be in straits that he might work gracious deliverances. Take a modern instance. One hundred and fifty years ago or so, there was a general religious lethargy in England, and ungodliness was master of the situation. The devil, as he flew over England, thought that he had drugged the church so that it would never wake again. How deceived he was! A student at Oxford, who had been a pot-boy down in Gloucester, found the Saviour and began to preach him. His first sermon was said to have driven nineteen people mad, because it awakened them to true life. Certain other scholars in Oxford met together and prayed, and were dismissed from the university for the horrible iniquity of holding a prayer-meeting. Out of the same university came another mighty evangelist, John Wesley, and he, with Whitefield, became the leader of the great Methodist revival: its effects are with us to this day. The arch-enemy soon found that his hopes were blighted, for the church awoke again. The poor miners were listening to the gospel; their tears were making gutters down their black cheeks, while seraphic men told them of pardoning love. Then respectable dissent awoke from its bed of sloth, and the Church of England began to rub her eyes and wonder where she was. An evil time brightened into a happy era. Shall it not be so again? Have no fear about it. 'All things' shall 'work together for good'. The Lord brings the people into the wilderness on purpose, that there it may be seen that it is not the earth, but he himself, that feeds the people.

FOR MEDITATION: Contemplate what was done in the wilderness by Moses (John 3:14), John the Baptist (Mark 1:2–5) and the Lord Jesus Christ (Matthew 4:1–11). Pray that once again in the spiritual wilderness of the present time (Amos 8:11) the Saviour will be lifted up, the gospel preached and the devil driven into retreat.

SERMON NO. 1885

8 FEBRUARY (1891)

A call to prayer and testimony

'I have set watchmen upon thy walls, O Jerusalem, which shall never hold their peace day nor night: ye that make mention of the LORD, *keep not silence, and give him no rest, till he establish, and till he make Jerusalem a praise in the earth.'* Isaiah 62:6–7

SUGGESTED FURTHER READING: Isaiah 21:6–12

Our hours are these: they 'shall never hold their peace day nor night'. St Augustine desired to be always found either praying or preaching, either speaking to God for men in prayer, or speaking for God to men in his ministry. Ministers of Christ especially should give themselves, not to the serving of tables, but 'to the ministry of the word' and to prayer. For us to give ourselves to getting up entertainments, to become competitors with theatres and music-halls, is a great degradation of our holy office. If I heard of a minister becoming a chimney-sweep to earn his living, I would honour him in both his callings, but for God's watchmen to become the world's showmen is a miserable business. God keep all of us who are ministers of Christ from entangling ourselves with the things of this life! The proverb says, 'Stick to your last, cobbler' and I would say, 'Stick to your pulpit, minister!' Keep to your one work, and you will find quite enough for all the strength you have, and even more. Oh, for preachers who 'shall never hold their peace'! You Christian people, you also must fulfil your watch. You also are called to ceaseless service. A policeman wears an armlet to show that he is on duty, and all believers should feel that such a badge is worn upon their very heart day and night. 'The love of Christ constraineth us', not now and then, but evermore. Our service of the Lord's cause comes not once a week on Sundays, but as often as we have opportunity. They must watch always who would be watchmen for souls, watchmen for God, watchers against error and sin, watchers for the coming of the Lord. 'I have set watchmen upon thy walls, O Jerusalem, which shall never hold their peace day nor night'.

FOR MEDITATION: Examine the role of God's watchman in Ezekiel 33:7–8. He is to 'hear the word' from God and proceed 'to warn the wicked from his way'. The apostle Paul was faithful to his appointed role as a watchman (Acts 22:14–15; 26:16–18). Are you doing your duty or are you absent without leave (2 Timothy 2:2–4)?

SERMON NO. 2189

9 FEBRUARY (1890)

Pleading, not contradiction

'*She said, Truth, Lord: yet.*' Matthew 15:27
SUGGESTED FURTHER READING: Psalm 73:1–28

Set one truth over against another. Do not contradict a frowning truth, but bring up a smiling one to meet it. Remember how the Jews were saved out of the hands of their enemies in the days of Haman and Mordecai. The king issued a decree that, on a certain day, the people might rise up against the Jews, slay them and take their possessions as a spoil. Now, according to the laws of the Medes and Persians, this could not be altered: the decree must stand. What then? How was it to be got over? Why, by meeting that ordinance by another. Another decree is issued, that although the people might rise against the Jews, yet the Jews might defend themselves and, if anybody dared to hurt them, they might slay them and take their property to be a prey. One decree thus counteracted another. How often we may use the holy art of looking from one doctrine to another! If a truth looks black upon me, I shall not be wise to be always dwelling upon it, but it will be my wisdom to examine the whole range of truth and see if there is not some other doctrine which will give me hope. Asaph practised this when he said of himself, 'So foolish was I, and ignorant: I was as a beast before thee.' And then he most confidently added, 'Nevertheless I am continually with thee: thou hast holden me by my right hand.' He does not contradict himself; and yet the second utterance removes all the bitterness which the first sentence left upon the palate. The two sentences together set forth the supreme grace of God, who enabled a poor beast-like being to commune with himself. I beg you to learn this holy art of setting one truth side by side with another, that thus you may have a fair view of the whole situation and may not despair.

FOR MEDITATION: (*Our Own Hymn Book,* no. 622 v.5—Anne Steele, 1760)
    'Hast Thou not bid me seek Thy face?
    And shall I seek in vain?
    And can the ear of sovereign grace
    Be deaf when I complain?'

SERMON NO. 2129

10 FEBRUARY (1887)

Essential points in prayer

'The LORD appeared to Solomon the second time, as he had appeared unto him at Gibeon. And the LORD said unto him, I have heard thy prayer and thy supplication, that thou hast made before me: I have hallowed this house, which thou hast built, to put my name there for ever; and mine eyes and mine heart shall be there perpetually.' 1 Kings 9:2–3

SUGGESTED FURTHER READING: Psalm 109:1–7

It is wrong for you, in a prayer-meeting, to pray with a view to an individual of importance, or with the remembrance of those present whose respect you would like to obtain. The mercy-seat is no place for the exhibition of your abilities. More evil still is it to take the opportunity of making personal remarks about others. I have heard of oblique hints having been given in prayer. I am sorry to say that I have even heard of remarks which have been so directly critical and offensive, that one knew what the brother was at and lamented it. Such a proceeding is altogether objectionable and irreverent. We do not even pray in prayer-meetings to correct doctrinal errors, nor to teach a body of divinity, nor to make remarks upon the errors of certain brethren, nor to impeach them before the Most High. These things should be earnest matters of supplication, but not of a sort of indirect preaching and scolding in prayer. It is conduct worthy of the accuser of the brethren to turn a prayer into an opportunity of finding fault with others. Our prayer must be 'before God,' or else it is not an acceptable prayer; and if eye, memory and thought can be shut to the presence of everybody else, except in that minor sense in which we must remember them in sympathy, then it is in the presence of God that we truly pray; and that, I say, may be done in public, if grace be given. For this we have need to pray, 'O Lord, open thou my lips; and my mouth shall shew forth thy praise.'

FOR MEDITATION: Others should be on our minds when we pray (Ephesians 6:18–19), but if it is with a view to impressing them or criticising them, it is only right and proper that such prayers should remain unanswered (Matthew 6:5; Luke 18:11–14).

SERMON NO. 2064

11 FEBRUARY (UNDATED SERMON)

Salt for sacrifice

'And every oblation of thy meat offering shalt thou season with salt; neither shalt thou suffer the salt of the covenant of thy God to be lacking from thy meat offering: with all thine offerings thou shalt offer salt.'
Leviticus 2:13

SUGGESTED FURTHER READING: Mark 9:42–50

Do not be deceived. You may be a great man in the church of God, hold office there and even be a leader, but if you lead an unholy life, neither you nor your sacrifice can ever be accepted with the Most High. God abhors that his priests should serve him with unwashed hands and feet. 'Be ye clean, that bear the vessels of the LORD.' I constantly preach to you free, rich and sovereign grace, without the slightest condition and I preach the same at this time, but remember that the grace of God brings sanctification with it, that the gift of God is deliverance from sin and that, if we abide in sin and remain in it, we cannot be the children of God. We must, dear friends, bring with all our oblations that salt in ourselves which shall purify our hearts from inward corruption and which shall have a power about it to purify others. Do you not know that the saints 'are the salt of the earth'? And if we are salt to others, we must have salt in ourselves. How can we conquer sin in others if sin be unconquered in ourselves? How can we give a light we have never seen? How can we have seed as sowers if we have never had bread as eaters? You know what the woman said concerning the well: 'our father Jacob,' she said, 'gave us the well, and drank thereof himself'. You cannot give other people wells if you do not drink thereof yourself. You cannot benefit a man by grace if you are not first benefited by grace yourself. Can anything come out of a man that is not in him? There must be a holy, sanctifying power about the child of God, making him to be as salt, or else he cannot act upon the putrid masses round him as the salt ought to do. With all your offerings, then, bring this salt. God give it to us!

FOR MEDITATION: Christians are to function as 'the salt of the earth' (Matthew 5:13). Consider what the outworkings of this should be both within the church (Mark 9:50) and towards those who are outside the church (Colossians 4:5–6).

SERMON NO. 1942

12 FEBRUARY (1888)

The Lord and the leper

'There came a leper to him, beseeching him, and kneeling down to him, and saying unto him, If thou wilt, thou canst make me clean. And Jesus, moved with compassion, put forth his hand, and touched him, and saith unto him, I will; be thou clean. And as soon as he had spoken, immediately the leprosy departed from him, and he was cleansed.' Mark 1:40–42
SUGGESTED FURTHER READING: Ephesians 4:17–24

To believe that the Lord Jesus Christ can make us love the good things which once we despised, and shun those evil things in which we once took pleasure, this is to believe in him indeed. Jesus can totally change the nature and make a sinner into a saint. This is faith of a practical kind, a faith worth having. None of us would imagine that this leper meant that the Lord Jesus could make him feel comfortable in remaining a leper. Some seem to fancy that Jesus came to let us go on in our sins with a quiet conscience, but he did nothing of the kind. His salvation is cleansing from sin and if we love sin, we are not saved from it. We cannot have justification without sanctification. There is no use in quibbling about it; there must be a radical change, a change of heart, or else we are not saved. I put it now to you: do you desire a moral and a spiritual change, a change of life, thought and motive? This is what Jesus gives. Just as this leper needed a thorough physical change, so you need an entire renewal of your spiritual nature, so as to become a new creature in Jesus Christ. Oh that many would desire this, for it would be a cheering sign. The man who desires to be pure is beginning to be pure; the man who sincerely longs to conquer sin has struck the first blow already. The power of sin is shaken in that man who looks to Jesus for deliverance from it. The man who frets under the yoke of sin will not long be a slave to it; if he can believe that Jesus Christ is able to set him free, he shall soon quit his bondage.

FOR MEDITATION: (*Our Own Hymn Book,* no. 546 v.5—Charlotte Elliott, 1836)
    'Just as I am—Thou wilt receive,
    Wilt welcome, pardon, cleanse, relieve;
    Because Thy promise, I believe,
    O Lamb of God, I come.'

SERMON NO. 2008

13 FEBRUARY (1887)

Who is this?

'Who is this that cometh from Edom, with dyed garments from Bozrah? this that is glorious in his apparel, travelling in the greatness of his strength? I that speak in righteousness, mighty to save.' Isaiah 63:1
SUGGESTED FURTHER READING: Luke 5:17–26

The answer which our Lord gives is twofold. He describes himself first as a *speaker*: 'I that speak in righteousness'. Is he not the Word? Every word that Christ speaks is true: he speaks not in falsehood, but in righteousness. The gospel which he proclaims is a just and righteous one, meeting both the claims of God and the demands of conscience. O soul, if you will hearken to Jesus, you shall hear that from him which you could never hear from any other lip! 'Never man spake like this man.' He will speak of God's holiness and yet he will speak to your comfort. He will reveal God's justice and yet God's love to you. Oh, hear what the Christ has to say, and believe every word of it without a cavil, for therein lies salvation; 'hear, and your soul shall live'. Our Lord also describes himself as *a Saviour*: 'I that speak in righteousness, mighty to save.' Now, observe that the word 'mighty' is joined with his saving and not with his destroying. Although he can crush his foes as easily as a man can crush with his feet the berries of the grape, the prophet does not speak of him as 'mighty to tread down his enemies.' He will prove himself thus mighty in that day of vengeance which is in his heart, but just now he reveals himself in the year of his redeemed as 'mighty to save.' Rejoice in this, my hearers! The Lord Jesus Christ is a Saviour, and he is grand in that capacity. Nothing is beyond his power in the line of salvation. He says, 'him that cometh to me I will in no wise cast out.' There is no manner of sin which he cannot forgive; there is no sort of hardness of heart which he cannot remove; there are no spiritual difficulties which he cannot surmount.

FOR MEDITATION: (*Our Own Hymn Book,* no. 315 v.2—Thomas Kelly, 1809)
   ''Tis the Saviour, now victorious, travelling onward in His might;
   'Tis the Saviour, oh how glorious to His people is the sight!
   Jesus now is strong to save; mighty to redeem the slave.'

SERMON NO. 1947

14 FEBRUARY (1886)

God's remembrance of his covenant

'Nevertheless he regarded their affliction, when he heard their cry: And he remembered for them his covenant, and repented according to the multitude of his mercies.' Psalm 106:44–45
SUGGESTED FURTHER READING: Luke 1:67–75

If God remembers for us his covenant, let us remember it. You that are the Lord's covenanted ones, think of the sacred promise, begin to enjoy it and live upon it practically. What is the covenant? Here is one form of it: 'I am the Almighty God; walk before me, and be thou perfect.' That is an early and condensed shape of it: that is to say, the Lord God Almighty gives himself up to be our portion, and we are to yield ourselves to him, to walk before him in perfect obedience. This also is the covenant: 'I will be their God, and they shall be my people.' Come, beloved, make God your God. This means make God your everything. Say not, 'I am poor.' Not so, for God is yours, and so all things are yours. Say not, 'I am weak.' Not so, God Almighty is yours: when you are weak, then you are strong. 'But I have no wisdom.' Is not the Lord Jesus made of God 'unto us wisdom, and righteousness, and sanctification'? He that has God has everything. Will you belittle your God and limit the Holy One of Israel? Come, find your all in God. This is your part of the covenant, to accept God as being to you what he says he is. He has made himself to be your all in all; accept him as such. Did not David say, 'this is all my salvation, and all my desire'? This is the portion and heritage of the children of God. 'Cursed be the man that trusteth in man, and maketh flesh his arm ... Blessed is the man that trusteth in the LORD, and whose hope the LORD is.' Cast yourself upon the covenant and find rest therein.

FOR MEDITATION: (*Our Own Hymn Book,* no. 229 v.4—Thomas Olivers, 1772)

    'He by Himself hath sworn, I on His oath depend;
    I shall, on eagles' wings upborne, to heaven ascend:
    I shall behold His face, I shall His power adore,
    And sing the wonders of His grace for evermore.'

SERMON NO. 1886

15 FEBRUARY (1891)

Bit and bridle: how to escape them

'I will instruct thee and teach thee in the way which thou shalt go: I will guide thee with mine eye. Be ye not as the horse, or as the mule, which have no understanding: whose mouth must be held in with bit and bridle, lest they come near unto thee.' Psalm 32:8–9
SUGGESTED FURTHER READING: James 3:1–13

Horses and mules have been so trained that they have needed neither bit nor bridle, but have performed marvellous feats at a word. It is possible for these animals to be brought to so high a training that they obey the word of command without the use of force. They come to have an understanding of their owner's intent and act as if they really entered into their master's designs. With the horses and mules of our streets and of David's day this is not the case; these display little understanding and we are not to be like them. You are a reasoning man; act reasonably. You have understanding; do not act under mere impulse, blind wilfulness or ignorant folly. What we need is to come to an understanding with God and to keep in that condition. The horse does not understand his driver's wishes, except as he intimates them through the bit and bridle. When he is to turn, when he is to quicken his pace and when he is to stand still, must be told to him through the rein, for apart from the bit in his mouth, he has no understanding of the man's mind. That thought which works in the mind of his driver is not working in the mule's mind, and therefore he has to feel a pull at his mouth to make him know his master's desire. We need to come to an understanding with God. 'Be ye not unwise, but understanding what the will of the Lord is.' Be sensitive to the Spirit of God. So dwell in God that he shall dwell in you, and his indwelling shall cause you to feel at once what he would have you do. May your will be so in accord with the Lord's will that you will only what he wills! This is the highest form of understanding that I know of; may we never rest till we have it. 'Give me understanding, and I shall keep thy law'.

FOR MEDITATION: (*Our Own Hymn Book*, no. 649 v.5—Charles Wesley, 1749)
   'If to the right or left I stray, that moment, Lord, reprove;
   And let me weep my life away, for having grieved Thy love.'

SERMON NO. 2190

16 FEBRUARY (1890)

The deceitfulness of sin

'But exhort one another daily, while it is called To day; lest any of you be hardened through the deceitfulness of sin.' Hebrews 3:13
SUGGESTED FURTHER READING: 2 Corinthians 11:1–15

Sin has a singular power to deceive. We have only to look back to the beginning of our race to be sure of this. Eve, in the garden, was pure, intelligent and filled with good dispositions: her faculties were well balanced, for no original sin or natural depravity had put her mind out of order. Yet that lovely woman, without a taint upon her heart or will, perfect as she came from her Maker's hand, was overcome by Satan, who embodied in himself the deceitfulness of sin. The serpent played his part right cunningly with the woman and soon withdrew her from her loyal obedience to the Lord God. She began to question, to parley, to argue with rebellious suggestions, and after a while she put forth her hand, took of the fruit which had been forbidden 'and gave also to her husband with her; and he did eat.' If man in his perfectness was so readily deceived by sin, what think you of yourself, fallen and inclined to evil as you are? Will not sin soon deceive you? I will even go further back than the garden, for the serpent who was the instrument of evil in the garden, was once an angel of God. Lucifer, the light-bearer, son of the morning, once stood high in the hierarchy of spirits, but sin entered into his heart and the sublime angel became a loathsome fiend. Lucifer became Satan, as prompt for evil as once he had been swift for good. If sin overcame angels, can we fight with it? If sin entangled in its thrice-accursed net even the pure spirits of heaven, will you, sons and daughters of fallen parents, not soon be deceived by it, unless the grace of God shall make you 'wise unto salvation'? Since your hearts are deceitful and sin is deceitful, you are in peril indeed.

FOR MEDITATION: (*Our Own Hymn Book*, no. 619 v.3—Isaac Watts, 1709)

'Trifles of nature, or of art,
With fair deceitful charms,
Intrude into my thoughtless heart,
And thrust me from Thy arms.'

SERMON NO. 2130

17 FEBRUARY (PROBABLY PREACHED APRIL 1888)

Nathanael; or, the ready believer and his reward

'Jesus answered and said unto him, Because I said unto thee, I saw thee under the fig tree, believest thou? thou shalt see greater things than these.' John 1:50

SUGGESTED FURTHER READING: Hebrews 11:1–6

Hear me, you that would be saved. The way of salvation is by believing in the Lord Jesus Christ, that is, by trusting him. There are two things I have to say to you. First, God commands you to believe in Jesus Christ and, secondly, nothing you can do will please God so much as for you at once to believe in his Only-begotten Son, whom he has set forth to be the propitiation for sin. These are two strong things to say and so I will not say them of myself, but give you God's Word for them. Please note these texts down, all of you. First Epistle General of John, third chapter, at the twenty-third verse: 'And this is his commandment, That we should believe on the name of his Son Jesus Christ'. If you are commanded to do it, do it. If you have salvation promised you when you believe on the name of Jesus, why then, believe and have salvation. 'Believe on the name of his Son Jesus Christ'. That is the first point. God commands you: will you disobey? The second thing I said was that nothing you can do will please God so much as for you now to believe in Jesus Christ. Look at the sixth chapter of John's gospel, and the twenty-eighth and twenty-ninth verses. There you have it. 'Then said they unto him, What shall we do, that we might work the works of God?' They meant, 'What are the best works, the works most pleasing to God?' 'Jesus answered and said unto them, This is the work of God, that ye believe on him whom he hath sent.' If you could build a row of almshouses, or endow a church, or pay the salaries of a hundred missionaries, it would not half so well please God as for you to believe on his Son Jesus Christ. Trust Christ.

FOR MEDITATION: (*Our Own Hymn Book*, no. 493 v.3—Joseph Swain, 1792)

'Blessèd are the eyes that see Him;
Blest the ears that hear His voice:
Blessèd are the souls that trust Him,
And in Him alone rejoice;
His commandments
Then become their happy choice.'

SERMON NO. 2021

18 FEBRUARY (UNDATED SERMON)

Zealous, but wrong

'Brethren, my heart's desire and prayer to God for Israel is, that they might be saved. For I bear them record that they have a zeal for God, but not according to knowledge. For they being ignorant of God's righteousness, have not submitted themselves unto the righteousness of God.' Romans 10:1–3

SUGGESTED FURTHER READING: Galatians 2:15–3:14

How many have been brought to Christ by reading Martin Luther upon the Galatians? What sledge-hammer words Martin uses! Only the other day I met a man who came to me like one of the old Puritans and said that he had traversed the line of the two covenants. He began to converse with me in that majestic style which comes of Puritanic theology. I thought, 'Bless the man! He has risen from the dead. He is one of Oliver Cromwell's grey Ironsides. He will be able to tell me of Naseby and Marston Moor.' So I said to him, 'Covenant and law, where did you pick that up?' 'Not at any church or chapel,' said he. 'There are none round about where I live who know anything at all about it. They are all in the dark together, dumb dogs that cannot bark.' 'How did you stumble on the true light?' I asked. The man replied, 'In the good providence of God, I met with Master Martin Luther on the Galatians. I bought it for sixpence out of a box in front of a bookseller's shop.' It was a good find for that man! Sixpenny worth of salvation according to the judgment of men, but infinite riches according to the judgment of God. He had found a jewel when he learned the truth of salvation by grace through faith. I recommend people, whether they will read Martin Luther or any other author, to be especially careful to read the Epistle to the Galatians itself. Paul hammers there against all hope of salvation by the law, and puts salvation on the basis of grace and grace alone, 'through faith which is in Christ Jesus.'

FOR MEDITATION: (*Our Own Hymn Book*, no. 563 v.2—John Kent, 1803)
  'We claim no merit of our own,
  But, self-condemned before Thy throne, our hopes on Jesus place;
  Though once in heart and life depraved,
  We now can sing as sinners saved, and praise redeeming grace.'

N.B. Martin Luther died on 18 February 1546.

SERMON NO. 1899

19 FEBRUARY (1888)

Job among the ashes

'I have heard of thee by the hearing of the ear: but now mine eye seeth thee. Wherefore I abhor myself, and repent in dust and ashes.' Job 42:5–6
SUGGESTED FURTHER READING: 2 Corinthians 7:2–16

All real repentance is joined with holy sorrow and self-loathing. I have read in the sermons of certain teachers that, 'Repentance is only a change of mind.' That may be true, but what a change of mind it is! It is not such a change of mind as some of you underwent this morning when you said, 'It is really too cold to go out,' but afterwards you braved the snow and came to the Tabernacle. Oh, no! Repentance is a thorough and radical change of mind, and it is accompanied with real sorrow for sin and self-loathing. A repentance in which there is no sorrow for sin will ruin the soul. Repentance without sorrow for sin is not the repentance of God's elect. If you can look upon sin without sorrow, then you have never looked on Christ. A faith-look at Jesus breaks the heart, both for sin and from sin. Try yourself by this test. But, next, repentance has comfort in it. It is to my mind rather extraordinary that the Hebrew word, which is justly translated 'repent,' is also used in two or three places at least in the Old Testament to express comfort. Isaac, it is said, took Rebekah to his mother's tent, and 'was comforted after his mother's death.' Here the word is the same as that which is here rendered 'repent.' Isaac's mind was changed as to the death of his mother. As then there is in the Hebrew word just a tinge of comfort, so in repentance itself, with all its sorrow, there are traces of joy. Repentance is a bitter-sweet or a sweet-bitter. After you have tasted it in your mouth as gall, it will go down into your stomach and be sweeter than honey and the honeycomb. The door of repentance opens into the halls of joy. Job's repentance in dust and ashes was the sign of his deliverance.

FOR MEDITATION: (*Our Own Hymn Book,* no. 186 v.3—Isaac Watts, 1706)
'Lord, what shall earth and ashes do?
We would adore our Maker too;
From sin and dust to Thee we cry,
The Great, The Holy, and the High!'

SERMON NO. 2009

20 FEBRUARY (1887)

A sermon for the worst man on earth

'And the publican, standing afar off, would not lift up so much as his eyes unto heaven, but smote upon his breast, saying, God be merciful to me a sinner.' Luke 18:13
SUGGESTED FURTHER READING (Spurgeon): Psalm 51:1–19

This man who was a sinner yet dared to approach the Lord. According to our version, he said, 'God be merciful to me *a* sinner', but a more accurate rendering is that which the Revised Version puts in the margin—'*the* sinner'. He meant to say that he was emphatically the sinner. The Pharisee yonder was *the* saint of his age: but this publican who stood afar off from the holy place was *the* sinner. If there was not another sinner in the world, he was one, and in a world of sinners he was a prominent offender—the sinner of sinners. Emphatically he applies to himself the guilty name. He takes the chief place in condemnation and yet he cries, 'God be merciful to me the sinner'. Now if you know yourself to be a sinner, you may plead with God, but if you mourn that you are not only a sinner, but *the* sinner with the definite article, the sinner above all others, you may still hope in the mercy of the Lord. The worst, the most profane, the most horrible of sinners may venture, as this man did, to approach the God of mercy. I know that it looks like a daring action; therefore you must do it by faith. On any other footing but that of faith in the mercy of God, you who are a sinner may not dare to approach the Lord lest you be found guilty of presumption. But with your eye on mercy you may be bravely trustful. Believe in the great mercy of God, and though your sins are abundant, you will find that the Lord will abundantly pardon; though they blot your character, the Lord will blot them out; 'though they be red like crimson,' yet the precious blood of Jesus will make you whiter than snow.

FOR MEDITATION: Note how God's mercy towards the tax-collector, who literally called himself '*the* sinner' in this parable, foreshadowed the actual cases not only of a tax-collector whom others called 'a sinner' (Luke 19:7–10), but also of a Pharisee who was to call himself the chief of sinners (1 Timothy 1:15–16). Can you identify with them? Or are you like the self-righteous Pharisee in the parable (Luke 18:11–12) whose attitude was soon echoed in the actual case of the rich young ruler (Luke 18:18–23)?

SERMON NO. 1949

21 FEBRUARY (1886)

Pleading for prayer

'Now I beseech you ... that ye strive together with me in your prayers to God for me; that I may be delivered from them that do not believe in Judæa; and that my service which I have for Jerusalem may be accepted of the saints; that I may come unto you with joy by the will of God, and may with you be refreshed.' Romans 15:30–32
SUGGESTED FURTHER READING: Deuteronomy 9:6–29

Never let us imagine that the doctrine of the fixity of events or the supremacy of law, as the philosophers call it, is at all contrary to the truth that prayer is effectual for its own ends and purposes. In olden times a warrior was going forth to battle for his country and a certain preacher of the word said to him, 'My prayer is made continually for you that you may be victorious.' The warrior, in his philosophic doubt, replied that he saw no use in the promised prayers, for if God had determined to give him victory, he would have it without prayer, and if fate had decreed that he should be defeated, prayers could not prevent it. To which the godly man very properly replied, 'Then take off your helmet and your coat of mail, and hang up your sword and buckler. Go not forth to battle at all with your men-at-arms, for, indeed, if the Lord is to conquer your enemies he can do it without your weapons, and if he will not prosper you, it is in vain for you to mount your war-horse.' The argument, when carried out, answers itself: there is, in truth, no force in it. The net result of such reasoning would be absolute inaction. Commonsense shows us how absurd it is. All means are to be used, notwithstanding the eternal purpose of God, for that purpose includes means and their uses. We declare that among the most potent means in all the world is prayer; and this must not be neglected. There are certain ascertained forces and among those forces, always to be reckoned with and relied upon, is the force of the cry of God's dear children to their great Father in heaven, in other words, the power of prayer. In prayer we present the sacrifice of God's own Son to God's own self, and prevail by its means.

FOR MEDITATION: Hezekiah was twice confronted by serious situations which seemed to be God's fixed will (2 Kings 18:25; 20:1). After he prayed to God (2 Kings 19:14–19; 20:2–3), Isaiah told him that God would grant his requests (2 Kings 19:20; 20:4–6). 'Prayer changes things.'

SERMON NO. 1887

22 FEBRUARY (1891)

Believing on Jesus, and its counterfeits

'Then said Jesus to those Jews which believed on him, If ye continue in my word, then are ye my disciples indeed.' John 8:31
SUGGESTED FURTHER READING: 2 Timothy 3:1–17

We need not think that some strange thing has happened to us as a church when the baser sort are found among us, for one such entered into that college of apostles, a man who, doubtless, believed the words of Jesus and thought him to be the Messiah: I mean Judas, who, with a traitor's hand, sold his Master. His intellect had been convinced, but his heart had never been renewed. He even dared to use his profession of religion and the position which it brought him as a means of unhallowed gain. Another notable believer of this sort was Simon Magus, who believed because he saw the signs and wonders wrought by the apostles, but, as he also sought to make gain of godliness, he remained 'in the gall of bitterness, and in the bond of iniquity', and never became 'a disciple indeed.' There is a greater one than these, even the devil. We read that 'the devils also believe, and tremble.' They hold the faith and feel something of the power of it, for they tremble, which is more than modern critics do. Devils know that Jesus is the Christ of God, for they have on occasion confessed it and have borne witness to the gospel in the open streets, crying after the preachers of the Word, and yet, with all their knowledge, with much of a sort of faith and with an apprehension which leads to trembling, they remain devils still and make no advance towards God. Beware of that faith which is a mere intellectual movement, which does not control the heart and life. To come to faith through a cold argument and to feel no spiritual life is a poor business. You want a faith that leads you to an entire reliance upon the person of Jesus, to the giving up of everything to him, to the reception of him as your Saviour and King, your all in all. You have not believed unto eternal life unless you have so believed on him.

FOR MEDITATION: Temporary belief is worse than the unbelief of Jesus' brothers (John 7:5), who disowned discipleship (John 7:3), doubted his deeds (John 7:4—in the Greek they said 'if', not 'since') and dictated their desires (John 7:3–4). It is less likely to lead to the true faith which they later obtained (Acts 1:14; 1 Corinthians 9:5; Galatians 1:19).

SERMON NO. 2191

23 FEBRUARY (1890)

Christ put on

'But put ye on the Lord Jesus Christ, and make no provision for the flesh, to fulfil the lusts thereof.' Romans 13:14
SUGGESTED FURTHER READING: Galatians 3:23–29

Paul does not say merely to one person, 'put *thou* on the Lord Jesus Christ,' but to all of us, 'put *ye* on the Lord Jesus Christ'. Can all the saints put on Christ, whether babes, young men, or fathers? You could not all of you wear my coat, I am quite certain, and I am equally certain that I could not wear the garments of many of the young people now present, but here is a matchless garment, which will be found suitable for every believer without expansion or contraction. Whoever puts on the Lord Jesus Christ has put on a robe which will be his glory and beauty. In every case the example of Jesus is admirably suited for copying. Suppose a child of God should be a king; what better advice could I give to him, when about to rule a nation, than this, 'put on the Lord Jesus Christ'? Be such a king as Jesus would have been. Copy his royal character. Suppose, on the other hand, that the person before us is a poor woman from the workhouse; shall I say the same to her? Yes, and with equal propriety, for Jesus was very poor and is a most suitable example for those who have no home of their own. Worker, put on Christ and be full of zeal! Sufferer, put on the Lord Jesus Christ and abound in patience! Yonder friend is going to the Sunday-school this afternoon. Well, in order to win those dear children to the Saviour, 'put on the Lord Jesus Christ,' who said, 'Suffer the little children to come unto me, and forbid them not'. In his sacred raiment you will make a good teacher. Are you a preacher and about to address thousands of grown-up persons? How better can I advise you than that you put on Christ and preach the gospel in his own loving, pleading, earnest style? The preacher's model should be his Lord. This is our preaching gown, our praying surplice, our pastoral robe: the character and spirit of the Lord Jesus.

FOR MEDITATION: (*Our Own Hymn Book,* no. 263 v.1—John Hampden Gurney, 1851)
'Lord, as to Thy dear Cross we flee, and plead to be forgiven,
So let Thy life our pattern be, and form our souls for heaven.'

SERMON NO. 2132

24 FEBRUARY (1889)

Breakfast with Jesus

'Jesus saith unto them, Come and dine [break your fast—Revised Version]. And none of the disciples durst ask him, Who art thou? knowing that it was the Lord.' John 21:12
SUGGESTED FURTHER READING: Philippians 4:10–20

Let us be satisfied with the Lord's great goodness to us when in trouble we have sought his face. 'This poor man cried, and the LORD heard him, and saved him out of all his troubles.' 'I sought the LORD, and he heard me'. Come, feed upon what you have already tasted and handled, both of his word and work. Rejoice in what you have seen him do in you and for you. Why, here are 'great fishes, an hundred and fifty and three'. The provision on the lone lakeshore was more than enough for seven men, however hungry they might be, was it not? They might eat as much as they liked without any fear of exhausting the supply, and, after the meal, they would not have left twelve baskets full alone, as there had been at the former feast, but a superabundance for their brethren or for any wanderers along the shore. Now, dear friends, try for a minute or two to dwell upon the wonders of God's truth and grace to you. Think of what he did in your conversion, what he has done in the time of temptation, how he has supplied your needs and how he has given you enjoyments of his love. I was looking back through former volumes of my sermons and I noticed how often a sermon occurs without a date upon it. I know what that denotes. It means that I was ill and in great pain. Two or three times in almost every year I have to hear the Lord preach to me in the chamber of sickness and I am unable, therefore, to preach to you. These were bitter things at the time, but I bless the Lord for them all and for raising me up again and again and renewing my strength. He will not leave me now. Cannot you also turn to your diaries, remember the lovingkindness of the Lord, and speak well of his name?

FOR MEDITATION: (*Our Own Hymn Book*, no. 820 v.3—Isaac Watts, 1734)
    'Oh, let my soul for ever lie
    Beneath the blessings of Thine eye;
    'Tis heaven on earth, 'tis heaven above,
    To see Thy face, and taste Thy love.'

SERMON NO. 2072

25 FEBRUARY (PREACHED 23 FEBRUARY 1890)

A mediator

'Now a mediator is not a mediator of one, but God is one.' Galatians 3:20
SUGGESTED FURTHER READING: 1 Timothy 2:1–6

'A mediator is not a mediator of one,' but he studies the interests of both parties. Such is our Lord Jesus Christ. Coming here on earth, did he come to save men? Yes. Did he come to glorify his Father's name? Yes. For which of these two purposes did he chiefly come? I will not say. He came for both and he blends the two. He looks after the interests of man and pleads the causes of his soul: he looks after the interests of God and vindicates the honour of God, even unto death. Is he obedient, that he might magnify the law of God, and make it honourable? Yes, but he is mediator that he may deliver us from the curse of the law. Beloved, our blessed mediator is not a mediator for one. An umpire must not take sides, and a mediator that did not understand more than one side and was not concerned for anybody but one side would be unworthy of the name. Our mediator, the Lord Jesus Christ, has both natures. Is he God? Verily, he is very God of very God. Is he man? Assuredly, of the substance of his mother, as truly man as any man among us. Is he most God, or is he most man? This is a question not to be asked and, therefore, not to be answered. He is my brother. He is God's Son. Yes, he is himself God. What better umpire can we want than this divine human being, who can lay his hands upon us both, who counts 'it not robbery to be equal with God', and yet calls man his brother? 'A mediator is not a mediator of one,' since he wears both natures and espouses both causes. How dear to the heart of Christ is the glory of God! He lives, he dies, he rises again to glorify the Father. How dear to Christ is the salvation of men! He lives, he dies, he rises again and pleads for the salvation of sinners.

FOR MEDITATION: (*Our Own Hymn Book,* no. 433 v.2—Isaac Watts, 1709)
  "'Tis by the merits of Thy death
  The Father smiles again;
  'Tis by Thine interceding breath
  The Spirit dwells with men.'

SERMON NO. 2180

26 FEBRUARY (1888)

Abram's call; or, half-way and all the way

'They went forth ... from Ur of the Chaldees, to go into the land of Canaan; and they came unto Haran, and dwelt there ... and they went forth to go into the land of Canaan; and into the land of Canaan they came.' Genesis 11:31; 12:5
SUGGESTED FURTHER READING (Spurgeon): Acts 7:1–5

To obey the Lord partially is to disobey him. If the Lord bids Abram go to Canaan, he cannot fulfil that command by going to Haran. Haran was not mentioned in the call. You cannot keep God's command by doing something else which pleases you better. The essence of obedience lies in its exactness. Although something else may seem to you to be quite as good as the thing commanded, what has that to do with it? This is what God bids you, and to refuse the thing commanded, professing to substitute a better thing, is gross presumption. You may not think it so, but so it is, that half obedience is whole disobedience. We can only obey the Lord's command as it stands; to alter it is as great a treason as to make erasures in a king's statute-book. It is will-worship, and not God's worship, if I do what I choose of the Lord's work and leave a part undone which does not please me quite so well. Moreover, half-way obedience increases our responsibility, because it is a plain confession that we know the Lord's will, though we do it not. Abram had received the call, and knew that he had done so, else why had he come to Haran? He admitted, by going as far as Haran, that he ought to go the whole way to Canaan; and so by his own action he left himself without excuse. And any of you who are doing in a measure what is right because of the fear of God and yet are acting in other matters contrary to what you know to be the Lord's will, you are left without excuse for such neglect. By the service which you do render to God you admit that he has right to your obedience; why, then, do you not obey him in all things? You call Jesus your Lord, and do some of the things which he says, but why not the rest?

FOR MEDITATION: The purpose of the test is to see whether we are 'obedient in all things' (2 Corinthians 2:9). Some have failed, but thought they had passed (1 Samuel 15:17–23; 2 Kings 10:15–16,30–31; 17:32–34; Mark 10:19–22). Anything short of full obedience makes us guilty (James 2:10–11). There but for the grace of God go all of us.

SERMON NO. 2011

27 FEBRUARY (1887)

Earthquake, but not heartquake

'God is our refuge and strength, a very present help in trouble. Therefore will not we fear, though the earth be removed, and though the mountains be carried into the midst of the sea; though the waters thereof roar and be troubled, though the mountains shake with the swelling thereof.'
Psalm 46:1–3
SUGGESTED FURTHER READING: Acts 27:13–44

If you are enabled to rise above fear in times of alarm, then those who see you will say, 'This is a man of God and this is God's work upon his soul.' I knew a youth near forty years ago, who was staying with relations when a thunderstorm of unusual violence came on at nightfall. A stack was struck by lightning and set on fire within sight of the door. The grown-up people in the house, both men and women, were utterly overcome with fright. The strong men seemed even more afraid than the women. All the inmates of the house sat huddled together. Only this youth was quietly happy. There was a little child upstairs in bed and the mother was anxious about it, but even her love could not give her courage enough to pass the staircase windows to bring that child down. The babe cried and this youth, whom I knew well and who was newly converted, went upstairs alone, took the child and, without hurry or alarm, brought it down to its mother. He needed no candle, for the lightning was so continuous that he could see his way well. He felt that the Lord was wonderfully near that night and so no fear was possible to his heart. He sat down and read a psalm aloud to his trembling relatives, who looked on the lad with loving wonder. That night he was master of the situation and those in the house believed that there was something in the religion which he had so lately professed. I believe that, if all of us can by God's grace get such a sense of God's nearness to us in times of danger and trouble that we remain calm, we shall bring much honour to the cause of God and the name of Jesus.

FOR MEDITATION: (*Our Own Hymn Book,* no. 673 v.3—Henry Kirke White, 1806; Fanny Fuller Maitland, 1827)

'Let not sorrow dim your eye,   Let not fears your course impede,
Soon shall every tear be dry;   Great your strength if great your need.'

SERMON NO. 1950

28 FEBRUARY (1886)

The blood of sprinkling

'And to Jesus the mediator of the new covenant, and to the blood of sprinkling, that speaketh better things than that of Abel. See that ye refuse not him that speaketh. For if they escaped not who refused him that spake on earth, much more shall not we escape, if we turn away from him that speaketh from heaven.' Hebrews 12:24–25
SUGGESTED FURTHER READING: Hebrews 9:11–22

This sprinkling of the blood, as mentioned by the Holy Spirit in this passage, is absolutely identical with Jesus himself. Read it: 'to Jesus the mediator of the new covenant, and to the blood of sprinkling, that speaketh better things than that of Abel. See that ye refuse not him that speaketh.' He says it is the blood 'that speaketh', and then he proceeds to say, 'See that ye refuse not him that speaketh.' This is a very unexpected turn, which can only be explained upon the supposition that Jesus and the blood are identical in the writer's view. By what we may call a singularity in grammar, in putting 'him' for 'it', the Spirit of God intentionally sets forth the striking truth that the sacrifice is identical with the Saviour. We have come to the Saviour, 'the mediator of the new covenant, and to the blood of sprinkling, that speaketh … See that ye refuse not him'. There is no Jesus if there is no blood of sprinkling; there is no Saviour if there is no sacrifice. I put this strongly, because the attempt is being made nowadays to set forth Jesus apart from his cross and atonement. He is held up as a great ethical teacher, a self-sacrificing spirit, who is to lead the way in a grand moral reformation and, by his influence, to set up a kingdom of moral influence in the world. It is even hinted that this kingdom has never had prominence enough given to it because it has been overshadowed by his cross. But where is Jesus apart from his sacrifice? He is not there if you have left out the blood of sprinkling, which is the blood of sacrifice. Without the atonement no man is a Christian and Christ is not Jesus. If you have torn away the sacrificial blood, you have drawn the heart out of the gospel of Jesus Christ and robbed it of its life.

FOR MEDITATION: (*Our Own Hymn Book,* no. 291 v.3—Isaac Watts, 1709)
   'How glorious was the grace when Christ sustained the stroke!
   His life and blood the Shepherd pays, a ransom for the flock.'

SERMON NO. 1888

29 FEBRUARY (PREACHED 28 FEBRUARY 1886)

The blood of sprinkling (second sermon)

'Ye are come ... to Jesus the mediator of the new covenant, and to the blood of sprinkling, that speaketh better things than that of Abel. See that ye refuse not him that speaketh.' Hebrews 12:24–25
SUGGESTED FURTHER READING: Romans 3:19–26

God is infinitely loving; in fact, God is love, but that love does not cause him to be unjust or unholy, for that in the long run would not be love. God is 'the Judge of all the earth' and he must 'do right'. The Lord, as the great moral governor, if he makes a law and threatens a penalty, must execute that penalty, or else his law will lose its authority. If the penalty threatened is not executed, there is a tacit acknowledgment that it was threatened in error. Could you believe in a fallible God? The Lord has made a law which is perfect, just and good. Would you rather be without law? What reasonable person desires anarchy? He has backed up that law with a threatening. What is the use of a law if to break it involves no evil consequences? A government that never punishes offenders is no government at all. God, therefore, as moral ruler, must be just and must display his indignation against wrong and evil of every kind. It is written on the conscience of men that sin must be punished. Would you have it go unpunished? If you are a just man, you would not. To meet the case, therefore, the Lord Jesus Christ, by himself bearing the penalty of death, has honoured the divine law. He has shown to all intelligences that God will not wink at sin, that even his infinite mercy must not come in the way of his justice. This is the doctrine: do not listen to those who twist and pervert it. It is the love of God which has provided the great atonement by which, in a judgment better than ours, the law finds a glorious vindication and the foundation of moral government is strengthened.

FOR MEDITATION: (*Our Own Hymn Book,* no. 294 v.4—Joseph Swain, 1792)
   'Angels here may gaze and wonder
   What the God of love could mean,
   When He tore the heart asunder,
   Never once defiled with sin!'

SERMON NO. 1889

1 MARCH (1891)

The joyous return

'O Israel, return unto the LORD thy God; for thou hast fallen by thine iniquity. Take with you words, and turn to the LORD: say unto him, Take away all iniquity, and receive us graciously.' Hosea 14:1–2
SUGGESTED FURTHER READING: Luke 11:1–4

The Lord helps us to return to him by giving a direction how to pray. A minister said to me last Thursday evening what I have often felt to be true: 'We need to make coming to Christ very plain, for many people are so ignorant that they almost need to have the words of confession and faith put into their mouths. They need somebody to kneel down side by side with them and utter the very words that they should speak to the Lord.' There is much more truth in this statement than inexperienced persons may think. So here the Lord does, as it were, put the words into the sinner's mouth. 'Take with you words, and … say unto him'. He says the words, that the sinner may make them his own and say them after him. In this condescending style he teaches the returning sinner how to pray. What a gracious God he is! Suppose a case. A great king has been grievously offended by a rebellious subject, but in kindness of heart he wills to be reconciled. He invites the rebel to sue for pardon. He replies, 'O King, I would be forgiven, but how can I properly approach your offended majesty? I am anxious to present such a petition as you can accept, but I know not how to draw it up.' Suppose this great king were to say, 'I will draw up the petition for you,' what confidence the supplicant would feel in presenting the petition! He brings to the king his own words. He prays the prayer he is bidden to pray. By the very fact of drawing up the petition, the monarch pledged himself to grant it. O my hearer, the Lord puts it into your mouth to say this morning, 'Take away all iniquity'. May you find it in your heart to pray in that fashion! That prayer is best which is offered in God's own way and is of God's own prompting. May you present such a prayer at once!

FOR MEDITATION: (*Our Own Hymn Book,* no. 600 v.1—H. W. Beecher's Plymouth Collection, 1855)
   'Jesus! who on Calvary's mountain poured Thy precious blood for me,
   Wash me in its following fountain, that my soul may spotless be.'

SERMON NO. 2192

2 MARCH (1890)

'Lama sabachthani?'

'And about the ninth hour Jesus cried with a loud voice, saying, Eli, Eli, lama sabachthani? that is to say, My God, my God, why hast thou forsaken me?' Matthew 27:46

SUGGESTED FURTHER READING: Mark 15:21–39

The soldier at the gate of Pompeii, remaining at his post as sentry when the shower of burning ashes is falling, was not more true to his trust than he who adheres to a forsaking God with loyalty of hope. Our Lord's suffering in this particular form was appropriate and necessary. It would not have sufficed for our Lord merely to have been pained in body, nor even to have been grieved in mind in other ways: he must suffer in this particular way. He must feel forsaken of God, because this is the necessary consequence of sin. For a man to be forsaken of God is the penalty which naturally and inevitably follows upon his breaking his relation with God. What is death? What was the death that was threatened to Adam? 'In the day that thou eatest thereof thou shalt surely die.' Is death annihilation? Was Adam annihilated that day? Assuredly not: he lived many a year afterwards. But in the day in which he ate of the forbidden fruit he died by being separated from God. The separation of the soul from God is spiritual death, just as the separation of the soul from the body is natural death. The sacrifice for sin must be put in the place of separation and must bow to the penalty of death. By this placing of the Great Sacrifice under forsaking and death it would be seen by all creatures throughout the universe that God could not have fellowship with sin. If even the Holy One, who stood 'the just for the unjust,' found God forsaking him, what must the doom of the actual sinner be! Sin is evidently always in every case a dividing influence, putting even the Christ himself, as a sinbearer, in the place of distance.

FOR MEDITATION: (*Our Own Hymn Book*, no. 299 vv.2&3—William Russell, 1861)
  'Oh, hear that piercing cry! What can its meaning be?
  "My God! my God! oh! why hast Thou in wrath forsaken me?"
  Oh 'twas because our sins on Him by God were laid;
  He who Himself had never sinned, for sinners, sin was made.'

SERMON NO. 2133

3 MARCH (1889)

Two essential things

'Testifying both to the Jews, and also to the Greeks, repentance toward God, and faith toward our Lord Jesus Christ.' Acts 20:21
SUGGESTED FURTHER READING: Mark 1:1–15

If there could be such a thing as a man who was a believer without repentance, he would be much too big for his boots and there would be no bearing him. If he were always saying, 'Yes, I know I am saved; I have a full assurance that I am saved,' and yet had no sense of personal sin, how loudly he would crow! But, O dear friends, while we mourn our sins, we are not puffed up by the privileges which faith receives. An old Puritan says that when a saint is made beautiful with rich graces, as the peacock with many-coloured feathers, let him not be vain, but let him recollect the black feet of his inbred sin, and the harsh voice of his many shortcomings. Repentance will never allow faith to strut, even if it had a mind to do so. Faith cheers repentance and repentance sobers faith. The two go well together. Faith looks to the throne and repentance loves the cross. When faith looks most rightly to the Second Advent, repentance forbids its forgetting the First Advent. When faith is tempted to climb into presumption, repentance calls it back to sit at Jesus' feet. Never try to separate these dear companions, which minister more sweetly to one another than I have time to tell. That conversion, which is all joy and lacks sorrow for sin, is very questionable. I will not believe in that faith which has no repentance with it any more than I would believe in that repentance which left a man without faith in Jesus. Like the two cherubs which stood gazing down upon the mercy-seat, so stand these two inseparable graces, and none must dare to remove the one or the other.

FOR MEDITATION: (*Our Own Hymn Book*, no. 579 vv.1&2—John S. B. Monsell, 1863)
'My sins, my sins, my Saviour! How sad on Thee they fall,
Seen through Thy gentle patience, I tenfold feel them all.
I know they are forgiven, but still their pain to me,
Is all the grief and anguish they laid, my Lord, on Thee.'

SERMON NO. 2073

4 MARCH (1888)

Grace abounding over abounding sin

'Moreover the law entered, that the offence might abound. But where sin abounded, grace did much more abound.' Romans 5:20
SUGGESTED FURTHER READING: Genesis 3:1–24

Sin abounded in its ruinous effects. It utterly destroyed humanity. In the third chapter of the Romans you see how, in every part of his nature, man is depraved by sin. Think of the havoc which the tyrant, sin, has made of our natural estate and heritage. Eden is withered; its very site is forgotten. Our restfulness among the trees of the field, freely yielding their fruit, is gone and God hath said, 'In the sweat of thy face shalt thou eat bread'. The field we till has lost its spontaneous yield of corn: 'Thorns also and thistles shall it bring forth to thee'. Our life has lost its glory and immortality, 'for dust thou art, and unto dust shalt thou return.' Every woman in her pangs of travail, every man in his weariness of labour, and all of us together in the griefs of death, see what sin has done for us as to our mortal bodies. Alas, it has gone deeper: it has ruined our souls. Sin has unmanned man. The crown and glory of his manhood it has thrown to the ground. All our faculties are out of gear; all our tendencies are perverted. Beloved, let us rejoice that the Lord Jesus Christ has come to redeem us from the curse of sin, and he will undo the evil of evil. Even this poor world he will deliver 'from the bondage of corruption' and he will create 'new heavens and a new earth, wherein dwelleth righteousness.' The groans and painful travail of the whole creation shall result in a full deliverance, through the grace of our Lord Jesus Christ, and somewhat more. As for ourselves, we are lifted up to a position far higher than that which we should have occupied had the race continued in its innocence. The Lord Jesus Christ found us in a horrible pit and in the miry clay, and he not only lifted us up out of it, but he set our feet upon a rock, and established our goings. Raised from hell, we are lifted not to the bowers of Eden, but to the throne of God.

FOR MEDITATION: (*Our Own Hymn Book*, no. 174 v.5—Thomas Davis, 1864)
  'Sin, which strove that love to quell, woke yet more its wondrous blaze;
  Eden, Bethlehem, Calvary, tell, more than all beside, His praise.'

5 MARCH (PREACHED 30 MARCH 1890)

Zedekiah; or, the man who cannot say 'No'.

'Then Zedekiah the king said, Behold, he is in your hand: for the king is not he that can do any thing against you.' Jeremiah 38:5
SUGGESTED FURTHER READING: John 19:1–16

Zedekiah was a gentleman of a sort wonderfully common nowadays, a good-natured, easy man; his nobles could get anything they liked from him. He would not act amiss of his own self, but he would follow the lead of others, wherever that might lead him. He had a great respect for the prophet; he liked to visit him and know what message he had received from God. He did not wish to have it known that he did consult him, but still he liked to steal away in private and have a talk with the man of God. He much respected the man so sorrowful and yet so heroic. But when the princes came round him, though he was an autocratic king and could have snuffed out those gentlemen at once, yet half-a-dozen of them, all very glib of speech, most easily persuaded him. He did not want to have any bother: he would do anything for a quiet life. 'The king is not he that can do any thing against you.' As much as to say: 'I cannot say "No" to you, if you wish it. I am sorry: I think you are wrong, but I will not insist upon my own idea. If you wish it, although I am a king and perhaps ought not to be so yielding, yet I so much wish to please everybody that I cannot refuse you anything. You may take the prophet and, if you like, you may put him into a dungeon, where he will die. I think you are too hard on a good man, for whom I have a great respect, but at the same time, gentlemen, I am not a man that can stand out against you; and so take him and do as you please.' This is that king Zedekiah: he does not rule, but is ruled by the princes whom he ought to command. 'Oh,' says one, 'you do not mean to insinuate that we have any Zedekiahs about now?' I shall not insinuate anything, but boldly declare that these soft, molluscous beings make up a large proportion of the population.

FOR MEDITATION: Failure to do what we know to be right is sin (James 4:17). The people of God are expected to have sufficient backbone to say 'No' to the enticements of others to sin (Proverbs 1:10; Titus 2:11–12). Nehemiah and Moses displayed true leadership in this matter (Nehemiah 6:2–4; Hebrews 11:24–25).

SERMON NO. 2178

6 MARCH (1887)

The pleading of the last messenger

'Those husbandmen said among themselves, This is the heir; come, let us kill him, and the inheritance shall be ours. And they took him, and killed him, and cast him out of the vineyard.' Mark 12:7–8
SUGGESTED FURTHER READING: Luke 19:11–27

The great reason, why these husbandmen determined to kill the heir was this: they said, 'the inheritance shall be ours.' This is what the heart of man vainly desires. It says, 'Let us be rid of this troublesome talk of religion, and then we can live for ourselves and study our own pleasure without remorse of conscience. Are we not our own? Who shall be lord over us? If we are rid of this Jesus, we shall not have this claim being always made upon us that we are God's creatures and that we ought to live to him. We do not intend to serve God. We will pay no rent to this householder. We will be our own proprietors. God shall have nothing from us. Who is the Lord, that we should obey his voice? If we can get rid of this Christ business we can live as we like and do as we please, and no one will call us to account. If we can persuade ourselves that religion is not true, we shall then care nothing for checks and warnings, but we shall take our full swing and enjoy ourselves without stint. A short life and a merry one will suit us. We might enjoy ourselves if this matter of God, Christ and eternity could be disposed of.' Yes, young man, this is what your prototype thought when he said to his father, 'give me the portion of goods that falleth to me.' Then he 'gathered all together,' went 'into a far country,' and spent 'his substance with riotous living.' This is what you hanker after. But your folly is exceeding great. I grieve as I look into your young face and read the idle dream of your heart. You little know what a tyrant he serves who lives as he likes. May God grant that I may never live as my sinful lusts would make me live!

FOR MEDITATION: (*Our Own Hymn Book*, no. 517 v.3—Charles Wesley, 1745)
　'Can I put my Lord to pain? Still to death my Lord pursue?
　Open all His wounds again? And the shameful cross renew?
　No, with all my sins I'll part; break, oh break my bleeding heart.'

SERMON NO. 1951

7 MARCH (1886)

Our Lord's prayer for his people's sanctification

'Sanctify them through thy truth: thy word is truth.' John 17:17
SUGGESTED FURTHER READING: 1 Thessalonians 4:1–12

Children of God should exhibit the love of God; they should be filled with zeal for his glory, they should live generous, unselfish lives, they should walk with God and commune with the Most High. Ours should be a purpose and an aim far higher than the best of the unregenerate can understand. We ought to reach unto a life and a kingdom of which the mass of mankind know nothing and care less. Now, I am afraid that this spiritual sense of the prayer is one that is often forgotten. Oh that God's Holy Spirit might make us to know it by experimentally feeling it in ourselves! May 'HOLINESS TO THE LORD' be written across the brow of our consecrated humanity! Beloved, this prayer of our Lord is most necessary, for without sanctification *how can we be saved*, since it is written that without holiness 'no man shall see the Lord'? How can we be saved from sin, if sin still has dominion over us? If we are not living holy, godly, spiritual lives, how can we say that we are redeemed from the power of evil? Without sanctification *we shall be unfit for service*. Our Lord Jesus contemplated sending each one of us into the world even as the Father sent him into the world, but how can he give a mission to unsanctified men and women? Must not the vessels of the Lord be clean? Without sanctification *we cannot enjoy the innermost sweets of our holy faith*. The unsanctified are full of doubts and fears, and what wonder? The unsanctified often say of the outward exercise of religion, 'what a weariness is it!' and no wonder, for they know not the internal joys of it, having never learned to delight themselves in God. If they walk not in the light of the Lord's countenance, how can they know the heaven below which comes of true godliness? Oh, it is a prayer that needs to be prayed.

FOR MEDITATION: (*Our Own Hymn Book,* no. 649 v.1—Charles Wesley, 1749)

'I want a principle within
Of jealous, godly fear;
A sensibility of sin,
A pain to feel it near.'

SERMON NO. 1890

8 MARCH (1891)

A poor man's cry and what came of it

'This poor man cried, and the LORD *heard him, and saved him out of all his troubles.'* Psalm 34:6
SUGGESTED FURTHER READING: 2 Timothy 4:9–18

Note that word '*all*'; it is large and comprehensive. If you will kindly look at the psalm, you will see the range of this delightful deliverance. We read in verse 4: 'he ... delivered me from *all my fears*.' Sometimes our fears are more painful than our troubles. We suffer more in dreading troubles than in enduring them, but prayer banishes such fears. We see that *all shame* was removed in the same way: 'They looked unto him, and were lightened: and their faces were not ashamed.' Happy men, for the shame of their sin is gone! Their shame and their fears went when their prayers were heard. They were no longer distressed about the past and no longer under apprehension of wrath in the future: he saved them out of all their fears. If you will look further on, you will find that the Lord saved them out of *all their wants* (verse 9): 'there is no want to them that fear him'; 'they that seek the LORD shall not want any good thing.' Oh, to be saved from the pinch of dire necessity within the soul, saved from all fear, all shame, all trouble, and then from all want! This is a grand salvation! But this is not all; for this poor man was saved from *all dangers* (verse 20): 'He keepeth all his bones: not one of them is broken.' The Lord saved him out of all real peril. And, lastly, he saved him from *all apprehension of desertion*: 'none of them that trust in him shall be desolate.' The salvation that God gives in answer to prayer is a perfect one and he gives it freely in answer to a poor man's cry, without money or merit. How complete is God's deliverance!

FOR MEDITATION: (*Our Own Hymn Book*, no. 116 song 1 v.1—Isaac Watts, 1719)
'I love the Lord: He heard my cries,
And pitied every groan:
Long as I live, when troubles rise,
I'll hasten to His throne.'

SERMON NO. 2193

9 MARCH (1890)

The rough hewer

'What shall I do unto thee? for your goodness is as a morning cloud, and as the early dew it goeth away. Therefore have I hewed them by the prophets; I have slain them by the words of my mouth.' Hosea 6:4–5
SUGGESTED FURTHER READING: 2 Chronicles 24:1–27

The love of approbation acts upon many with great force. Especially will young people follow each other and follow leaders, if they are praised for it. Converts may easily be made by mutual admiration. If it happens to be a religious time and it is the fashion to profess conversion, many of all ages go with the rush and yet are by no means truly called into the kingdom of God. That religion which lives upon companionship is apt to die when the company is changed. Beware of the godliness which is carried off its feet by the crowd: true religion is the personal conviction of one who has repented and believed on his own account. No man can be carried to heaven by the stream of outside influence—there must be a work within: 'Ye must be born again.' No doubt we have many who disappoint our hopes, because they are moving in the right way, but they are not going there from a force within, but are being compelled to go by an influence from without. One person of great strength of mind may have a vast influence over others, but subjecting to the best influence can never take the place of personal conversion. We read, in the Word of God, of a young king who 'did that which was right in the sight of the LORD all the days of' the venerable high priest who had been his guardian, but when the gracious man was gone, then the king went his own way and that way was an evil one. Many persons are under the holy influence of godly relatives and friends, but they are by no means gracious themselves: their real character is concealed by the godly one who overshadows them. Oh, how sad, to be going the right way openly and yet in heart to be treading the downward road! We are before God what we are in heart, not what our surroundings compel us to be.

FOR MEDITATION: The loss of a father-figure is likely to expose those like Joash whose godliness is only skin-deep (2 Chronicles 24:15–19), but can confirm those like Elisha who are genuine (2 Kings 2:9–15). Paul and Peter prepared their true children in the faith for the time of spiritual bereavement (Acts 20:29–32; 2 Timothy 4:5–6; 2 Peter 1:12–15).

SERMON NO. 2134

10 MARCH (1889)

Intimate knowledge of the Holy Spirit

'The Spirit of truth; whom the world cannot receive, because it seeth him not, neither knoweth him: but ye know him; for he dwelleth with you, and shall be in you.' John 14:17
SUGGESTED FURTHER READING: Acts 10:34–48

When our Lord Jesus Christ came upon the earth and was beheld as God in human flesh, that was to us the pledge of the indwelling of the Holy Spirit in us, for, as God dwelt in the human person of the Lord Jesus Christ, even so does the Spirit abide in our humanity. Our Lord's life on earth was the picture of the Spirit's indwelling. As he was anointed of the Spirit, even so are we in our measure. He 'went about doing good'. He lived consecrated to God, loving the sons of men; thus will the Spirit of God within us cause us to live: we shall imitate the Christ of God through the Spirit of God. The death of Christ was the way by which the Spirit was enabled to come to sinful men. By his great sacrifice the stone is rolled away which once blocked the road.

> ''Tis through the purchase of his death,
> Who hung upon the tree,
> The Spirit is sent down to breathe
> On such dry bones as we.'

When our Lord rose from the dead, we had the guarantee that even so the Spirit of God would quicken our mortal bodies and renew us into newness of life. But it was when our Lord ascended up on high, leading captivity captive, that the Holy Spirit was, to the full, actually given. When our Redeemer returned to his Father's throne, he scattered the largess of heaven: he gave the Holy Spirit to men of various offices and to his whole church; then were the days of refreshing by divine visitation. Your ascended Lord gives you this token of his love, the indwelling of the Holy Spirit in you: prize it above all things. Do you know it?

FOR MEDITATION: (*Our Own Hymn Book*, no. 454 v.5—Isaac Watts, 1709)
> 'Come, Holy Spirit, heavenly Dove, with all Thy quickening powers,
> Come, shed abroad a Saviour's love, and that shall kindle ours.'

SERMON NO. 2074

11 MARCH (1888)

The infallibility of Scripture

'The mouth of the LORD hath spoken it.' Isaiah 1:20
SUGGESTED FURTHER READING: Hebrews 13:5–15

'The mouth of the LORD hath spoken it' is the foundation of our confidence. There is forgiveness, for God has said it. Look, friend; you are saying, 'I cannot believe that my sins can be washed away, I feel so unworthy.' Yes, but 'the mouth of the LORD hath spoken it'. Believe over the head of your unworthiness. 'Ah,' says one, 'I feel so weak I can neither think, nor pray, nor do anything else, as I should.' Is it not written, 'when we were yet without strength, in due time Christ died for the ungodly'? 'The mouth of the LORD hath spoken it'; therefore, over the head of your inability, still believe it, for it must be so. I think I hear some child of God saying, 'God has said, "I will never leave thee, nor forsake thee", but I am in great trouble; all the circumstances of my life seem to contradict the promise': yet, 'the mouth of the LORD hath spoken it,' and the promise must stand. 'Trust in the LORD, and do good; so shalt thou dwell in the land, and verily thou shalt be fed.' Believe God in the teeth of circumstances. If you cannot see a way of escape or a means of help, yet still believe in the unseen God, and in the truth of his presence, 'for the mouth of the LORD hath spoken it.' I think I have come to this pass with myself, at any rate for the time present, that when circumstances deny the promise, I believe it none the less. When friends forsake me, foes belie me, my own spirit goes down below zero and I am depressed almost to despair, I am resolved to hang to the bare word of the Lord and prove it to be in itself an all-sufficient stay and support.

FOR MEDITATION: (*Our Own Hymn Book,* no. 191 v.2—Isaac Watts, 1709)
   'Praise to the goodness of the Lord,
   Who rules His people by His word;
   And there, as strong as His decrees,
   He sets His kindest promises.'

12 MARCH (PREACHED 31 MARCH 1889)

The gospel of the glory of Christ

'The light of the glorious gospel of Christ.' 2 Corinthians 4:4
SUGGESTED FURTHER READING: 1 Thessalonians 2:1–8

We have heard of preachers who secretly believe very differently from what they say openly. The trust-deed requires some little consonance with evangelical doctrine, but they loathe it in their souls and tell their brethren so in private. But as for us, we 'have renounced the hidden things of dishonesty, not walking in craftiness, nor handling the word of God deceitfully'. We dare preach everything that we believe, and preach it as plainly as possible. The more you know us through and through, the more glad we shall be. Our gospel is one which may be advertised on every hoarding: we have nothing to conceal. I have heard of William Gadsby of Manchester, that, travelling on a coach one day, he asked two heretical divines to tell him how a sinner is justified in the sight of God. 'No,' said they, 'you don't catch us in that fashion. Whatever answer we gave you would be repeated all over Manchester within a week.' 'Oh,' said he, 'then I will tell you. A sinner is justified in the sight of God by faith in the blood and righteousness of Jesus Christ. Go and tell that all over Manchester and all over England as quickly as you like, for I believe nothing that I am ashamed of.' Light rejoices to proclaim itself. The gospel is a light, and lights are not meant to be hidden under bushels or beds. If they are buried in that way, they will burn their way to resurrection, and the bushels and the beds will be consumed and make all the greater light. The gospel of the blessed God is intended to be conspicuous as the lighthouse on the rock, which is seen afar. It is so illuminating that everyone in the house may see by it. The gospel which is not known is of no value: it is as much intended to be understood as light is meant to be seen.

FOR MEDITATION: The word of God, if handled properly (2 Timothy 2:15), can be preached boldly (Acts 4:31; Philippians 1:14), but this will not be the case when it is treated corruptly (2 Corinthians 2:17) or deceitfully (2 Corinthians 4:2).

SERMON NO. 2077

13 MARCH (1887)

The Holy Ghost the need of the age

'*O thou that art named the house of Jacob, is the spirit of the* LORD *straitened? are these his doings? do not my words do good to him that walketh uprightly?*' Micah 2:7
SUGGESTED FURTHER READING: Revelation 3:1–6

The words of Micah imply that the descendants of Jacob in his day were proud of the name of 'house of Jacob,' but that they were not worthy of it. Nothing is more mischievous than to cling to a name when the thing for which it stands has disappeared. May we never come to such a stage of declension, that even the Spirit of God will be compelled, in speaking to us, to say, 'O thou that art called the church of God!' To be named Christians and not to be Christians is to be deceivers or deceived. The name brings with it great responsibility and, if it be a name only, it brings with it terrible condemnation. It is a crime against the truth of God, if we dare to take the name of his people when we are not his people. It is a robbery of honour from those to whom it is due; it is a practical lie against the Holy Spirit; it is a defamation of the character of the bride of Christ to take the name of Christian when the Spirit of Christ is not among us. This is to honour Christ with our lips and disgrace him by our lives. What is this but to repeat the crime of Judas and betray 'the Son of man with a kiss'? Brothers and sisters, I say again, may we never come to this! Truth, not names, facts, not professions, are to be the first consideration. Better to be true to God and bear the names of reproach which the adversary is so apt to coin, than to be false to our Lord and yet to be decorated with the names of saints and regarded as the most orthodox of believers. Whether named 'the house of Jacob' or not, let us be wrestlers like Jacob and like him may we come off as prevailing princes.

FOR MEDITATION: It is a privilege to be called Christians (Acts 11:26; James 2:7), but many a church would be more appropriately named Ichabod (1 Samuel 4:21) or Loammi (Hosea 1:9)—check the references to discover the meanings of these names. By God's grace things can still be put right (Hosea 1:10; Romans 9:25–26).

SERMON NO. 1952

14 MARCH (1886)

The sermon of the seasons

'While the earth remaineth, seedtime and harvest, and cold and heat, and summer and winter, and day and night shall not cease.' Genesis 8:22
SUGGESTED FURTHER READING (Spurgeon): Jeremiah 33:17–26

Our text takes us back to the time when the waters of the flood had just assuaged, and God opened the door of the ark and bade Noah and his family come forth into a new world. For a time there had been a confusion: the seasons were mixed up, the perpetual downpour of the rain had almost turned day into night, and whether it was summer or winter could scarcely be told. The frame of nature seemed to be out of joint, her order suspended. And now the Lord, in making a promise to Noah that he would never destroy the earth again with a flood, also declares that while the earth remains there shall be no more of the confusion of the seasons and mingling of day and night which had brought such destruction upon all living things. As there should be no more a general deluge, so should there be no more a serious disarrangement of the course of the seasons and the temperature appropriate thereto. 'Seedtime and harvest, and cold and heat, and summer and winter, and day and night', are to succeed each other in their perpetually unchanging change, so long as the present reign of forbearance shall last. Till comes the close of time, the rolling year, made up of alternate day and night, shall pass through cold and heat in due order. We are grateful to God for thus settling in his mind that so it shall be. We are at ease because we know that he will not lift his hand again to destroy every living thing with a flood of water. He will deal with men in longsuffering, tender mercy and forbearance. He will not use the stern weapons of destruction, but will try the tender ministrations of patience and grace, that men may be led to repentance. There will come an end to this dispensation, but while the reign of forbearance lasts, nature shall keep her appointed marches and we need not fear a disorderly rush or a destructive chaos.

FOR MEDITATION: 'God is not the author of confusion' (1 Corinthians 14:33); his ordering of the seasons produced confident deductions from which Jesus made spiritual applications (Luke 21:29–31; John 4:35). He was not satisfied if men were weather-experts only (Matthew 16:1–3).

SERMON NO. 1891

15 MARCH (1891)

Between the two appearings

'Now once in the end of the world hath he appeared to put away sin by the sacrifice of himself.' Hebrews 9:26
SUGGESTED FURTHER READING: 1 Corinthians 15:1–11

The text tells us that in his first coming our Lord 'appeared to put away sin'. By his coming and sacrifice he accomplished many things, but his first end and object was 'to put away sin'. The modern babblers declare that he appeared to reveal to us the goodness and love of God. This is true, but it is only the fringe of the whole truth; he revealed God's love in the provision of a sacrifice 'to put away sin'. Then they say that he appeared to exhibit perfect manhood and to let us see what our nature ought to be. Here also is a truth, but it is only part of the sacred design. He appeared, say they, to manifest self-sacrifice and to set us an example of love to others. By his self-denial he trampled on the selfish passions of man. We deny none of this, and yet we are indignant at the way in which the less is made to hide the greater. To put the secondary ends into the place of the grand object is to turn the truth of God into a lie. It is easy to distort truth by exaggerating one portion of it and diminishing another, just as the drawing of the most beautiful face may soon be made a caricature rather than a portrait by neglect of proportion. You must observe proportion if you would take a truthful view, and in reference to the appearing of our Lord, his first and chief purpose is 'to put away sin by the sacrifice of himself.' The great object of our Lord's coming here was not to live, but to die. He appeared, not so much to subdue sin by his teaching, as to put it away 'by the sacrifice of himself.' The master purpose which dominated all that our Lord did was not to manifest goodness, nor to perfect an example, but to put away sin by sacrifice. That which the moderns thrust into the background our Lord placed in the forefront.

FOR MEDITATION: (*Our Own Hymn Book,* no. 289 vv.1&2—Isaac Watts, 1709)

'Nature with open volume stands, to spread her Maker's praise abroad;
And every labour of His hands shows something worthy of a God.
But in the grace that rescued man His brightest form of glory shines;
Here, on the cross, 'tis fairest drawn in precious blood and crimson lines.'

SERMON NO. 2194

16 MARCH (1890)

The warnings and rewards of the Word of God

'Moreover by them is thy servant warned: and in keeping of them there is great reward.' Psalm 19:11
SUGGESTED FURTHER READING: 2 Peter 3:1–10

The Bible warns us all of certain great events, especially of the Second Advent of the Lord and the coming judgment. It does not clearly tell us when our Lord will appear, but it warns us that to the unprepared he will come 'as a thief in the night.' It warns us of the general judgment and of the day when all men shall live again and stand before the great white throne. It warns us of the day when every secret shall be revealed and when every man shall receive for the things that he has 'done in his body, according to that he hath done, whether it be good or bad.' 'By them is thy servant warned'. If I live like one of yonder cattle, in the immediate present, if I have no eye for the future that is hurrying on, if my soul never places herself in vision before the judgment-seat of Christ, if I never foresee the day when heaven and earth, before the presence of the great Judge, shall flee away, why, then I cannot be a diligent reader of the Word of God. If I search the Scriptures I shall be called to walk in the light of the last day and shall be made to gird up my loins to face the dread account. Oh that we might all be warned to be ready, that we may give in our account with joy! Oh that we may so take the warnings of holy scripture as to be ready for death, ready for judgment and ready for that final sentence which can never be reversed! If we were truly wise, these warnings would put salt into our lives and preserve them from 'the corruption that is in the world through lust.' Beloved, I trust that every one of us who knows the Lord will use his holy Book as the constant guard of his life.

FOR MEDITATION: (*Our Own Hymn Book*, no. 19 v.5—Isaac Watts, 1719)
 'Thy noblest wonders here we view,
 In souls renewed, and sins forgiven:
 Lord, cleanse my sins, my soul renew,
 And make Thy word my guide to heaven.'

SERMON NO. 2135

17 MARCH (1889)

Our Lord's entrance within the veil

'Neither by the blood of goats and calves, but by his only blood he entered in once into the holy place, having obtained eternal redemption for us.' Hebrews 9:12
SUGGESTED FURTHER READING: Galatians 4:1–7

When the Lord Jesus Christ died, he paid our redemption price and when he entered within the veil, he entered as one who not only desired to give us redemption, but as one who had 'obtained eternal redemption'. He has won for us redemption both by price and by power. We do not fully know what the word 'redemption' means, for we were born free, but if we could go back a few years and mix with the negro slaves of America, they could have told us what redemption meant, if ever by any good fortune any one of them was able to buy his freedom. You that have groaned under the tyranny of sin, you know what redemption means in its spiritual sense and you prize the ransom by which you have been made free. Brethren, we are today redeemed from our far-off condition in reference to the Lord God: we do not now stand outside the veil. This is a great redemption. We are also delivered from guilt, for he has 'washed us from our sins in his own blood'. This is a great redemption. We are rescued from the power of sin that we should not live any longer therein. We overcome sin through the blood of the Lamb. This also is a great redemption. We are now saved from the curse of sin, for he was 'made a curse for us: for it is written, Cursed is every one that hangeth on a tree'. This is, indeed, a great redemption. We are redeemed from all the bondage that ensued from sin. We are no longer the serfs of Satan, nor the slaves of the world, neither are we 'subject to bondage' 'through fear of death'. That last enemy shall be destroyed, and we know it. The Son has set us free, and we are 'free indeed'. He entered into the heavenly places with this for his everlasting renown, that he has obtained redemption for his people.

FOR MEDITATION: (*Our Own Hymn Book,* no. 412 v.7—Isaac Watts, 1709)
   'Thou hast redeemed our souls with blood,
    Hast set the prisoners free;
    Hast made us kings and priests to God,
    And we shall reign with Thee.'

SERMON NO. 2075

18 MARCH (1888)

'As we have heard, so have we seen'

'As we have heard, so have we seen in the city of the LORD of hosts, in the city of our God: God will establish it for ever.' Psalm 48:8
SUGGESTED FURTHER READING: 1 John 4:1–6

Some, nowadays, are inclined to hear everything, bad, good and indifferent. I believe that hearing everything will end in hearing nothing. That text is often quoted and misunderstood, which says, 'Prove all things'. If men really mean what they say and are going to prove all things, I would persuade them to begin with their bodies and not at first to run great risks with their souls. Gentlemen, I invite you to begin with commoner things than the gospel; for instance, commence with proving all the patent medicines and next prove all the drugs of the chemist. If you survive the process, it will then be time to go round and prove all the ministers and all the different doctrines of this wretched period. If you survive the drugs and poisons, you will not survive the false doctrines. False doctrines cannot be proved and you need not make the attempt. It is only the truth which is capable of proof. The text does not mean 'experiment upon everything', but receive nothing until it has been proved to be true and good. The most of us are not appointed to the office of Universal Taster: we are not commissioned to taste all deadly things that we may know their precise effect: we are far better employed in holding 'fast that which is good.' The truths which we have already proved to be the truth of God, we hold as with a death-grip, and, as we hold them fast, we also hold them forth. That which we accept for ourselves we commend to others: this is a far safer and healthier exercise than imitating the Athenians in their desire to be for ever hearing 'some new thing.' Take heed what you hear, lest you be not able to say, 'As we have heard, so have we seen'.

FOR MEDITATION: (*Our Own Hymn Book*, no. 675 v.4—Philip Doddridge, 1755)
'Thus far we prove that promise good,
Which Jesus ratified with blood:
Still He is gracious, wise, and just
And still in Him let Israel trust.'

SERMON NO. 2014

19 MARCH (PREACHED 23 MARCH 1890)

Possessing possessions

'But upon mount Zion shall be deliverance, and there shall be holiness; and the house of Jacob shall possess their possessions.' Obadiah 17
SUGGESTED FURTHER READING: Isaiah 52:7–12

Heart-passion for souls is not found in unholy men. Unless you are thoroughly consecrated to God and then sanctified by the Spirit, you will not speak with that accent of conviction which carries truth home to the hearer. Do you not know yourselves that when you have listened to a clever preacher who has no spirituality, but is a mere actor and known to be of worldly habits, his preaching has no power in it for you? What he said was all very well, but it fell flat: he was a clever and eloquent man, but he did not touch you. When I heard George Müller, some years ago, there was nothing of oratory in what he said, but then there was George Müller behind it, and every syllable had weight. That blessed man spoke as one who had experience of what he said. His long life of faith in God made every word powerful with the heart and conscience. Teachers of Bible-classes and schools, a holy life must be your power in your classes, or your words will be to your children as idle tales! If they see your lives to be unholy, the ungodly will reject your testimony and it will be no wonder that they do so. They want to reject it; they are looking out for excuses for rejecting it and they will gladly find an argument in your unhallowed behaviour. They will say, 'The man does not believe it himself, or else he would not live as he does.' I heard of one who was asked by her minister whether she remembered last Sunday's sermon. 'No,' she said, 'it is all gone.' 'But you ought to remember it,' said the minister. 'No,' she replied, 'I am not to be expected to do so, for you did not remember it yourself—you read it all from a paper.' The argument is, if the preacher does not remember his own preaching to put it into practice, how can he expect others to do so?

FOR MEDITATION: Whether you are a pastor or one of the flock, it is vital to recognise the qualities to be seen in God's servants—holy living (1 Timothy 3:1–3; Titus 1:6–8), ability in leadership (1 Timothy 3:4–5), maturity (1 Timothy 3:6), a good reputation (1 Timothy 3:7), gentleness (2 Timothy 2:24) and faithfulness in holding to and teaching the Scriptures (Titus 1:9). God cannot be expected to own and bless anything less.

SERMON NO. 2136

20 MARCH (1887)

The breaker and the flock

'I will surely assemble, O Jacob, all of thee; I will surely gather the remnant of Israel. I will put them together as the sheep of Bozrah, as the flock in the midst of their fold.' Micah 2:12
SUGGESTED FURTHER READING: Hebrews 6:13–20

Our hope of the salvation of God's elect lies in the fact that it is God himself who undertakes to gather them. Remember his word by the prophet Ezekiel, 'For thus saith the Lord GOD; Behold, I, even I, will both search my sheep, and seek them out.' Following the text closely, we notice that this gathering is to be performed *surely*. I dwell with great pleasure upon that word 'surely,' because it is spoken twice: 'I will *surely* assemble, O Jacob, all of thee; I will *surely* gather the remnant of Israel'. There are no 'ifs' where there is a God: there are no 'maybes' where divine predestination rules the day. Let Jehovah speak and it is done; let him command and it shall stand firm. Inasmuch as he says 'surely' twice, it reminds me of Joseph's word to the Egyptian king: 'And for that the dream was doubled unto Pharaoh twice, it is because the thing is established by God'. God will not change his purpose, nor turn from his promise, nor forget his covenant: he will surely gather together his chosen people wherever they may be. You that are buffeted by opposition and driven to sore distress in your holy service, be not dismayed, for the purpose of the Lord shall stand. *You* may fail, but the eternal God will not. Your work may be washed away like the work of little children in the sand of the seashore, but that which God does endures for ever. God shakes the earth out of its place, but who can move *him*? When God says *'surely'*, who shall cast doubt in the way? The Lord will without fail call out his redeemed from among men. As a worker and a soul-winner I grasp at these words, 'I will surely gather the remnant of Israel', and I feel that I shall not labour in vain, nor spend my strength for nothing.

FOR MEDITATION: We can make our calling and election sure (2 Peter 1:10) because everything to do with God is sure, including his covenant (2 Samuel 23:5), his testimony (Psalm 19:7; 93:5), his commandments (Psalm 111:7), his foundation (Isaiah 28:16; 2 Timothy 2:19), his mercies (Isaiah 55:3; Acts 13:34) and his promise (Romans 4:16).

SERMON NO. 1954

21 MARCH (1886)

Why they leave us

'Father, I will that they also, whom thou hast given me, be with me where I am; that they may behold my glory, which thou hast given me: for thou lovedst me before the foundation of the world.' John 17:24
SUGGESTED FURTHER READING: Hebrews 2:5–13

Where did our Lord's glory come from? 'Thou gavest me', says Jesus. Hence it is the Father's glory passed over to the Son. Yet Jesus calls it 'my glory,' for it is truly his own. The saints are to behold this and it will be their glory to see it. Here we have the Father, the Elder Brother, the many brethren and a wonderful communism of interests and possessions. It is ever so in a loving family. There we draw no hard and fast lines: 'all mine are thine, and thine are mine'. We ask not whose is this or that when we are at home. If you were to go into a stranger's house, you would not think of taking this or that, but as your father's own son you make yourself at home and no one enquires, 'What are you doing?' Bridegroom and bride do not quarrel about property whether it be his or hers. Laws have been made lately to settle different estates for those who are one: this is well enough when love is gone, but true conjugal love laughs at all that can make separate that which 'God hath joined together'. The wife says, 'That is mine.' 'No' says the caviller, 'it is your husband's.' Her answer is, 'and therefore it is mine.' In that blessed union, into which divine love has admitted us, Christ is ours, and we are Christ's; his Father is our Father; we are one with him; he is one with the Father: hence all things are ours and the Father himself loves us. So when the Lord brings his people home, we shall be one with him, and he one with the Father, and we also in him one with the Father, so that we shall then find boundless glory in beholding the glory of our Lord and God.

FOR MEDITATION: (*Our Own Hymn Book,* no. 855 v.4—Isaac Watts, 1709)
    'Adoring saints around Him stand,
    And thrones and powers before Him fall;
    The God shines gracious through the Man,
    And sheds sweet glories on them all.'
N.B. This sermon was 'suggested by the death of Charles Stanford, D.D., Minister of Denmark Place Chapel, Camberwell'.

SERMON NO. 1892

22 MARCH (PALM SUNDAY 1891)

Hosanna!

'And the multitudes that went before, and that followed, cried, saying, Hosanna to the son of David: Blessed is he that cometh in the name of the Lord; Hosanna in the highest.' Matthew 21:9
SUGGESTED FURTHER READING (Spurgeon): John 12:12–19

I want you to notice in our text, that our Saviour was received with the shout of Hosanna! The best interpretation I can give is—'Save, oh, save! Save, oh, save!' Different nations have different ways of expressing their goodwill to their monarchs. A Roman would have shouted, 'Io triumphe!' We sing, 'God save our gracious Queen.' The Persians said, 'O King, live for ever.' The Jews cried, 'Hosanna!' 'Save,' or, 'God save the King!' The French have their 'Vivas,' by which they mean, 'Long live the man.' Hosanna is tantamount to all these. It is a shout of homage, welcome and loyalty. It wishes wealth, health and honour to the king. In the Saxon we say, 'Hurrah', in Hebrew, 'Hosanna.' That mighty shout startled all the streets of the old city: 'Hosanna, Hosanna, the King is come. Save him, O Lord! Save us through him! Long live the King!' While it was a shout of homage, it was also a prayer *to* the King. 'Save, Lord; save us, O King! O King, born to conquer and to save, deliver us!' It was, moreover, a prayer *for* him—'God save the King; God bless and prosper his majesty.' 'Prayer also shall be made for him continually; and daily shall he be praised.' We never cease to pray, 'Thy kingdom come. Thy will be done in earth, as it is in heaven.' Let us then cry 'Hosanna', making it at once a loyal shout, a prayer to our King and a prayer for him. All these things appear in the benediction which follows: 'Blessed is he that cometh in the name of the Lord; Hosanna in the highest.'

FOR MEDITATION: (*Our Own Hymn Book,* no. 909 v.3—Isaac Watts, 1719)
   'Hosannah to th'anointed King,
   To David's holy Son!
   Help us, O Lord! descend and bring
   Salvation from Thy throne.'

SERMON NO. 2196

23 MARCH (1890)

The shank-bone sermon; or, true believers and their helpers

'Who, when he was come, helped them much which had believed through grace.' Acts 18:27
SUGGESTED FURTHER READING: Exodus 12:1–28

Reading yesterday, in *Israel my Glory*, a book by Mr Wilkinson, who is the director of the Jewish mission at Mildmay, I saw a statement there which was quite new to me. He is speaking of the Jewish Passover at the present day. Now, you know what the Passover was according to the law of Moses, how a lamb was killed and the blood was sprinkled on the lintel and the two side-posts, while the flesh was roasted and eaten. The Jews at this day observe the Passover, but they observe it in a way which is according to the Rabbis and not according to Moses. On the table there are Passover cakes, lettuce, chervil and parsley, as the bitter herbs. This I understand, but what is this charoseth, a mixture of lime and mortar? And whence come the egg and the salt water? Moses knows nothing of eggs and mortar. What is there, do you suppose, besides? 'Oh,' say you, 'the Paschal Lamb.' No, no; they have left that out. What is there at the Jewish Passover at the present time instead of the lamb? A shank-bone! A shank-bone, mark you, with no meat upon it! Only a shank-bone! The blood is gone and in place of it is an egg. The Lamb is gone and instead of it there is a shank-bone. 'Ah, me! How can they thus make void the law of God?' This I said involuntarily, but very soon I remembered that I could not blame the Jews, for they are only imitating the Christians. Go and hear many who pretend to preach the gospel. Where is the Lamb, the Sacrifice, to be fed upon? Where is the sprinkled blood? Why, they are ashamed to speak of 'the blood.' They think the very word is vulgar. But what do they give us? A bone! A bone! A bone that no dog would care for, a bone of modern thought put in the place of the Lamb, who ought to be fed upon by all the living Israel of God. I thank Mr Wilkinson for such a simile.

FOR MEDITATION: (*Our Own Hymn Book,* no. 414 v.6—Isaac Watts, 1709)

> 'Blessings for ever on the Lamb,
> Who bore the curse for wretched men:
> Let angels sound His sacred name,
> And every creature say, Amen.'

SERMON NO. 2138

24 MARCH (1889)

Sounding out the word of the Lord

'For from you sounded out the word of the Lord, not only in Macedonia and Achaia, but also in every place your faith to God-ward is spread abroad; so that we need not to speak anything.' 1 Thessalonians 1:8
SUGGESTED FURTHER READING: Ezekiel 33:1–9

Their testimony was distinct, clear, resonant and far-sounding. We may find an illustration in the silver trumpets of the sanctuary which were sounded to gather the people together. Let your trumpets ring out the call to assemble to our Lord Jesus, the true 'Shiloh', unto whom 'shall the gathering of the people be.' We may further think of the Jubilee trumpet, which proclaimed clearance of debts, release from bondage and restoration to lost heritages. Such are the glad announcements of the gospel; let us hasten to make them. Trumpets are also blown in time of war: many are the allusions to this in Scripture. Oh that the church of God may boldly sound the war-trumpet against impurity, intemperance, false doctrine and loose living! Our Lord has come to send a sword upon earth in these matters. Oh that the war-blast may be sounded without fear or hesitation! May we earn the name given to the apostles, 'These that have turned the world upside down', for at present it is wrong-side up. A trumpet is also used simply for musical purposes and the testimony of the church to her Lord Jesus should be the most melodious sound the ears of man have ever heard. *'How sweet the name of Jesus sounds!'* Oh to sound forth the glorious name, 'with trumpets and sound of cornet', that multitudes might be compelled to hear it! Oh to make all earth and heaven ring with that dear name! Somebody, writing upon this verse, compares the sounding forth to the voices of church bells. Each church should find in its living members its best peal of bells. Every individual, great and little, should give forth his sound: not one should be dumb. Oh that everyone would constantly show forth the praises of the Lord!

FOR MEDITATION: (*Our Own Hymn Book*, no. 888 v.1—Charles Wesley, 1740)
> 'Partners of a glorious hope, lift your hearts and voices up;
> Jointly let us rise and sing Christ our Prophet, Priest, and King.
> Monuments of Jesu's grace, speak we by our lives His praise,
> Walk in Him we have received; show we not in vain believed.'

SERMON NO. 2076

25 MARCH (1888)

The rent veil

'*Jesus ... yielded up the ghost. And, behold, the veil of the temple was rent in twain from the top to the bottom.*' Matthew 27:50–51
'*Enter into the holiest by the blood of Jesus, by a new and living way, which he hath consecrated for us, through the veil.*' Hebrews 10:19–20
SUGGESTED FURTHER READING: John 14:1–6

The way is not worn away by long traffic: it is always new. If Jesus Christ had died yesterday, would you not feel that you could plead his merit today? You can plead that merit after all these centuries with as much confidence as at the first hour. The way to God is always newly laid. In effect the wounds of Jesus incessantly bleed our expiation. The cross is as glorious as though he were still upon it. So far as the freshness, vigour and force of the atoning death are concerned, we come by a new way. Let it be always new to our hearts. Let the doctrine of atonement never grow stale, but let it have dew upon your souls. Then, the apostle adds, it is a 'living way'. The way by which the high priest went into the holy place was of course a material way and so a dead way. We come by a spiritual way, suitable to our spirits. The way could not help the high priest, but our way helps us abundantly. Jesus says, 'I am the way, the truth, and the life'. When we come to God by this way, the way itself leads, guides, bears and brings us near. This way gives its life with which to come. It is a dedicated way, 'which he hath consecrated for us'. When a new road is opened, it is set apart and dedicated for the public use. Sometimes a public building is opened by a king or a prince and so is dedicated to its purpose. The way to God through Jesus Christ is dedicated and ordained by Christ for the use of poor believing sinners, such as we are. He has consecrated the way towards God and dedicated it for us that we may freely use it. Surely, if there is a road set apart for me, I may use it without fear; the way to God and heaven through Jesus Christ is dedicated by the Saviour for sinners; it is the King's highway for wayfaring men, who are bound for the City of God; therefore, let us use it.

FOR MEDITATION: (*Our Own Hymn Book,* no. 296 v.7—Horatius Bonar, 1856)
  ''Tis finished all: the veil is rent, the welcome sure, the access free;
  Now then, we leave our banishment, O Father, to return to Thee.'

SERMON NO. 2015

26 MARCH (PREACHED 24 MARCH 1887)

Three sights worth seeing

'For this cause also thank we God without ceasing, because, when ye received the word of God which ye heard of us, ye received it not as the word of men, but as it is in truth, the word of God, which effectually worketh also in you that believe.' 1 Thessalonians 2:13

SUGGESTED FURTHER READING: James 1:16–25

These people had doubly received the word of God; at least, the word is twice mentioned in our version. 'When ye received the word of God which ye heard of us, ye received it'. In the Greek those are two different words altogether. The second 'received' might, perhaps, better be read, 'accepted.' I do not think that I should be straining a point if I read it, 'ye welcomed it'. They first received it by eagerly hearing it. They wanted to know what it was all about: they were attentive to it and wanted to understand it. When they had heard it they rejoiced, and said, 'Oh, yes, yes, yes, this is the very thing we want!' They embraced it. That word will do: they embraced it. They put their arms around it and would not let it go. They were hospitable to the gospel, and said, 'Come in, thou blessed of the Lord: come and live in our hearts!' They assented and they consented to the word of the Lord. They first appreciated the gospel and then they apprehended it by faith. They were like the man that was hungry in a foreign land and he could not make the people quite understand, but, as soon they brought an article of food which he liked, he fell to directly and made them comprehend that he would be glad of more of that sort of thing. By his hearty reception of what they brought, the hungry man said plainly, 'Bring some more of that.' So we have a people about us that are looking out for the gospel! They are always willing to hear it, if men will preach it, and when they do get it they mean business and feed upon the word with hearty appetite. How glad I am to feed men that will eat! It is a pleasure indeed. The spiritually hungry welcome heavenly food.

FOR MEDITATION: (*Our Own Hymn Book*, no. 483 v.2—Isaac Watts, 1709)

    'But souls enlightened from above
    With joy receive the Word;
    They see what wisdom, power, and love,
    Shine in their dying Lord.'

SERMON NO. 1979

27 MARCH (1887)

Jesus declining the legions

'Thinkest thou that I cannot now pray to my Father, and he shall presently give me more than twelve legions of angels? but how then shall the scriptures be fulfilled, that thus it must be?' Matthew 26:53–54
SUGGESTED FURTHER READING (Spurgeon): Luke 22:31–38,47–53

For a man to abstain from using force when he has none to use is no great virtue: it reminds one of the lines of Cowper's ballad: *'Stooping down, as needs he must who cannot sit upright.'* But for a man to have force ready to his hand, and then to abstain from using it, is a case of self-restraint, and possibly of self-sacrifice, of a far nobler kind. Our Saviour had his sword at his side that night, though he did not use it. 'What!' say you, 'how can that be true?' Our Lord says, 'Can I not now pray to my Father, and he will give me twelve legions of angels?' Our Lord had thus the means of self-defence; something far more powerful than a sword hung at his girdle, but he refused to employ the power within his reach. His servants could not bear this test; they had no self-restraint; the hand of Peter is on his sword at once. The failure of the servants in this matter seems to me to illustrate the grand self-possession of their Master. 'Alas,' he seems to say, 'you cannot be trusted even with swords, much less could you be entrusted with greater forces. If you had the angelic bands at your command, down they would come streaming from the sky to execute works of vengeance and so mar my great life-work of love.' Brethren, we are better without swords and other forms of force than with them, for we have not yet learned, like our Lord, to control ourselves. Admire the glorious self-restraint of our Lord Jesus Christ, who, armed not with a sword but with the embattled hosts of 'helmed cherubim and sworded seraphim,' yet refused even by a prayer to bring them down to his relief. Peter's passionate use of the sword illustrates the happy self-control of his Lord, and this is the use of the incident.

FOR MEDITATION: This was not the first time that the gracious self-restraint of the Lord Jesus Christ was seen in stark contrast to the fierce impetuosity of his disciples (Luke 9:51–56). Nor was it the last time that he was to resist all challenges to resort to the powers at his disposal (Matthew 27:40–42; Luke 23:37–39).

SERMON NO. 1955

28 MARCH (1886)

Jesus angry with hard hearts

'And when he had looked round about on them with anger, being grieved for the hardness of their hearts, he saith unto the man, Stretch forth thine hand.' Mark 3:5
SUGGESTED FURTHER READING: Psalm 119:1–11

Let us feel an intense desire to submit ourselves unto the Lord Jesus. If he is in the synagogue, let us ask him to heal us and to do it in his own way. Let us become his disciples and follow him wherever he goes. Yield yourselves to God. Be as melted wax to the seal. Be as the water of the lake, which is moved with every breath of the wind. All he wills is our salvation. Lord Jesus, let thy will be done! *Let us be careful to keep away from all hardening influences*, whether of books, or men, or habits, or pleasures. If there is any company which deadens us as to spiritual things, which hinders our prayers, shakes our faith, or damps our zeal, let us get out of it and keep out of it. If any amusement lessens our hatred of sin, let us never go near it; if any book clouds our view of Jesus, let us never read it. We grow hard soon enough through the needful contact with the world which arises out of work-day life and business pursuits; let us not increase these evils. Shun the idler's talk, the scorner's seat and the way of the ungodly. Shun false doctrine, worldliness and strife. Keep clear of frivolity and trifling. Be in earnest and be pure; live near to God and keep far off from the throne of iniquity. Lastly, *use all softening influences*. Ask to have your heart daily rendered sensitive by the indwelling of the quickening Spirit. Go often to hear the word: it is like a fire and like a hammer breaking the rock in pieces. Dwell at the foot of the cross; it is there that tenderness is born into human hearts. Jesus makes all hearts soft and then stamps his image on them. Entreat the Holy Spirit to give you a very vivid sense of sin and a very intense dread of it.

FOR MEDITATION: Hardness of heart is not confined to unbelievers, but was displayed by the apostles of the Lord Jesus Christ (Mark 6:52), on one occasion leading him to question them (Mark 8:17) and on another occasion causing him to rebuke them (Mark 16:14). Beware of where hardness of heart can lead (Proverbs 28:14; Romans 2:5).

SERMON NO. 1893

29 MARCH (EASTER 1891)

Christ's resurrection and our newness of life

'Therefore we are buried with him by baptism into death: that like as Christ was raised up from the dead by the glory of the Father, even so we also should walk in newness of life.' Romans 6:4
SUGGESTED FURTHER READING: 1 Peter 3:18–4:2

Quickening is a needful part of the process of sanctification. Sanctification, in its operation upon our character, consists of three things. First, we die unto sin. A wondrous death! By this Jesus strikes at the heart of evil. The death of Christ makes us die to sin. After this comes burial. We are buried with Christ, and of this burial, baptism is the type and token. Covered up to be forgotten, we are to sin as a dead shepherd to his flock. As the sheep pass over the dead shepherd's grave or even feed thereon, and yet he regards them not, so our old sins and habits come about us, but we, as dead men, know them no more. We are buried to them. To complete our actual sanctification we receive heavenly quickening. 'If we be dead with Christ, we believe that we shall also live with him'. Yes, we do live in him and by him, for 'he that believeth on him ... hath everlasting life.' I trust you know what this means. Have you been thus dead, thus buried with Christ? Are you now thus quickened in the likeness of his resurrection? This is your joyful privilege, if you are indeed believers in Christ and joined unto the Lord in one spirit. Being thus quickened you are partakers of a new life. You are not like Lazarus, who, when he was raised from the dead, had the same life restored to him. True, you have that same life about you. Alas, that you should have it, for it will be your burden and plague. But your true life has come to you by your being born again from above. 'This is the record, that God hath given to us eternal life, and this life is in his Son. He that hath the Son hath life'. The Holy Spirit has wrought in us a higher life than nature possessed.

FOR MEDITATION: (*Our Own Hymn Book,* no. 309 v.2—Thomas Kelly, 1804)
    '"The Lord is risen indeed:"
    The grave has lost its prey;
    With Him is risen the ransomed seed,
    To reign in endless day.'

SERMON NO. 2197

30 MARCH (1890)

Christ precious to believers

'Unto you therefore which believe he is precious.' 1 Peter 2:7
SUGGESTED FURTHER READING: Hebrews 1:1-14

For a thing to be called precious, it should have three qualities: it should be rare, have an intrinsic value of its own, and possess useful and important properties. All three meet in our adorable Lord and make him precious to discerning minds. As for *rarity*: talk not of the rarity of gold or of gems: he is absolutely unique. 'Other foundation can no man lay than that is laid'. He is the one sacrifice for sin. Neither the infinite God nor all the wealth of heaven could supply another like him. As God and man he alone combines the two natures in one person. There is 'one mediator between God and men, the man Christ Jesus'. If we can never find another like him, after searching all the ages through, we may well call him precious. It is also clear that he is *intrinsically valuable*: who shall estimate his worth? I should darken 'counsel by words without knowledge' if I were to attempt in detail to tell you what he is. Dwell on the simple fact that while he is God over all and has thus the fullness of the Godhead, he is also true man of the substance of his mother and so has all the adaptation of perfect manhood. 'Consider how great this man was'. Not even heaven itself can be compared with Christ Jesus. He is incomparably, immeasurably, inconceivably precious. As for *useful qualities*, where else shall we find such a variety of uses in one place? He is eyes to the blind, ears to the deaf, feet to the lame, healing to the sick, freedom to the slave, joy to the mourner and life to the dead. Think how his life gives life to the believer! Think how his death redeems from hell all those who trust in him! Think how his resurrection justifies believers and how his second coming delights our hearts! Think of our Lord in all his offices as Prophet, Priest, and King, in all his relationships as husband, brother, friend, and under all the types and figures with which Scripture delights to set him forth! Think of him in all positions and conditions, as you will and as you can, but in every one of these he has a blessed use for the supply of some terrible need which afflicts his redeemed.

FOR MEDITATION: (*Our Own Hymn Book,* no. 817 v.1—John Kent, 1841)
    'Precious is the name of Jesus, who can half its worth unfold?
    Far beyond angelic praises, sweetly sung to harps of gold.'

SERMON NO. 2137

31 MARCH (1887)

Sweet peace for tried believers

'These things I have spoken unto you, that in me ye might have peace. In the world ye shall have tribulation: but be of good cheer; I have overcome the world.' John 16:33
SUGGESTED FURTHER READING: Isaiah 26:1–12

'These things have I spoken unto you, that in me ye might have peace.' Our Lord Jesus Christ delights to see his people firm, calm, happy. I do not think that he is so pleased to see them excited, although we have those around us who seem to think that great grace can only display itself by raving and raging. The religion of the quiet Jesus was never intended to drive us to the verge of insanity. 'He shall not strive, nor cry; neither shall any man hear his voice in the streets.' His Holy Spirit is no raven or eagle, but a dove: his holy influences are powerful and therefore calm. Weakness hurries, rages and shouts, for it needs to do so. Strength moves with its own deliberate serenity and effects its purpose. To those who think that saints should be maniacs, Jesus says, 'Peace! Peace!' On the other hand we are quite certain that our Lord Jesus does not desire his disciples to be depressed. To some the fit colour for piety seems to be grey, drab or full mourning. But it is not so: the saints are arrayed in white linen, which is the emblem of gladness as well as of purity. The Saviour does not wish his disciples to go through the world as through a twilight of sadness, whispering in fear because of judgments to come, and suppressing all joy because of the evils with which they are surrounded. No, brethren, Jesus wishes us all to be happy in himself, with a quiet peacefulness like his own. He was no laughing maker of merriment, but still he was serenely confident, and he would have us keep to his pitch and be at peace. 'These things have I spoken unto you, that in me ye might have peace.'

FOR MEDITATION: (*Our Own Hymn Book*, no. 779 v.4—Jeanne Marie Guyon, 1790; tr. by William Cowper, 1801)

   'Ah, then! to His embrace repair;
   My soul, thou art no stranger there:
   There love divine shall be thy guard,
   And peace and safety thy reward.'

SERMON NO. 1994

1 APRIL (EASTER 1888)

Jesus affirmed to be alive

'Against whom when the accusers stood up, they brought none accusation of such things as I supposed: but had certain questions against him of their own superstition, and of one Jesus, which was dead, whom Paul affirmed to be alive.' Acts 25:18–19

SUGGESTED FURTHER READING: 1 Corinthians 15:12–24

Paul teaches us to preach in our gospel all the sweet inferences which flow from the resurrection of Jesus from the dead. Here they are. He rose from the dead, and therefore *his sacrifice has been accepted.* God has 'brought again from the dead our Lord Jesus, that great Shepherd of the sheep, through the blood of the everlasting covenant'. The work he has done has pleased the Father, and therefore he has brought him back from among the dead. His acceptance is ours: we are 'accepted in the beloved'. Next, *Jesus himself is clear.* He had, as our sponsor, become our hostage. Sin was laid on him and he was laid in the grave, but now the sinner's surety is as clear as the sinner himself, for the Lord Jesus is released from the prison of the tomb. He 'was delivered for our offences, and was raised again for our justification.' Now, also, *we live unto God.* Our Lord Jesus 'died unto sin once: but in that he liveth, he liveth unto God': so is it with us. This is our joy: his work is accepted, his bearing of our curse is finished and life in us is made manifest. And now, beloved, we see in the resurrection of Jesus Christ from the dead that *he is divine.* He is 'declared to be the Son of God with power, according to the spirit of holiness, by the resurrection from the dead'. So says Paul in the first chapter of his Epistle to the Romans. Jesus raised himself from the dead by his own will. 'I have power to lay down my life,' said he, 'and I have power to take it again.' Who could possess and exercise such a power but a divine being? From the resurrection of our Lord we draw the comfortable inference of the resurrection unto eternal life of all who are in Christ.

FOR MEDITATION: (*Our Own Hymn Book,* no. 326 v.1—Anne Steele, 1760)
  'He lives, the great Redeemer lives,
  (What joy the blest assurance gives!)
  And now before His Father God,
  Pleads the full merit of His blood.'

SERMON NO. 2016

2 APRIL (PREACHED EASTER 1 APRIL 1888)

The miracles of our Lord's death

'Jesus, when he had cried again with a loud voice, yielded up the ghost. And, behold, the veil of the temple was rent in twain from the top to the bottom; and the earth did quake, and the rocks rent: and the graves were opened; and many bodies of the saints which slept arose, and came out of the graves after his resurrection, and went into the holy city, and appeared unto many.' Matthew 27:50–53
SUGGESTED FURTHER READING: Romans 6:1–11

Which way did these people go after they had come out of their graves? We are told that they 'went into the holy city'. He that has felt the power of the cross may well make the best of his way to holiness. He will long to join himself with God's people; he will wish to go up to God's house and to have fellowship with the thrice-holy God. I should not expect that quickened ones would go anywhere else. Every creature goes to its own company, the beast to its lair and the bird to its nest; and the restored and regenerated man makes his way to the holy city. Does not the cross draw us to the church of God? I would not wish one to join the church from any motive that is not fetched from the five wounds and bleeding side of Jesus. We give ourselves first to Christ and then to his people for his dear sake. It is the cross that does it. We are told that they 'went into the holy city, and appeared unto many.' That is, some of them who had been raised from the dead, I do not doubt, appeared unto their wives. What rapture as they saw again the beloved husband! It may be that some of them appeared to father and mother and I doubt not that many a quickened mother or father would make the first appearance to their children. What does this teach us, but that, if the Lord's grace should raise us from the dead, we must take care to show it? Let us appear unto many. Let the life that God has given us be manifest. Let us not hide it, but let us go to our former friends and make our appearances as Christ made his. For his glory's sake let us have our appearance unto others. Glory be to the dying Saviour! All praise to the great Sacrifice!

FOR MEDITATION: (*Our Own Hymn Book,* no. 280 v.4—Samuel Stennett, 1787)
   'So great, so vast a sacrifice may well my hope revive:
   If God's own Son thus bleeds and dies, the sinner sure may live.'

SERMON NO. 2059

3 APRIL (1887)

On the cross after death

'For these things were done, that the scripture should be fulfilled, A bone of him shall not be broken. And again another scripture saith, They shall look on him whom they pierced.' John 19:36–37
SUGGESTED FURTHER READING: Luke 24:25–47

This case was singularly complicated. It was negative and positive: the Saviour's bones must not be broken and he must be pierced. In the type of the Passover lamb it was expressly enacted that not a bone of it should be broken; therefore not a bone of Jesus must be broken. At the same time, according to Zechariah 12:10, the Lord must be pierced. He must not only be pierced with the nails and so fulfil the prophecy, 'they pierced my hands and my feet', but he must be conspicuously pierced, so that he can be emphatically regarded as a pierced one. How were these prophecies, and a multitude more, to be accomplished? Only God himself could have brought to pass the fulfilment of prophecies which were of all kinds and appeared to be confused and even in contradiction to each other. It would be an impossible task for the human intellect to construct so many prophecies, types and foreshadowings and then to imagine a person in whom they should all be embodied. But what would be impossible to men has been literally carried out in the case of our Lord. There are prophecies about him and about everything connected with him, from his hair to his garments, from his birth to his tomb, and yet they have all been carried out to the letter. That which lies immediately before us was a complicated case, for if reverence to the Saviour would spare his bones, would it not also spare his flesh? If a coarse brutality pierced his side, why did it not break his legs? How can men be kept from one act of violence, and that an act authorized by authority, and yet how shall they perpetrate another violence which had not been suggested to them? Infinite wisdom knew how to work it out in all points and it did so. The Christ is the exact substance of the foreshadowings of the Messianic prophecies.

FOR MEDITATION: All parts of the Old Testament give details about the crucifixion: the Pentateuch (Exodus 12:46; Numbers 9:12), the Psalms (22:1,7–8,16–18; 31:5; 41:9; 69:21) and the Prophets (Isaiah 53:12; Zechariah 9:9; 11:12–13; 12:10; 13:7). What a privilege it was to hear the risen Lord expounding on such themes (Luke 24:25–27,44–46)!

SERMON NO. 1956

4 APRIL (1886)

The two appearings and the discipline of grace

'For the grace of God that bringeth salvation hath appeared to all men, teaching us that, denying ungodliness and worldly lusts, we should live soberly, righteously, and godly, in this present world; looking for that blessed hope, and the glorious appearing of the great God and our Saviour Jesus Christ.' Titus 2:11–13
SUGGESTED FURTHER READING: Romans 6:12–17

The word rendered 'teaching' is a scholastic term and has to do with the education of children, not merely teaching, but training and bringing up. The grace of God has come to be a schoolmaster to teach, train and prepare us for a more developed state. Christ has manifested in his own person that wonderful grace of God which is to deal with us as sons and to educate us unto holiness and so to the full possession of our heavenly heritage. We are the many sons who are to be brought to glory by the discipline of grace. We generally think of law when we talk about schoolmasters and discipline, but grace itself has a discipline and a wonderful training power too. The manifestation of grace is preparing us for the manifestation of glory. What the law could not do, grace is doing. The free favour of God instils new principles, suggests new thoughts and, by inspiring us with gratitude, creates in us love to God and hatred of that which is opposed to God. Happy are they who go to school to the grace of God! This grace, entering us, shows us what was evil even more clearly than the commandment does. We receive a vital, testing principle within, whereby we discern between good and evil. The grace of God provides us with instruction, but also with chastisement, as it is written, 'As many as I love, I rebuke and chasten'. As soon as we come under the conscious enjoyment of the free grace of God, we find it to be a holy rule, a fatherly government, a heavenly training. We do not find self-indulgence, much less licentiousness; on the contrary, the grace of God restrains and constrains us; it makes us free to holiness and delivers us 'from the law of sin and death' by 'the law of the Spirit of life in Christ Jesus'.

FOR MEDITATION: (*Our Own Hymn Book,* no. 639 v.7—Philip Doddridge, 1755)
  'Thou know'st I love Thee, dearest Lord; but oh, I long to soar
  Far from the sphere of mortal joys, and learn to love Thee more.'

SERMON NO. 1894

5 APRIL (1891)

The census of Israel

'These are they that were numbered by Moses and Eleazar the priest, who numbered the children of Israel in the plains of Moab by Jordan near Jericho. But among these there was not a man of them whom Moses and Aaron the priest numbered, when they numbered the children of Israel in the wilderness of Sinai. For the LORD *had said of them, They shall surely die in the wilderness. And there was not left a man of them, save Caleb the son of Jephunneh, and Joshua the son of Nun.'* Numbers 26:63–65

SUGGESTED FURTHER READING: 2 Corinthians 12:14–21

Our text is from the Book of Numbers and the book well answers to its title, for it continually deals with numbers and numberings. The numbering on this occasion was not of the women and children or the infirm, for the order ran thus, 'Take the sum of all the congregation of the children of Israel, from twenty years old and upward, throughout their fathers' house, all that are able to go to war in Israel.' If the numbers of our churches were taken in this fashion, would they not sadly shrink? We have many sick among us that need to be carried about, nursed and doctored. Half the strength of the church goes in ambulance service towards the weak and wounded. Another diminution of power is occasioned by the vast numbers of undeveloped believers, to whom the apostle would have said, 'when for the time ye ought to be teachers, ye have need that one teach you again which be the first principles of the oracles of God; and are become such as have need of milk, and not of strong meat.' They should have become men, but they remain babes in grace. They are sadly slow in reaching the fullness of the stature of men in Christ Jesus. How many are quite unable to bear arms against the foe, for they need to be themselves guarded from the enemy! To revise the church rolls so as to leave none but vigorous soldiers on the muster-roll would make us break our hearts over our statistics. May the Lord send us, for this evil, health and cure!

FOR MEDITATION: (*Our Own Hymn Book,* no. 87 v.5—Isaac Watts, 1719)
  'When God makes up His last account of natives in His holy mount,
  'Twill be an honour to appear as one new-born or nourished there.'
N.B. This sermon was preached on the day of the 1891 census.

SERMON NO. 2198

6 APRIL (EASTER 1890)

The Prince of life

'And killed the Prince of life, whom God hath raised from the dead; whereof we are witnesses.' Acts 3:15
SUGGESTED FURTHER READING: Acts 13:26–41

Could they really kill the Prince of life? Go and extinguish the sun; go and stop the heart of this great earth, so that there shall be no more pulsings in her tides; but you can never in very deed destroy him 'Who only hath immortality'. Yet they thought they had killed the Prince of life and, in a sense, they had done so. And this is the idle dream of men to this day: they hope to quench the gospel, to silence the doctrines of grace, to exterminate the ancient orthodoxy and to put modern heresies in its place. Vanity of vanities! Even as the resurrection mocked the guards, the watch, the stone, so shall the revival of true godliness and the restoration of true doctrine baffle the devices of men. They that count the towers, to pull them down, and go about Zion in the hope of destroying her bulwarks, shall yet know that the virgin 'daughter of Zion ... hath shaken her head at' them, and laughed them to scorn. As the Lord Jesus lives, 'the way, the truth, and the life' shall remain eternally the same. Fools, when will you be wise and quit your vain rebellions? The text also exhibits the triumph of his life. 'The Prince of life, whom God hath raised from the dead'. His Godhead raised him, his Father raised him, his Spirit raised him. He resumed his life and thus was 'declared to be the Son of God with power'. This glorious resurrection of Christ should cause the universe to sing. Rejoice, for Jesus has left the dead, no more to die. A dead Christ? Then there would have been a dead gospel! What had we to preach to you if Jesus had not risen? Now that he has risen again we have justification to proclaim. Go and tell it all the world over: 'The Lord is risen indeed'. His resurrection is the cornerstone of the good news which the Lord has sent to believing men.

FOR MEDITATION: (*Our Own Hymn Book*, no. 306 v.3—Charles Wesley, 1739)
   'Vain the stone, the watch, the seal,
   Christ has burst the gates of hell;
   Death in vain forbids His rise,
   Christ hath opened paradise.'

SERMON NO. 2139

7 APRIL (1887)

Not bound yet

'Wherein I suffer trouble, as an evil doer, even unto bonds; but the word of God is not bound.' 2 Timothy 2:9
SUGGESTED FURTHER READING: Psalm 19:7–14

Paul is bound, 'but the word of God is not bound.' Read it thus: the preacher has had a bad week, he is full of aches and pains, he feels ill: *but the word of God is not ill.* Oh, what a blessing that is! We preach a healthy gospel if we are unhealthy ourselves. In this let the invalid rejoice. Dear suffering worker, your work shall not suffer, for it is a sound gospel which you preach, though you yourself are hampered by a poor, weak body! 'What will become of the congregation when a certain minister dies?' Well, he will be dead, *but the word of God is not dead.* God buries his workmen, but his work goes on. One light goes out, but another torch flames forth. Star by star sinks beneath the horizon, but another star appears on the other side to make glad the night. The word of God is not dead when the preacher is dead. 'Oh, but the worker is so feeble!' *The word of God is not feeble.* 'But the worker feels so stupid.' *But the word of God is not stupid.* 'But the worker is so unfit.' *But the word of God is not unfit.* You see it all comes to this: the preacher is bound, 'but the word of God is not bound': the worker is feeble, but the word of God is not feeble. You are nothing and nobody, but the word of God cannot be said to be nothing and nobody: it is everything and everybody: it is girt about with all power. But you bitterly and truthfully lament that Christian men are nowadays very devoid of zeal. 'All hearts are cold in every place'; the old fire burns low. *But the word of God is not cold*, nor lukewarm, nor in any way losing its old fire. 'Such and such a congregation is as frozen as the North Pole.' Yes, *but the word of God is not frozen*: divine truth is not turned into an iceberg. Do not fret yourself into despair as to the condition of the church, since the Lord lives.

FOR MEDITATION: (*Our Own Hymn Book*, no. 484 v.1—Isaac Watts, 1709)
'This is the word of truth and love,
Sent to the nations from above;
Jehovah here resolves to show
What His almighty grace can do.'

SERMON NO. 1998

8 APRIL (1888)

Cured at last!

'And a woman having an issue of blood twelve years, which had spent all her living upon physicians, neither could be healed of any, came behind him, and touched the border of his garment: and immediately her issue of blood stanched.' Luke 8:43–44
SUGGESTED FURTHER READING: John 1:9–13

Many under their burden of sin go first to one, then to another, practice this, agonize after that and pine for the other, perseveringly and still without avail! Travel as fast as you may in a wrong direction, you will not reach the place you seek. Vain are all things save Jesus our Lord. Have you been to Dr Ceremony? He is the fashionable doctor. Has he told you that you must attend to forms and rules? Has he prescribed you so many prayers and services? Many go to him and persevere in a round of religious observances, but these yield no lasting ease to the conscience. Have you tried Dr Morality? He has a large practice and is a fine old Jewish physician. 'Be good in outward character,' says he, 'and it will work inwardly and cleanse the heart.' A great many are supposed to have been cured by him and by his assistant, Dr Civility, but I have it on good evidence that neither of them apart, nor even the two together, could ever deal with an inward disease. Your own doings will not stanch the wounds of a bleeding heart. Dr Mortification has also a select practice, but men are not saved by denying themselves until they first deny their self-righteousness. Dr Excitement has many patients, but his cures seldom outlive sunset. Dr Feeling is much sought after by tender spirits; these try to feel sorrow and remorse, but the way of cure does not lie in that quarter. Let everything be done that can be done apart from our blessed Lord Jesus Christ, and the sick soul will be nothing bettered. You may try human remedies for a lifetime, but sin will remain in power, guilt will cling to the conscience and the heart will abide as hard as ever.

FOR MEDITATION: (*Our Own Hymn Book*, no. 493 v.1—Joseph Swain, 1792)

'Come, ye souls by sin afflicted, bowed with fruitless sorrow down;
By the broken law convicted, through the cross behold the crown.
Look to Jesus—mercy flows through Him alone.'

SERMON NO. 2018

9 APRIL (PREACHED 7 APRIL 1889)

The believing thief

'And he said unto Jesus, Lord, remember me when thou comest into thy kingdom. And Jesus said unto him, Verily I say unto thee, To day shalt thou be with me in paradise.' Luke 23:42–43
SUGGESTED FURTHER READING: Revelation 7:1–17

Have you never heard of him who dreamed that he stood outside the gate of heaven and heard sweet music from a band of venerable persons who were on their way to glory? They entered the celestial portals and there was great rejoicing and shouts. Enquiring 'What are these?' he was told that they were the goodly fellowship of the prophets. He sighed and said, 'Alas! I am not one of those.' He waited a while and another band of shining ones drew nigh, who also entered heaven with hallelujahs, and when he enquired, 'Who are these and whence came they?' the answer was, 'These are the glorious company of the apostles.' Again he sighed and said, 'I cannot enter with them.' Then came another body of men white-robed and bearing palms in their hands, who marched amid great acclamation into the golden city. These he learned were the noble army of martyrs; again he wept and said, 'I cannot enter with these.' In the end he heard the voices of many people and saw a greater multitude advancing, among whom he perceived Rahab, Mary Magdalene, David, Peter, Manasseh, Saul of Tarsus and especially the thief, who died at the right hand of Jesus. These all entered in, a strange company. Then he eagerly enquired, 'Who are these?' and they answered, 'This is the host of sinners saved by grace.' Then was he glad and said, 'I can go with these.' He thought there would be no shouting at the approach of this company and that they would enter heaven without song, instead of which there seemed to rise a seven-fold hallelujah of praise unto the Lord of love, for 'there is joy in the presence of the angels of God over' sinners that repent.

FOR MEDITATION: (*Our Own Hymn Book*, no. 506 v.3—Albert Midlane, 1865)
   'Love which made Him, "Prince of Glory", come to die, the "Sinner's Friend",
   Love beyond the reach of mortals' deepest thoughts to comprehend.
   Sinner, make this love thy portion, slight not love so vast and free;
   Still unblest, if unforgiven, come, the Saviour calleth thee.'

SERMON NO. 2078

10 APRIL (EASTER 1887)

The first appearance of the risen Lord to the eleven

'Jesus himself stood in the midst of them, and saith unto them, Peace be unto you. But they were terrified and affrighted, and supposed that they had seen a spirit. And he said unto them, Why are ye troubled? and why do thoughts arise in your hearts? Behold my hands and my feet, that it is I myself: handle me, and see.' Luke 24:36–39
SUGGESTED FURTHER READING (Spurgeon): Mark 16:1–14

They are as slow of heart and as fearful as ever. If *they* are convinced that Jesus has risen from the dead, it must be so. If they go forth to tell the tidings of his resurrection and to yield up their lives for it, you may be sure that their witness is true, for they are not the sort of men to be deceived. In our day there has been a buzz about certain miracles of faith, but the statements usually come from those whose impartiality is questionable, credulous persons who saw what they evidently wished to see. I know several good people who would not wilfully deceive, who nevertheless upon some points are exceedingly unreliable, because their enthusiasm is prepared to be imposed upon. Any hawker of wonders would expect them to be buyers; they have a taste for the marvellous. As witnesses, the evidence of such people has no value in it as compared with that of these eleven men, who evidently were the reverse of credulous or excitable. In the apostles' case the facts were tested to the utmost and the truth was not admitted till it was forced upon them. I am not excusing the unbelief of the disciples, but I claim that their witness has all the more weight in it, because it was the result of such cool investigation. These apostles were in special manner to be witnesses of the resurrection and it makes assurance doubly sure to us when we see them arrive at their conclusion with such deliberate steps. These were men like ourselves, only perhaps a little less likely to be deceived: they needed to be convinced by overwhelming witness: ever afterwards they declared boldly that their crucified Lord had indeed risen from the dead.

FOR MEDITATION: The apostles who said 'we cannot but speak the things which we have seen and heard' (Acts 4:20) were the very men who a little earlier had been unable to believe their own ears (Mark 16:11,13; John 20:24–25) and eyes (Matthew 28:17; Luke 24:36–41). We cannot see what they saw, but we can believe their word (John 17:20; 20:29).

SERMON NO. 1958

11 APRIL (1886)

Love abounding, love complaining, love abiding

'But now thus saith the LORD *that created thee, O Jacob, and he that formed thee, O Israel, Fear not: for I have redeemed thee, I have called thee by thy name; thou art mine.' 'But thou hast not called upon me, O Jacob; but thou hast been weary of me, O Israel.' 'Remember these, O Jacob and Israel; for thou art my servant ... thou shalt not be forgotten of me.'* Isaiah 43:1,22; 44:21
SUGGESTED FURTHER READING: Micah 6:1–8

'Thou hast been weary of me, O Israel.' The Lord has delighted in us, for he joyously recounts his dealings towards us, saying, 'I have created thee and formed thee. I have redeemed thee, and called thee, and made thee mine.' If he had been weary of us we need not have wondered, but we ought to blush and be silent for shame, because we have wearied of him. Brothers, are we tired of our God? If not, how is it that we do not walk with him from day to day? Really spiritual worship is not much cared for in these days, even by professing Christians. Many will go to a place of worship if they can be entertained with fine music or grand oratory, but if communion with God is the only attraction, they are not drawn thereby. They can spend many an evening where all sorts of levity and nonsense waste the hour, but when do they spend an evening with their God? If some of you had ever done such a thing, it would be marked down in your diaries as a wonder. Can any of you say, 'I did once spend a night with God'? Is it not, then, true, 'thou hast been weary of me'? Some of my hearers have never spoken with God in all their lives: they are not on speaking terms with him; they do not know him. Small wonder is it that you do not believe in him: he alone truly believes in God who has come to know him. He that lives with God and walks with God has no questions or doubts about his existence: he has risen long ago above that wretched state of mind. God grant that any of you who are weary at the very mention of eternal things may be delivered from your earth-bondage and made to rejoice in the Lord.

FOR MEDITATION: (*Our Own Hymn Book*, no. 735 v.6—William Cowper, 1771)

'Lord, it is my chief complaint, that my love is weak and faint;
Yet I love Thee and adore—oh for grace to love Thee more!'

SERMON NO. 1895

12 APRIL (1891)

The covenant promise of the Spirit

'And I will put my spirit within you.' Ezekiel 36:27
SUGGESTED FURTHER READING: 1 John 1:1–5

Our dearly beloved friend Adolph Saphir passed away last Saturday and his wife died three or four days before him. When my dear brother, Dr Sinclair Patteson, went to see him, the beloved Saphir said to him, 'God is light, and in him is no darkness at all.' Nobody would have quoted that passage but Saphir, the Biblical student, the lover of the word, the lover of the God of Israel. 'God is light, and in him is no darkness at all.' His dear wife has gone and he himself is ill, but 'God is light, and in him is no darkness at all.' This is a deep well of overflowing comfort, if you understand it well. God's providence is light as well as his promise and the Holy Spirit makes us know this. God's word and will and way are all light to his people 'and in him is no darkness at all' for them. God himself is purely and only light. What if there be darkness in me, there is no darkness in him, and his Spirit causes me to fly to him! What if there be darkness in my family, there is no darkness in my covenant God, and his Spirit makes me rest in him. What if there be darkness in my body by reason of my failing strength, there is no failing in him, and there is no darkness in him: his Spirit assures me of this. David says, 'God my exceeding joy', and such he is to us. 'Yea, mine own God is he'! Can you say, 'My God, my God'? Do you want anything more? Can you conceive of anything beyond your God? Omnipotent to work all for ever! Infinite to give! Faithful to remember! He is all that is good. Light only: 'in him is no darkness at all.' I have all light, yes, all things, when I have my God. The Holy Spirit makes us apprehend this when he is put within us. Holy Comforter, abide with us, for then we enjoy the light of heaven.

FOR MEDITATION: (*Our Own Hymn Book,* no. 468 v.1—Isaac Watts, 1709)

> 'Why should the children of a King
> Go mourning all their days?
> Great Comforter, descend and bring
> Some tokens of Thy grace.'

SERMON NO. 2200

13 APRIL (1890)

A homily for humble folks

'Surely I am more brutish than any man, and have not the understanding of a man.' Proverbs 30:2
SUGGESTED FURTHER READING: Romans 1:16–25

Because God had taught Agur much, he felt that he knew little. Especially I think the truth of our text relates to one particular line of things. This man was a naturalist. We have nothing of his save this chapter, but his allusions to natural history all through it are exceedingly abundant. He was an instructed scientist, but he felt that he could not by searching find out God, nor fashion an idea of him from his own thoughts. When he heard of the great discoveries of those who judged themselves to be superior persons, he disowned such wisdom as theirs. Other men with their great understanding might be fishing up pearls of truth from the sea; as for himself, he knew nothing but that which he found in God's Word. He had none of that boasted understanding which climbed the heavens, bound the winds, swathed the sea and so found out the sacred name; he was content with revelation, and felt that 'Every word of God is pure'. Not in any earthly school learned he the knowledge of the Holy: all that he knew he had been taught by God's Book. He had in thought climbed to heaven and come down again: he had listened to the speech of winds, waves and mountains, but he protested that in all this he had not discovered God's name nor his Son's name by his own understanding. All his light had come through the Lord's own Word and he shrewdly gave this caution to those who thought themselves supremely wise, above what is written: 'Add thou not unto his words, lest he reprove thee, and thou be found a liar.' Philosophy had failed him and revelation was his sole confidence. As for himself, he did not claim that degree of perception and profundity which enabled him to think out God, but he went to God himself and learned from him at first hand, through his revealed wisdom.

FOR MEDITATION: In Proverbs 30 contrast Agur's lowly view of self (vv.2–3) with his inspired views of Scripture (vv.5–6), sin (vv.7–14), science and society (vv.15–33). Having a good opinion of oneself is not a good idea (Proverbs 3:7; Romans 12:3; 1 Corinthians 8:2; Galatians 6:3); such a thing is safer left to the discernment of another (Proverbs 27:2).

SERMON NO. 2140

14 APRIL (1889)

Man unknown to man

'The heart knoweth his own bitterness; and a stranger doth not intermeddle with his joy.' Proverbs 14:10
SUGGESTED FURTHER READING: Job 2:1–13

If we desire to show sympathy to our brethren, let us not dream that this is an easy task. It is not a simple matter to square two unknown quantities, yourself and your friend. It would take me long to learn to correspond with the inhabitants of the planet Mars: in all probability I should never achieve the task. I doubt not that there are many people so peculiar, both in their sorrows and in their joys, that I shall no more be able to commune with them in real sympathy than with the people of the aforesaid planet. Study the art of sympathy. It is easy enough for a captain of a steam-vessel to lay his ship alongside the quay, but if I had the doing of it, I should probably break down the wall of the dock and injure the vessel too. It is not easy to lay your soul side by side with another man's soul. It is difficult to do as Elijah did, when he laid himself upon the dead child, putting his mouth upon the child's mouth, his hands upon the child's hands, his feet upon the child's feet and so, by God's power, breathing life into the cold form. It is not easy to be effectively sympathetic: some cannot manifest tenderness even when they have a mind to do so. I once knew a minister who had never suffered pain or illness in his life. I was unwell in his house and he most kindly tried to sympathize with me. He did it almost as wonderfully as an elephant picks up a pin. It was a marvel that he could attempt a thing so altogether out of his line. Many of the trials which are experienced by Christians are sent as an education in the art of sympathy. Be thankful for that which enables you to be a minister of consolation to your fellow-men, but feel that in this matter you are a learner yet and will frequently meet with sorrows and with joys into which you cannot enter.

FOR MEDITATION: The Christian who has experienced affliction receives from God a comfort which can be passed on to others in the same position (2 Corinthians 1:3–4). But there will be times when the well-intentioned comforter will be no more successful than Jacob's children (Genesis 37:35) or Job's 'miserable comforters' (Job 16:2).

SERMON NO. 2079

15 APRIL (1888)

'She was not hid'

'And when the woman saw that she was not hid, she came trembling, and falling down before him, she declared unto him before all the people for what cause she had touched him, and how she was healed immediately.' Luke 8:47
SUGGESTED FURTHER READING: Luke 12:1–12

If it is right for one Christian not to confess Christ but to join a church, it must be allowable for other Christians to do the same. Where would be churches, where would be the continuance of gospel ordinances and who would be bound to be a preacher if no one is even bound to make an open profession? If you may go to heaven by the backstairs, so may I, and God's grand entrance to the kingdom may be deserted. Who will care to go to heaven by the open way, with all its responsibility and opposition, if you can just as easily take the snug road behind the hedges and slink into glory without observation? It will not do, if we consider what the Lord Jesus Christ deserves of us and how our open confession tends to certify his mission. The change wrought in the spiritual and moral condition of the saved is God's attestation of the gospel and, if this is not to be spoken of, how is the world to know that God has sent the gospel at all? Further, remember that our Lord's miracles were illustrative of his teaching. Properly viewed, the miracles of Christ are the pictures of a volume of which his sermons are the letterpress. You take *The Illustrated London News* and you get the description of a public building or the account of a grand ceremony: you are glad of the printed account, but you are much helped to form an idea of the whole business by the engravings. You would not like to lose the woodcut, which is the chief feature of value in the paper. Now, in our Saviour's ministry his words were the letterpress and his miracles the engravings. If the engraving is to be torn away or pasted over, a great injury is done to the paper; even so our Lord's teaching would be greatly marred if its miracles were concealed.

FOR MEDITATION: (*Our Own Hymn Book*, no. 671 v.1—Isaac Watts, 1721)

'Am I a soldier of the cross,   And shall I fear to own His cause,
A follower of the Lamb?   Or blush to speak His name?'

SERMON NO. 2019

16 APRIL (PREACHED 18 APRIL 1886)

The three hours' darkness

'Now from the sixth hour there was darkness over all the land unto the ninth hour.' Matthew 27:45
SUGGESTED FURTHER READING: Luke 23:39–49

This darkness tells us all that the Passion is a great mystery, into which we cannot pry. I try to explain it as substitution and I feel that where the language of Scripture is explicit, I may and must be explicit too. But yet I feel that the idea of substitution does not cover the whole of the matter and that no human conception can completely grasp the whole of the dread mystery. It was wrought in darkness, because the full, far-reaching meaning and result cannot be beheld by finite minds. Tell me the death of the Lord Jesus was a grand example of self-sacrifice—I can see that and much more. Tell me it was a wondrous obedience to the will of God—I can see that and much more. Tell me it was the bearing of what ought to have been borne by myriads of sinners of the human race, as the chastisement of their sin—I can see that and found my best hope upon it. But do not tell me that this is all that is in the cross. No, great as this would be, there is much more in our Redeemer's death. God only knows the love of God: Christ only knows all that he accomplished when he bowed his head and gave up the ghost. There are common mysteries of nature into which it would be irreverence to pry, but this is a divine mystery, before which we put our shoes from off our feet, for the place called Calvary is holy ground. God veiled the cross in darkness and in darkness much of its deeper meaning lies, not because God would not reveal it, but because we have not capacity enough to discern it all. God was manifest in the flesh, and in that human flesh he put away sin by his own sacrifice: this we all know, but 'without controversy great is the mystery of godliness'.

FOR MEDITATION: (*Our Own Hymn Book,* no. 279 v.3—Isaac Watts, 1709)
    'Well might the sun in darkness hide,
    And shut his glories in,
    When God, the mighty Maker died
    For man, the creature's sin.'

SERMON NO. 1896

17 APRIL (1887)

The watchword for today: 'Stand fast'

'Stand fast in the Lord, my dearly beloved.' Philippians 4:1
SUGGESTED FURTHER READING: 2 Thessalonians 2:13–3:5

'Stand fast' *without wavering in your trust*. Permit no doubt to worry you. Know that Jesus can save you and, what is more, know that he has saved you. So commit yourself to his hands, that you are as sure of your salvation as of your existence. 'The blood of Jesus Christ' this day 'cleanseth us from all sin'; his righteousness covers us and his life quickens us into newness of life. Tolerate no doubt, mistrust, suspicion or misgiving. Believe in Christ up to the hilt. As for myself, I will yield to be lost for ever if Jesus does not save me. I will have no other string to my bow, no second door of hope or way of retreat. I could risk a thousand souls on my Lord's truth and feel no risk. 'Stand fast', without wishing for another trust and without wavering in the trust you have. Moreover, 'stand fast' *without wandering into sin*. You are tempted this way and that way: 'stand fast'. Inward passions rise, lusts of the flesh rebel, the devil hurls his fearful suggestions, the men of your own household tempt you: 'stand fast'. Only so will you be preserved from the torrents of iniquity. Keep close to the example and spirit of your Master 'and having done all,' still stand. 'Stand fast' without wandering; next I must say 'stand fast' *without wearying*. You are a little tired. Never mind, take a little rest and brush up again. 'Oh,' you say, 'this toil is so monotonous.' Do it better and that will be a change. Your Saviour endured his life and labour without this complaint, for zeal had eaten him up. 'Alas!' you cry, 'I cannot see results.' Never mind; wait for results, even as 'the husbandman waiteth for the precious fruit of the earth'. 'Oh, sir, I plod along and make no progress.' Never mind; you are a poor judge of your own success. Work on, 'for in due season we shall reap, if we faint not.' Practise perseverance.

FOR MEDITATION: (Philip P. Bliss, 1870)
   '"Hold the Fort, for I am coming,"
   Jesus signals still;
   Wave the answer back to Heaven,
   "By Thy grace we will."'

SERMON NO. 1959

18 APRIL (1889)

A dirge for the down-grade, and a song for faith

'Rejoice for joy with her, all ye that mourn for her.' Isaiah 66:10
SUGGESTED FURTHER READING: Amos 6:1–6

Things are done in our churches which thirty years ago were not so much as dreamed of. In the matter of amusements, professors have gone far in the way of laxity. What is worse, the churches have now conceived the idea that it is their duty to amuse the people. Dissenters, who used to protest against going to the theatre, now cause the theatre to come to them. Ought not many schoolrooms to be licensed for stage-plays? If someone were to see to the rigid carrying out of the law, would they not be required to take out a license for theatricals? I dare not touch upon what has been done at bazaars and fancy fairs. If these had been arranged by decent worldly people, could they have gone further? What folly has been left untried? What absurdity has been too great for the consciences of those who profess to be the children of God, who are not of the world but called to walk with God in a separated life? The world regards the high pretensions of such men as hypocrisy and truly I do not know another name for them. Think of those who enjoy communion with God playing the fool in costume! They talk of wrestling with the Lord in secret prayer, but they juggle with the world in unconcealed gambling. Can this be right? Have right and wrong shifted places? Surely there is a sobriety of behaviour which is consistent with a work of grace in the heart and there is a levity which indicates that the spirit of evil is supreme. There may have been a time when Christians were too precise, but it has not been in my day. There may have been such a dreadful thing as Puritanic rigidity, but I have never seen it. We are quite free from that evil now, if it ever existed. We have gone from liberty to libertinism. We have passed beyond the dubious into the dangerous and none can prophesy where we shall stop. Where is the holiness of the church of God today?

FOR MEDITATION: (*Our Own Hymn Book*, no. 888 v.3—Charles Wesley, 1740)
    'Still, O Lord, our faith increase; cleanse from all unrighteousness:
    Thee the unholy cannot see; make, oh make us meet for Thee!
    Every vile affection kill; root out every seed of ill;
    Utterly abolish sin; write Thy law of love within.'

SERMON NO. 2085

19 APRIL (1891)

The sword of the Spirit

'Take ... the sword of the Spirit, which is the word of God.' Ephesians 6:17
SUGGESTED FURTHER READING: Luke 4:1–19

What is the matter this morning? 'Oh,' says one, 'I have been in the habit of sinning and the habit is very strong upon me.' Fight with sinful habits with the word of God, as the sword of the Spirit: so only will you conquer your evil self. Find a text of Scripture that will cleave your sin down to the bone or stab it to the heart. 'Alas! Satan tempts me horribly,' cries one; 'I have been lately assailed in many ways.' Have you? You are not the first. Our divine Lord in the wilderness was tempted by the devil. He might have fought Satan with a thousand weapons, but he chose to defeat him with this one only. He said, 'It is written; it is written; it is written.' He pricked the foeman so sorely with this sharp point that the arch-adversary thought to try the same sword and also began to say, 'it is written'. But he cut himself with this sword, for he did not quote the passages correctly nor give the whole of them, and the Master soon found the way to knock aside his sword and wound him still more. Follow your Lord's example. 'Oh, but,' says one, 'I am so low in spirits.' Very well; fight lowness of spirits with the word of God. 'The doctor recommended me,' says one, 'to take a little spirits to raise my spirits.' Those doctors are always having this sin laid to their charge. I am not so sure that they are not often maligned. You like the dose and that is why you take it. Try the word of God for lowness of spirits and you will have found a sure remedy. I find, if I can lay a promise under my tongue like a sweet lozenge and keep it in my mouth or mind all the day long, I am happy enough. If I cannot find a Scripture to comfort me, then my inward troubles are multiplied. Fight despondency and despair with the sword of the Spirit. I cannot tell what your particular difficulty may be at this moment, but I give you this direction for all holy warfare: 'take ... the sword of the Spirit, which is the word of God'.

FOR MEDITATION: (*Our Own Hymn Book*, no. 673 v.1—Henry Kirke White, 1806; Fanny Fuller Maitland, 1827)

'Oft in sorrow, oft in woe,   Fight the fight, maintain the strife,
Onward, Christians, onward go;   Strengthened with the bread of life.'

SERMON NO. 2201

20 APRIL (1890)

The question of questions

'Jesus heard that they had cast him out; and when he had found him, he said unto him, Dost thou believe on the Son of God?' John 9:35
SUGGESTED FURTHER READING: 1 John 2:1–17

There are marks and evidences of true faith by which you can readily test yourself. If you enquire, 'Do I believe on the Son of God?' answer this: *is Christ precious to you*? 'Unto you' who 'believe he is precious'. If you love and prize him as the most precious thing in earth or heaven, you could not have this appreciation of him if you were not a believer. Tell me again, *have you undergone the change called the new birth*? Have you passed through a process which could be described as being brought 'out of darkness into his marvellous light'? If so, your new birth is a sure evidence of faith, for these things go together: while faith is a proof of regeneration, regeneration is also a proof that you have faith in the Son of God. Again, *are you obedient to Christ*? Faith works by love and purifies the soul. Is it so with you? Has sin become bitter? Do you loathe it? Has holiness become sweet? Do you follow after it? I do not ask whether you are perfect, but is the whole current of your soul towards being perfect? Can you say that if you could live entirely without sin it would be the greatest delight you could have, that absolute perfection would be heaven to you? Then it shows which way your mind goes; it shows that there is a change of nature, for no unrenewed heart pines after perfect holiness. Your heart is bending towards Christ's perfect rule and sovereignty and I am sure that you have believed that he is the Son of God. You are resting upon him with a true and living faith, if you take up his cross heartily and follow him. Again, *do you love God*? Do you love his people? 'We know that we have passed from death unto life, because we love the brethren.' Do you love his Word? Do you delight in his worship? Do you bow in patience before his rod, so that you take up the bitter cup and say, 'Thy will be done'? These things prove that you have faith in Jesus. Look well to them.

FOR MEDITATION: Read 1 John 3:23–24. The presence of genuine saving faith can be tested by examining whether we possess life through our believing (1 John 5:12–13), light in our behaviour (1 John 1:5–7; 2:3–6) and love towards our brethren (1 John 3:14; 4:7–8).

SERMON NO. 2141

21 APRIL (EASTER 1889)

The power of his resurrection

'That I may know him, and the power of his resurrection.' Philippians 3:10
SUGGESTED FURTHER READING: Romans 8:9–13

The resurrection of Christ is operating at this present time with a quickening power on all who hear the word aright. The sun is, to the vegetable world, a great quickener. In this month of April he goes forth with life in his beams and we see the result. The buds are bursting, the trees are putting on their summer dress, the flowers are smiling and even the seeds which he buried in the earth are beginning to feel the vivifying warmth: they see not the lord of day, but they feel his smile. Over what an enormous territory is the returning sun continually operating! How potent are his forces when he crosses the line and lengthens the day! Such is the risen Christ. In the grave he was like the sun in his winter solstice, but he crossed the line in his resurrection; he has brought us all the hopes of Spring and is bringing us the joys of Summer. He is quickening many at this hour and will yet quicken myriads. This is the power with which the missionary goes forth to sow; this is the power in which the preacher at home continues to scatter the seed. The risen Christ is the great harvest-producer. By the power of his resurrection men are raised from their death in sin to eternal life. I said eternal life, for wherever Jesus gives life, it is everlasting life. 'Christ being raised from the dead dieth no more; death hath no more dominion over him' and as we have been raised 'in the likeness of his resurrection', so we are raised into a life over which death has no more dominion. We shall not die again, but the water which Jesus gives us shall be in us 'a well of water springing up into everlasting life.'

FOR MEDITATION: (*Our Own Hymn Book*, no. 306 v.4—Charles Wesley, 1739)
    'Lives again our glorious King!
    "Where, O death, is now thy sting?"
    Once He died our souls to save;
    "Where's thy victory, boasting grave?"'

SERMON NO. 2080

22 APRIL (1888)

'Is anything too hard for the Lord?'

'Then came the word of the LORD *unto Jeremiah, saying, Behold, I am the* LORD, *the God of all flesh: is there any thing too hard for me?'* Jeremiah 32:26–27
SUGGESTED FURTHER READING: John 1:43–51

God had caused Jeremiah to know his omnipotence so far, but he was to see still more of it. Faith has led you into marvellous places, but there are greater things before you, and the Lord presses truth upon you that you may receive more of it. Did you ever climb a mountain? A friend of mine, when among the Alps, asserted confidently that he could reach the top of a certain mountain in half-an-hour. It certainly looked very near us, but my eye had been better educated to estimate distances among mountains and I assured him that it would take him all the day to stand upon that ridge. The fact is, that when you have climbed one stiff bit of hill you find yourself bound to go down into a valley before you can tackle the next ascent. There are hills above hills and one summit is a sort of lookout from which you see that you have much further to go. That which looked like a part of the side of the hill may really be a mountain by itself and when you have ascended it, you have the cheering privilege of seeing that you are now at the bottom of the next. In fact, although you are decidedly higher, you often seem to have further to go than when you started. It is just so with our experience of divine things: when we know the Lord to the full of our capacity, that capacity enlarges and we begin to learn again. We know more and for that very reason are far more conscious of our ignorance than we were at the first. The Lord himself came to his servant Jeremiah and thus prepared him for those greater things which he was about to reveal.

FOR MEDITATION: (*Our Own Hymn Book*, no. 209 v.2—Ambrose Serle, 1787)
   'With feeble light and half obscure,
   Poor mortals Thy arrangements view;
   Not knowing that the least are sure,
   And the mysterious just and true.'

SERMON NO. 2020

23 APRIL (PREACHED 19 APRIL 1885)

First healing and then service

'And when Jesus was come into Peter's house, he saw his wife's mother laid, and sick of a fever. And he touched her hand, and the fever left her: and she arose, and ministered unto them.' Matthew 8:14–15
SUGGESTED FURTHER READING: Genesis 13:1–18

This took place at Capernaum, but Peter's residence was at Bethsaida, for we read, 'Philip was of Bethsaida, the city of Andrew and Peter.' How came Peter to have a house at Capernaum? Poor fishermen do not often have two houses. May it not be highly probable that, finding the Lord Jesus Christ was frequently at Capernaum, Peter thought it best to have a dwelling there, that he might always be present when the Master was preaching and that he might entertain him between whiles? I like to think that the servant changed his place of abode for his Master's sake. Would it not be well if many Christian people had some little consideration, when they are choosing a house, as to whether it will be convenient for the hearing of the word? Do you not think that a great many look chiefly for every other kind of advantage and, when they have virtually made their choice, afterwards enquire into the very secondary item of their nearness to a place where they may worship God, enjoy Christian fellowship and be useful? Some in this congregation have moved to this part of town to become members of an earnest, prayerful church. Such believers feel that the first consideration in life must be the health of their souls, the benefiting of their children and their usefulness in promoting the cause of Christ. When they have made the selection of a house in that way and for that reason, they have found a blessing resting upon them according to the promise, 'seek ye first the kingdom of God, and his righteousness; and all these things shall be added unto you.' Some who have forgotten this rule and, like Lot, have chosen the well-watered plains of Sodom, have lived to rue their choice. Although the house may be commodious and the position convenient, these advantages will not make up for losing the means of grace and missing opportunities of holy service.

FOR MEDITATION: Living in spiritual isolation amongst the ungodly caused Lot great distress (2 Peter 2:7–8). The Psalmist also lamented such an experience (Psalm 120:5–7). A company of believers, however, can stand firm in an ungodly environment (Revelation 2:12–13).

SERMON NO. 1836

24 APRIL (1887)

The servants and the pounds

'A certain nobleman went into a far country to receive for himself a kingdom, and to return. And he called his ten servants, and delivered them ten pounds, and said unto them, Occupy till I come.' Luke 19:12–13
SUGGESTED FURTHER READING: Matthew 25:14–30

What they had to do with the pound was prescribed in general terms. They were to trade with it, not to play with it. I dare say they were inclined to argue, 'Our master's cause is assailed; let us fight for him'; yet he did not say, 'fight,' but trade. Peter drew his sword. Oh, yes, we are eager combatants, but slow merchants. Many manifest a defiant spirit, and are never more satisfied than when they are in noise and strife. The servants in this parable were not to fight, but to trade, which is a much more cool-blooded and ignoble thing in common esteem. We may leave our Lord's enemies to himself; he will end their rebellions one of these days. We are to follow a much lowlier line of things. No doubt certain of them might have thought that the pound would be useful to purchase comforts or even luxuries: one would buy a new coat, another would bring home a piece of furniture for his house and others would solemnly say, 'We have our families to think of.' Yes, but their lord did not say so; the master said, 'Trade therewith until I come.' They were neither to fight with it, nor hoard it, nor spend it, nor waste it, but to trade with it for him. The pound was not put into their hands for display. They were not to glory over others who had not so much as a penny to bless themselves with, for though they were little capitalists, that capital was their lord's. It is a pity when graces or talents are boasted of as if they were our own. A tradesman who is prospering seldom has much money to show; it is all wanted in his business. Sometimes he can scarcely put his hand upon a five-pound note, because his cash is all absorbed: his golden grain is all sown in the field of his trade. Our pound is not to be hung on our watch-chain, but to be traded with.

FOR MEDITATION: As God's stewards Christians are required to be faithful (1 Corinthians 4:1–2). How do you employ the 'pounds' God has entrusted to you, such as your possessions (1 Chronicles 29:12–14), your abilities (Romans 12:6–8; 1 Peter 4:10–11) and your body (1 Corinthians 6:19–20)?

SERMON NO. 1960

25 APRIL (EASTER 1886)

Mouth and heart

'That if thou shalt confess with thy mouth the Lord Jesus, and shalt believe in thine heart that God hath raised him from the dead, thou shalt be saved.' Romans 10:9
SUGGESTED FURTHER READING: Romans 1:1–8

Why, my dear brethren, is salvation promised here especially to a belief with the heart that God has raised Christ from the dead? Is not our faith to be fixed upon the death of Christ rather than upon the resurrection of Christ? I answer, it is probably here stated because in the resurrection of our Lord all the rest of his history is implied and included. If he was raised from the dead, then he must have died. If he died, then he must have been a man and have been born into the world. In mentioning that God raised our Lord from the dead, the apostle has really mentioned all the great redeeming work of Jesus, since all the other items are involved therein. Moreover, the raising from the dead is not only inclusive of the rest, but confirmatory of the whole. By raising him from the dead the Father gave confirmation of the mission of his Son. He set his seal upon his person as divine, upon his office as commissioned of God to be the Messiah, upon his life as well-pleasing and upon his death as being accepted of God for full atonement. Therefore the Most High raised him from the dead, so that he might be 'declared to be the Son of God with power,' and that in and through him believers might be justified. We should not have had firm ground for our faith in Jesus if the seal of resurrection had not been set to his work, but now, when we believe in the seal, we believe also in that which is sealed. His resurrection is the seal of all that our Lord is and does and, believing in this with our heart, we believe in that which brings salvation.

FOR MEDITATION: (*Our Own Hymn Book,* no. 909 v.2—Isaac Watts, 1719)
'Today He rose and left the dead;
And Satan's empire fell;
Today the saints His triumph spread,
And all His wonders tell.'

SERMON NO. 1898

The good Ananias: a lesson for believers

'And there was a certain disciple at Damascus, named Ananias; and to him said the Lord in a vision, Ananias. And he said, Behold, I am here, Lord.' Acts 9:10

SUGGESTED FURTHER READING (Spurgeon): Acts 22:1–16

Notice how faithful Ananias was. He said, 'arise, and be baptized, and wash away thy sins'. The tendency with many evangelists is to say nothing upon that point. The main thing is to get this man to be a believer in the Lord Jesus Christ, but to say, 'arise, and be baptized', is that not far less important? We have nothing to do with altering Christ's message, but are bound to deliver it as a whole without addition or diminution. The tendency is to say, 'Baptism should not be mentioned; it is sectarian.' Who said so? If our Lord commanded it, who dares to call it sectarian? We are not commanded to preach a part but the whole of the gospel, and this Ananias did. Is it not written, 'He that believeth and is baptized shall be saved'? Why omit one clause? I question whether God's blessing has not been withheld from some preachers because they have failed to repeat their message in its entirety. A brother will write to me next week and say, 'I am sorry that I cannot circulate your sermon, because you allude to baptism.' My dear brother, if you cannot circulate the sermon, I must be content without your kind help, but I cannot amend the Lord's word to please the best man upon the earth. What prominence is given to baptism here! We should greatly err if we believed in baptismal regeneration or even in the efficacy of washing in water for the removal of sin, but, on the other hand, we are not to place in the background an ordinance which, by the language of Scripture, is placed in the forefront. Ananias said to Paul, 'arise, and be baptized, and wash away thy sins'. And this tallies with that other text, 'He that believeth and is baptized shall be saved'. In both of these passages the Lord puts a special honour upon baptism and it would be ill for us to neglect that which he so evidently esteems.

FOR MEDITATION: The Lord Jesus Christ commanded the apostles to baptize converts (Matthew 28:19) and they commanded converts to be baptized (Acts 2:38; 10:48). But gospel-preaching must take precedence (1 Corinthians 1:17). If you are unbaptized, what is hindering you (Acts 8:36), lack of trust in the Saviour or disobedience to his command?

SERMON NO. 1838

27 APRIL (1890)

Our Lord's triumphant ascension

'Thou hast ascended on high, thou hast led captivity captive: thou hast received gifts for men; yea, for the rebellious also, that the LORD *God might dwell among them.'* Psalm 68:18
SUGGESTED FURTHER READING (Spurgeon): Ephesians 4:7–13

The gifts here spoken of are those brought by the Holy Spirit. 'The water that I shall give him', said Christ 'shall be in him a well of water springing up into everlasting life.' He said again, 'If any man thirst, let him come unto me, and drink.' We read that he spoke 'of the Spirit, which they that believe on him should receive'. 'If ye then, being evil, know how to give good gifts unto your children: how much more shall your heavenly Father give the Holy Spirit to them that ask him?' To conquer the world for Christ we need nothing but the Holy Spirit and in the hour of his personal victory he secured us this boon. If the Holy Spirit is given, we have in him all the weapons of our holy war. But observe, according to Paul, these gifts which our Lord gave are *embodied in men*, for the Holy Spirit comes upon men whom he has chosen and works through them according to his good pleasure. Hence 'he gave some, apostles; and some, prophets; and some, evangelists; and some, pastors and teachers'. No one may be judged to be given by God to the church in any of these offices except as the Spirit dwells upon him. All are given by God upon whom the Holy Spirit rests, whatever their office may be. It is ours to accept with great joy the men who are chosen and anointed to speak in the name of the Lord, be they what they may. Paul, Apollos, Cephas, they are all the gifts of the risen Christ to his redeemed ones for their edifying and perfecting. The Holy Spirit, in proportion as he abides in these servants of God, makes them to be precious blessings of heaven to his people, and they become the champions by whom the world is subdued to the Lord Jesus Christ.

FOR MEDITATION: All good gifts come from God (James 1:17), people as well as things. The Levites were God's gift to the Old Testament priests to assist them in their service (Numbers 8:19; 18:6) and we should thank God not only for giving us the Lord Jesus Christ (John 3:16; 2 Corinthians 9:15) and the Holy Spirit (Luke 11:13; Acts 2:38), but also for the additional gift of Christian leaders (Ephesians 4:11).

SERMON NO. 2142

28 APRIL (1889)

One lost sheep

'How think ye? if a man have an hundred sheep, and one of them be gone astray, doth he not leave the ninety and nine, and goeth into the mountains, and seeketh that which is gone astray? And if so be that he find it, verily I say unto you, he rejoiceth more of that sheep, than of the ninety and nine which went not astray.' Matthew 18:12–13
SUGGESTED FURTHER READING: Luke 15:1–7

The great deeps of Christ's love are the same to all his flock, but on the surface there is sometimes a holy storm of joy when any one of them has been newly restored after wandering. Learn the occasion of this demonstrative joy. The wandering one has caused *great sorrow*. We were all grieved that our brother should become a gross backslider, that such an earnest Christian as he seemed to be should disgrace his profession. Our Lord is still more grieved than we are. When the erring one comes back, we feel a new joy in him. In proportion to the sorrow felt over the wanderer, is the joy manifested when he is restored. Moreover, *great apprehensions* were aroused; we feared that he was not the Lord's and that he would go back unto perdition. We trembled for him. That black dread is all over now: the sheep is safe; the doubtful one is saved and restored to the fold. In proportion to the weight of the apprehension is the intensity of the relief. The Shepherd had exercised also *great labour* over the lost one. He went up among the mountains to find his sheep, but now his labour is fully rewarded, for he has found his lost sheep. He remembers no more his travel and travail, for joy that the sheep is safe. Besides, in this newly-restored one, there are marks of salvation which cause joy. He has been torn with the briars, but he is resting now. See how he lies down in the tender grass! He was weary, worn and almost dead with his wanderings, but now, how happy he is in the presence of his shepherd! How closely he keeps to his shepherd's footsteps! All this goes to make the shepherd glad!

FOR MEDITATION: Consider the causes of joy which follow the finding of the lost sheep—there will be restoration (Galatians 6:1), salvation (James 5:20), life (1 John 5:16) and rescue (Jude 23). God rejoices in the end product (Jude 24).

SERMON NO. 2083

29 APRIL (PREACHED 25 APRIL 1890)

Our manifesto

'But I certify you, brethren, that the gospel which was preached of me is not after man.' Galatians 1:11
SUGGESTED FURTHER READING: James 2:1–9

'The poor have the gospel preached to them.' Yet there are not a few nowadays who despise a gospel which the common people can hear and understand; we may be sure that a plain gospel never came from them, for their taste does not lie in that direction. They want something 'thoughtful'. Do we not hear this sort of remark, 'We are an intellectual people and need a cultured ministry. Those evangelistic preachers are all very well for popular assemblies, but we have always been select and require that preaching which is abreast of the times'? Their man will be one who will not preach the gospel unless it is in a clouded manner, for if he does declare the gospel of Jesus, the poor will be sure to intrude and shock my lords and ladies. Brethren, our gospel does not know anything about high and low, rich and poor, black and white, cultured and uncultured. If it makes any difference, it prefers the poor and downtrodden. The great Founder of it says, 'I thank thee, O Father, Lord of heaven and earth, because thou hast hid these things from the wise and prudent, and hast revealed them unto babes.' We praise God that he has chosen the 'base things', and 'things which are despised'. I hear it boasted of a man's ministry, although it gradually diminishes the congregation, that it is doing a great work among thoughtful young men. I confess that I am not a believer in the existence of these thoughtful young men: those who mistake themselves for such I have generally found to be rather conceited than thoughtful. Young men are all very well and so are young women and old women also, but I am sent to 'preach the gospel to every creature,' and I cannot limit myself to thoughtful young men.

FOR MEDITATION: Man's standards do not apply when it comes to identifying those who will believe the gospel (1 Corinthians 1:26–28). The unrighteous cannot inherit the kingdom of God but can be saved (1 Corinthians 6:9–11) and enter it before those who, humanly speaking, are the more likely candidates (Matthew 21:31–32).

N.B. This sermon was preached 'at an assembly of ministers of the gospel.'

SERMON NO. 2185

30 APRIL (PREACHED 26 APRIL 1891)

'Lo, I come': exposition

'Then said I, Lo, I come: in the volume of the book it is written of me, I delight to do thy will, O my God: yea, thy law is within my heart.' Psalm 40:7–8
'When he cometh into the world, he saith ... a body hast thou prepared me ... Then said I, Lo, I come (in the volume of the book it is written of me,) to do thy will, O God.' Hebrews 10:5–7
SUGGESTED FURTHER READING: Proverbs 8:22–31

It was delightful to our Lord to come here. 'What did he delight in?' says one. Evidently he delighted in God's *law*. 'Thy law is within my heart.' He resolved that the beauties of the law of the Lord should be displayed by being embodied in his own life and that its claims should be vindicated by his own death. To achieve this he delighted to come to keep and honour it by an obedience both active and passive. He delighted in God's *will* also, and that is somewhat more, for law is the expression of will and this may be altered, but the will of the great King never changes. Our Lord delighted to carry out all the purposes and desires of the Most High God. He so delighted in the will of God that he came to do it, and to bear it, 'By the which will we are sanctified through the offering of the body of Jesus Christ once for all.' He delighted also in *God*. He took an intense delight in glorifying the Father. He came to reveal the Father and make him to be beloved by men. He did all things to please God. Moreover, he took a delight in *us*, and here, though the object of his love is less, the love itself is heightened by the conspicuous condescension. The Lord Jesus took a deep delight in his people, whose names were written on his heart, and graven on the palms of his hands. His heart was fixed on their redemption and therefore he would present himself as a sacrifice on their behalf. The people whom the Father gave him from before the foundation of the world lay on his very soul; for them he had 'a baptism to be baptized with', and he was 'straitened till it be accomplished'. He gave himself no rest till he had left both joy and rest to ransom his own.

FOR MEDITATION: If this is what delighted the Saviour, God surely delights in those who likewise delight in his law (Psalm 1:2; 119:70,77,92,174; Romans 7:22), his will (Isaiah 58:2), his person (Job 22:26; Psalm 37:4; Isaiah 58:14) and his people (Psalm 16:3).

SERMON NO. 2202

1 MAY (1887)

S. S. or, the sinner saved

'The Gentiles, which followed not after righteousness, have attained to righteousness, even the righteousness which is of faith. But Israel, which followed after the law of righteousness, hath not attained to the law of righteousness. Wherefore? Because they sought it not by faith, but as it were by the works of the law.' Romans 9:30–32
SUGGESTED FURTHER READING: Matthew 23:23–28

Israel did not follow after righteousness, but after *the law of righteousness*. They missed the spirit, which is righteousness, and followed after the mere letter of the law. To be really righteous was not their aim, but to do righteousness was their utmost notion. They looked at 'Thou shalt not kill. Thou shalt not commit adultery', 'Remember the Sabbath day, to keep it holy' and so forth, but to love God with all their heart was not thought of and yet this is the essence of righteousness. They looked at the letter of the law and were careful to 'pay tithe' upon 'mint and anise' and to attend to all sorts of small points and niceties, but to cleanse the heart and purify the motive did not occur to them. They thought of what a man *does*, but they forgot the importance of what a man *is*. Love to God and likeness to God were forgotten in a servile attempt to observe the letter of the law. So we see everywhere; people nowadays consider what kind of dress a clergyman ought to wear on a certain day, which position he should occupy at the communion, what should be the decoration of the place of worship, what should be the proper music for the hymn and so forth, but to what purpose is all this? To be right in heart with God, to trust in his dear Son and to be renewed in his image is better than all ritual. Among us there are certain people who are nothing if they are not orthodox: they make a man an offender for a word and are never so happy as when they are up to their necks in controversy. In each case the external and the letter are preferred to the inward and the spiritual. Escape from this error; be not so eager for the shell as to lose the kernel, so zealous for the 'form of godliness' as to deny 'the power thereof'!

FOR MEDITATION: (*Our Own Hymn Book,* no. 554 v.4—Isaac Watts, 1709)
   'The best obedience of my hands dares not appear before Thy throne;
   But faith can answer Thy demands, by pleading what my Lord has done.'

SERMON NO. 1961

2 MAY (PREACHED 3 MAY 1891)

'Lo, I come': application

'Then said I, Lo, I come.' Psalm 40:7
SUGGESTED FURTHER READING: Mark 10:32–45

Mr Moody tells a story, which I hope may be true, for one would like to hear something good about a Czar of Russia and especially about our once enemy, the Emperor Nicholas. The story concerns a soldier in the barracks who was much distressed by his heavy debts. He was in despair, for he owed a great deal of money and could not tell where to get it. He took a piece of paper and made a list of his debts and underneath the list he wrote, 'Who will pay these debts?' He then lay down on the barrack bed and fell asleep with the paper before him. The Emperor of Russia passed by and, taking up the paper, read it, and being in a gracious mood signed at the bottom, 'Nicholas.' Was that not a splendid answer to the question? When the soldier woke up and read it, he could scarcely believe his own eyes. 'Who will pay these debts?' was the despairing question. 'Nicholas' was the all-sufficient answer. So are we answered. Who will bear our sins? The grand reply is 'JESUS.' He puts his own name to our liabilities and in effect, that he may meet them, says, 'Lo, I come'. Your debt of sin is discharged when you believe in Christ Jesus. 'Without shedding of blood is no remission', but 'the blood of Jesus Christ', God's dear 'Son cleanseth us from all sin.' You are not now to bear your own sins. Behold the scapegoat, who carries them away into the wilderness! Yes, Jesus says, 'Lo, I come'. He takes our sins upon himself, he bears their penalty and we go free. Blessed word: 'Lo, I come': I come to take your weight of sin, your burden of punishment. I come to be made a curse for you, that you may be made the righteousness of God in me. Sinner, stand out of the way and let Jesus appear for you and fill your place! He sets you on one side and then he sets himself where you have been. Jesus is now the one pillar on which to lean, the one foundation on which to build, the one and only rest of our weary souls.

FOR MEDITATION: It was by means of his death on the cross that the Lord Jesus Christ came to seek us (Luke 19:10; Isaiah 53:6), to serve us (Matthew 20:28) and to save us (John 12:47; 1 Corinthians 1:18).

SERMON NO. 2203

3 MAY (1885)

Delight in the Almighty

'For then shalt thou ... lift up thy face unto God.' Job 22:26
SUGGESTED FURTHER READING (Spurgeon): Psalm 63:1–11

What does it mean? Does it not mean *joy in God*? When a man hangs his head down, he is unhappy, but when our thoughts of God and relationship to God are changed, we lift up our faces and sun our countenances in the light of God's favour. The face of God is toward the believer and so the believer's face is toward the Most High. He has said, 'Seek ye my face'; how can we seek his face but with our own faces? 'Look unto me, and be ye saved, all the ends of the earth', is the divine call and the believer looks to God with intense joy, knowing that in him is his salvation. Does it not signify that this man is *reconciled to God* and clear before him? How can the guilty look up? Guilt makes a man hang his head. 'Conscience doth make cowards of us all', but when the atoning sacrifice comes to us with all its power, when we are washed in the blood of the Lamb and are clean, we lift up our 'face unto God.' In that tremendous day when heaven and earth shall flee before the face of the Judge, we shall be bravely calm, fearing no word of doom, because we are cleansed by the atoning sacrifice and justified by the righteousness in which we trust. What a blessed thing to lift up one's 'face unto God' in confidence towards him through Christ Jesus! Does not our text indicate *fearlessness*? Fear covers her face and would hide herself altogether, even though to accomplish concealment the rocks must fall upon her. That sacred bravery which the Holy Spirit breathes into the child of God makes him cry, 'Abba, Father', and in the spirit of adoption he lifts up his 'face unto God.' May it not signify *expectation*? 'I will lift up mine eyes unto the hills, from whence cometh my help.' 'My expectation is from him', says David. Oh to lift one's face toward God, looking for deliverance, safety and rest, and expecting grace and glory from his right hand!

FOR MEDITATION:(*Our Own Hymn Book*, no. 688 v.1—John Ryland, 1777)
   'O Lord, I would delight in Thee, and on Thy care depend;
   To Thee in every trouble flee, my best, my only Friend.'

SERMON NO. 1839

4 MAY (1890)

The shining of the face of Moses

'Till Moses had done speaking with them, he put a veil on his face. But when Moses went in before the Lord to speak with him, he took the veil off, until he came out ... And the children of Israel saw the face of Moses, that the skin of Moses' face shone: and Moses put the veil upon his face again, until he went in to speak with him.' Exodus 34:33–35

SUGGESTED FURTHER READING (Spurgeon): 2 Corinthians 3:7–18

Are not many suffering from veiled hearts? In your circle there is a rare man of God: you have heard of his faith: he walks with God: others have told you what beauties they see in his character. You cannot see anything particular in him; on the contrary you despise him and avoid his company. He wears a veil for you. Here is the Bible. 'O book, exquisite sweetness!' Your dear mother calls it beyond all things precious. How her face brightens when she tells you how she has been sustained by it in the day of trouble! You read it now and then, but you do not see anything remarkable in it, certainly nothing that charms you: the Book is veiled to you. Here is the glorious gospel of the blessed God. You have heard us say what a wonderful gospel it is. We have been overjoyed in describing it. You feel no enthusiasm. The gospel is veiled to you. You have heard a sermon on some grand doctrine. Believers are ready to leap for joy, but you are utterly indifferent. The truth is veiled to you. This is a sad omen of a lost estate. The veil is on your heart and your soul is in darkness. Am I not speaking the truth about many of you? When you hear about Christ and do not admire him, conclude that you must be blinded; when you hear the glorious gospel of the blessed God and it does not charm you, conclude that the veil is on your hearts. Oh that you would turn to the Lord! When you turn to God, the veil shall be taken away. Oh that God the Holy Spirit would come and turn you by his almighty power! May he constrain you to seek the Lord today. Then shall the veil be taken away and you shall see the beauty of the Lord Jesus in his salvation.

FOR MEDITATION: Satan is responsible for blinding the minds of perishing unbelievers to stop them seeing the glories of the gospel (2 Corinthians 4:3–4). God can keep these things hidden from some and reveal them to others (Luke 10:21–22). Are you concerned enough to pray that he will shine into the darkness of your heart (2 Corinthians 4:6)?

SERMON NO. 2143

5 MAY (1889)

The Bible tried and proved

'The words of the LORD *are pure words: as silver tried in a furnace of earth, purified seven times.'* Psalm 12:6
SUGGESTED FURTHER READING: 1 Corinthians 14:33–40

Do not drop into the semi-blasphemy of some who think the New Testament vastly superior to the Old. I would not err by saying that in the Old Testament you have more of the bullion of truth than in the New, for therein I should be falling into the evil which I condemn, but this I will say, that they are of equal authority and that they cast such light upon each other that we could not spare either of them. 'What therefore God hath joined together, let not man put asunder.' In the whole Book, from Genesis to Revelation, the words of Jehovah are found, and they are always pure words. Neither is it right for any to say, 'Thus spoke Christ himself, but such and such a teaching is Pauline.' No, it is not Pauline; if it is here recorded, it is of the Holy Spirit. Whether the Holy Spirit speaks by Isaiah, Jeremiah, John, James or Paul, the authority is still the same. Even concerning Jesus Christ our Lord this is true, for he says of himself, 'the word which ye hear is not mine, but the Father's which sent me.' In this matter he puts himself upon the level of others who were as the mouth of God. He says again, 'For I have not spoken of myself; but the Father which sent me, he gave me a commandment, what I should say, and what I should speak.' We accept the words of the apostles as the words of the Lord, remembering what John said: 'We are of God: he that knoweth God heareth us; he that is not of God heareth not us. Hereby know we the spirit of truth, and the spirit of error' (1 John 4:6). A solemn judgment is thus pronounced upon those who would set the Spirit of Jesus against the Spirit which dwelt in the apostles. The words of the Lord are not affected in their value by the medium through which they came.

FOR MEDITATION: (*Our Own Hymn Book,* no. 191 v.3—Isaac Watts, 1709)
   'Firm are the words His prophets give,
   Sweet words, on which His children live:
   Each of them is the voice of God,
   Who spoke, and spread the skies abroad.'

SERMON NO. 2084

6 MAY (1888)

'The wedding was furnished with guests'

'The wedding was furnished with guests.' Matthew 22:10
SUGGESTED FURTHER READING: Revelation 19:6–9

It is the Father's aim in the work of grace to glorify his Son, who, as God and man in one nature, is the channel of grace to fallen men. He proposes to do this now that the Lord Jesus takes his church into marriage union with himself. The incarnate God calls a chosen company, the bride, the Lamb's wife, and celebrates thus early in the day this happy union by a wedding breakfast, to which he invites multitudes to come. It is a feast of mercy, grace and peace, a marriage feast of delight and joy. The feast is for the glorifying of the Lord Jesus Christ in a very special manner. Can any of us measure the glory which comes to our Lord Jesus by his union with the church? Angels, principalities and powers, intelligences now existing and all intelligences yet to be created, will wonderingly gaze upon the riches of his inheritance in the saints. What a spectacle is this! The Word made flesh that he might dwell among us! Immanuel, God with us, taking unto himself a company of chosen men, to be one with him for ever. In the union of Christ and his church all wisdom centres, all grace shines forth. 'The excellency of our God' is to be seen in the salvation of the elect and the joining of them to the Christ. Our glorious Second Adam was like the first Adam in the garden, for whom no helpmeet was found. Neither cherubim nor seraphim, angels nor spirits, could be fit companions for him. He says, 'my delights were with the sons of men.' He willed that his chosen church should stand to him in the same relation as Eve stood to Adam, to be the solace of his heart and the rest of his love. He chose men to be his companions, his friends, his joy, his crown.

FOR MEDITATION: (*Our Own Hymn Book,* no. 504 vv.2&3—Albert Midlane, 1862)
>'"All things are ready," Come, the invitation's given,
>Through Him who now in glory sits at God's right hand in heaven.
>"All things are ready," Come, the door is open wide,
>Oh feast upon the love of God, for Christ, His Son, has died.'

SERMON NO. 2022

7 MAY (1891)

'Am I a sea, or a whale?'

'Am I a sea, or a whale, that thou settest a watch over me?' Job 7:12
SUGGESTED FURTHER READING: Mark 4:35–41 & 6:45–51

Hardship, want and pain are meant to bring you back and God uses them to that end; may the day come when you will say, 'I bless God for the rough wave which washed me on shore. I bless God for the stormy providence which drowned my comfort, but saved my soul.' God will not always deal roughly with you. Perhaps tonight he will say his last sharp word. Will you yield to softer means? They say that oil poured on troubled waters will make them smooth: God the Holy Spirit can send to your troubled soul a lifelong calm. The winds and waves on the Galilean sea all went to sleep in an instant. How? Why, when Jesus came walking on the water he said to the warring elements, 'be still.' The waves crouched like whipped dogs at his feet, though they had roared like lions before. He said to the winds, 'Hush!' and they breathed as softly as the lips of a babe. Jesus is here at this hour. He that died on Calvary looks down on us: believe on him. He lifts his pierced hands, and cries, 'Look unto me, and be ye saved'. Will you not look to him? Oh that his grace may lead you at once to say, 'He is all in all to me!' Here is a soul-saving text for you: 'God so loved the world, that he gave his only begotten Son, that whosoever believeth in him should not perish, but have everlasting life.' Accept the Saviour, and though you be as 'a sea, or a whale,' you shall no longer complain of the Lord's watching you, but you shall rejoice in perfect liberty. He is free who loves to serve his God. He makes it his delight that he is watched of the Lord.

FOR MEDITATION: (*Our Own Hymn Book,* no. 590 v.1—Charlotte Elliott, 1834)
   'With tearful eyes I look around,
   Life seems a dark and stormy sea;
   Yet 'mid the gloom, I hear a sound,
   A heavenly whisper, "Come to Me."'

N.B. This sermon was preached 'on behalf of the British and Foreign Sailors' Society'.

SERMON NO. 2206

8 MAY (1887)

The friend of God

'Thou, Israel, art my servant, Jacob whom I have chosen, the seed of Abraham my friend.' Isaiah 41:8
'And he was called the Friend of God.' James 2:23
SUGGESTED FURTHER READING (Spurgeon): John 15:9–17

Jesus himself invites us to live and act and be his friends. Surely none of us will neglect any gracious attainment which lies within the region of the possible. None of us will be content with a scanty measure of grace, when we may have life more abundantly. I trust you are not so foolish as to say, 'If I may but get to heaven by the skin of my teeth, I shall not care about what I am on the road.' This would be wicked talk, and, if you speak thus, I am afraid you will never get to heaven at all. He that is being prepared for glory is always hungry after the largest measure of grace. He who is born of God desires his Father's love while he is yet a child, and has no idea of waiting for it till he comes of age and enters upon his estate. Let me have as much of heaven, even now, as I can have. Yes, let me now be the friend of God. The other day there landed on the shores of France a boatful of people sodden with rain and saltwater; they had lost all their luggage and had nothing but what they stood upright in: they were glad, indeed, to have been saved from a wreck. It was well that they landed at all, but when it is my lot again to cross to France, I trust I shall put my foot on shore in a better plight than that. I would prefer to cross the Channel in comfort and land with pleasure. There is all this difference between being 'saved ... so as by fire', and having an abundant entrance 'ministered unto' us into the kingdom. Let us enjoy heaven on the road to heaven. Why not? Instead of being fished up as castaways, stranded upon the shores of mercy, let us take our passage on board the well-appointed Liner of Free Grace; let us, if possible, go in the first cabin, enjoying all the comforts of the way and having fellowship with the great Captain of our Salvation. Why should we think it enough to be mere stowaways?

FOR MEDITATION: (*Our Own Hymn Book,* no. 770 v.2—Horatius Bonar, 1856)
   'Go up, go up, my heart, be not a trifler here:
   Ascend above these clouds, dwell in a higher sphere.'

SERMON NO. 1962

9 MAY (PREACHED 10 MAY 1885)

The bond of the covenant

'I will bring you into the bond of the covenant' Ezekiel 20:37
SUGGESTED FURTHER READING: Romans 6:16–23

> 'Oh to grace how great a debtor
> Daily I'm constrained to be!
> Let that grace, now, like a fetter
> Bind my wandering heart to Thee.'

Can grace ever be a fetter? Yes, it is the most blessed of all fetters, for it holds us fast and yet never violates our liberty. It binds the very heart in willing captivity. This is the bond of the covenant. 'Oh,' says one, 'I do not want to be under any bond.' Then, in all probability, you are bound by the chains of self-will. In grace you can be under bonds, yet not in bondage. I am in the bonds of wedlock, but I feel no bondage; on the contrary, it is a joy to be so bound. The bonds of love and the 'cords of a man' cause no chafing. The bond of grace is a marriage bond, inviting us to him whom we love above all, even the altogether lovely Bridegroom of our souls. It is our joy to look up to our Covenant-Head and obey him in all things. This bond holds us back from doing what it would be to our injury to do; it restrains us from sinning against God. Instead of wishing to be free of this bond, we desire to realize it in its most stringent form by being crucified with Christ, nailed up hands and feet, so as to be incapable of following the wandering wishes of the unregenerate nature. O that we were utterly incapable of sin! Would God we were bound to holiness as with belts of steel. I hope many of you feel the blessed restraint of covenant relationship, so that you cry with Joseph, 'how then can I do this great wickedness, and sin against God?' The love of Christ both restrains and constrains us, 'because we thus judge, that if one died for all, then were all dead: and that he died for all, that they which live should not henceforth live unto themselves, but unto him which died for them and rose again.' Blessed bond of the covenant!

FOR MEDITATION: (*Our Own Hymn Book,* no. 228 v.1—Philip Doddridge, 1755)
> 'My God, the covenant of Thy love abides for ever sure;
> And in its matchless grace I feel my happiness secure.'

SERMON NO. 1840

10 MAY (1891)

Sin: its spring-head, stream, and sea

'Our fathers understood not thy wonders in Egypt; they remembered not the multitude of thy mercies; but provoked him at the sea, even at the Red sea.' Psalm 106:7

SUGGESTED FURTHER READING: Psalm 116:1–19

True gratitude shows itself in acts and deeds. A gentleman had been the means of making a position for a tradesman and by a misfortune he came to be himself in want of immediate help to tide over a season of great pressure. He called at the house of the person he had so successfully helped and found the wife at home. He told her the case and she answered at once, 'My husband will be ready to lend you his name to the full amount required. He will hasten to you the moment you need him and be glad to do so.' A prudent neighbour afterwards said, 'But you may have to pay away all you have in the world.' 'Yes', said the grateful wife, 'we do not mind that: he was the making of us and, if we have to lose everything for his sake, we shall do it very cheerfully, for we shall only be back to where we were when he first helped us.' That is a form of gratitude which is rare enough in this world, though I have seen it here and there. Beloved, if the Lord were to take all away that we have, we should only be back where we were at the beginning. We have nothing but what we have received from him. He takes nothing from us but what he first gave us: let us bless a taking as well as a giving God. Oh for this practical gratitude towards the Lord, that we may in all things either do his will cheerfully, or suffer it patiently! If we remember the multitude of his mercies practically we shall be ready to surrender honour, ease, health, estate, yes, life itself for him who gave himself for us. Oh to remember God's mercies practically in everyday life, in thought, word and deed!

FOR MEDITATION: The truly grateful humbly acknowledge the source of their possessions (Deuteronomy 8:17–18; 1 Corinthians 4:7; James 1:17) and are therefore much better prepared to accept the sacrifice of their possessions (Job 1:20–21; Matthew 10:8).

SERMON NO. 2204

11 MAY (1890)

Believers sent by Christ, as Christ is sent by the Father

'As thou hast sent me into the world, even so have I also sent them into the world.' John 17:18
SUGGESTED FURTHER READING: John 12:47–13:20

Our Lord's mission involved complete subjection to the Father's will. He said, 'my Father is greater than I': this did not relate to his essential nature and dignity as God, but to the position which he took up in reference to the Father when he was sent to be our Saviour. He that sends is greater than he that is sent: the Saviour took up that subordinate position that he might do the Father's will. From that time forth, so long as he remained under his commission, he did not speak his own words, nor do his own deeds, but he listened to the Father's will and what the Father said to him he both spoke and did. That is exactly where you and I have to place ourselves now, deliberately and unreservedly. Our Lord sends us and we are to be, in very deed, subordinate to his command in all things. We are no longer masters; we have become servants. Our will is lost in the will of our glorious superior. If we are ambitious and our ambition is guided by wisdom, it will take us down to that basin and the towel and we shall be willing to wash the disciples' feet, to show that we are sent by our condescending Lord. We shall henceforth have no respect unto our own dignity or interest, but shall lay ourselves out to serve him to whom we belong. Whatsoever he says unto us we shall aim to do. Although we are sons of God, yet now we are also servants and we would not do our own will, but the will of him that sent us. Oh to be sound on this point, so as to yield our members in perfect obedience and even bring every thought into subjection to Christ! Oh to die to self and live in Christ!

FOR MEDITATION: (*Our Own Hymn Book*, no. 262 v.2—Isaac Watts, 1709)
    'Such was Thy truth, and such Thy zeal,
    Such deference to Thy Father's will,
    Such love, and meekness so divine,
    I would transcribe and make them mine.'

SERMON NO. 2144

12 MAY (1889)

Taking possession of our inheritance

'Moses my servant is dead; now therefore arise, go over this Jordan, thou, and all this people, unto the land which I do give to them, even to the children of Israel. Every place that the sole of your foot shall tread upon, that have I given unto you, as I said unto Moses.' Joshua 1:2–3
SUGGESTED FURTHER READING (Spurgeon): Ephesians 1:1–23

'Every place that the sole of your foot shall tread upon, that have I given unto you'. This is an easy way of taking land: to put your foot down upon it. I delight in that word of the Lord to Jacob, when he lay asleep: 'the land whereon thou liest, to thee will I give it, and to thy seed'. If you can, by faith, lie down on a promise and find rest in it, it is yours. Every place in the grace-country upon which 'the sole of your foot shall tread' is yours. You will remember that the Red Indians agreed to sell to William Penn as much land as a man could walk round in a day; I do not wonder that at the end of the day they complained that the white brother had made a big walk. I think I should have put my best leg foremost, if whatever I could put my foot upon would be mine; would not you? Why, then, do you not hurry up in spiritual matters? Do you value earthly things more than spiritual? Mark, then, that if you put your foot down upon a blessing and say, 'This is mine,' it is yours. What a very simple operation is the claim of faith! You do not want to pass through the universities to learn that: it is grasping with the hand or appropriating with the foot. Many of the Lord's poor and unlearned ones obtain more from the promise than the more cultured ever do. The learned man lifts his head up, but the simple put their foot down and this is the way to the inheritance. By criticism you may put your foot in it, but by faith you put your foot on it. Strangers cavil, children claim. He that can trust his Lord may say, 'In the name of the living God this blessing is mine.' Come, then, brother, if there be more holiness, put your foot on it; if there be more happiness, put your foot on it; if there be more usefulness, put your foot on it. Lay your claim to all that is put within your reach in Scripture.

FOR MEDITATION: (*Our Own Hymn Book*, no. 757 v.2—Isaac Watts, 1721)
   'All things are ours; the gift of God, the purchase of a Saviour's blood;
   While the good Spirit shows us how to use and to improve them too.'

SERMON NO. 2086

13 MAY (1888)

The blessing of full assurance

'These things have I written unto you that believe on the name of the Son of God; that ye may know that ye have eternal life, and that ye may believe on the name of the Son of God.' 1 John 5:13
SUGGESTED FURTHER READING: 2 Thessalonians 1:1–4

According to the Authorized text, though not according to the Revised Version, John desired the increase and confirmation of their faith. He says, 'that ye may believe on the name of the Son of God.' John wrote to those who believed, that they might believe in a more emphatic sense. As our Saviour has come not only that we may have life, but that we may 'have it more abundantly', so does John write, that having faith we may have more of it. Come, beloved, listen for a moment to this! You have the milk of faith, but God wills that you should have this cream of assurance! He would increase your faith. May you believe more extensively. Perhaps you do not believe all the truth, because you have not yet perceived it. There were members of the Corinthian church who had not believed in the resurrection of the dead, and there were Galatians who were very cloudy upon justification by faith. Many a Christian man is narrow in the range of his faith from ignorance of the Lord's mind. Like certain tribes of Israel, they have conquered a scanty territory as yet, though all the land is theirs from Dan to Beersheba. John would have us push out our fences and increase the enclosure of our faith. Let us believe all that God has revealed, for every truth is precious and practically useful. Perhaps your doctrinal belief has been poor and thin. Oh that the Lord would turn the water into wine! Many of you live upon milk and yet your years qualify you to feed on meat. Why keep the babes' diet? You that believe are exhorted to 'go in and out, and find pasture'; range throughout the whole revelation of God.

FOR MEDITATION: A Christian may be weak (Romans 14:1) and lacking (1 Thessalonians 3:10) in faith, but should regard this as an opportunity for that faith to be increased (Luke 17:5; 2 Corinthians 10:15), to be furthered (Philippians 1:25), to grow (2 Thessalonians 1:3) and to be supplemented (2 Peter 1:5).

SERMON NO. 2023

14 MAY (PREACHED 19 MAY 1889)

Grace for grace

'Now we have received, not the spirit of the world, but the spirit which is of God; that we might know the things that are freely given to us of God.' 1 Corinthians 2:12

SUGGESTED FURTHER READING: Romans 8:28–34

Salvation is not granted to men as the result of anything they are, or do, or resolve to be, but it is the undeserved gift of heaven. If it were of works, it would not be of grace, but it is of faith, that it might be of grace alone. The blessings of salvation are freely given us by God; therefore they are not a loan, handed to us for a time and to be one day recalled. Our heavenly heritage is not held on lease, upon terms of annual payment: it is an unencumbered freehold to every man that has by faith put his foot upon it. To give a thing and take a thing is for little children in their play and even among them it is the subject of ridicule. But 'the gifts and calling of God are without repentance' on his part. When he has given it, the deed is done outright and can never be reversed. O believer, if your sin is blotted out, it can never be written in again! God has declared that he has forgiven our transgressions and then he adds, 'their sins and iniquities will I remember no more.' There is no playing fast and loose in connection with the everlasting love of God and its glorious acts; if you have God, you have him by an eternal holding, of which none can deprive you. 'This God is our God for ever and ever'. The better part which Jesus gives to his beloved shall not be taken away from us. The things of God are all of them free gifts, with no legal condition appended to them which would make their tenure one of payment rather than of absolute gift. We may not say that the blessings of salvation, such as pardon, justification and eternal life, are gifts with an 'if' in the core of them, rendering them uncertain. No, 'the gift of God is' not temporary life, but 'eternal life through Jesus Christ our Lord.'

FOR MEDITATION: (*Our Own Hymn Book*, no. 491 v.6—Samuel Medley, 1789)

'To sinners poor, like me and you,
He saith He'll "Freely give;"
Come, thirsty souls, and prove it true;
Drink, and for ever live.'

SERMON NO. 2087

15 MAY (1887)

The search for faith

'Nevertheless when the Son of man cometh, shall he find faith on the earth?' Luke 18:8
SUGGESTED FURTHER READING: Hebrews 10:19–39

When Jesus comes he will look for precious faith. He has more regard for faith than for all else that earth can yield him. Our returning Lord will care nothing for the treasures of the rich or the honours of the great. He will not look for the abilities we have manifested, nor for the influence we have acquired, but he will look for our faith. It is his glory that he is 'believed on in the world,' and to that he will have respect. This is the jewel for which he is searching. This heavenly merchantman counts faith to be the 'pearl of great price': faith is precious to Jesus as well as to us. The last day will be occupied with a great scrutiny, and that scrutiny will be made upon the essential point: where is there faith and where is there no faith? 'He that believeth' is saved; 'he that believeth not is condemned'. A search-warrant will be issued for our houses and our hearts, and the enquiry will be: Where is your faith? Did you honour Christ by trusting his word and his blood, or did you not? Did you glorify God by believing his revelation and depending upon his promise, or did you not? The fact that our Lord, at his coming, will seek for faith should cause us to think very highly of faith. It is no mere act of the intellect; it is a grace of the Holy Spirit which brings glory to God and produces obedience in the heart. Jesus looks for it because he is the proper object of it and it is by means of it that his great end in his first advent is carried out. Dear hearers, conceive for a minute that our Saviour is searching for faith now. 'His eyes behold, his eyelids try, the children of men.' This is the gold he seeks after amid the quartz of our humanity. This is the object of his royal quest: Do you believe in the Lord Jesus Christ?

FOR MEDITATION: The Lord Jesus Christ had already found it hard to find any people with faith during his life on earth (Mark 4:40; 6:6; Luke 7:9; 8:25). The prospect of his second coming is a challenge to persevere in faith (Revelation 13:10; 14:12) rather than to be finally exposed as an unbeliever whose name is omitted from the book of life (Revelation 20:15; 21:8).

SERMON NO. 1963

16 MAY (PREACHED 17 MAY 1891)

'My times are in thy hand'

'My times are in thy hand.' Psalm 31:15
SUGGESTED FURTHER READING: Matthew 6:25–34

A full belief in the statement of our text is a cure for present worry. O Lord, if 'my times are in thy hand', I have cast my care on thee, and I trust and am not afraid! Why is it, my sister—for this habit of worrying abounds among the gracious sisterhood—why do you vex yourself about a matter which is in the hand of God? If he has undertaken for you, what cause have you for anxiety? And you, my brother—for there are plenty of men who are nervous and fretful—why do you want to interfere with the Lord's business? If the case is in his hand, what need can there be for you to be prying and crying? You were worrying this morning, fretting last night, distressed now and will be worse tomorrow morning. May I ask you a question? Did you ever get any good by fretting? When there was not rain enough for your farm, did you ever fret a shower down? When there was too much wet, or you thought so, did you ever worry the clouds away? Tell me, did you ever make a sixpence by worrying? It is a very unprofitable business. Do you answer, 'What, then, are we to do in troubled times'? Why, go to him into whose hand you have committed yourself and your times. Consult with infinite wisdom by prayer; console yourself with infinite love by fellowship with God. Tell the Lord what you feel and what you fear. Ten minutes' praying is better than a year's murmuring. He that waits upon God and casts his burden upon him, may lead a royal life: indeed, he will be far happier than a king. To leave our times with God is to live as free from care as the birds upon the bough. If we fret, we shall not glorify God.

FOR MEDITATION: (*Our Own Hymn Book,* no. 701 v.3—William Freeman Lloyd, 1835)

> 'Our times are in Thy hand,
> Why should we doubt or fear?
> A Father's hand will never cause
> His child a needless tear.'

SERMON NO. 2205

17 MAY (1885)

Divine forgiveness admired and imitated

'Forbearing one another, and forgiving one another, if any man have a quarrel against any: even as Christ forgave you, so also do ye.'
Colossians 3:13
SUGGESTED FURTHER READING: Ephesians 4:1–6

'Forbearing one another, and forgiving one another': you see, it has two sides. 'Ah,' says one, 'I cannot understand it; people ought to be far more forbearing to me.' Just so; but the first point is that you should be forgiving towards them. What numbers of church members think that the duties of a church are all one-sided. 'I was ill and nobody came to see me.' 'Did you send for anybody to see you?' 'No, I did not.' Brother, before you find fault, remember your own fault; you have violated the command, 'Is any sick among you? let him call for the elders of the church'. 'But nobody exhibits Christian love,' says one. Is that true of yourself? I have noticed that the man who says that love is dead is usually rather short of love himself. How very different the church looks to different eyes: one sees a thousand virtues to admire, but another a world of evil to expose. One gratefully cries, 'When I was ill, the dear brethren came to see me so often that I had even to ask them not to stay very long.' Another grumbles, 'I might have laid there a month and nobody would ever have come near me.' We understand the reason for this difference: the tone of the speech is the key to the riddle. As a rule, 'with what measure ye mete, it shall be measured to you again.' I do not find Christ's people to be one half so faulty as I am myself. I meet with many Christians whom I think it an honour to know and commune with; those of another sort are useful to me as warnings and as fields for exercising my graces. The forgiveness and the forbearance are needed all round and we must both give and take.

FOR MEDITATION: The word 'rich' not only expresses the value of God's forbearance and forgiveness towards sinners (Romans 2:4; Ephesians 1:7; 2:4,7), but also exposes the cheapness of sinners' abuse of his forbearance and forgiveness (Romans 2:4). Imitation of God's approach is a good sign (Matthew 6:14; Ephesians 4:32–5:1), but the same cannot be said of the alternative (Matthew 6:15; 18:23–35).

SERMON NO. 1841

18 MAY (1890)

Scriptural salvation

'For the scripture saith, Whosoever believeth on him shall not be ashamed.' Romans 10:11
SUGGESTED FURTHER READING: Acts 17:1–12

Here is an old-fashioned way of proof: 'the scripture saith'. In this enlightened age little is made of Scripture; the tendency is to undermine men's faith in the Bible and persuade them to rest on something else. It is not so with us, as it certainly was not so with Paul. He enforced and substantiated his teaching by declaring, 'the scripture saith'. In this he follows the manner of Christ Jesus our Lord. Though quite able to speak of himself, our Lord continually referred to Holy Scripture. His first public sermon was founded upon the book of the prophet Isaiah. All along to the very end he was always quoting the Old Testament. So did his apostles. One is struck with their continual reference to Moses and the prophets. While they set the truth in a fresh light, they fell back continually upon the old revelation. 'What saith the scripture?' 'According to the scriptures': these are phrases constantly repeated. Paul declared that he spent his life 'witnessing both to small and great, saying none other things than those which the prophets and Moses did say should come'. Evidently they regarded the statements of Scripture as conclusive. They took counsel of the Scriptures and so ended the matter. 'It is written,' was to them proof positive and indisputable. 'Thus saith the LORD,' was the final word, enough for their mind, heart, conscience and understanding. To go behind Scripture did not occur to the first teachers of our faith: they heard the Oracle of divine testimony and bowed their heads in reverence. So it ought to be with us: we have erred from the faith and shall pierce ourselves 'through with many sorrows', unless we feel that if the Scripture says it, it is even so. 'Holy men of God spake as they were moved by the Holy Ghost', and therefore spoke not erroneously, nor even dubiously.

FOR MEDITATION: The Old Testament points us to eternal life in the Lord Jesus Christ (John 5:39–40). Abraham's experience in the first book (Genesis 15:6) gave clear teaching about justification by faith to which the New Testament writers could refer with complete confidence (Romans 4:3; Galatians 3:8; James 2:23). See 1 Peter 2:6 for another reference to Isaiah 28:16, the verse recalled by today's text.

SERMON NO. 2145

19 MAY (1889)

A straight talk

'I cannot come.' Luke 14:20
SUGGESTED FURTHER READING: 1 Corinthians 7:10–16

This man said, 'I cannot come.' Why? Because he had a wife! Strange plea! Surely that was a reason why he should come and bring her with him. If any man, unhappily, has a wife opposed to the things of God, instead of saying, 'I cannot be a Christian, for I have an unconverted wife,' he should seek for double grace that he may win his wife to Christ. If a woman laments that she has an unconverted husband, let her live the nearer to God that she may save her husband. If a servant has an unconverted master, let him labour with double diligence to glorify God, that he may win his master. Thus you see there are two reasons why you should come to the gospel banquet, not only for your own sake, but for the sake of your unconverted relatives. My neighbour's candle has blown out; is that a reason why I must not light mine? No, but that is a reason why I should be all the more careful to keep mine burning, that I may light my neighbour's candle too. It is a pity that my wife should be lost, but I cannot help her by being lost myself. No, but I may help her if I take my stand and follow Christ the more resolutely because my wife opposes me. Good man, do not allow your wife to draw you aside! Good woman, do not let your husband hinder you! Do not say, 'I cannot attend the house of God, nor be a Christian while I have such a husband as I have.' No, that is the reason why you should take your stand the more bravely in the name of God that, by your example, those whom you love may be rescued from destruction. 'What knowest thou, O wife, whether thou shalt save thy' unbelieving 'husband? or how knowest thou, O man, whether thou shalt save thy' unbelieving 'wife?'

FOR MEDITATION: (*Our Own Hymn Book,* no. 504 v.1—Albert Midlane, 1852)
   '"All things are ready," Come,
   Come to the supper spread;
   Come, rich and poor, come, old and young,
   Come, and be richly fed.'

SERMON NO. 2122

20 MAY (1888)

What is the wedding garment?

'*And when the king came in to see the guests, he saw there a man which had not on a wedding garment: and he saith unto him, Friend, how camest thou in hither not having a wedding garment? And he was speechless.*' Matthew 22:11–12
SUGGESTED FURTHER READING: Isaiah 61:10–62:5

It was a wedding and the guests must put on a suitable dress. This man refused to put it on. He was proud and would not wear the gift of grace; he was self-willed and must be singular and show his independence of mind. The regulation was by no means irksome and to the rest of the guests the commandment was not grievous, but this man would have his own way in defiance of the Lord of the feast. What could come of such folly? Now, one of the requirements of the feast is that you with your heart believe on the Lord Jesus and take his righteousness to be your righteousness. Do you refuse this? If you will not accept the Lord Jesus as your substitute, bearing your 'sins in his own body on the tree,' you have not the wedding garment. Another requirement is that you should repent of sin and forsake it and that you should follow after holiness and endeavour to copy the example of the Lord Jesus. You are to possess, as the work of divine grace, a godly and upright character. Have you such a character? Even though you are not perfect, yet, inasmuch as you follow after righteousness, you have the wedding garment. You say that you are a Christian; do you live like a Christian? Are you in a position and condition which agree with the gospel feast? If so, you have on the wedding garment. Those who came to the feast were 'both bad and good', so that the wedding garment relates not to their past character but to something with which they were invested when they came to the banquet. The putting on of a wedding robe cannot refer to an elaborate ceremony, a feat of the intellect or a deep experience of the heart, yet it involved joining in the wedding or not. It involved reverence for the King, homage to the Prince and sympathy with the whole matter. Look well and see whether you truly yield yourselves to the Lord.

FOR MEDITATION: (*Our Own Hymn Book*, no. 721 v.5—Isaac Watts, 1709)
   'The Spirit wrought my faith and love, and hope, and every grace;
   But Jesus spent His life to work the robe of righteousness.'

SERMON NO. 2024

21 MAY (PREACHED 23 MAY 1886)

Mysterious meat

'In the mean while his disciples prayed him, saying, Master, eat. But he said unto them, I have meat to eat that ye know not of. Therefore said the disciples one to another, Hath any man brought him ought to eat? Jesus saith unto them, My meat is to do the will of him that sent me, and to finish his work.' John 4:31–34

SUGGESTED FURTHER READING: 1 Thessalonians 2:17–3:10

I do not know anything that can make a man forget his pain and weariness like grasping the hand of a sinner saved. 'Oh,' says the saved one, 'God Almighty bless you! You have brought me to Jesus.' This nerves us to new effort. I speak here from experience, for yesterday evening, when I was thinking of this subject, I was myself somewhat dull through pain and weakness and, as God would have it, I took up the Report of the Baptist Missionary Society and, as I glanced over it, I saw my own name. It seems that our missionary in San Domingo has had a discouraging year, but it was lit up with one most pleasing incident. A man had come down from the interior of Haiti to ask for baptism. Finding him to be a most intelligent Christian, well instructed in the gospel, the missionary asked how he came to know anything about it. In reply he told him that he had fallen in with a sermon translated into the French language which was preached by Mr Spurgeon. I was dull no longer. I had meat to eat. Had an angel stood in the study, I could not have felt more delighted with his visit than I did when I read of a sinner saved. Here was a sermon translated into French, which was carried far away to Haiti, I do not know how, and there was read by a Romanist, who found by it salvation. God bless him! You cannot faint after such a success, can you? As for myself, despite my sickness, I resolve to go on again, preach with all my might, print more sermons and send them out to the ends of the earth. Never say die. Never dream of giving up. Let God's blessing on your work refresh you.

FOR MEDITATION: The apostle Paul was upset when people rejected the gospel (Romans 9:1–3; Philippians 3:18–19) and uneasy when churches went astray (2 Corinthians 11:2–4; Galatians 1:6), but uplifted when converts produced genuine fruit (2 Corinthians 7:4; Philippians 4:1; Philemon 7). Church leaders are required to be affected by the spiritual condition of those in their care (Hebrews 13:17).

SERMON NO. 1901

22 MAY (1887)

Why is faith so feeble?

'And he said unto them, Why are ye so fearful? how is it that ye have no faith?' Mark 4:40
SUGGESTED FURTHER READING: Jeremiah 11:18–12:6

Jesus censured his friends because he foresaw that such unbelief as theirs would unfit them for their future lives. That ship was the symbol of the church of Christ and the crew were the apostles of Christ. The storm represented in parable the persecutions which the church would have to endure and they, if they were cast down as cowards in a storm on the paltry lake of Galilee, would be proving themselves altogether unfit for those more tremendous spiritual storms which in after years tossed the church and mingled earth and hell in dire confusion. Peter, James, John and the rest were to steer the ship of the church of God through seas of blood and stand at the helm in the midst of hurricanes of error; therefore fearfulness was a sad evil, because it would render them unfit for their solemn task. Jesus might have said to them, 'If you have run with the footmen, and they have wearied you, then how can you contend with horses? If these winds and waves have been too much for you, what will you do when you wrestle with principalities, powers and spiritual wickedness in high places? If natural causes destroy your peace, how will spiritual influences distract you?' Our present trials may be a training-ground for more serious conflicts. We do not know what we have yet to endure; the adversities of today are a preparatory school for the higher learning. If we do not play the man now, what shall we do by-and-by? If because of some little domestic discomfort we are ready to give up, what shall we 'do in the swelling of Jordan?' If a little toil oppresses us, what shall we do when the death sweat trickles from our brow? Let us hear our Lord as he lovingly rebukes us, shake off our fears and resolve that by his grace we will have no more of them, but will trust and not be afraid.

FOR MEDITATION: (*Our Own Hymn Book*, no. 683 v.3—William Hiley Bathurst, 1831)
  'On Thy sure mercy I depend
  In all my trials, wants, and woes;
  For Thou art an unchanging Friend,
  Sweet is the peace Thy hand bestows.'

SERMON NO. 1964

23 MAY (1886)

The master-key, opening the gate of heaven

'And thou saidst, I will surely do thee good.' Genesis 32:12
SUGGESTED FURTHER READING: Hebrews 11:8–22

You notice that Jacob puts it, 'thou saidst,' and then quotes the words, 'I will surely do thee good'. It is an essential part of the education of a Christian to learn the promises. I always admire that fact in the life of General Gordon (who, whatever mistakes he made, was a grand believer, a very Abraham among us in these latter days), that he always carried with him that little book called Clark's *Precious Promises*, which is an arrangement of the various promises of the Old and New Testaments under different heads. The General used to consult that collection of divine promises and seek out that holy text which best suited his particular condition; then he sought solitude and pleaded before the Lord that inspired word, believing that it was true and that the Lord would do as he had said. By faith he looked for an answer and acted upon it. He went down through the Sudan alone, daring all manner of dangers because he believed in God. The heroism of his life grew out of his confidence in the promises. If we would be heroes, here is the food with which to sustain a noble life. I would have all Christian people know God's promises. If you had in your house a number of cheques which you believed to be good, I do not suppose that you would long be unaware of their nature and value. No merchant here would say, 'I have a number of bills, drafts and cheques at home somewhere: I have no doubt that they are all good and that they are my lawful property, but I do not know much about them. Their value is quite unknown to me.' Such ignorance would argue insanity. Will you know your earthly wealth and never consider your heavenly riches? In the Bible there are 'exceeding great and precious promises'; shall it be said that some of God's children do not know what those promises contain?

FOR MEDITATION: (*Our Own Hymn Book*, no. 192 v.6—Isaac Watts, 1709)
    'His very word of grace is strong, as that which built the skies;
    The voice that rolls the stars along speaks all the promises.'

N.B. General Gordon died at the fall of Khartoum on 26 January 1885, two days before relief arrived on what would have been his 52nd birthday.

SERMON NO. 1938

24 MAY (WHITSUN 1885)

The private tutor

'These things have I spoken unto you, being yet present with you. But the Comforter, which is the Holy Ghost, whom the Father will send in my name, he shall teach you all things, and bring all things to your remembrance, whatsoever I have said unto you.' John 14:25–26
SUGGESTED FURTHER READING: 1 Corinthians 2:6–16

Christ in his sayings gave us our class-book, complete and infallible, but through our dullness we need more. That young man has gone to college: he has with him all necessary books and in them is to be found all that he will need to learn; even thus the Lord Jesus has given us in his sayings all that we need to know. But the young man's father wishes him to become a learnèd man and therefore he engages for him a private tutor, who will teach him what the books contain. With his tutor's help his book is of far greater use to him than before. If any passage is difficult the tutor explains it; he puts the youth into the way of reading his class-books, so as to get the full value of them. Spiritually this is the office of the Holy Spirit: he finds us the key wherewith to open up the mystery which otherwise would be out of our reach. He really teaches us. To *teach* you is a very different thing from speaking to you. A person may speak to a company of young people and yet teach them nothing. If I am anxious to instruct a brother on any point, I do not merely speak to him, but I go over the ground carefully, set out each point distinctly, repeat my statements deliberately and illustrate them appropriately. The Spirit of God, when he takes the child of God out of the company and speaks privately to his heart, goes over the truth with him till it is made clear and happily apprehended. We need to have truth opened up to the understanding, impressed upon the heart, made real to the apprehension, applied to the mind, wrought into the affections and endeared to the soul. It is one thing to hear the Word, but it is another thing to learn the Word: it is one thing to be told, but quite another thing to be taught.

FOR MEDITATION: (*Our Own Hymn Book,* no. 455 v.2—Charles Wesley, 1740)
  'Come, Holy Ghost (for moved by Thee the prophets wrote and spoke),
  Unlock the truth, Thyself the key, unseal the sacred book.'

SERMON NO. 1842

25 MAY (1890)

Joy, joy for ever

'But let all those that put their trust in thee rejoice: let them ever shout for joy, because thou defendest them: let them also that love thy name be joyful in thee.' Psalm 5:11
SUGGESTED FURTHER READING: Psalm 98:1–9

You see in my text *a permit* to be glad: 'let all those that put their trust in thee rejoice'. You have here a ticket to the banquets of joy. You may be as happy as ever you like. You have divine permission to shout for joy. Yonder is the inner sanctuary of happiness. You cry, 'May I come in?' Yes, if by faith you can grasp the text, 'let all those that put their trust in thee rejoice'. 'But may I be happy?' asks one. 'May I be glad? May I? Is there joy for me?' Do you trust in the Lord? Then you have your passport; travel in the land of light. But the text is not only a permit, it is *a precept*. When it says, 'let them ever shout for joy,' it means that they are commanded to do so. Blessed is that religion wherein it is a duty to be happy. Come, you mournful ones, be glad. You discontented grumblers, come out of that dog-hole! Enter the palace of the King! Quit your dunghills; ascend your thrones. The precept commands it: 'Rejoice in the Lord alway: and again I say, Rejoice.' We have here more than a permit and a precept; it is *a prayer*. David prays it; the Lord Jesus prays it by David. Let them rejoice, let them be joyful in thee! Will he not grant the prayer which he has inspired by causing us to rejoice through lifting upon us the light of his countenance? Pray for joy yourself, saying with David, 'Restore unto me the joy of thy salvation'. The text might be read as *a promise*: 'all those that put their trust in thee *shall* rejoice'. God promises joy and gladness to believers. Light is sown for them: the Lord will turn their night into day.

FOR MEDITATION: (*Our Own Hymn Book,* no. 136 song 1 v.1—John Milton, 1645)
    'Let us, with a gladsome mind,
    Praise the Lord, for He is kind:
    For His mercies shall endure,
    Ever faithful, ever sure.'

SERMON NO. 2146

26 MAY (1889)

Filling with the Spirit, and drunkenness with wine

'And be not drunk with wine, but be filled with the Spirit.' Ephesians 5:18

SUGGESTED FURTHER READING: Proverbs 23:19–24:7

Wine causes riot; the Spirit causes peace. Drunkenness causes contention; the Spirit of God causes submission. Furthermore, drunkenness makes men foolish, but the Spirit of God makes them wise. I am keeping to the connection of my text. Read the fifteenth verse: 'See then that ye walk circumspectly, not as fools, but as wise.' The drunken man cannot walk at all, because he has not made up his mind as to which way he will go. He attempts to go two ways and ends up staggering till he falls. The man filled with the Spirit has a very definite idea of which way he is going. He knows the right and he deliberately chooses it; he perceives the strait and narrow way and he steadfastly follows it, for God has made him wise. Folly clings to the wine-cup, but wisdom comes with the Holy Spirit. Drunkenness wastes time, but the Spirit of God, when we are filled with him, makes us save it. Read the sixteenth verse: 'Redeeming the time, because the days are evil. Wherefore be ye not unwise, but understanding what the will of the Lord is. And be not drunk with wine, wherein is excess'. How much of time is wasted over the unholy cup! But the child of God, when the Spirit of God enters into him, makes a conscience of his odd moments and leisure minutes. As goldsmiths sweep up the very dust of their shops, that no filings of the precious metal may be lost, so does the Christian man, when filled with the Spirit, use his brief intervals. It is wonderful what may be done in odd minutes. Little spaces of time may be made to yield a great harvest of usefulness and a rich revenue of glory to God. May we be filled with the Spirit in that respect!

FOR MEDITATION: (*Our Own Hymn Book,* no. 464 v.2—Andrew Reed, 1842)

    'Come as the *light*—to us reveal
    Our emptiness and woe:
    And lead us in those paths of life
    Where all the righteous go.'

27 MAY (PREACHED 26 MAY 1889)

The curse; and the curse for us

'Christ hath redeemed us from the curse of the law, being made a curse for us: for it is written, Cursed is every one that hangeth on a tree.'
Galatians 3:13
SUGGESTED FURTHER READING: 2 Corinthians 5:16–21

I do not like to use a word of my own, in trying to open up this mystery: I will not even try to explain it, but will bid you look down into the depths of it for yourselves. He was 'made a curse for us': he was not such by nature; it needed a special arrangement to put him in that condition. Not only did the curse pass over him in its results, but the word says that he was 'made a curse'. It is wonderfully expressive; and yet more wonderfully it veils the inexpressible. He was 'made a curse'. O thou divine Son, thou ever-blessed One, thou perfect One, thou altogether lovely One, how can such words apply to thee? Yet they do so apply, for the Holy Spirit speaks of thee in this wise. Here is our hope and here our joy, even in this abyss of woe: He was 'made a curse for us'. The penal consequences of sin were so visited upon the great Substitute that he vindicated the law of God in the highest conceivable manner. Remember those words: 'Who his own self bare our sins in his own body on the tree'. These are the echo of that prophetic sentence, 'the LORD hath laid on him the iniquity of us all.' 'He bare the sin of many'. 'Behold the Lamb of God, which taketh away the sin of the world.' He 'bare our sins' that he might bear them away by the fact of bearing them himself. This is the central doctrine of the gospel and, although today it is slighted, here I stand, by God's grace, to declare it in plain terms while my tongue can move. I know no other hope for lost men but this, that the justice of God has been vindicated by the death of the Lord Jesus Christ and it is by faith in him that men are delivered 'from the curse of the law,' because he was 'made a curse' for them.

FOR MEDITATION: (*Our Own Hymn Book*, no. 406 v.2—John Kent, 1803)
   'Shout, believer, to thy God,
   He hath once the wine press trod;
   Peace procured by blood divine,
   Cancelled all thy sins and mine.'

SERMON NO. 2093

28 MAY (PREACHED 29 MAY 1887)

God's thoughts of peace, and our expected end

'For I know the thoughts that I think toward you, saith the LORD, thoughts of peace, and not of evil, to give you an expected end.' Jeremiah 29:11

SUGGESTED FURTHER READING: Isaiah 55:6–11

Sometimes a man may hardly know his own thoughts, because he has scarcely made up his mind. There are several subjects now upon the public mind, concerning which it is wise to say little or nothing, because it is not easy to decide about them. Upon a certain matter one asks you this question and another asks you another question; it is possible that you have so carefully weighed and measured the arguments both pro and con that you cannot come to a conclusion either way. Your thoughts differ from day to day and therefore you do not yet know them. You need not be ashamed of this: it shows that you have a just sense of your own imperfect knowledge. A fool soon makes up his mind, because there is so very little of it, but a wise man waits and considers. The case is far otherwise with the only wise God. The Lord is not a man that he should need to hesitate; his infinite mind is made up and he knows his thoughts. With the Lord there is neither question nor debate: 'he is in one mind, and who can turn him?' His purpose is settled and he adheres to it. He is resolved to reward 'them that diligently seek him' and to honour those that trust in him. He is resolved to remember his covenant for ever and to keep his promises to those who believe him. His thought is that the people whom he has formed for himself shall show forth his praise. 'The Lord knoweth them that are his'; he knows whom he gave to his Son and he knows that these shall be his jewels for ever and ever. Beloved, when you do not know your own mind, God knows *his* mind.

FOR MEDITATION: (*Our Own Hymn Book*, no. 734 v.3—John Newton, 1779)

> 'His love in time past forbids me to think
> He'll leave me at last in trouble to sink;
> Each sweet Ebenezer I have in review,
> Confirms His good pleasure to help me quite through.'

SERMON NO. 1965

29 MAY (1887)

'Sitting by'

'And it came to pass on a certain day, as he was teaching, that there were Pharisees and doctors of the law sitting by.' Luke 5:17
SUGGESTED FURTHER READING: Mark 2:1–12

It is a very poor business to go to the house of God to criticize a fellow-mortal who is sincerely trying to do us good. In no case can ungenerous criticisms do any good; but the pity of it is, that when we earnestly desire to show to you the way of salvation, some of you should hinder us by petty observations upon a faulty mannerism, a slight blunder, a mispronunciation of a word, or an inaccurate accent. Alas, what small things put eternal truth on one side! I do not know, and I should not like to say if I did know, what petty trifles people will carry away and talk of, after we have been solemnly pleading with them about heaven, hell, the judgment-day, the wrath to come and the way to escape from it. Was it Carlyle who spoke of the cricket as chirping amid the crack of doom? I am apt to think that many people are like that cricket; they go on with their idle chit-chat when Christ himself is set before them on the cross. Assuredly this is poor work. I am hungry; I come to a banquet; but instead of feasting upon the viands, I begin to criticize the dress of the waiters, abuse the arrangements of the banqueting-hall and vilify the provisions. I shall go home as hungry as I came and who will be blamed for it? The best criticism that you can possibly give of your friend's entertainment is to be hearty in partaking of it. The greatest honour that we can do to Christ Jesus is to feed upon him, to receive him, to trust him, to live upon him. Merely to carp and to question will bring no good to the most clever of you. How can it? It is a pitiful waste of time for yourself, and a trial of temper to others. Yet there are many who, like the scribes and Pharisees, are in this manner 'sitting by'.

FOR MEDITATION: Negative responses to the words of the Lord Jesus Christ assumed various forms—some were offended (Matthew 15:12), some reasoned (Luke 5:21–22), some derided (Luke 16:14) and others murmured (John 6:41,60–61). But all of these boiled down to the same conclusion—they all rejected God's ways (Luke 7:29–30).

SERMON NO. 1991

30 MAY (1886)

The happy duty of daily praise

'I will extol thee, my God, O king; and I will bless thy name for ever and ever. Every day will I bless thee; and I will praise thy name for ever and ever.' Psalm 145:1–2
SUGGESTED FURTHER READING: Psalm 71:1–24

Observe that David is firmly resolved to praise God. My text has four 'I wills' in it. Frequently it is foolish for us poor mortals to say 'I will,' because our will is so feeble and fickle; but when we resolve upon the praise of God, we may say, 'I will' and 'I will' and 'I will' and 'I will' till we make a solid square of determinations. You will have need to say 'I will' a great many times, for many obstacles will hinder your resolve. There will come depression of spirit and then you must say, 'I will extol thee, my God, O king'. Poverty, sickness, losses and crosses may assail you and then you must say, 'and I will bless thy name for ever and ever.' The devil will come and tell you that you have no interest in Christ, but you must say, 'Every day will I bless thee'. Death will come and perhaps you will be under the fear of it; then it will be incumbent upon you to cry, 'and I will praise thy name for ever and ever.'

> 'Sing, though sense and carnal reason
> Fain would stop the joyful song:
> Sing, and count it highest treason
> For a saint to hold his tongue.'

A bold man took this motto: 'While I live I'll crow', but our motto is, 'While I live I'll praise.' An old motto was, 'Dum spiro spero', but the saint improves upon it, and cries, 'Dum expiro spero'—not only 'While I live I will hope', but 'When I die I will hope': he even gets beyond all that and determines, 'Whether I live or die I will praise my God.' 'My heart is fixed, O God, my heart is fixed: I will sing and give praise.'

FOR MEDITATION: (*Our Own Hymn Book*, no. 100 version 2 v.3—William Kethe, 1562)
   'O enter then His gates with praise, approach with joy His courts unto:
   Praise, laud, and bless His name always, for it is seemly so to do.'

SERMON NO. 1902

31 MAY (1885)

A question for a questioner

'Hath God forgotten to be gracious?' Psalm 77:9
SUGGESTED FURTHER READING: Romans 10:1–17

Believe in the Lord Jesus Christ now and you are saved; then you will no more ask the question, 'Is his mercy clean gone for ever?' 'Oh,' says one, 'but I have been looking to reform myself and grow better and I have done a good deal in that way.' That is not the gospel; it is all very right and proper, but the gospel is, 'He that believeth on him is not condemned'. The other day I saw my bees swarming; they hung on a branch of a tree in a living mass; the difficulty was to get them into a hive. My man went with his veil over his face and began to put them into the hive; I noticed that he was particularly anxious to get the queen bee into it, for once he had her in the hive the rest would be sure to follow and remain with her. Now, faith is the queen bee. You may get temperance, love, hope and all those other bees into the hive, but the main thing is to get simple faith in Christ and all the rest will come afterwards. Get the queen bee of faith and all the other virtues will attend her. 'Alas!' cries one, 'I have been listening to the gospel for years.' That is quite right, for 'faith cometh by hearing,' but we are not saved by mere listening, nor even by knowing, unless we advance to believing. The letter of the word is not life; it is the spirit of it which saves. When tea was first introduced into this country a person favoured a friend with a pound of it. It was exceedingly expensive and when he met his friend next, he enquired, 'Have you tried the tea?' 'Yes, but I did not like it at all.' 'How was that? Everybody else is enraptured with it.' 'Why,' said the other, 'we boiled it in a saucepan, threw away the water and brought the leaves to table, but they were very hard and nobody cared for them.' Thus many people keep the leaves of form and throw away the spiritual meaning. They listen to our doctrines, but fail to come to Christ. They throw away the true essence of the gospel, which is faith in Jesus. I pray you, do not act thus.

FOR MEDITATION: (*Our Own Hymn Book,* no. 502 v.2—William Freeman Lloyd, 1835)
    '"Come," it is His invitation; "come to Me," the Saviour says,
    Why, oh why such hesitation, gloomy doubts, and base delays?'

SERMON NO. 1843

1 JUNE (1890)

Noah's faith, fear, obedience, and salvation

'By faith Noah, being warned of God of things not seen as yet, moved with fear, prepared an ark to the saving of his house; by the which he condemned the world, and became heir of the righteousness which is by faith.' Hebrews 11:7

SUGGESTED FURTHER READING (Spurgeon): Genesis 6:5–22

Noah had a very humble distrust of himself. I wish we all had such a fear. Let us fear God because of his greatness; let us fear ourselves because of our sinfulness. Let us fear lest we should fall into sin and perish with the rest of the sinners. Let no man say, 'I shall never fall.' Alas! Those are the most likely to slip. Did you never note that those who seem least likely to fall into a sin are the very people who commit it? You would not have dreamed that sober Noah should be found drunk, nor that righteous Lot should commit incest, nor that David, whose heart smote him when he only cut off the lap of Saul's garment, should be guilty of murder, nor that Peter, who said, 'Though all men shall be offended because of thee, yet will I never', would have denied his Master with oaths and cursing. We may not trust ourselves, but we ought to stand in daily fear lest we be guilty before God. Here was Noah filled with such a holy fear of himself, that he took care to do what the Lord bade him, even to the most minute particular. He did not choose another sort of wood, nor alter the shape of the vessel, nor make more stories, nor more windows, nor more doors, but he distrusted his own judgment and leaned not to his own understanding. He did exactly what he was told to do and thus left the consequences with the Lord who commanded him. He feared his own wisdom, for he knew that 'Man is like to vanity' and no more to be relied upon than the mist of the morning. Fear made Noah hew the trees, square the timbers and wield the axe and the hammer. Fear wrought in him diligence and speed. It made him despise the observations of onlookers and build for his life in brave defiance of the spirit of the age and the judgment of the wise.

FOR MEDITATION: Fear of failure can lead to disobedient inaction (Luke 19:12–13,20–23) but 'In the fear of the LORD is strong confidence: and his children shall have a place of refuge' (Proverbs 14:26). Noah proved it (Genesis 6:18; 7:1,7,13) by trusting God and not himself.

SERMON NO. 2147

2 JUNE (1889)

The form of godliness without the power

'Having a form of godliness, but denying the power thereof: from such turn away.' 2 Timothy 3:5
SUGGESTED FURTHER READING: Jude 8–19

What is the general history of those who have not this power? Well, dear friends, their course usually runs thus: they do not begin with denying the power, but they begin by trying to do without it. They would like to become members of the church and, as they fear that they are not fit for it, they look about for something which looks like conversion and the new birth. They try to persuade themselves that they have been changed: they accept emotion as regeneration and a belief of doctrine for belief in Christ. It is rather hard at first to reckon brass as gold, but it grows easier as it is persisted in. Patching up a conversion and manufacturing a regeneration, they venture forward. At the first they are a good deal suspicious of themselves, but they industriously kill every question by treating it as a needless doubt. Thus, by degrees, they believe a lie. The next step is easy: they deceive themselves and come to believe that they are surely saved. All is now right for eternity, so they fancy, and they fold their arms in calm security. Meeting with godly people, they put on a bold front and speak up as bravely as if they were the true soldiers of King Jesus. Good people are charmed to meet with fresh brethren and at once take them into their confidence. Thus they deceive others and help to strengthen themselves in their false hope. They use the choice phrases of earnest Christians. Mixing with them, they pick up their particular expressions and pronounce 'Shibboleth' in the most approved fashion. At last they take the daring step of denying the power. Being without it themselves, they conceive that others are without it also. Judging from their own case, they conclude that it is all an affair of words. They get on very well without any supernatural power and others, no doubt, do the same; only they add a little cant to it to please the very godly folk.

FOR MEDITATION: (*Our Own Hymn Book,* no. 399 v.3—John Adams, 1776)
> 'Save us from a mere profession! Save us from hypocrisy;
> Give us, Lord, the sweet possession of Thy righteousness and Thee:
> Best of favours! None compared with this can be.'

SERMON NO. 2088

3 JUNE (WRONGLY DATED 17 MAY 1887)

The word a sword

'For the word of God is quick, and powerful, and sharper than any two-edged sword, piercing even to the dividing asunder of soul and spirit, and of the joints and marrow, and is a discerner of the thoughts and intents of the heart.' Hebrews 4:12

SUGGESTED FURTHER READING: Jeremiah 23:21–32

There is not an inert passage in the Scriptures; every line has its virtues. Have you never heard of one who heard read, as the lesson for the Sabbath-day, that long chapter of names, wherein it is written that each patriarch lived so many hundred years, 'and he died'? Thus it ends the notice of the long life of Methuselah with 'and he died.' The repetition of the words, 'and he died', woke the thoughtless hearer to a sense of his mortality and led to his coming to the Saviour. I should not wonder that, away there in the Chronicles, among those tough Hebrew names, there have been conversions wrought in cases unknown to us as yet. Anyhow, any bit of Holy Scripture is very dangerous to play with and many a man has been wounded by the Scriptures when he has been idly or even profanely reading them. Doubters have meant to break the Word to pieces and it has broken them. Fools have taken up portions and studied them on purpose to ridicule them and they have been sobered and vanquished by that which they repeated in sport. There was one, a member of the 'Hell-fire Club,' a desperate fellow, who went to hear Mr Whitefield. He stood up at the next meeting of his abominable associates and delivered Mr Whitefield's sermon with wonderful accuracy, imitating his very tone and manner. In the middle of his exhortation he converted himself, came to a sudden pause, sat down broken-hearted and confessed the power of the gospel. That club was dissolved. That remarkable convert was Mr Thorpe of Bristol, whom God so greatly used afterwards in the salvation of others. I would rather have you read the Bible to mock at it than not read it at all. I would rather that you came to hear the Word of God out of hatred to it than that you never came at all.

FOR MEDITATION: (*Our Own Hymn Book,* no. 957 v.1—Albert Midlane, 1861)

'Revive Thy work, O Lord, Thy mighty arm make bare;
Speak with the voice that wakes the dead, and make Thy people hear.'

SERMON NO. 2010

4 JUNE (PREACHED 30 MAY 1886)

Truth stranger than fiction

'And I will restore to you the years that the locust hath eaten.' Joel 2:25
SUGGESTED FURTHER READING: Jeremiah 29:1–14

Lost years can never be restored literally. Time once past is gone for ever. Let no man make any mistake about this, or trifle with the present moment under any notion that the flying hour will ever wing its way back to him. As well recall the north wind, or fill again the emptied raincloud, or put back into their quiver the arrows of the lord of day. As well bid the river, which has hastened onward to the sea, bring back its rolling floods, as imagine that the years that have once gone can ever be restored to us. It will strike you at once that the locusts did not eat the years: the locusts ate the fruits of the years' labour, the harvests of the fields, so that the meaning of the restoration of the years must be the restoration of those fruits and of those harvests which the locusts consumed. You cannot have back your time, but there is a strange and wonderful way in which God can give back to you the wasted blessings, the unripened fruits of years over which you mourned. The fruits of wasted years may yet be yours. It is a pity that they should have been locust-eaten by your folly and negligence, but if they have been so, be not hopeless concerning them. 'All things are possible to him that believeth.' There is a power which is beyond all things and can work great marvels. Who can make the all-devouring locust restore his prey? No man, by wisdom or power, can recover what has been utterly destroyed. God alone can do for you what seems impossible, and here is the promise of his grace: 'I will restore to you the years that the locust hath eaten'.

FOR MEDITATION: (*Our Own Hymn Book*, no. 605 v.3—John Morrison, 1781)
> 'Long hath the night of sorrow reigned;
> The dawn shall bring us light;
> God shall appear, and we shall rise
> With gladness in His sight.'

SERMON NO. 2081

5 JUNE (1887)

The death of Moses

'So Moses the servant of the LORD *died there in the land of Moab, according to the word of the* LORD.*'* Deuteronomy 34:5
SUGGESTED FURTHER READING (Spurgeon): Deuteronomy 3:21–28

It never was the work of Moses to lead Israel into the Promised Land. It was his wish, but not his work. His work he saw, but his wish he saw not. Moses did really finish his own proper work, but the desire of his heart was to have seen the people settled in their land and this was not granted him. Thus David gathered together gold and silver with which to build the Temple, but he was not to build it; Solomon, his son, undertook the work. Even thus great reformers rise and speak the truth and cause colossal systems of error to tremble, but they do not themselves utterly destroy those evils. Their successors continue the work. Most men have to sow that others may reap. The prayer of Moses is fulfilled to others as well as to himself: 'Let thy work appear unto thy servants, and thy glory unto their children.' We must not hope to engross all things: let us be content to do our own part in laying the foundation upon which other men may build in due course. It is according to the divine appointment which links us with each other that one plants and another waters, one brings out of Egypt and another leads into Canaan. And I may here notice that Moses thus 'died according to the word of the LORD', for a deep dispensational reason. It was not for Moses to give the people rest, for the law gives no man rest and brings no man to heaven. The law may bring us to the borders of the promise, but only Joshua or Jesus can bring us into grace and truth. If Moses had given them Canaan, the allegory would have seemed to teach us that rest might be obtained by the law, but as Moses must be laid asleep and buried by divine hands, so must the law cease to rule that the covenant of grace may lead us into the fullness of peace.

FOR MEDITATION: (*Our Own Hymn Book,* no. 875 v.6—Isaac Watts, 1709)
   'Could we but climb where Moses stood,
   And view the landscape o'er,
   Not Jordan's stream, nor death's cold flood,
   Should fright us from the shore!'

SERMON NO. 1966

6 JUNE (1886)

Who found it out?

'*And there were four leprous men at the entering in of the gate: and they said one to another, Why sit we here until we die? ... And they rose up in the twilight, to go unto the camp of the Syrians: and when they were come to the uttermost part of the camp of Syria, behold, there was no man there.*' 2 Kings 7:3,5

SUGGESTED FURTHER READING: Psalm 34:1–10

He knows the grace of God best who, in all his leprosy, defilement, hunger, faintness and weariness, has come to Christ, fed on the bread of heaven, drank the water of life, taken the blessings of the covenant and made himself rich with hidden treasure. Such a man will speak convincingly, because he will bear a personal witness. This man has no doubts upon the vital points, for Christ is his life: he does not argue, but testify; he is not a special pleader, but a witness. The leper, fed and enriched, stands outside the city gate, calls to the porter and wakes him up at the dead of night, for he has news worth telling. The experienced believer speaks with the accent of conviction and therein imitates his Master, who spoke with authority. 'Why,' says the porter, 'I used to speak to you over the city wall; are you the leper to whom I said that there was no more food for you? I have thrown you nothing for a week and thought you were dead; are you the man?' He answers, 'I am: I do not want your wretched rations now; I am filled and where I have fed there is enough for you all. Come out and feast yourselves.' 'I should not know you,' says the porter. All four join in saying, 'No, you would not know us; we are new men since we have been to the camp. Believe the story and tell it to all in the city, for it is true. There is enough and to spare, if they will but come out and have it.' The Lord made a good choice when he selected these lepers to be discoverers of his great work. He does wisely when he takes those who are saddest and fills their mouths with laughter and their tongues with singing, for these will command attention.

FOR MEDITATION: The Lord Jesus Christ came into the world to seek the lost (Luke 19:10), to give sight to the blind (John 9:39; 12:46) and to give life to the dead (John 10:10), in short to save sinners (1 Timothy 1:15). Consider the responses and testimonies of some who then came to him (Luke 19:6–8; John 9:24–25; Ephesians 2:4–5; 1 Timothy 1:15–16).

SERMON NO. 1903

7 JUNE (1891)

The statute of David for the sharing of the spoil

'David came to the two hundred men, which were so faint that they could not follow David ... he saluted them. Then answered all the wicked men ... Because they went not with us, we will not give them aught of the spoil ... Then said David, Ye shall not do so ... with that which the LORD *hath given us, who hath preserved us ... but as his part is that goeth down to the battle so shall his part be that tarrieth by the stuff.'* 1 Samuel 30:21–24
SUGGESTED FURTHER READING: Joshua 24:14–31

If you could see our Captain, you would get down on your knees and beg him to let you enter the ranks of those who follow him. It is heaven to serve Jesus. I am a recruiting sergeant and I would find a few recruits at this moment. Every man must serve somebody: we have no choice as to that fact. Those who have no master are slaves to themselves. Depend upon it, you will either serve Satan or Christ, either self or the Saviour. You will find sin, self, Satan and the world to be hard masters, but if you wear the livery of Christ, you will find him so meek and lowly of heart that you will 'find rest unto your souls.' He is the most magnanimous of captains. There never was his like among the choicest of princes. He is always to be found in the thickest part of the battle. When the wind blows cold, he always takes the bleak side of the hill. The heaviest end of the cross lies ever on his shoulders. If he bids us carry a burden, he carries it also. If there is anything that is gracious, generous, kind, tender, lavish and super abundant in love, you always find it in him. These forty years and more have I served him, blessed be his name! I have had nothing but love from him. I would be glad to continue yet another forty years in the same dear service here below if so it pleased him. His service is life, peace, joy. Oh that you would enter on it at once! God help you to enlist under the banner of Jesus even this day! Amen.

FOR MEDITATION: (*Our Own Hymn Book,* no. 917 v.1—John Mason, 1683)
　'My Lord, my love, was crucified, He all the pains did bear;
　But in the sweetness of His rest He makes His servants share.'
N.B. With these words Spurgeon ended his preaching ministry in London.

SERMON NO. 2208

8 JUNE (1890)

The tenderness of Jesus

'We have not an high priest which cannot be touched with the feeling of our infirmities; but was in all points tempted like as we are, yet without sin.' Hebrews 4:15

SUGGESTED FURTHER READING: Job 29:11–16

I noticed a very able address delivered by Mr Hutchinson before the Lord Mayor last Friday, in which he advises a person who mourns his lack of sympathy to go for a week to his usual city vocation with a black patch over one eye or wearing a wooden leg. 'If this does not effect the business,' he says, 'let him choose some leisure day in the country in bright spring and resolutely for twenty-four hours keep a bandage firmly placed over both eyes. His organization is, I fear, in this direction, well-nigh hopeless, if next morning he does not feel inclined to send a liberal donation to some hospital that has for its mission the prevention of blindness.' I have no doubt that improvable persons might be all the better for some such attempt to gain fellow-feeling. The principle is good and might be tried in other directions. Suppose the squire of the parish should say to his lady, 'We have always said that our agricultural labourers have quite enough money to live upon; let us try their fare. We will leave this house for a week, take one of the old cottages in the village and live, all of us, on the wage we pay our men.' What a capital school for social economy! Only we should like members of parliament to have a longer experience than one week, lest it might be a pleasant change from feasting to fasting. Say six months for the honourable member! This might foster sympathy. Our blessed Lord had real experience and the faculty of being able to put himself into the place of sufferers and so to be 'acquainted with grief'. His quick understanding made him realize, as High Priest, the sorrows of his people.

FOR MEDITATION: (*Our Own Hymn Book*, no. 328 v.1—Isaac Watts, 1709)
    'With joy we meditate the grace of our High Priest above;
    His heart is made of tenderness, His bowels melt with love.'

N.B. Spurgeon mentioned that he was a governor of St Thomas's Hospital during this sermon preached on Hospital Sunday, an annual event since 1876. For other Hospital Sunday sermons see 14, 19, 23 and 27 June.

SERMON NO. 2148

9 JUNE (1889)

Profitable mixture

'For unto us was the gospel preached, as well as unto them: but the word preached did not profit them, not being mixed with faith in them that heard it.' Hebrews 4:2
SUGGESTED FURTHER READING (Spurgeon): Hebrews 3:7–19

A man that has no faith in what he hears does not appropriate it. A hungry man passes by where there is entertainment for needy travellers. Believing that there is food for his hunger, he tarries at the door, but if unbelief mutters, 'There is a bare table within; you might as soon break your neck as break your fast in that place,' then the traveller hurries on. Unbelief palsies the hand and it appropriates nothing. That which is not appropriated can be of no use to you. Look at your food. How is it that it builds up your body? Because you take it into the mouth and it descends into the stomach, is mixed with certain fluids, digested, ultimately taken up into the system and becomes a life-sustaining force. Being properly mixed, it is taken up and assimilated. So it is with heavenly truth: if it is taken into the heart and mixed with faith, it is digested and becomes food to every part of the spiritual nature. Without faith the gospel passes through the soul undigested and rather feeds disease than promotes life. What a dreadful lack is the lack of faith! These people could not enter in because they had no faith. They could go to the border of the land, but they must die even there. They could send their spies into the country, but they could not see the fertile valleys themselves. Without faith they could not enter Canaan. Shall it be so with us, that, for want of faith, we shall hear the gospel, know something about its power and yet miss its glories and never enter into possession of the life eternal which it reveals? Here is the point: 'they could not enter in because of unbelief.'

FOR MEDITATION: (*Our Own Hymn Book,* no. 95 song 2 vv.5&6—Isaac Watts, 1719)
'But if your ears refuse the language of His grace,
And hearts grow hard, like stubborn Jews, that unbelieving race:
The Lord, in vengeance dressed, will lift His hand and swear,
"You that despise My promised rest shall have no portion there."'

SERMON NO. 2089

10 JUNE (PREACHED 7 JUNE 1885)

Israel and Britain. A note of warning

'But though he had done so many miracles before them, yet they believed not on him: that the saying of Esaias the prophet might be fulfilled, which he spake, Lord, who hath believed our report? and to whom hath the arm of the Lord been revealed?' John 12:37–38
SUGGESTED FURTHER READING (Spurgeon): Isaiah 6:1–13

I am growingly fearful lest our own country should furnish a parallel to all this. Read the story of England, beginning where you will, and see how gracious God has been to us. Note well our great deliverances, from the destruction of the Spanish Armada to the overthrow of Napoleon. Do not forget how often this little country has been made victorious in wars against great peoples, who thought to swallow her up. Then reflect how God sent the light to us, how the gospel spread all over England and how it has in many ways been rejected. How often since the days of Cromwell Rome has been allowed to dim the light of our Protestantism and how it labours to do so still! See how this people have received the truth of heaven, but again and again have proved false to it, turning at one time to superstition and at another time to infidelity. At this moment we are rich and, despite depression in business, we are less tried by it than any other nation. What comes of all this mercy but increased sin? At this moment we have sin rampant among us almost beyond precedent. Think how the poor are oppressed and ground down with awful poverty in many parts of this great city. Shall not God avenge the cry of starving women? Worse still, those who dare walk our streets after sundown tell us that Sodom, in its most putrid days, could scarce exceed this metropolis for open vice. To our infinite disgust and horror, the names of certain of the greatest in the land are openly mentioned in connection with the filthiest debauchery. It is a hideous evil that the dregs of vice should be the chosen luxury of certain of our hereditary legislators and rulers. Woe unto thee, O land!

FOR MEDITATION: (*Our Own Hymn Book,* no. 12 vv.1&2—Isaac Watts, 1719)

'Lord, when iniquities abound, and blasphemy grows bold,
When faith is hardly to be found, and love is waxing cold,
Is not Thy chariot hastening on? Hast Thou not given this sign?
May we not trust and live upon a promise so divine?'

SERMON NO. 1844

11 JUNE (PREACHED 7 JUNE 1885)

Immeasurable love

'For God so loved the world, that he gave his only begotten Son, that whosoever believeth in him should not perish, but have everlasting life.'
John 3:16
SUGGESTED FURTHER READING: 2 Peter 1:1–15

The higher truths, those truths which belong to a more enlightened experience, those richer truths which tell of the fellowship of the higher life—all these are helpful to holy fellowship, but I am sure not more so than those elementary and foundation truths which were the means of our first entrance into the kingdom of God. Babes in Christ and men in Christ here feed upon one common food. Come, you aged saints, be children again, and you that have long known your Lord, take up your first spelling-book and go over your A B C again, by learning that 'God so loved the world', that he gave his Son to die, that man might live through him. I do not call you to an elementary lesson because you have forgotten your letters, but because it is a good thing to refresh the memory and a blessed thing to feel young again. What the old folks used to call the Christ-cross Row contained nothing but the letters, and yet all the books in the language are made out of that line: therefore do I call you back to the cross and to him who bled thereon. It is a good thing for us all to return at times to our starting-place and make sure that we are in the way everlasting. The love of our espousals is most likely to continue if we again and again begin where God began with us and where we first began with God. It is wise to come to him afresh, as we came in that first day, when helpless, needy, heavy-laden, we stood weeping at the cross and left our burden at the pierced feet. There we learned to look, live and love; there would we repeat the lesson till we rehearse it perfectly in glory.

FOR MEDITATION: (*Our Own Hymn Book,* no. 539 v.3—Isaac Watts, 1709)
   'High on the cross the Saviour hung,
   High in the heavens he reigns;
   Here sinners, by th'old serpent stung,
   Look, and forget their pains.'

N.B. Spurgeon had no record of having preached on John 3:16 before!

SERMON NO. 1850

12 JUNE (1887)

Plain gospel for plain people

'For this commandment which I command thee this day, it is not hidden from thee, neither is it far off.' 'But the word is very nigh unto thee, in thy mouth, and in thy heart, that thou mayest do it.' Deuteronomy 30:11,14
SUGGESTED FURTHER READING: Hebrews 10:1–18

Even in the days of Moses, how plain some things were! It must have been plain to every Israelite that *man is a sinner*, else why the sacrifices, purgations and cleansings? The whole Levitical economy proclaimed aloud that man has sinned: all the Ten Commandments thundered out this truth! They could not avoid knowing it. It was plain also that *salvation is by sacrifice*. Not a day passed without its morning and evening lambs. All the year round there were special sacrifices by which the doctrine of atonement by blood was clearly declared. It was written clear as a sunbeam, 'without shedding of blood is no remission.' Plain enough also was *the doctrine of faith*, for each bringer of a sacrifice laid his hand upon the victim, confessing his sin, and by that act he transferred his sin to the offering. Thus faith was typically described as that act by which we accept the propitiation prepared by God and recognize the God-given Substitute. It was also clear to every Israelite that *this cleansing was not the effect of the typical sacrifices* themselves, otherwise they would not have been repeated year by year and day by day, otherwise, the conscience being once purged, there would be no necessity for further sacrifice. The remembrance of sin was made over and over again, to let Israel know that the visible sacrifices pointed to the real way of cleansing and were meant to set forth that blessed 'Lamb of God, which taketh away the sin of the world.' In many ways the Jew was put off from resting in forms and ceremonies and was directed to the inner truth, the spiritual substance, which is Christ. Equally clear it must have been to every Israelite that *the faith which brings the benefit of the great sacrifice is a practical and operative faith* which affects the life and character. Continually were they exhorted to serve the Lord with their whole heart.

FOR MEDITATION: The plainness with which the law was to be written up (Deuteronomy 27:8) was itself a foreshadowing of the plainness with which the Lord Jesus Christ spoke (John 11:14; 16:25,29). If God's word is not plain to us, it isn't his fault (Proverbs 8:8–9).

SERMON NO. 1967

13 JUNE (WHITSUN 1886)

The personal Pentecost and the glorious hope

'And hope maketh not ashamed; because the love of God is shed abroad in our hearts by the Holy Ghost which is given unto us.' Romans 5:5
SUGGESTED FURTHER READING: Ephesians 3:14–21

The shedding abroad of the love of God in the heart by the Holy Spirit means this: he imparts to us an *intense appreciation* and sense of that love. We have heard of it, believed in it, meditated upon it and at last are overpowered by its greatness! 'God so loved the world, that he gave his only begotten Son'. We cannot measure such love. We become affected by it; we are filled with wonder and admiration. Its greatness, its singularity, its speciality, its infinity—all these amaze us. It 'is shed abroad in our hearts'. Then there comes an *appropriation* of it. We cry, 'He loved me, and gave himself for me.' We begin to feel that God's love was not only love to men in general, but love to ourselves in particular, and we are now fairly carried off our feet. In a belief of this special love to us we are ready to dance for joy. Faith perceives that it is even so and then we praise the Lord 'upon the high sounding cymbals.' Then follows, as a matter of course, that *return of love* which the human heart must feel: 'We love him, because he first loved us.' We did doubt his love once; we cannot doubt it now. If we were asked three times, 'lovest thou me?' we should answer humbly, but most emphatically, 'Lord, thou knowest all things; thou knowest that I love thee. I could not live without loving thee. I would rather a thousand times that I had never been born than be without love to thee; and though I do not love thee as I ought and my heart craves after a far greater love, yet I do love thee in deed and in truth. Thou knowest that I do and I should be false to my own consciousness if I denied it.' This is to have the love of God shed abroad in the heart 'by the Holy Ghost which is given unto us': to know it, enjoy it, appropriate it, rejoice in it and come under its divine influence.

FOR MEDITATION: (*Our Own Hymn Book*, no. 250 v.3—Thomas Kelly, 1809)

'But though His love no measure knows,
The Saviour to His people shows
Enough to give them joy, when known,
Enough to make their hearts His own.'

SERMON NO. 1904

14 JUNE (1885)

The pitifulness of the Lord the comfort of the afflicted

'Behold, we count them happy which endure. Ye have heard of the patience of Job, and have seen the end of the Lord; that the Lord is very pitiful, and of tender mercy.' James 5:11
SUGGESTED FURTHER READING: Ezekiel 14:12–20

Of the Book of Job it has been said that it is a drama, a fiction, a fine piece of Oriental imagination. But see how the New Testament protects the Old. How can Job be an imaginary character? Does the Spirit of God quote for our guidance a fictitious person? Does he set Job before us as an example when Job never existed? The thing is too absurd to contemplate. There was such a person as Job and possibly the passage may confirm us in the belief that the patriarch lived in the earliest ages, since this apostle, when mentioning the prophets, places Job in the forefront and quotes his case in preference to any other. 'Take, my brethren, the prophets, who have spoken in the name of the Lord, for an example of suffering affliction, and of patience ... Ye have heard of the patience of Job'. He might have mentioned Jacob, Moses or David as examples of heroic endurance, but he cites Job, in all probability as being first in order of time and in degree of trial. I conceive him to have been one of the earliest of those gracious persons who walked with God 'through much tribulation' and 'endured, as seeing him who is invisible.' We are certain that James does not bring before us the imaginary actor in an Oriental tale as an argument for patience, for when men are suffering they have no patience with fiction and are in no humour for amusement; suffering men will only endure to be comforted by the story of real persons who have literally known the sufferings of life. Should you try to stimulate the afflicted to patience by a piece of fiction, they would turn upon you with indignation and say: 'You demand a patience of me which was never found in mortal man; you ask me to display a virtue which was never actually exemplified in history and so you are driven to invent a person for my imitation.' It is too absurd.

FOR MEDITATION: (*Our Own Hymn Book,* no. 103 version 3 v.2—Henry Francis Lyte, 1834)
  'Praise Him for His grace and favour to our fathers in distress!
  Praise Him still the same as ever, slow to chide and swift to bless!
  Praise Him! praise Him, glorious in His faithfulness!'

SERMON NO. 1845

15 JUNE (1890)

Everlasting love revealed

'The LORD hath appeared of old unto me, saying, Yea, I have loved thee with an everlasting love: therefore with lovingkindness have I drawn thee.' Jeremiah 31:3
SUGGESTED FURTHER READING: Isaiah 54:4–10

Such a magnificent text as ours ought to make us consider two things. The first is, Is it so? *Am I drawn?* If God loves you 'with an everlasting love', he has drawn you by his lovingkindness: is it so or not? Has he drawn you by his Holy Spirit, so that you have followed on? Are you a believer? Do you carry Christ's cross? You have been drawn to this. Then take home these gracious words: 'I have loved thee with an everlasting love'. If you have not been so drawn, do you not wish you were? Oh, it would be worth dying a thousand deaths to be a Christian after that fashion of Christianity which is based on everlasting love! Here is a glorious foundation: love without beginning, love without end, free, sovereign, unchangeable love, not bought by merit in us, nor produced by our efforts or entreaties, love which comes to us because God will love and has chosen in his divine sovereignty to love *us*. 'Everlasting love'! Why, the syllables are music. If you can climb that height, you have climbed where it is worth while to abide for ever. If you cannot claim this, at any rate desire it; go humbly on your knees to Christ Jesus, look to him and live! But, child of God, if you know these drawings and if it is true that God loves you 'with an everlasting love,' then *are you resting?* 'I have a feeble hope,' says one. What? How can you talk so? He who is 'loved with an everlasting love' and knows it, should swim in an ocean of joy. Not a wave of trouble should disturb the glassy sea of his delight. What is to make a man happy if this will not? Come, come; we must have no more hanging heads. Hallelujah! Hallelujah! If the Lord has loved me 'with an everlasting love', I will not be cast down, 'though the earth be removed'.

FOR MEDITATION: (*Our Own Hymn Book,* no. 220 v.2—Josiah Conder, 1856)
  ''Twas sovereign mercy called me, and taught my opening mind;
  The world had else enthralled me, to heavenly glories blind.
  My heart owns none above Thee; for Thy rich grace I thirst;
  This knowing, if I love Thee, Thou must have loved me first.'

SERMON NO. 2149

16 JUNE (1889)

A delicious experience

'For we which have believed do enter into rest, as he said, As I have sworn in my wrath, if they shall enter into my rest.' Hebrews 4:3
SUGGESTED FURTHER READING (Spurgeon): Psalm 23:1–6

What are the excellencies of this rest which comes by believing? I answer, they are very many. It brings us *honour*. Unto you that believe, he is an honour. It is a glorious thing to rest where God rests. Many people would give their eyes to be invited to stay with the Queen, but, oh, to dwell where God dwells and to rejoice where God rejoices! Every believer has this dignity. This rest is also a wonderful source of *strength*. When the tree strikes deep root it gets vigour for fruitage. No man has any great power to work successfully while he is worried. The fulcrum must rest, or the lever will not work. Fret creates a great leakage in a man and his force runs away uselessly, but when care is ended and he enters into rest with Christ, then all the force and energy of his being turns to holy service for God and man. Rest in Christ Jesus also gives an *incentive to diligence*, for we feel that, since we have such sweet rest ourselves, we would wish others to have it. We tell out the news which gladdens us. We cannot hide from the multitudes around us the glad tidings which have charmed away our griefs. This rest also *brightens life*. When you enter into rest, life is not a dull and dreary round, such as the blind horse finds at the mill. Life is not a chain, which we must drag behind us, but wings on which we soar into the joyous blue and hold converse with the choristers of heaven. I know not how to express my thankfulness that ever I had a being, seeing it is crowned with well-being in Christ Jesus. I could not say, ''Tis something better not to be.' No, life is a favour now that I know my Lord. This rest in Christ is a fair foretaste of heaven.

FOR MEDITATION: (*Our Own Hymn Book*, no. 917 v.2—John Mason, 1683)
'How sweetly rest Thy saints above
Which in Thy bosom lie!
The church below doth rest in hope
Of that felicity.'

SERMON NO. 2090

17 JUNE (1888)

'Let him deliver him now'

'He trusted in God; let him deliver him now, if he will have him: for he said, I am the Son of God.' Matthew 27:43
SUGGESTED FURTHER READING: John 15:18–27

That which appears in many a psalm to relate to David is found in the Gospels to refer to Jesus, our Lord. Often the student of the Psalm will say to himself, 'of whom speaketh the prophet this?' He will have to disentangle the threads sometimes and mark off that which belongs to David and that which relates to the Son of God; frequently he will not be able to disentangle the threads at all, because they are one and may relate both to David and to David's Lord. This is meant to show us that the life of Christ is an epitome of the life of his people. He not only suffers for us as our substitute, but he suffers before us as our pattern. In him we see what we have in our measure to endure. 'As he is, so are we in this world.' We also must be crucified to the world and we may look for somewhat of those tests of faith and taunts of derision which go with such a crucifixion. 'Marvel not, my brethren, if the world hate you.' You, too, must suffer 'without the gate.' Not for the world's redemption, but for the accomplishment of divine purposes in you and through you to the sons of men, you must be made to know the cross and its shame. Christ is the mirror of the church. What the head endured every member of the body will also have to endure in its measure. Let us read the text in this light and come to it saying to ourselves, 'Here we see what Jesus suffered in our stead and we learn hereby to love him with all our souls. Here, too, we see, as in a prophecy, how great things we are to suffer for his sake at the hands of men.' May the Holy Spirit help us in our meditation.

FOR MEDITATION: The apostles not only promised that Christians would suffer persecution (Acts 14:22; 2 Timothy 3:12), but took the trouble to explain why. Peter said that in suffering we follow Christ's pattern (1 Peter 2:20–21); Paul went further and stated the purpose of his own suffering (Colossians 1:24–25).

SERMON NO. 2029

18 JUNE (PREACHED 22 JUNE 1890)

Three important precepts

'Hear thou, my son, and be wise, and guide thine heart in the way.'
Proverbs 23:19
SUGGESTED FURTHER READING: Jeremiah 6:16–21

I love to think of friends in glory: their footprints cheer me. I love *'The way the holy prophets went, the road that leads from banishment.'* The moderns have struck out a new path altogether; their road is both new and broad. What! Were the saints of former ages all mistaken? Did the martyrs die for a falsehood and shed their blood for doctrines which criticism explodes? The men 'Of whom the world was not worthy', were they all the dupes of theories which time has disproved? Did nobody know anything till Darwin appeared? Were those who believed that the 'things which are seen were not made of things which do appear', downright fools? Is it quite so certain as some think it, that the things which were made grew out of things already existing? Of course, I know that nowadays men are so wonderfully intelligent, that they have discovered that human life has been 'evolved' from lower life. We are the heirs of oysters and the near descendants of apes. It has taken some time to compass the evolution and yet I will grant that very hard shells are still to be met with and some men are not much above animals, especially such men as can be duped by this hypothesis. Were the old-fashioned believers all wrong? No, my brethren, they were not wrong: their lives and their deaths prove that they were right. We shall be wrong if we leave the old and tried paths for these new cuts which lead into fathomless bogs of unbelief. It was enough to condemn the idols of Israel that they were new gods, newly set up, and it is enough to condemn the gospels of the hour that they are such as were never heard of in the golden ages of the church. 'The old is better.'

FOR MEDITATION: (*Our Own Hymn Book,* no. 518 v.4—Jonathan Allen, 1801)
'Who hath our report believèd? Who received the joyful word?
Who embraced the news of pardon spoken to you by the Lord?
Can you slight it? Spoken to you by the Lord.'

SERMON NO. 2152

19 JUNE (1887)

Jubilee joy; or, believers joyful in their King

'Let the children of Zion be joyful in their King.' Psalm 149:2
SUGGESTED FURTHER READING: Daniel 7:9–14

Fifty years is a long time for Her Majesty to have reigned. May her days yet be many! Fifty years as we measure life is a long space, but fifty years in the measurement of human history is far less and fifty years as compared with eternity is nothing. King Jesus has a kingdom of which 'there shall be no end.' This is our joy, that the ages past have not taken away from the length of his reign. So much the less has any king to reign as he has already reigned, but it is not so with him, for still is the voice heard, even the same voice that made the Red Sea resound, 'The LORD shall reign for ever and ever.' Hallelujah! Let us this day be right glad concerning our King, since he 'only hath immortality,' and therefore will live for ever. He communicates that immortality to all his people and thus is the undying King of an undying kingdom. True we shall pass through that river which is named Death, but it is a misnomer; like the Jordan when Israel passed into Canaan, the Lord has rebuked it and it is dried up. We shall pass 'through the valley of the shadow of death,' and that is all; thus we shall reach a higher stage of being, in which we shall 'ever be with the Lord.' Shall not those whom the King has made to live be joyful that their King lives and reigns world without end? The age of our King has not enfeebled him. John in vision saw him with his head and hair 'white like wool, as white as snow', but to his well-beloved spouse he is not grey with age, for she sings of him, 'his locks are bushy, and black as a raven.' He is as youthful and vigorous as ever. His age is eternity and eternity has not the fretting tooth of time. He is the same Christ still, as mighty in power as when he routed the hosts of hell. Let us be joyful in our King.

FOR MEDITATION: (*Our Own Hymn Book*, no. 417 v.5—Edward Perronet, 1780)
  'Babes, men, and sires, who know His love, who feel your sin and thrall,
  Now joy with all the hosts above, and crown Him Lord of all.'

N.B. Queen Victoria attended a Jubilee service at Westminster Abbey on 21 June 1887, having succeeded to the throne on 20 June 1837, one day after Spurgeon's third birthday.

SERMON NO. 1968

20 JUNE (1886)

Healing and pardon

'And the inhabitant shall not say, I am sick: the people that dwell therein shall be forgiven their iniquity.' Isaiah 33:24
SUGGESTED FURTHER READING: Psalm 32:1–11

When we once begin to feel what sin is, to discern its true nature, and to understand the just punishment which must follow upon it, we cannot rest under its condemnation. Though God should give us dainties from day to day, clothe us in scarlet and fine linen and set us among the princes of the earth, we should be restless and wretched as long as sin preyed upon our heart. Sin casts darkness upon the sun, eclipsing its meridian light. Sin is the blast which withers all the flowers of life. Sin is the gall of bitterness; a drop of it would turn an ocean of pleasure into wormwood. Sin would again blight Paradise, could it be restored; it would turn heaven into hell could it enter there. Sin is a burden which an awakened conscience cannot bear; it crushes the spirit into the dust and threatens further to bear it down, even to the lowest hell. But when sin is pardoned, then our hymn which we have just now been singing leaps joyfully to our lips: *'Now, oh joy! my sins are pardoned'*. Is this not a necessary ingredient in that overflowing cup which the Lord puts to the lips of his redeemed ones? 'Therefore being justified by faith, we have peace with God through our Lord Jesus Christ', but without that justification there can be no peace and no enjoyment of life. Believers are spoken of as a blessed people who joy in God: they are bidden to rejoice evermore: the apostle says, 'Rejoice in the Lord alway: and again I say, Rejoice.' Such rejoicing would be impossible if sin were not pardoned and therefore we conclude that sin may be pardoned, that it may be pardoned now and that we may know it. If forgiveness is essential to a state of mind which we are exhorted to exhibit, then forgiveness may be enjoyed at this present hour.

FOR MEDITATION: (*Our Own Hymn Book*, no. 566 v.1—Albert Midlane, 1865)
   'Now, oh joy! my sins are pardoned, now I can, and do believe;
   All I have, and am, and shall be, to my precious Lord I give;
   He aroused my deathly slumbers, He dispersed my soul's dark night;
   Whispered peace, and drew me to Him—made Himself my chief delight.'

SERMON NO. 1905

21 JUNE (1885)

The purging of the conscience

'For if the blood of bulls and of goats, and the ashes of an heifer sprinkling the unclean, sanctifieth to the purifying of the flesh: How much more shall the blood of Christ, who through the eternal Spirit offered himself without spot to God, purge your conscience from dead works to serve the living God?' Hebrews 9:13–14
SUGGESTED FURTHER READING: Hebrews 5:11–6:12

Without going into what the world calls actual sin, you and I may come into contact with spiritual death; we carry death about us, from which we daily cry to be delivered. For instance, in prayer: our prayer in its form and fashion may be right enough, but if it lacks earnestness and importunity, it will be a dead work. A sermon may be orthodox and correct, but if it is devoid of that holy passion, that divine inspiration, without which sermons are but mere harangues, it is a dead work. An alms given to the poor is good as a work of humanity, but it will be only a dead work if a desire to 'be seen of men' is found at the bottom of it. Like the almsgiving of the Pharisee, it will be a mockery of God. Without a spiritual motive the best work is dead. I confess that I never appear before you without a fear that my preaching may be a dead work among you. It must be so, as it comes from myself; its life must depend upon the spiritual power with which the Lord clothes it. Do you not think that very much of common Christian conversation is dead, or very near to it? You stand and sing, but your hearts do not sing: you bow your heads in prayer, but you are not praying: you read the Scripture, but it is not inspired to you, so as to breathe its own life into you. Even our meditations and thoughts about God's work may be mere intellectual exercises and so may be devoid of that power which alone can make them living works, fit for the service of the living God. Beloved friends, we want the precious blood of Christ to purge our consciences from this death and its working and to lift us into holy and heavenly life.

FOR MEDITATION: All kinds of so-called spiritual activities can be spiritually dead (1 Corinthians 13:1–3). It takes a work of God to bring life to us in areas such as praising (Psalm 51:15), praying (Psalm 80:18), precepts (Psalm 119:18) and preaching (Ephesians 6:19–20).

SERMON NO. 1846

22 JUNE (1890)

'All the day long'

'Let not thine heart envy sinners: but be thou in the fear of the LORD *all the day long. For surely there is an end; and thine expectation shall not be cut off.'* Proverbs 23:17–18
SUGGESTED FURTHER READING: 1 Peter 1:10–17

Certain professors are Christians 'off and on' and nobody respects them. Such seed as this will not grow: there is no vitality in it. Constancy is the proof of sincerity. 'Be thou in the fear of the LORD all the day long': this is to be happy. God has spoiled the believer for being easy in sin. If you are a Christian you will never find happiness in departing from God. I say again, God has spoiled you for such pleasure. Your joy lies in a closer walk with God: your heaven on earth is in communion with the Lord. If you abide in the fear of the Lord, how useful you will be! Your 'off and on' people are worth nothing: nobody is influenced by them. What little good they do, they undo. The abiding man is also the growing man. He that is 'in the fear of the LORD all the day long' gets to have more of that fear and it has more practical power over his life and heart. What a poor life they lead who are alternately zealous and lukewarm! Like Penelope, they weave by day, but unravel by night. They blow hot and cold, and so melt and freeze by turns. They build and then break down, and so are never at rest. Children of God, let your conduct be consistent. Let not your lives be like a draught-board, with as many blacks as whites. Do not be speckled birds, like magpies, more famed for chatter than anything else. Oh that God would make us white doves! I pray you be not bold one day and cowardly another; be not one day sound in the faith and the next day on the down-grade. Be not under excitement generous and in cool blood mean as a miser. Oh that we might become like our Father in heaven in holiness and then become like him in immutability, so as to be for ever holy!

FOR MEDITATION: The Old Testament saints displayed their 'fear of the LORD' in what they did 'day and night', whether meditating on God's law (Joshua 1:8; Psalm 1:2), being employed in God's service (1 Chronicles 9:33), praying (Nehemiah 1:6), watching (Nehemiah 4:9) or even weeping (Jeremiah 9:1; 14:17; Lamentations 2:18).

SERMON NO. 2150

23 JUNE (1889)

'Jesus wept'

'Jesus wept.' John 11:35
SUGGESTED FURTHER READING: Luke 19:41–48

We read of other men that they wept. Abraham, when he buried Sarah, wept; Jacob had power with the angel, for he wept and prevailed; of David we are continually reading that he wept. His friend Jonathan and he once wept together and were not unmanned, but were the more truly men for weeping. Of Hezekiah we read that he 'wept sore', and of Josiah that he poured forth tears over the sins of Judah. Jeremiah was a weeping prophet; I might continue the list, but if I did, it would not be at all remarkable that the sons of a fallen father should weep. With all the sin and sorrow that surrounds our manhood, it is no marvel that it should be said of any man, 'He wept.' The earth brings forth thorns and thistles and the heart brings forth sorrow and sighing. Is there a man or woman here who has not wept? Have we not all, sometimes, felt a sweet relief in tears? Looking round upon this great assembly, I could point to you, one by one, and say, '*He* wept and *he* wept; *she* wept and *she* wept', and none would wonder that such has been the case. The marvel is that the sinless Son of God should, 'in the days of his flesh,' know the meaning of 'strong crying and tears'. The fact worthy to be noticed and recorded is that 'Jesus wept.' On that subject we shall meditate. First, I would remind you that 'Jesus wept', because *he was truly man*: secondly, 'Jesus wept', for *he was not ashamed of his human weakness*, but allowed himself to reveal the fact that he was, in this point also, 'made like unto his brethren'. Thirdly, 'Jesus wept', and therein *he is our instructor*. Fourthly, *he is our comforter*, and lastly, *he is our example.*

FOR MEDITATION: (*Our Own Hymn Book,* no. 265 vv.2&3—Benjamin Beddome, 1818)
  'The Son of God in tears, angels with wonder see!
  Be thou astonished, O my soul, He shed those tears for thee.
  He wept that we might weep; each sin demands a tear:
  In heaven alone no sin is found, and there's no weeping there.'

SERMON NO. 2091

24 JUNE (1888)

Moses: his faith and decision

'By faith Moses, when he was come to years, refused to be called the son of Pharaoh's daughter; choosing rather to suffer affliction with the people of God, than to enjoy the pleasures of sin for a season; esteeming the reproach of Christ greater riches than the treasures in Egypt: for he had respect unto the recompence of the reward.' Hebrews 11:24–26
SUGGESTED FURTHER READING: Acts 7:17–38

Moses should be imitated by us. First, brethren, *we should have Moses' faith*. The things which Moses believed are true and therefore ought still to be believed. They are as important today as when he believed them; let us lay hold upon them and feel their practical bearings this very morning. Young men especially, I entreat you to believe in God and in his work of grace among his people, that you may be numbered with his chosen now and in the day of his appearing. Next, we must imitate Moses in this, that if we do believe *we must come out on the Lord's side*. Now that you have 'come to years,' do let it be seen on whose side you are. Let there be no doubt, no hesitation, no vacillation, but let those who see you in the house or in business know that you are on the Lord's side. Let me exhort you also to *see things in the eternal light*. Do not look at things in their bearings upon today, or tomorrow, or the next few years. Judge by eternity. For the present the good man may be a loser. You must look further than your foot. Take the measuring line of the sanctuary and use it when you judge of spiritual things. Note another important matter: I pray that you may *get into fellowship with Christ*. Oh to know Christ and love him, to have him to be your Saviour and then to feel that you can wear 'the reproach of Christ' as a chain of gold! This is a great help in the life of a tried child of God. Dear friend, if you are a believer in Christ, *give yourself up to God without reserve*: say, 'I will follow thee, my Lord, through flood or flame. I will follow thee up hill or down dale. I will follow wherever the Lord shall lead the way. I will follow at all cost and hazard.' Say this in your soul.

FOR MEDITATION: Meditate on Hebrews 11:23–28. The faith displayed by Moses' parents (v.23) was continued by his own preference (vv.24–26) and bore fruit in his dealings with Pharaoh (v.27) and the Passover (v.28).

SERMON NO. 2030

25 JUNE (1885)

The lowly King

'Rejoice greatly, O daughter of Zion; shout, O daughter of Jerusalem: behold, thy King cometh unto thee: he is just, and having salvation; lowly, and riding upon an ass, and upon a colt the foal of an ass.'
Zechariah 9:9
SUGGESTED FURTHER READING (Spurgeon): Matthew 11:25–30

Since the Lord Jesus Christ is so 'meek and lowly', poor, trembling, guilty one, you may come to him! You may come to him now! I was sitting the other night amongst some excellent friends, who, I suppose, were none of them rich and some of them poor. I am sure it never entered into my head to think how much money they owned, for I felt myself very much at home with them, until one of them remarked, 'You do not mind mixing with us poor folk?' Then I felt quite ashamed for myself that they should think it necessary to make such a remark. I was so much one with them that I felt honoured by having fellowship with them in the things of God and it troubled me that they should think I was doing anything remarkable in conversing with them. Dear friends, do not think hardly of any of us who are ministers of Christ; you will think hardly of us if you conceive that we think it a coming-down to associate with any of you! We are in heart and soul your brothers, bone of your bone, your truest friends whether you are rich or poor. We desire your good, for we are your servants for Christ's sake. Above all, do not think hardly of our Lord and Master by supposing that it will be a strange thing for him to come to your house or to your heart. It is his habit to forgive the guilty and renew the sinful. Come to him at once and he will accept you now. Jesus is exceedingly approachable. He is not hedged about with guards to keep off the poor or the sinful. Your room may be very humble; what cares he for that? He will come and hear your prayer.

FOR MEDITATION: The range of characters invited by the Lord Jesus Christ to come to him included fishermen (Mark 1:16–17), children (Mark 10:13–14), a rich ruler (Mark 10:21), a greedy tax collector (Luke 19:1–5), an immoral woman (John 4:16–18) and even a dead man (John 11:43–44)! He still makes wonderful promises to all who will take up his kind invitation (John 6:35,37).

SERMON NO. 1861

26 JUNE (1887)

Loving persuasion

'Persuading them concerning Jesus.' Acts 28:23
SUGGESTED FURTHER READING: Acts 18:1–17

Are we right trying to persuade men? Are not human hearts too hard to be broken by so feeble a hammer as our persuasion? Yes, I most solemnly believe they are: but that is not the question. 'What is the use of persuading them, if you know that they will not be won by your persuasion in and of itself?' Well, brethren, I feel safe in doing what Paul did. I will not stop to solve difficulties, but merely say, Paul persuaded, and so will I. 'Knowing therefore the terror of the Lord, we persuade men'. 'Oh,' says one, 'we may persuade awakened sinners, but not dead sinners!' But I reply that Paul persuaded these chief men of the Jews, some of whom never believed in Jesus, for their hearts were gross and their eyes were blinded. Paul persuaded them, though they were judicially blinded. He knew that they were living men and that they were possessed of reason, even though they had no grace, and so he appealed to what remained in them and he persuaded them. Again, I say, I will do what Paul did. But I know, as Paul also knew, that all the human persuasion in the world will fall short of the mark without divine power. I never dreamed that my persuasion was of the slightest avail without the Holy Spirit. If the Holy Spirit will cause the persuasion to reach the inward ear, then it will prevail and not else: if he will drive home the persuasion, so that it touches the heart which is encased in the fat of worldly pleasure, indifference, prejudice and pride, then men will yield and men will be persuaded indeed. But the Holy Spirit will do this! He has done it; he is doing it; he will do it; and therefore we persuade. Brothers, why should we not expect the Holy Spirit to display his power? We have sought it with fervent prayer.

FOR MEDITATION: (*Our Own Hymn Book,* no. 385 v.1—Philip Doddridge, 1755)

'Jesus, I love Thy charming name,
'Tis music to mine ear;
Fain would I sound it out so loud
That earth and heaven should hear.'

SERMON NO. 1970

27 JUNE (1886)

'The tender mercy of our God'

'Whereby the dayspring from on high visited us, to give light to them that sit in darkness and in the shadow of death, to guide our feet into the way of peace.' Luke 1:78–79

SUGGESTED FURTHER READING: Psalm 107:1–9

Imagine a caravan in the desert, which has lost its way and is famishing. The sun has long gone down and the darkness has caused every one's heart to droop. All around them is a waste of sand and an Egyptian darkness. There they must remain and die unless they can find the track. They feel themselves to be in a fearful case, for, hungry and thirsty, their soul faints in them. They cannot even sleep for fear. Heavier and heavier the night comes down and the damps are on the tents chilling the souls of the travellers. What is to be done? How they watch! Alas, no star comforts them! At last the watchmen cry, 'The morning cometh'. It breaks over the sea of sand and, what is better, reveals a heap which had been set up as a way-mark; the travellers have found the track. The 'dayspring' has saved them from swift destruction by discovering the way of peace. When the Lord Jesus Christ visits us, he actually brings light to our darkness, really leads into the way and makes that way a way of peace to us. Remember what the Lord has done for you. You did not know the way once and all the preaching in the world would not have made you know it, if Jesus had not by his Spirit visited you as 'the dayspring'. When you did know the way, you could not reach it by yourself: you saw it from a distance and could not enter upon it, but when Jesus came near, he actually guided your feet into that way. He put your 'feet upon a rock, and established' your goings. That way would have been to you a way of doubt, fear and hesitation, if the Lord had not so sweetly shone upon you that your road became a way of perfect peace. Peace in our text means prosperity, plenty, rest, joy. I ask you whether you have not found it so.

FOR MEDITATION: (*Our Own Hymn Book,* no. 912 v.5—Philip Doddridge, 1755)

'O long-expected day, begin;
Dawn on these realms of woe and sin:
Fain would we leave this weary road,
And sleep in death, to rest with God.'

SERMON NO. 1907

28 JUNE (1885)

Before sermon, at sermon, and after sermon

'Wherefore lay apart all filthiness and superfluity of naughtiness, and receive with meekness the engrafted word, which is able to save your souls. But be ye doers of the word, and not hearers only, deceiving your own selves.' James 1:21–22

SUGGESTED FURTHER READING: Matthew 13:1–23

We should endeavour to gather the most we can from the means of grace and not pluck at them at random. A farmer may feel that there will be sure to be some crop upon his land if he only seeds it, yet, if he is a wise man, he is not satisfied with a bare crop, but manures his land heavily and tills it well, that it may bring forth a large return to him, for in these times the largest harvest is no more than he needs. So, my brethren, let us so use the holy ordinance of preaching that we may extract the largest possible amount of gold from the ore. Let us so come into the solemn assembly that we may hope to meet with God there, for this is the chief end of our gathering together; let us so behave ourselves before coming, in coming and after coming to the sanctuary, that we may gain the greatest possible profit by our coming together. To hear the word of the Lord is often made by the Spirit of God to be life to dead souls and the most eminent means of further quickening to those who are already alive unto God. Let us not lose a grain of the blessing through our own fault. The word of the Lord is precious in these days; let us not trifle with it. First, let us note what to do *before sermon*: 'lay apart all filthiness and superfluity of naughtiness'. Secondly, let us learn how to behave *during sermon*: 'receive with meekness the engrafted word, which is able to save your souls.' And thirdly, here is the instruction for *after sermon*: 'be ye doers of the word, and not hearers only, deceiving your own selves.'

FOR MEDITATION: In Psalm 119 note how carefully the Psalmist put this into practice before hearing (vv.29, 37, 101), while hearing (vv.11, 15, 18, 103) and after hearing (vv.16, 32–35, 60, 106, 112) God's word. Let us seek God's help to go and do likewise.

SERMON NO. 1847

29 JUNE (1890)

Holy longings

'I opened my mouth, and panted: for I longed for thy commandments. Look thou upon me, and be merciful unto me, as thou usest to do unto those that love thy name. Order my steps in thy word: and let not any iniquity have dominion over me.' Psalm 119:131–133
SUGGESTED FURTHER READING: Romans 12:1–8

'*Order* my steps'. We wish to put the right foot foremost, but the right foot to move may not always be that which is called the right. The left foot may sometimes be the right and we must not take things for granted. We wish to put down our right foot in the right place, at the right time, with the right degree of force and turned in the right direction. A great deal of holiness depends upon order, punctuality and proportion. If order is not heaven's *first* law, it is certainly one of its laws, and proportion is another. Some men's lives are out of perspective. Do you remember Hogarth's caricature of a picture without perspective wherein a man appears to be fishing in a river, but is really standing far away from it; a sparrow in a tree looks like a huge eagle and a man on the top of a hill is borrowing a light from a candle held out of the window of a house down below on the other side of the river. Without perspective good drawing is impossible, and without proportion a complete life is impossible. A man may be, in many points, a good man; you may say of him, bit by bit, 'Yes, *that* is good, and *that* is good'; yet he may have so much of one virtue that it may become a vice, and he may have so little of another virtue that it may be a grave defect. We can never attain to the right proportion of the virtues unless the Lord himself arranges them in order for us. Do not tell me it is easy to be holy: you want not only the different graces, but all these in due order and fit measure. O Lord, help us! Order our steps.

FOR MEDITATION: (*Our Own Hymn Book*, no. 119 song 2 v.2—Isaac Watts, 1719)
  'Oh send Thy Spirit down, to write
  Thy law upon my heart!
  Nor let my tongue indulge deceit,
  Nor act the liar's part.'

SERMON NO. 2151

30 JUNE (1889)

God's own gospel call

'Incline your ear, and come unto me: hear, and your soul shall live; and I will make an everlasting covenant with you, even the sure mercies of David.' Isaiah 55:3
SUGGESTED FURTHER READING: Revelation 22:16–21

'How can I come to God?' says one. Come to him at least *by thinking much of him*. At present God is not in all your thoughts. Some of you are busy just now with sightseeing, but you seek not a sight of God: should it be so? Others of you are busy in moneymaking; you go out to business early and come home late, and all those hours you are as little mindful of heaven as if there were no God at all. We have not much doctrinal atheism abroad, but we are drenched with practical atheism. The nations forget God. The Lord bids you turn your face Godward and seek after him. Consider eternity, how you will spend it and what it must be for you if you pass into it without God. When you have come to him in thought, then *come by your desires*. The son in the far-off country began to return to his father's house, where there was 'bread enough and to spare,' before he had put a foot on the ground to go thither; his heart was on the road before his feet. If you feel as if you could not come to God anyhow else, come by desire at least; desire to be reconciled to God, long to become his child, hunger to taste of his love. This is a true coming. Come to God *by confession of sin*. You have lived hitherto without him; confess that neglect. You have thought that repentance and faith might safely be put off to a more convenient season, and thus you have given your God a contemptuous putting-off. Confess the wrong you have done in this. You have violated the law, for you have not loved the Lord with all your heart, with all your soul, with all your strength, and with all your mind. Besides this, you have broken every command. Thus have you insulted your Maker; yet come to him with filial sorrow, and say, 'Father, I have sinned'. Come to God in humble, believing prayer; ask him to save you and believe that he 'that asketh receiveth'. What! Will you not do that?

FOR MEDITATION: (*Our Own Hymn Book*, no. 494 v.2—Joseph Humphreys, 1743)
   'God loved the church, and gave His Son to drink the cup of wrath:
   And Jesus says, He'll cast out none that come to Him by faith.'

SERMON NO. 2092

1 JULY (1888)

David dancing before the ark because of his election

'And David said unto Michal, It was before the LORD, which chose me before thy father, and before all his house, to appoint me ruler over the people of the LORD, over Israel: therefore will I play before the LORD.'
2 Samuel 6:21
SUGGESTED FURTHER READING: 2 Timothy 2:1–10

David had a missionary spirit, and often does it flame out in his Psalms. They say that those of us who believe that we are the chosen of God are narrow and selfish. We will prove the contrary by our evangelistic zeal. The greatest missionaries that have ever lived have believed in God's choice of them and, instead of this doctrine leading to inaction, it has ever been an irresistible motive power and it will be so again. It was the secret energy of the Reformation. It is because free grace has been put into the background that we have seen so little done in many places. It is in God's hand the great force which can stir the church of God to its utmost depth. It may not work superficial revivals, but for deep work it is invaluable. Side by side with the blood of Christ it is the world's hope. How can men say that the doctrine of distinguishing grace makes men careless about souls? Did they never hear of the evangelical band which was called the Clapham Sect? Was Whitefield a man who cared nothing for the salvation of the people? He who flew like a seraph throughout England and America unceasingly proclaiming the grace of God, was he selfish? Yet he was distinctly a free-grace preacher. Did Jonathan Edwards have no concern for the souls of others? Oh how he wept, cried and warned them of the wrath to come! Time would fail me to tell of the lovers of men who have been lovers of this truth. This doctrine first makes sure to the man himself that he is the Lord's and then fills him with a desire to see myriads brought to bow before the Lord of love. Oh that the Lord would speedily accomplish the number of his elect!

FOR MEDITATION: (*Our Own Hymn Book*, no. 219 v.1—George Keith, 1787)
    'In songs of sublime adoration and praise,
    Ye pilgrims to Zion who press,
    Break forth, and extol the great Ancient of days,
    His rich and distinguishing grace.'

SERMON NO. 2031

2 JULY (UNDATED MIDSUMMER SERMON)

The Lord's Supper: a remembrance of Jesus

'This do in remembrance of me.' Luke 22:19
SUGGESTED FURTHER READING: Matthew 26:20–29

Whether or not I may come to the Lord's table must depend upon whether I know the Lord Jesus, or do not know him. If I am a stranger to him, I may not come, for I may only come to remember him, and I cannot come to remember him if I do not know him; it would be a profanation of this blessed institution for any man to draw near to the table who does not know Christ already. O sirs, this is no saving ordinance: it was never meant to be; its intent relates only to those who are saved. To know Jesus Christ is eternal life and, as you may not come without that knowledge, it is clear that you may not come unless you are saved. If any of you dream that your participation in your last moments in what is called 'the sacrament' will save you, you are under a deep delusion. You may as well trust to the incantations of a witch as to the performance of any ceremony whatever, by whomsoever, in order to convey salvation to you. Salvation is by faith in Jesus Christ and that is not wrought by the bodily act of swallowing bread and wine. 'Ye must be born again' and that is not effected by material substances, however consecrated; it is the work of the Holy Spirit. Until you have believed in Jesus, known him and his power within you and come to personal dealings with him, instead of getting a blessing from the ordinance, you would eat and drink condemnation to yourselves, 'not discerning the Lord's body.' You are not capable of discerning that body if you have no faith. Let every 'man examine himself' as to his knowledge of our Lord, 'and so let him eat of that bread and drink of that cup.' If you do not know him you cannot remember him and, therefore, hands off from the tokens of remembrance.

FOR MEDITATION: (*Our Own Hymn Book*, no. 555 vv.4&5—Isaac Watts, 1706)
  'My soul looks back to see the burdens Thou didst bear,
  When hanging on the cursèd tree, and hopes her guilt was there.
  Believing, we rejoice to see the curse remove;
  We bless the Lamb with cheerful voice, and sing His bleeding love.'

SERMON NO. 2038

3 JULY (1887)

The blood shed for many

'For this is my blood of the new testament, which is shed for many for the remission of sins.' Matthew 26:28
SUGGESTED FURTHER READING: Acts 2:22–42

Our blessed Saviour would have us hold his death in great reverence: it is to be our chief memory. Both the emblems of the Lord's Supper set forth the Saviour's death. This peculiarly Christian ordinance teaches nothing if it does not teach this. Christ's death for men is the great doctrine of the church. We profess ourselves partakers of the merit of his death when we come to this table; our Lord's death is then remembered, shown, declared, testified and trusted in. Evidently the Lord Jesus means us to treat the fact of his death as a truth to be made pre-eminently prominent: he would not have instituted an ordinance specially to remind us of the shedding of his blood, if he had not regarded it as the forefront of his whole earthly career. The other ordinance of our holy faith also sets forth our Lord's death. Are we not 'buried with him by baptism into death'? Is not baptism an emblem of his being immersed beneath the waves of sorrow and death? Baptism shows us that participation in Christ's suffering by which we begin to live; the Lord's Supper shows us that participation in Christ's suffering by which that life is sustained. Both institutions point to his death. Besides, beloved, we know from Holy Scripture that this doctrine of the death of Christ is the very core of Christianity. Leave out the cross and you have killed the religion of Jesus. Atonement by the blood of Jesus is not an arm of Christian truth; it is the heart of it. Even as the Lord said of the animal, 'the blood of it is for the life thereof', so is it true of the gospel; the sacrificial death of Jesus is the vital point of our profession. I know nothing of Christianity without the blood of Christ. No teaching is healthy which throws the cross into the background.

FOR MEDITATION: (*Our Own Hymn Book,* no. 296 v.5—Horatius Bonar, 1856)
  'The ever-blessed Son of God
  Went up to Calvary for me:
  There paid my debt, there bore my load
  In His own body on the tree.'

SERMON NO. 1971

4 JULY (PREACHED 12 JULY 1885)

Coming judgment of the secrets of men

'The day when God shall judge the secrets of men by Jesus Christ according to my gospel.' Romans 2:16
SUGGESTED FURTHER READING (Spurgeon): Revelation 20:11–15

We must preach the coming of the Lord and preach it somewhat more than we have done, because it is the driving power of the gospel. Too many have kept back these truths and thus the bone has been taken out of the arm of the gospel. Its point has been broken; its edge has been blunted. The doctrine of judgment to come is the power by which men are to be aroused. There is another life; the Lord will come a second time; judgment will arrive; the wrath of God will be revealed. Where this is not preached, I am bold to say the gospel is not preached. It is absolutely necessary to the preaching of the gospel of Christ that men be warned as to what will happen if they continue in their sins. Ho, ho, sir surgeon, you are too delicate to tell the man that he is ill! You hope to heal the sick without their knowing it. You therefore flatter them; and what happens? They laugh at you; they dance upon their own graves. At last they die! Your delicacy is cruelty; your flatteries are poisons; you are a murderer. Shall we keep men in a fool's paradise? Shall we lull them into soft slumbers from which they will awake in hell? Are we to become helpers of their damnation by our smooth speeches? In the name of God we will not. It becomes every true minister of Christ to cry aloud and spare not, for God has set a day in which he will 'judge the secrets of men by Jesus Christ according to my gospel.' As surely as Paul's gospel was true the judgment will come. Wherefore flee to Jesus this day, O sinners. O saints, come hide yourselves again beneath the crimson canopy of the atoning sacrifice, that you may be now ready to welcome your descending Lord and escort him to his judgment-seat.

FOR MEDITATION: (*Our Own Hymn Book*, no. 364 v.3—Reginald Heber, 1811; Thomas Cotterhill, 1815)
   'The Lord shall come! a dreadful form,
   With rainbow wreath and robes of storm;
   On cherub wings, and wings of wind,
   Appointed Judge of all mankind.'

SERMON NO. 1849

5 JULY (1885)

The looking-glass

'For if any be a hearer of the word, and not a doer, he is like unto a man beholding his natural face in a glass: for he beholdeth himself, and goeth his way, and straightway forgetteth what manner of man he was. But whoso looketh into the perfect law of liberty, and continueth therein, he being not a forgetful hearer, but a doer of the work, this man shall be blessed in his deed.' James 1:23–25

SUGGESTED FURTHER READING: Exodus 25:10–22

The picture I have in my mind's eye at this moment is that of the cherubim upon the mercy-seat: these are models for us. Their standing is upon the golden mercy-seat and our standing-place is the propitiation of our Lord: there is the resting-place of our feet and, like the cherubs, we are joined thereto and therefore continue therein. They stand with their eyes looking downward upon the mercy-seat, as if they desired to look into the perfect law of God which was treasured within the ark: even so do we look through the atonement of our Lord Jesus, which is to us as pure gold like transparent glass, and we behold the law, as a 'perfect law of liberty,' in the person of our Mediator. Like the cherubim, we are in happy company and like them, we look towards each other, by mutual love. Our common standing is the atonement, our common study is the law in the person of Christ and our common posture is that of angels with outstretched wings prepared to fly at the Master's bidding. Oh that we might in this sense be as the cherubim and like them abide in the secret-place of the Most High, where the light is the light of God and the glory is the Divine Presence! We are not to look casually at the Word as though it were a mere looking glass, but we are to gaze earnestly upon it as our law under the new covenant. As the apostles stooped down and looked into the sepulchre, so are we to search diligently into the blessed law of the Lord and delight in it after the inner man.

FOR MEDITATION: The privilege of looking into God's saving gospel was not only suggested by the posture of model cherubim, but was stressed by the prophets and is still sought for even by angels (1 Peter 1:10–12). Do you share their eagerness about such things (1 Peter 2:2)?

SERMON NO. 1848

6 JULY (1890)

The iniquity of our holy things

'And thou shalt make a plate of pure gold, and grave upon it, like the engravings of a signet, HOLINESS TO THE LORD.*' 'And it shall be upon Aaron's forehead, that Aaron may bear the iniquity of the holy things, which the children of Israel shall hallow in all their holy gifts; and it shall be always upon his forehead, that they may be accepted before the* LORD.*'* Exodus 28:36,38

SUGGESTED FURTHER READING: Hebrews 7:23–8:12

This high priest was altogether given up to his people. He has a heart: his people's names are on the breast-plate which covers it. He has shoulders: his people's names are written on his shoulder-pieces and thus he lends them his power. He has feet: there were no sandals for the priest; he ministered barefooted before God. Why? Because it is the only way in which the Lord can be worshipped, according to his command, 'put off thy shoes from off thy feet, for the place whereon thou standest is holy ground.' Christ has given to us the heart of his love, the shoulders of his strength, the feet of his humiliation. He 'loved me, and gave himself for me.' But, observe that his head is left. He must give us his head. The power to think is supposed to dwell in the temples and the forehead. The golden plate covered Aaron's forehead from temple to temple and it was always conspicuous there. Thus Christ has given up his thought, his judgment, his mind, his every faculty to his people. He is all ours. The high priest reserved nothing of himself: he gave all of himself to all his people. Christ is ours. From head to foot he serves us personally and constantly. The point I want to bring out most prominently is that the high priest bore 'the iniquity of the holy things'. You and I have been guilty of iniquity in our holy things, but here is our joy, that Jesus bears it all. Putting on his heavenly mitre, marked as 'HOLINESS TO JEHOVAH', he bears for us the iniquity. 'The LORD hath laid on him the iniquity of us all.' He was made 'sin for us, who knew no sin'. It is a wonderful mystery, the transference of sin and of merit: it staggers human reason; faith alone apprehends it.

FOR MEDITATION: (*Our Own Hymn Book*, no. 325 v.3—Augustus M. Toplady, 1771)
   'For all that come to God by Him, salvation He demands;
   Points to their names upon His breast, and spreads His wounded hands.'

SERMON NO. 2153

7 JULY (1889)

Foundation work

'And the king commanded, and they brought great stones, costly stones, and hewed stones, to lay the foundation of the house.' 1 Kings 5:17
SUGGESTED FURTHER READING: 1 Corinthians 3:10–17

Lay the foundation well; look to that part which is out of sight, because in this way you will secure the superstructure. There was a bit of a flaw in the foundation, but nobody saw it, for the builder covered it up and ran up the whole concern as quickly as possible. The walls were built well. It seemed clear that the fault down below was of no consequence whatever and, as it had a little cheapened the underground construction, was it not so much the better? How long was this the case? Well, the next year nothing happened: time passed, then an ugly crack came down the wall. Had there been an earthquake? No. Had a cyclone beaten upon the work? No: the weather was the same as usual. What was the cause of that gaping space which marred the beauty of the building and threatened to bring it down? It was that blunder long ago: that underground neglect produced the terrible mischief above, which would involve a great expense and perhaps render it needful to take all the building down. That which was out of sight did not always remain out of mind; it only needed time to produce a dangerous settlement. If certain men had been soundly converted at first, backsliding and apostasy would not have followed. If certain preachers had done their work in the church of God better in years past, those sad departures from the truth, which now vex the saints, would not have occurred. If today you do not teach your children the gospel fully and clearly, the evil may not be seen in your present classes, nor possibly even in this generation, but children's children will bear the impress of the slight work done at this hour. Years may be needed for the development of the full result of a false doctrine.

FOR MEDITATION: (*Our Own Hymn Book,* no. 732 v.1—George Keith, 1787)
'How firm a foundation, ye saints of the Lord,
Is laid for your faith in His excellent word!
What more can He say than to you He hath said,
You who unto Jesus for refuge have fled?'

SERMON NO. 2094

8 JULY (1888)

The charge of the angel

'The angel of the Lord by night opened the prison doors, and brought them forth, and said, Go, stand and speak in the temple to the people all the words of this life.' Acts 5:19–20

SUGGESTED FURTHER READING: Acts 10:1–33

Do you not think that the angels must often wonder at us? When they see men eager upon politics and negligent of souls, are they not astonished? Do they never say, 'We wish the great Lord would let us go and speak to perishing souls. We would speak with all our hearts'? Do they not sometimes say to one another, 'What are these men at? Do they disdain their high calling? God has given to them the great privilege of preaching and teaching his holy word, but they do not care to do it. They speak as if they were half asleep. Where is their zeal for God, their love to men, their earnestness for Christ'? Brethren, these holy spirits must feel ashamed of us! True, they are our servants and bear us up in their hands, lest we dash our feet against a stone, but must they not sometimes wish that we were stronger on our feet and more eager to dash our hands against the enemies of God? We are carried as invalids, when we ought to be fighting like champions. I charge you by the angels of God, who are not permitted to touch this holy work, 'Preach the word; be instant in season, out of season'. Preach with a vigour worthy of the divine exercise. Preach the word in some such style as you would expect from those who are bought with the precious blood of Jesus. So have I spoken to you who are men. As for you, angel of God, you have opened the prison doors and set free the men of God, but you must now go back to him that sent you. Bright spirit, I dare not offer you my pulpit. Feeble as I am, I must do the preaching. Oh that your Lord and mine may help me and enable me to make full proof of my ministry! Farewell, angel of God, go your way!

FOR MEDITATION: Angels long to look into the gospel message we have been commanded to preach (1 Peter 1:12), but their active role is one of planning evangelistic opportunities, not of evangelism itself (Acts 8:26; 11:13–14). Perhaps we should leave more of the organising to them and concentrate more on getting on with the preaching!

SERMON NO. 2032

9 JULY (PREACHED 14 JULY 1889)

The Lamb in glory

'In the midst of the throne and of the four beasts, and in the midst of the elders, stood a Lamb as it had been slain, having seven horns and seven eyes.' Revelation 5:6
SUGGESTED FURTHER READING: Revelation 14:1–12

Let us look at the peculiar marks of him, and we see that he has 'seven horns and seven eyes'. His power is equal to his vigilance and these are equal to all the emergencies brought about by the opening of the seven seals of the Book of Providence. When plagues break forth, who is to defend us? Behold the seven horns. If the unexpected occurs, who is to forewarn us? Behold the seven eyes. Every now and then some foolish person brings out a pamphlet stuffed with horrors which are going to happen in a year or two. The whole of it is about as valuable as the Norwood Gipsy's Book of Fate, but still, if it were all true that these prophecy-mongers tell us, we are not afraid; for the Lamb has seven horns and will meet every difficulty by his own power, having already foreseen it by his own wisdom. The Lamb is the answer to the enigma of providence. Providence is a riddle, but Jesus explains it all. During the first centuries, the Church of God was given up to martyrdom: every possible torment and torture was exercised upon the followers of Christ: what could be God's meaning in all this? What but the glory of the Lamb? And now today the Lord seems to leave his Church to wander into all kinds of errors: false doctrines are, in some quarters, fearfully paramount. What does this mean? I do not know, but the Lamb knows, for he sees with seven eyes. As a Lamb, as our Saviour, God and man, he understands all and has the clues of all labyrinths in his hands. He has power to meet every difficulty and wisdom to see through every embarrassment. We should cast out fear and give ourselves wholly up to worship.

FOR MEDITATION: (*Our Own Hymn Book,* no. 412 vv.4&5—Isaac Watts, 1709)
> 'Eternal Father, who shall look into Thy secret will?
> Who but the Son shall take that book, and open every seal?
> He shall fulfil Thy great decrees, the Son deserves it well;
> Lo! in His hand the sovereign keys of heaven, and death, and hell.'

SERMON NO. 2095

10 JULY (1887)

A bit of history for old and young

'And he blessed Joseph, and said, God, before whom my fathers Abraham and Isaac did walk, the God which fed me all my life long unto this day, the Angel which redeemed me from all evil, bless the lads.'
Genesis 48:15–16
SUGGESTED FURTHER READING: Proverbs 4:1–19

Those of us who are parents are bound to do our best, that our children may be partakers with us of the divine inheritance. As Joseph took Ephraim and Manasseh to see their aged grandfather, let us bring our children where blessings may be expected. Let us be careful of the company into which we take our sons and daughters. Let us never conduct them where they may get harm rather than benefit. Carefully, lovingly, wisely, using no undue severity, let us guide them into likely places for the divine benediction and encourage them to seek the blessing for themselves by the fact that their parents are seeking it for them. The father who will not seize every opportunity of getting a blessing for his Ephraim and Manasseh is not likely to see the lads seeking the blessing for themselves. Especially should this care be taken by parents who are growing rich, whose offspring will be tempted by this very fact to seek grander society than the poor people of God can afford them. I doubt not that these two sons of Egypt's prime minister were exposed to exceedingly great temptations. As the sons of a very wealthy and distinguished parent, their tastes might lie in an Egyptian direction. I believe that they were nevertheless greatly swayed to the right side and led to worship the God of Abraham, Isaac and Jacob by the zeal of the father, Joseph, and by the recollection of the benediction of their dying grandfather. There is no trace of their having inclined to the religion of the king and the nobles of Egypt, but they adhered to the faith of their father. Oh that all the descendants of Puritan fathers might be steadfast to the pure truth of God in these evil days!

FOR MEDITATION: (*Our Own Hymn Book,* no. 214 v.4—Joseph Addison, 1712)
  'When in the slippery paths of youth with heedless steps I ran,
  Thine arm unseen conveyed me safe, and led me up to man.'

SERMON NO. 1972

11 JULY (1886)

A seasonable exhortation

'Wherefore gird up the loins of your mind, be sober, and hope to the end for the grace that is to be brought unto you at the revelation of Jesus Christ.' 1 Peter 1:13
SUGGESTED FURTHER READING: Luke 12:35–44

'Gird up the loins of your mind'. My brethren, that certainly teaches us, in the first place, *earnestness*. A man going to work tucks up his sleeves and tightens his robes. He has something to do which demands all his strength and, therefore, he cannot afford to have anything hanging loosely about him, to hinder him. We brace ourselves for a supreme effort: the Christian life is always such. We must always be in earnest if we would be disciples of our earnest Lord. Does it not also mean *preparedness*? When a man has girt his garments about him, he is ready for his work. A true believer should be ready for suffering or service, ready, indeed, for anything. A servant standing with his loins girt signifies that whatever the message may be from his Master, he is ready to deliver it; whatever the errand, he is ready to run upon it. He only needs the word and he will not hesitate, but will obey at once. This is the position which Christian people should always occupy; you should be earnestly prepared for the will of the Lord, let it be what it may. The future is to you unknown, but you are in a fit condition to meet it, whatever form it may assume. But the figure means more than this, does it not? It means *determination* and hearty resolution. The man who girds himself up for a work means that he is resolved to do it at once. He has made up his mind; no shilly-shallying remains with him, no hesitancy, no questioning, no holding back: he is set upon his course and is not to be moved from it. You will never get to heaven, any of you, by playing at religion. There will be no climbing the hill of the Lord without effort, no going to glory without the violence of faith.

FOR MEDITATION: (*Our Own Hymn Book*, no. 678 v.1—Isaac Watts, 1709)

'Stand up, my soul, shake off thy fears,
And gird the gospel armour on;
March to the gates of endless joy,
Where thy great Captain-Saviour's gone.'

SERMON NO. 1909

12 JULY (1888)

Driving out the Canaanites and their iron chariots

'For thou shalt drive out the Canaanites, though they have iron chariots, and though they be strong.' Joshua 17:18
SUGGESTED FURTHER READING (Spurgeon): Ephesians 6:10–20

Canaan is hardly a full type of heaven. It may be used so in a modified sense, but it is a far better emblem of that state and condition of soul in which a man is found when he has become a believer and by believing has entered into rest, but not into an absolutely perfect deliverance from sin. He has come to take possession of the covenant heritage, but finds the Canaanite of sin and evil still in the land, both in the form of original sin within and of temptation from without. Before he can fully enjoy his privileges he must drive out his sins. It is absolutely needful, before he can experience the blessings of the covenant of grace to the full, that he should contend with the iniquities and evils which are within him and around him. He must drive out the various tribes of enemies which, for a long time, have been dwellers in the land of his nature. No doubt, many young Christians think that, when they are converted, the warfare is all over. No, the battle has just begun. You have not come to the winning-post: you have only come to the starting-point. You have entered upon the land in which you will have to fight, wrestle, weep and pray until you get the victory. That victory will be yours, but you will have to agonize to obtain it. He that has brought you into this condition will not fail you nor forsake you, but, at the same time, not without strong contentions and earnest strivings will you be able to win your inheritance. Be not deluded with the idea that you may sit down at your ease, for the very reverse will happen to the true heir of heaven.

FOR MEDITATION: (*Our Own Hymn Book*, no. 672 v.6—Charles Wesley, 1749)
  'From strength to strength go on,
  Wrestle, and fight, and pray,
  Tread all the powers of darkness down,
  And win the well-fought day.'

N.B. A footnote indicates that 'On this occasion several soldiers from Woolwich were baptized in the Tabernacle.'

SERMON NO. 2049

13 JULY (1890)

The pastor's joy and confidence

'I thank my God upon every remembrance of you, always in every prayer of mine for you all making request with joy, for your fellowship in the gospel from the first day until now; being confident of this very thing, that he which hath begun a good work in you will perform it until the day of Jesus Christ.' Philippians 1:3–6

SUGGESTED FURTHER READING: Philippians 3:12–4:1

Paul says that God 'will perform it until the day of Jesus Christ'. Shall we be absolutely perfect until then? I think not. Perfection in a modified sense is possible through divine grace, but not absolute perfection. Old Master Trapp very well says a Christian may be perfect, but not perfectly perfect. Perfection in the Scriptural use of it is not at all what those make of it who boast of perfection in the flesh. A child is perfect when it is newly born; there is every toe on the tiny foot; its eyes, ears, nose and other organs are all there, but if you tell me that a child is a perfect man, I smile at you. So the Christian may be perfect as to all his parts, 'perfect and entire, wanting nothing', and yet he may not be perfect as to development by a very long way. One says, 'We shall be perfect at death, shall we not?' It is not so written here; but he 'will perform it *until the day of Jesus Christ*'. We may be perfect in death as to the moral and spiritual nature, but a man has a body as well as a soul and it needs both parts to make the perfect man. While the worms are devouring the body, the man is not yet perfect. He will be perfect as to his whole manhood when the Lord shall come, 'the trumpet shall sound, and the dead shall be raised incorruptible'. Paul delights to make the Christian leap over that little rivulet called death and swallow up the thought of dissolution in the far grander fact of the coming of the Lord. The second advent ought to be much more on our minds than the hour of our death. The Lord will perform the sacrifice which he has begun, until he perfects it in the day when the Lord Jesus Christ shall receive his church to himself.

FOR MEDITATION: The Christian should aim at perfection in holiness (2 Corinthians 7:1), faith (1 Thessalonians 3:10), good works (2 Timothy 3:17; Hebrews 13:21) and love (1 John 2:5; 4:17–18), but those considered to 'be perfect' (Philippians 3:15) are to have the mind of Paul and press on towards the goal of perfect perfection (Philippians 3:12).

SERMON NO. 2154

14 JULY (1887)

'Eyes right'

'Let thine eyes look right on, and let thine eylids look straight before thee.' Proverbs 4:25
SUGGESTED FURTHER READING: Luke 7:18-23

If you begin to look two ways at a time, you will miss the Lord Jesus, who is your way. Under the Jewish law no man who had a squint was allowed to be a priest. He is described as one who had 'a blemish in his eye'. I wish they would make a similar law with regard to spiritual sight in preachers nowadays, for certain of them are sadly cross-eyed. When they preach free grace, they squint fearfully towards free-will; if they look to the atonement, they must see in it more of man than of Christ. See how they look to Moses and to Darwin, to revelation and to speculation! A great many people want to be saved, but they squint: they look a little towards sin, the flesh and the world, and they make provision for personal gain and personal ease. In this case they fail to see Christ's strait and narrow way of the denial of self and the crucifixion of the flesh. If you would have salvation, 'Let thine eyes look right on, and let thine eyelids look straight before thee.' Look not a little this way and a little that way, or you will never run aright. 'I could believe that I was a Christian,' says one, 'if I felt more happy. I could trust Christ if I felt my nature changed.' That is a squint which ruins the faith-look. That is trying to look two ways at once. You cannot do it: it will ruin you. It would spoil the beauty of the sweetest countenance if we could use our eyes to look otherwise than straight on. We have some friends who, if they wish to see us, look over there and yet we are not there. Avoid this spiritual blemish; it has no advantages. 'Let thine eyes look right on'. Look to Christ alone, to him as your whole salvation.

FOR MEDITATION: (*Our Own Hymn Book*, no. 527 v.5—Jared Bell Waterbury, 1844)
  'Wretched, ruined, helpless soul,
  To a Saviour's blood apply;
  He alone can make thee whole,
  Fly to Jesus, sinner, fly.'

SERMON NO. 2058

15 JULY (1888)

Plain directions to those who would be saved from sin

'Stand in awe, and sin not: commune with your own heart upon your bed, and be still. Selah. Offer the sacrifices of righteousness, and put your trust in the LORD.' Psalm 4:4–5
SUGGESTED FURTHER READING: Lamentations 3:25–33

'Commune with your own heart upon your bed, and be still.' Do you know what that means? There comes a time with men whom God is saving when all grows quiet within them. Their old pleasures and desires are hushed; the voice of the outside world is still and they hear in the silence of their souls the 'still small voice' of conscience. Oh that you were at this moment still enough to hear that warning note! Memory also commences her rehearsals: it tells of the past and brings forgotten things before the soul. Oh that all of you would remember that God requires that which is past. Best of all, God speaks in the soul. It was at night, when young Samuel was on his bed, that the Lord said to him, 'Samuel, Samuel', and it is when the heart at last has grown still that God's voice of mercy is heard calling to the man by name. Oh that in such a case you may have grace to answer, 'Speak, LORD; for thy servant heareth'! I beseech you, give yourselves space for thought, before thought becomes the worm of eternal misery to you. Remember, before you hear that voice from heaven which spoke to the rich man in hell and said to him, 'Son, remember'. You slaves of fashion and frivolity, think, I pray you! You serfs of daily money-grubbing, rest a while and hear what God the Lord shall speak to you! You can hardly hear the great bell of St Paul's when the traffic is thundering around, but it sounds solemnly in the stillness of night. We who live in the more remote suburbs hear Big Ben of Westminster at night, but we seldom note it amid the stir and noise of the day. Do give an opportunity for the eternal voices to pierce the clamours of the hour.

FOR MEDITATION: (*Our Own Hymn Book*, no. 525 v.4—John Newton, 1779)
   'Lord, prepare us by Thy grace! Soon we must resign our breath!
   And our souls be called to pass through the iron gate of death:
   Let us now our day improve, listen to the gospel-voice;
   Seek the things that are above, scorn the world's pretended joys.'

SERMON NO. 2033

16 JULY (PREACHED 18 JULY 1889)

Faith's firm resolve

'I will go in the strength of the Lord GOD: I will make mention of thy righteousness, even of thine only.' Psalm 71:16
SUGGESTED FURTHER READING: Psalm 35:22–28

Bear your testimony to the righteousness of God in *providence*. Stand to it that the Lord never does wrong. He is never mistaken; whatever he ordains is and must be unquestionably right. Bear witness, next, to his righteousness in *salvation*, that he does not save without an atonement, that he does not put away sin without being strictly just, that he does by no means spare the guilty, but has laid on Christ that which was due to human sin, 'that he might be just, and the justifier of him which believeth'. Go on to tell everybody that the righteousness which saves you is the righteousness of God, not your own righteousness. There is no such thing as human righteousness: the two worlds make up a contradiction. Any righteousness that you could gain by your own works would be 'filthy rags' at the best; filthy rags are not righteousness. We have no personal merit, but are justified by imputed righteousness. Make mention of the righteousness of Christ, which covers you from head to foot.

> 'Jesus, Thy blood and righteousness
> My beauty are, my glorious dress;
> Midst flaming worlds, in these arrayed,
> With joy shall I lift up my head.'

Declare the righteousness of God *as to a future state*. Declare that whatever Scripture speaks of the ungodly is true and that God is righteous in it. Never mind the cavils and inventions of this present age: God's character can never be harmed by these dreamers. Stand by your God and you may rest assured that time shall never change the essential truth that he is a holy and righteous God and will justify his ways to men.

FOR MEDITATION: God's righteousness benefits those who are righteous in Christ. He knows their way (Psalm 1:6), blesses them (Psalm 5:12), looks upon them (Psalm 34:15), upholds them (Psalm 37:17) and loves them (Psalm 146:8). He is their 'righteous Father' (John 17:25) who will reward them as 'the righteous judge' (2 Timothy 4:8). Are you one of them?

SERMON NO. 2164

17 JULY (1887)

God's nearness to us

'Though he be not far from every one of us.' Acts 17:27
SUGGESTED FURTHER READING: Psalm 119:145–152

All through history God has been familiar with man. He has spoken to him in various ways, but principally through chosen men. One after another he has raised up prophets and by their warning voices he has pleaded with men and invited them to seek his face. His own voice might have caused dismay and distance, and so he has used human voices, that he might come nearer to the heart. All the history of the chosen nation, as we read it in the Old Testament, reveals the nearness of Jehovah; whatever we read upon the page, we know that within, above, or behind it, the Lord is near, even when he appears to have hidden himself. In these latter days, the Lord has come nearer to us still, for he has 'spoken unto us by his Son'. The Son of God became the Friend of sinners: could he come nearer than that? 'The Word was made flesh, and dwelt among us, (and we beheld his glory)'. Bone of our bone and flesh of our flesh is the Christ, yet he is very God of very God. In him God is next-of-kin to man and manhood is brought near to the eternal throne. Christ Jesus is God and man in one person and thus the closest union is formed between God and man. Verily, verily, the Lord God is 'not far from' each one of us in his own dear Son. Today, though Jesus has gone up on high, the Spirit of God abides in the midst of the church and thus again the Lord is near. The Comforter is at work still; the Convincer still presses upon man's conscience sin, righteousness and judgment to come. Still does the Holy Spirit work with the Word of God, directing his ministers so to speak that their hearers shall perceive a personality and pointedness in the word delivered. Oh, you that hear the gospel, be sure of this, 'that the kingdom of God is come nigh unto you' in a very special sense! I may say of you with an emphasis, that he is 'not far from' any of you, and you are 'not far from the kingdom'.

FOR MEDITATION: (*Our Own Hymn Book,* no. 185 v.4—Isaac Watts, 1719)
   'Oh wondrous knowledge, deep, and high:
   Where can a creature hide?
   Within Thy circling arms I lie,
   Beset on every side.'

SERMON NO. 1973

18 JULY (1886)

The heart of the gospel

'Now then we are ambassadors for Christ, as though God did beseech you by us: we pray you in Christ's stead, be ye reconciled to God. For he hath made him to be sin for us, who knew no sin; that we might be made the righteousness of God in him.' 2 Corinthians 5:20–21

SUGGESTED FURTHER READING: 1 Thessalonians 1:1–10

I have found by long experience that nothing touches the heart like the cross of Christ; when the heart is touched and wounded by the two-edged sword of the law, nothing heals its wounds like the balm which flows from the pierced heart of Jesus. The cross is life to the spiritually dead. There is an old legend which can have no literal truth in it, but, if it be regarded as a parable, it is then most instructive. They say that when the Empress Helena was searching for the true cross they dug deep at Jerusalem and found the three crosses of Calvary buried in the soil. Which out of the three crosses was the actual cross upon which Jesus died they could not tell, except by certain tests. So they brought a corpse and laid it on one of the crosses, but there was neither life nor motion. When the same dead body touched another of the crosses it lived and then they said, 'This is the true cross.' When we see men quickened, converted and sanctified by the doctrine of the substitutionary sacrifice, we may justly conclude that it is the true doctrine of atonement. I have not known men made to live to God and holiness except by the doctrine of the death of Christ on man's behalf. Hearts of stone that never beat with life before have been turned to flesh through the Holy Spirit causing them to know this truth. A sacred tenderness has visited the obstinate when they have heard of Jesus crucified for them. Those who have lain at hell's dark door, wrapped about with a sevenfold death-shade, even upon them has a great light shone. The story of the great Lover of the souls of men who gave himself for their salvation is still in the hand of the Holy Spirit the greatest of all forces in the realm of mind.

FOR MEDITATION: Christ crucified is an offence to many (1 Corinthians 1:23; Galatians 5:11), but to all who trust him, Christ crucified represents power (1 Corinthians 1:17–18) plus wisdom (1 Corinthians 1:24), reconciliation (Ephesians 2:16) and peace (Colossians 1:20). No wonder Paul refused to glory in anything else (Galatians 6:14).

SERMON NO. 1910

19 JULY (1885)

'And we are': a jewel from the Revised Version

'Behold what manner of love the Father hath bestowed upon us, that we should be called children of God: and such we are' [literally 'and we are']. 1 John 3:1 [R.V.]
SUGGESTED FURTHER READING: Romans 8:14–23

Who calls the saints the sons of God? *The Father himself* does so. He speaks unto them as unto children. He deals with them as with sons. He is pleased in infinite love to bid them say, 'Our Father', and he answers to them by calling them children and heirs. He acknowledges their sonship and pities them 'as a father pitieth his children'. He has called them sons, saying, 'I will be a Father unto you, and ye shall be my sons and daughters, saith the Lord Almighty.' Oh what a blessing it is to have God calling you his child, the great Almighty and Infinite One looking upon you with a Father's love and saying, 'Thou art my son'! He speaks the truth; we may believe it and be sure: he knows his own children and gives the name of sons to none whom he will in the end disown. He calls us his children 'and we are'. Who has called us the sons of God? *Jesus himself*, 'the firstborn among many brethren', has called us so. Did he not speak of 'my Father, and your Father'? What did he mean when he was 'not ashamed to call' us 'brethren'? Everywhere our dear Lord and Master speaks of us as belonging to the one family of which he is the Head. By sweetly taking us into union with himself Jesus practically calls us Sons of God 'and we are'. *The Holy Spirit* also dwells in all the heirs of heaven and thereby calls them sons of God. He bears 'witness with our spirit, that we are the children of God'; and it is he who is given to us to be 'the Spirit of adoption, whereby we cry, Abba, Father.' That 'Abba, Father' of ours is prompted by the Spirit of grace, who would never prompt a stranger and an alien to claim kinship with the Lord. Oh no! The witness of the Holy Spirit is the witness of truth. A filial spirit implanted by the Spirit of God cannot deceive us. Thus Father, Son and Holy Spirit call us the children of God 'and we are'.

FOR MEDITATION: (*Our Own Hymn Book*, no. 728 v.1—Isaac Watts, 1709)

'Behold what wondrous grace   On sinners of a mortal race,
The Father hath bestowed   To call them sons of God!'

SERMON NO. 1934

20 JULY (1890)

The beginning of miracles which Jesus did

'This beginning of miracles did Jesus in Cana of Galilee, and manifested forth his glory; and his disciples believed on him.' John 2:11
SUGGESTED FURTHER READING: John 3:13–18

Will you that read your Greek Testament notice the expression here? Is it said, 'his disciples believed him'? No. Is it 'believed *in* him'? No. 'Believed *on* him'? Yes. It is so in our version, but *'into'* would be more correct. The Greek is *'eis'*: 'his disciples believed *into* him.' They so believed that they seemed to submerge themselves in Jesus. 'Into him'—think what that means! John, Andrew, Nathanael and the others cast their lifelong concerns upon Jesus and felt that they need never have another care. Jesus would see them through to the end. They would leave everything to him. Mary took the matter a little into her own hands, but she erred therein; the disciples entered into Jesus by the open door of this confirming miracle and there they rested. Let this be your condition: 'Casting all your care upon him, for he careth for you.' They believed right into Jesus. It is one thing to believe in him and another thing to believe him; it is a restful thing to believe on him, but best of all to believe right into him so that your very personality is swallowed up in Christ and you feel the bliss of living, loving, lasting union with him. Those six men could not have produced a drop of wine for the wedding, but count their Master in with them and the seven could flood the streets with it, if there had been need. Entering into partnership with Jesus, their faith rose as a morning without clouds. Now were they sure, steadfast, strong, for their weak and watery faith had gained the fullness and richness of generous wine.

FOR MEDITATION: Christian faith includes not only believing *that* (John 14:10–11; 16:27,30; 17:8,21; 20:31; 1 John 5:1,5), but also believing *into* the Lord Jesus Christ (John 12:11; Galatians 2:16) as the Son of God (1 John 5:10), the Son of man (John 9:35) and the Light of the world (John 12:36). Do you believe *into* his name (John 1:12; 2:23; 1 John 5:13)? See also 5 August on 'looking *into* Jesus'.

SERMON NO. 2155

21 JULY (1889)

'The marriage of the Lamb'

'Let us be glad and rejoice, and give honour to him: for the marriage of the Lamb is come, and his wife hath made herself ready. And to her was granted that she should be arrayed in fine linen, clean and white: for the fine linen is the righteousness of saints.' Revelation 19:7–8

SUGGESTED FURTHER READING: Ephesians 5:21–33

What could be more beautiful than pure white linen? In the Greek our text runs thus: 'Fine linen, clean and white, for fine linen is the righteousnesses of the saints.' Our Revised Version has, in this case, not given us a translation, but an explanation, and that explanation is a contraction of the sense. The revisers word it, 'Fine linen is the righteous acts of saints.' That word 'acts' is of their own insertion. The word 'righteousnesses' has a fuller meaning: it is exceeding broad, but they have narrowed it and misapplied it. We shall have a complete array of righteousnesses in Christ's righteousness, active and passive, a garment for the head, a garment for the feet and a garment for the loins. What righteousnesses we have! Righteousness imparted by the power of the Spirit, righteousness imputed by the decree of God. Every form of righteousness will go to make up the believer's outfit, only, all of it is *granted* and none of it is of our own purchasing. We shall not have Christ's righteousness to cover up our sin, as some blasphemously say, for we shall have no sin to cover. We shall not want Christ's righteousness to make an evil heart seem pure: we shall be as perfect as our Father in heaven is perfect. Washed in the blood of the Lamb, we shall have no spot upon us or within us. We shall have a complete righteousness and, in this arrayed, we shall be covered with the beauty of holiness. This garment is most befitting, for it is 'the righteousness of saints.' Saints ought to have righteousness. They are themselves made holy and therefore they ought to be adorned in visible holiness; and so they shall be.

FOR MEDITATION: The beautiful righteousness with which God clothes the bride of Christ (Isaiah 61:10–11) is in stark contrast to our own righteous acts, which are likened to 'filthy rags' (Isaiah 64:6) and 'dung' (Philippians 3:8–9). Whose design of wedding dress are you intending to wear when you meet God—God's, or your own?

SERMON NO. 2096

22 JULY (1888)

Peter's restoration

'*And immediately, while he yet spake, the cock crew. And the Lord turned, and looked upon Peter. And Peter remembered the word of the Lord, how he had said unto him, Before the cock crow, thou shalt deny me thrice. And Peter went out, and wept bitterly.*' Luke 22:60–62
SUGGESTED FURTHER READING: Galatians 6:1–10

Note what sacred teaching is here. The teaching is of practical value and should be at once carried out by the followers of Jesus. You, dear friend, are a Christian man or a Christian woman; you have been kept, by divine grace, from anything like disgraceful sin. Thank God it is so. I dare say, if you look within, you will find much to be ashamed of, yet you have been kept from presumptuous and open sins. Alas! One who was once a friend of yours has disgraced himself: he was a little while ago a member of the church, but he has shamefully turned aside. You cannot excuse his sin; on the contrary, you are forced to feel great indignation against his folly, his untruthfulness, his wickedness. He has caused the enemies of the Lord to blaspheme and has done awful mischief to the cause of righteousness. Now I know what will be suggested to you. You will be inclined to cut his acquaintance, to disown him altogether and scarcely to look at him if you meet him in the street. This is the manner of men, but not the manner of Jesus. I charge you, act not in so un-Christlike a manner. 'The Lord turned, and looked upon Peter'; will not his servants look on him? You are not perfect like your Lord; you are only a poor sinful creature like your fallen brother. What! Are you too proud to look at the fallen one? Will you not give him a helping hand? Will you not try to bring him back? The worst thing you can do with a backslider is to let him keep on sliding back. Your duty should be your pleasure and your duty is to 'restore such a one in the spirit of meekness; considering thyself, lest thou also be tempted.'

FOR MEDITATION: This was only the first step in the process by which the Lord Jesus Christ restored Peter. Note how he followed it up after his resurrection with a message (Mark 16:7), a meeting (Luke 24:34; 1 Corinthians 15:5) and a mandate (John 21:15–17). Each one of these can be a valuable first move in seeking to reclaim the backslider.

SERMON NO. 2034

23 JULY (PREACHED 19 JULY 1885)

The modern Dead Sea, and the living waters

'The waters shall be healed.' Ezekiel 47:8
SUGGESTED FURTHER READING (Spurgeon): Revelation 22:1–15

The world, the city and the heart are each symbolized by the Dead Sea. Can they ever be purified? Can these waters be healed? According to our text, the Lord says expressly, *'the waters shall be healed.'* Let us believe his promise and take heart of hope from this good hour. Here is room, my brethren, for the faith which, like charity, 'believeth all things, hopeth all things'. If any of you desire to exercise a faith by which you can glorify God, believe that the world can yet be delivered from sin; believe that London can yet be made a holy city; believe that your own heart, by the power of God's Spirit, can be purified even as Christ is pure. Even when it seems to be furthest off from hope, even when we are staggered at the sin which surrounds us, we are still to believe that the Lord shall reign for ever and ever, and sin and Satan shall be crushed under our Redeemer's foot. Let us believe in God as God deserves to be believed in: let us rely implicitly upon Omnipotence and trust without a doubt in that strong will which can never be turned from its purpose of grace. *'The waters shall be healed'*: all the brine and bitumen of the Dead Sea shall not prevent the divine work. The putrid waters of London shall be made sweet as the well of Bethlehem. The atrocities of war and oppression shall cease and the reign of evil shall end; for the Lord has purposed it and it shall be done. 'The kingdoms of this world' must 'become the kingdoms of our Lord, and of his Christ;' London must be won for Jesus and our own hearts must be wholly his. *'The waters shall be healed.'*

FOR MEDITATION: (*Our Own Hymn Book*, no. 874 v.5—Samuel Stennett, 1787)
  'No chilling winds, or poisonous breath,
  Can reach that healthful shore:
  Sickness and sorrow, pain and death,
  Are felt and feared no more.'

SERMON NO. 1852

24 JULY (PREACHED 2 AUGUST 1888)

The Lord's own salvation

'But I will have mercy upon the house of Judah, and will save them by the LORD *their God, and will not save them by bow, nor by sword, nor by battle, by horses, nor by horsemen.'* Hosea 1:7
SUGGESTED FURTHER READING: Acts 3:1–4:4

Let every man work as he feels called to do, provided he follows the rules of his Lord; but we have seen revivals of which it was said at the first, 'We will get up a revival.' Revivals can be got up, but are they worth the trouble? What has been the end of them all? A few years after where is the result? I hear an echo say, 'Where is it?' I cannot tell you what has become of it; in many cases I fear that the disappointed church has become more hard to stir than it was before. Brethren, I hopefully believe that there will soon come a deep, widespread, lasting revival of religion and it may be it will come just as it used to in apostolic times. How did they act in Jerusalem? What did they do throughout Asia Minor? What was the apostles' plan? I cannot find, for the life of me, that they did anything else but preach the gospel, while at the same time they went from house to house and held meetings for prayer; and thus the kingdom of Christ came. They did not work up a revival, but they prayed it down. They simply waited upon the Lord in supplication and service. They might have tried other plans had they been so unwise as to think of them. They would never have tolerated the dodges of the present period, the adaptations of the gospel and the degrading of it by secular lectures, entertainments and so forth. They never dreamed of keeping abreast of the times with liberal philosophical teaching, but I recollect that Paul was so resolutely ignorant as to say, 'I determined not to know anything among you, save Jesus Christ, and him crucified.' Standing all together the chosen preachers of the first days could assert, 'we preach Christ crucified'. They could all say that and say it emphatically. All the men of the college of the apostles stuck to that theme; and see the effect!

FOR MEDITATION: In one sense the Jews' enemies were correct to deny that revival was within their grasp (Nehemiah 4:1–2). Ezra was careful to give all the credit for revival to God (Ezra 9:8–9) and spiritual people have always looked to God alone for revival (Psalm 85:6; Habakkuk 3:2).

SERMON NO. 2057

25 JULY (1886)

Hideous discovery

'From within, out of the heart of men, proceed evil thoughts, adulteries, fornications, murders, thefts, covetousness, wickedness, deceit, lasciviousness, an evil eye, blasphemy, pride, foolishness: all these evil things come from within, and defile the man.' Mark 7:21-23
SUGGESTED FURTHER READING: Proverbs 6:12-19

How evil each of these sins may be it is not possible for us to know, but none of them is defensible. They are each vile before God and some of them are mischievous towards men. *Evil thoughts* mainly blacken the man's own mind, but when he expresses them they destroy the love of truth in others: *adulteries*, as violations of the marriage vow, shake the very foundations of family life: *fornications*, which today are winked at as though they were scarcely offences, defile two people at once in body and soul. Actual *murders* follow frequently upon unbridled passion, but forget not that the command, 'Thou shalt not kill', may be broken by anger, hate, malice and the desire for revenge. Many a murderer in heart may be among us this day, being 'angry with his brother without a cause'. He that conceives and hides malice in his soul is a murderer before God. This form of evil breeds all manner of harm to society. *Thefts* in all their shapes are also injurious to the commonwealth. By this we mean not only robberies, but all taking from others unjustly, such as the oppression of the poor in their wages, the taking of undue advantage in trading, the incurring of debts without hope of being able to pay: these are varied forms of dishonesty and are full of injury to others. *Covetousness*: the greed to get and keep, the adding field to field until the man seems eager to be left alone in the earth, the grasping of excessive riches and the creation of poverty in others by crushing their humbler enterprises: all this is evil, though some applaud it as business sharpness. Need I mention the ills which come of *wickedness, deceit and lasciviousness*? These are poisons in the air deadly to all who breathe them. I sicken as I think how man has plagued his fellow-men by his sins.

FOR MEDITATION: This list of sins is not exhaustive. Consider what Paul included (Romans 1:29-30; Galatians 5:19-21; 2 Timothy 3:2-5), but rejoice that the Lord Jesus Christ can save us from all these (1 Corinthians 6:9-11; Titus 3:3-7) and cleanse us from all unrighteousness (1 John 1:7,9).

SERMON NO. 1911

26 JULY (PREACHED 5 AUGUST 1886)

The great sin of doing nothing

'But if ye will not do so, behold, ye have sinned against the LORD: and be sure your sin will find you out.' Numbers 32:23
SUGGESTED FURTHER READING: Nehemiah 4:1–15

It is no slight sin to discourage holy zeal and perseverance in others. May we never be guilty of killing holy desires even in children! How often has a burning desire in a boy's heart been quenched by his own father, who has thought him too impulsive, or too ardent! How frequently the conversation of a friend, so called, has dried up the springs of holy desire in the person with whom he has conversed! Let it not be so. Yet without cold words our chill neglects may freeze. I know a terrace where the shutting up of one or two shops has a deadening effect upon the trade of the other shops. Somehow the closed shutters give a gloomy look to the place and customers are repelled. Does not the same thing happen to groups of workers when one grows idle? Does not the one dull brother deaden the rest? We cannot neglect our own gardens without injuring our neighbours. Do you live anywhere near a house that is not let, which has a back garden left to run to waste? All manner of seeds are blown over upon your ground and, though you keep the hoe going, yet the weeds baffle you, for there is such a nursery for them just over the wall. One mechanic coming late among a set of workmen may throw the whole company out of order for the day. One railway truck off the rails may block the entire system. Depend upon it, if we are not serving the Lord our God, we are committing the sin of discouraging our fellowmen. They are more likely to imitate our lethargy than our energy. Why should we wish to hinder others from being earnest? How dare we rob God of the services of others by our own neglect? O God, deliver us from this sin!

FOR MEDITATION: Consider some who opted out of their share in God's work (Nehemiah 3:5; Psalm 78:9). The discouraging attitude of a few can bring many others to a standstill (Numbers 32:6–9; Deuteronomy 1:28), but an encourager can spur others to action (Deuteronomy 1:38; 3:28).

27 JULY (1890)

Robbers of God

'Will a man rob God? Yet ye have robbed me.' Malachi 3:8
SUGGESTED FURTHER READING: John 12:1–8

'Will a man rob God?' What! God, whose eyes are fixed upon him? Will he thus defy *his Maker*? We lift up our hands in amazement that such a crime should be even conceived, much less committed. Yet, I shall have to show that many of us, in various ways, have been guilty of this audacious crime. 'Will a man rob God?' Furthermore, it is shamefully ungrateful! God 'hath made us, and not we ourselves'; therefore we are bound to serve him and every righteous instinct forbids our robbing him. Shall a creature injure *its Creator*? If we live, it is by his forbearance. 'Will a man rob God' who spares him? If saved, it must be by his divine redemption; will a man rob *his Redeemer*? If provided with food for the body, it must be by God's daily bounty; will a man rob *his constant Benefactor*? O thou Preserver of men, will men rob thee? Believers in the Lord Jesus, God is your Father, and from you this crime would have a sevenfold heinousness. Will a man rob *his own Father*? Can it be that one, in whose heart there pulses the life of God, would be guilty of such an infamy as to rob God? I fear it is so, but in such a case it is ingratitude of so black a type as to be well-nigh incredible. Ingratitude in every land and in every age has been abhorred of just men. It is a fiendish vice. It is at once contemptible and unendurable: we not only despise, but hate it. Every voice hoots down ingratitude. Yet when a man robs God, it is ingratitude written in capital letters, ingratitude that will sink the soul into the lowest hell. 'Will a man rob God?' The Lord deliver us from conduct so base!

FOR MEDITATION: (*Our Own Hymn Book,* no. 576 v.1—Mrs J. L. Gray, 1843)

> 'Am I called? And can it be!
> Has my Saviour chosen me?
> Guilty, wretched as I am,
> Has He named my worthless name?
> Vilest of the vile am I,
> Dare I raise my hopes so high?'

SERMON NO. 2156

28 JULY (1889)

The Mediator—the Interpreter

'The people saw the thunderings, and the lightnings, and the noise of the trumpet, and the mountain smoking ... And they said unto Moses, Speak thou with us, and we will hear: but let not God speak with us, lest we die. And Moses said ... Fear not: for God is come to prove you, and that his fear may be before your faces, that ye sin not.' Exodus 20:18–20
SUGGESTED FURTHER READING: Hebrews 12:3–11

The dealings of the Lord are meant to keep us from sin. The Psalmist says, 'Before I was afflicted, I went astray: but now have I kept thy word.' Hezekiah tells us that 'by these things men live, and in all these things is the life of' our 'spirit'. We are so worldly that we need our nest to be stirred to keep us on the wing. Six days we are taken up with business, mixing with those who despise heavenly things; we would think lightly of them too, were it not that God comes to us in his dread majesty and makes us think, consider and fear. This holy trembling drives off the shams which else would grow over us like mould on decaying matter. Our inward tempests clear the air and keep us from stagnation and the pestilence which breeds in it. God's love will not let us settle down in mere pretences and glide into gross sins: he empties us 'from vessel to vessel', discovers our evil sediment and cleanses us from it. Many, when they hear a sermon, say, 'How did you enjoy it?' If you always enjoy sermons, the minister is not a good steward. He is not acting wisely who deals out nothing but sweets. God's people need the word at times to be medicine to them and we do not enjoy medicine. The word is like fire; the iron does not like the fire, yet it is vital to its melting. It is like a hammer; the rock does not love the hammer, yet it is vital to its breaking. Experiences which are painful may be all the more profitable. That which makes us hate sin is a thing to be valued. Thus read the dispensations of God with you. When he chides he loves; when he chastens he shows fatherly affection; when he scourges he receives into peculiar familiarity. Do not therefore run away from a chastening God.

FOR MEDITATION: If God deals firmly with his children, it is to discipline them (Hebrews 12:7), not to punish sin (Psalm 103:10). The right response is repentance (Zechariah 1:6). When you think God is being harsh with you, consider how much worse Moses felt (Numbers 11:11,15).

SERMON NO. 2097

29 JULY (1888)

The whole-heartedness of God in blessing his people

'Yea, I will rejoice over them to do them good, and I will plant them in this land assuredly with my whole heart and with my whole soul.'
Jeremiah 32:41

SUGGESTED FURTHER READING: Psalm 33:1–12

There are some works of God in which his heart does not go. He smites the guilty with his left hand, but he says, 'I have no pleasure in the death of the wicked; but that the wicked turn from his way and live'. But when he is dealing with his right hand of loving-kindness, his heart goes out with his hand. O beloved, you that receive his grace may know assuredly that, besides the blessings which you receive, you also have God's whole heart therewith. He blesses you with his whole soul or life. He concentrates his nature upon you, that he may bless you to the full. He is slow to wrath, but he is swift to mercy, for he delights in it. When he deals out his grace to his people, then you see the loving God, 'for God is love', and you see the living God, for he blesses you with his whole soul. His Godhead is displayed in the deeds of his love. There is a way of doing things and there is another way of doing things: a work can be done according to rule and no great fault can be found with it, yet it may be done listlessly and as a matter of routine. Another worker takes pleasure in his work and throws his heart and soul into it. The result will show the difference in points which one can hardly mention in words. A painting with a great painter's heart and soul in it is a rare treasure. When the worker puts himself forth to his utmost, that he may do the work in the noblest fashion, the product is most precious. Even so has God determined that in the wonders of his grace, through Jesus Christ, he will show himself more fully than in any other labour to which he has set his hand. No other work so clearly displays the heart of Jehovah.

FOR MEDITATION: (*Our Own Hymn Book*, no. 230 v.3—John Kent, 1803)
   'Preserved in Jesus, when
   My feet made haste to hell;
   And there should I have gone
   But Thou dost all things well;
   Thy love was great, Thy mercy free,
   Which from the pit delivered me.'

SERMON NO. 2036

30 JULY (PREACHED 2 AUGUST 1885)

A discourse upon true blessedness here and herafter

'Blessed is the man that endureth temptation: for when he is tried, he shall receive the crown of life, which the Lord hath promised to them that love him.' James 1:12

SUGGESTED FURTHER READING: Matthew 5:1–12

The text is a beatitude. It begins with BLESSED. We should all like to be blessed. What a more than golden word 'blessed' is! It begins the Psalms of David: there is sweetest poetry in it. It begins the sermon of the Son of David; it is the end of all holy teaching. 'Happiness' is the earthly word, 'blessedness' the heavenly one. Happiness may prove to be a superficial appearance; blessedness is deep as the abyss. Happiness ripples like a flowing brook; blessedness is a springing well. Happiness may be wholly human; blessedness has the divine element in it. Happiness is transient; blessedness is eternal. Happiness may lie in our own conception of things; blessedness is God's verdict, God's truthful statement of a man's condition. Happiness may prove but tinsel; blessedness is solid gold. Oh to be 'blessed of the LORD which made heaven and earth'! Where are these blessed men? There are such still upon the earth, for the text says, 'Blessed is the man': it speaks not of a phantom, but of a man, not of an ideal man, but of one who is tried and made to endure temptation. I hear in this verse the echo of many a psalm chanted by the saints hundreds of years before. James took pen in hand concerning blessed men; of the like persons David long before had sung. There are such people as blessed men, or the eminently practical James would not have written concerning them. It is true the curse has fallen on the world and man is born to endure toil and suffering in tilling a thorn-bearing earth and earning his bread with the sweat of his face, but, for all that, there are men so blessed that the wilderness and solitary place are glad for them and by their presence the desert is made to rejoice and blossom as the rose.

FOR MEDITATION: 'Blessed [or 'Happy'] is the man', 'whom God correcteth' (Job 5:17), 'that walketh not in the counsel of the ungodly' (Psalm 1:1), 'unto whom the LORD imputeth not iniquity' (Psalm 32:2), 'that trusteth in him' (Psalm 34:8), 'that maketh the LORD his trust' (Psalm 40:4), 'that feareth the LORD' (Psalm 112:1), 'that findeth wisdom' (Proverbs 3:13). Are you blessed?

SERMON NO. 1874

31 JULY (1887)

The covenanter

'All the paths of the LORD are mercy and truth unto such as keep his covenant and his testimonies.' Psalm 25:10
SUGGESTED FURTHER READING: 2 Chronicles 34:29–33

In my bedroom I have hung up the picture of an old Covenanter. He sits in a wild glen with his Bible open before him on a huge stone. He leans on his great broadsword and his horse stands quietly at his side. Evidently he smells the battle afar off and is preparing for it by drinking in some mighty promise. As you look into the old man's face you can almost hear him saying, 'For the crown of Christ and the covenant, I would gladly lay down my life this day.' They did lay down their lives, too, right gloriously and Scotland owes to her covenanting fathers far more than she knows. It was a grand day when they spread the Solemn League and the Covenant upon the tombstones of the old kirkyard in Edinburgh and all sorts of men came forward to set their names to it. Glorious was that roll of worthies. There were the lords of the Covenant and the common men of the Covenant; some pricked a vein and dipped the pen into their blood, that they might write their names with the very fluid of their hearts. All over England also there were men who entered into a like solemn league and covenant, and met together to worship God according to their right and not according to human order-books. They were resolved that Rome should not come back to place and power while they could lift a hand against her, neither should any other power in throne or Parliament prevent the free exercise of their consciences for Christ's cause and covenant. These stern old men, with their stiff notions, have gone. And what have we in their places? Indifference and frivolity. We have no Roundheads and Puritans, but then we have scientific dress-making and we play lawn-tennis! We have no contentions for the faith, but then our amusements occupy all our time. This wonderful century has become a child and put away manly things. Self-contained men, in whom is the true grit, are now few and far between as compared with the old covenanting days.

FOR MEDITATION: God usually made the covenants, but sometimes, under a godly influence, his people did so (2 Chronicles 15:12–15). Job made one of his own (Job 31:1). God meant his covenants (2 Samuel 23:5), but human covenants may be empty words (Hosea 10:4).

SERMON NO. 1975

1 AUGUST (1886)

The holy road

'And an highway shall be there, and a way, and it shall be called The way of holiness; the unclean shall not pass over it; but it shall be for those: the wayfaring men, though fools, shall not err therein.' Isaiah 35:8
SUGGESTED FURTHER READING: Isaiah 40:1-5

We might gather from our text that this way was cast up at great expense, for road-making over a long and rugged country is a costly business. It might be read, 'a causeway shall be there'; it is a way thrown up and raised by art. Engineering has done much to tunnel mountains and bridge abysses, but the greatest triumph of engineering is that which made a way from sin to holiness, from death to life, from condemnation to perfection. Who could make a road over the mountains of our iniquities but Almighty God? None but the Lord of love would have wished it; none but the God of wisdom could have devised it; none but the God of power could have carried it out. It cost the great God the Jewel of heaven: he emptied out the treasury of his own heart, for he 'spared not his own Son, but delivered him up for us all'. In the life and death of the Well-beloved infinite wisdom laid a firm foundation for the road by which sinners in all ages may journey home to God. The highway of our God is such a masterpiece that even those who travel it every day often stand and wonder how such a way could have been planned and constructed. That prophecy is fulfilled to the letter: 'I will even make a way in the wilderness, and rivers in the desert. The beast of the field shall honour me, the dragons and the owls'. This road has lasted now thousands of years; it is still in good travelling condition and will never be closed till all the chosen wayfarers shall have reached the many mansions of the Father's house. The everlasting causeway remains unbroken and unaltered, and fresh caravans of pilgrims continually traverse it.

FOR MEDITATION: (*Our Own Hymn Book,* no. 408 vv.1&2—John Cennick, 1743)
'Jesus, my all, to heaven is gone, He whom I fixed my hopes upon,
His track I see, and I'll pursue the narrow way, till Him I view.
The way the holy prophets went, the road that leads from banishment,
The King's highway of holiness, I'll go, for all His paths are peace.'

SERMON NO. 1912

2 AUGUST (1885)

Up from the country, and pressed into the service

'They compel one Simon a Cyrenian, who passed by, coming out of the country, the father of Alexander and Rufus, to bear his cross.' Mark 15:21

SUGGESTED FURTHER READING: Colossians 1:21–29

It has always been part of the divine counsel that for the salvation of men from sin the Lord should be associated with his church. So far as atonement is concerned, the Lord has 'trodden the winepress alone; and of the people there was none with' him, but as far as the conversion of the world is concerned and its rescue from the power of error and wickedness, Christ is not alone. We are 'workers together with' God. We are ourselves to be in the hands of God part-bearers of the sorrow and travail by which men are to be delivered from the bondage of sin and Satan and brought into the liberty of truth and righteousness. Hence it became important that in the bearing of the cross, though not in the death upon it, there should be yoked with the Christ one who should follow close behind him. To bear the cross after Jesus is the office of the faithful. Simon the Cyrenian is the representative of the whole church of God and of each believer in particular. Jesus said, 'whosoever doth not bear his cross, and come after me, cannot be my disciple'; now at last he embodies that sermon in an actual person. The disciple must be as his Master: he that would follow the Crucified must himself bear the cross: this we see visibly set forth in Simon of Cyrene with the cross of Jesus laid upon his shoulder.

> 'Shall Simon bear the cross alone,
> And all the rest go free?
> No, there's a cross for every one,
> And there's a cross for me.'

FOR MEDITATION: Simon was once required to take up the cross and follow Jesus (Luke 23:26); the Christian is to do this daily (Luke 9:23). For the two thieves crucifixion with Christ was temporary (Mark 15:27–28,32); for the Christian it is permanent (Romans 6:6; Galatians 2:20). This should have far-reaching effects upon the Christian's relationships with the world (Galatians 6:14) and the flesh (Galatians 5:24).

SERMON NO. 1853

3 AUGUST (1890)

The peace of the devil, and the peace of God

'When a strong man armed keepeth his palace, his goods are in peace.'
Luke 11:21
'The LORD will bless his people with peace.' Psalm 29:11
SUGGESTED FURTHER READING: 1 Thessalonians 5:1–11

Peace caused by the devil is often the awful prelude of the last tremendous storm. One who described to me the earthquake in the south of France said, 'That morning when we rose, I never saw more lovely weather. Everything smiled deliciously across the blue Mediterranean and the azure sky was without a cloud. Suddenly, without a moment's warning, a tremor seized the earth and there was a great cry of men and women in their fright.' It usually happens, before tremendous convulsions of nature, that there is an ominous calm. You must have noticed, a few minutes before a storm, how awfully still everything becomes. The air is motionless, the birds sit mute upon the bough, not a leaf is stirring; all is silent expectation. Deceive not yourself; the tempest is hurrying on and while you speak, it bursts upon you, casting all things into confusion. Before the last dread hurricane of doom a soul may be asleep and all around it there may be a deep calm. Beware of the treacherous peace! Beware of insensibility! Your unfeeling state should warn you that you are given over to destruction. In the higher and colder latitudes, when men feel sleepiness stealing over them, their companions stir them up, rub them and will not let them slumber, for to sleep is to wake no more. The man pleads, 'Let me sleep a half-an-hour and I shall be so refreshed.' Alas! If he sleeps he will grow rigid in the death which frost brings to one. Go on, wise friends, and compassionately shake him! Hurry him to and fro or rub him vigorously till he grows sore. Oh that I could do this spiritually and wake you up! I cannot leave you to sleep your soul into perdition.

FOR MEDITATION: (*Our Own Hymn Book,* no. 734 v.1—John Newton, 1779)
> 'Begone, unbelief, my Saviour is near,
> And for my relief will surely appear;
> By prayer let me wrestle, and He will perform,
> With Christ in the vessel, I smile at the storm.'

SERMON NO. 2157

4 AUGUST (1889)

Whither goest thou?

'But he knoweth the way that I take: when he hath tried me, I shall come forth as gold.' Job 23:10
SUGGESTED FURTHER READING (Spurgeon): Psalm 139:1–12

Is it a comfort to you that God knows your way? Solemnly, I believe that one of the best tests of human character is our relation to the great truth of God's omniscience. If it startles you that God sees you, then you ought to be startled. If it delights you that God sees you, you may reasonably conclude that there is within your heart that which is right and true, which God will approve of. You are among those who do the truth, for you come to the light, and cry, 'Search me, O God'. Allow me to apply the test to you now, by asking what you think of the truth that the Lord knows you altogether. Remember, 'if our heart condemn us, God is greater than our heart, and knoweth all things', but 'if our heart condemn us not, then have we confidence toward God.' Dear friend, it is quite certain that God does know the way that you take. The Hebrew may be read, 'he knoweth the way that is in me', from which I gather that the Lord not only knows our outward actions, but our inward feelings. He knows our likes and dislikes, our desires and our designs, our imaginations and tendencies. He knows not only what we do, but what we would do if we could. He knows which way we should go if the restraints of society and the fear of consequences were removed, and that, perhaps, is a more important proof of character than the actions of which we are guilty. God knows what you think of, what you wish for, what you are pleased with: he knows not only the surface-tint of your character, but the secret heart and core of it. The Lord knows you altogether. Think of that.

FOR MEDITATION: (*Our Own Hymn Book,* no. 701 v.1—William Freeman Lloyd, 1835)
   'Our times are in Thy hand,
   Father, we wish them there:
   Our life, our soul, our all, we leave
   Entirely to Thy care.'

SERMON NO. 2098

5 AUGUST (1888)

The rule of the race

'Let us run with patience the race that is set before us, looking unto Jesus the author and finisher of our faith; who for the joy that was set before him endured the cross, despising the shame, and is set down at the right hand of the throne of God.' Hebrews 12:1–2
SUGGESTED FURTHER READING: Philippians 3:7–11

The instructive original has in it the word '*eis*', which is translated 'unto,' but in addition has the force of 'into.' We shall do well if we look unto Jesus, but better still if we are found 'looking *into* Jesus.' I want you, when you begin your divine life, to take care that you look to Jesus with so penetrating a gaze that your 'unto' grows to an 'into.' Read not only the outside of the volume of his life, but loose the seals thereof and read his heart. Dive into the meaning of what he has done for you. Look at his enduring the cross, know what it means and enter into 'the fellowship of his sufferings'. Study well the sin-bearing, the curse-bearing, the forsaking and the sorrow unto death. Think how the Lord Jesus came under shame for your sakes and see how he rose above it all. Look to him till you are familiar with the different views of the one great Sacrifice. Under the law, a poor man brought his two young pigeons, and the birds were divided in the middle and so offered. A richer man brought a lamb or a bullock; this was divided carefully and all its anatomy laid bare: *this* was to be done with the leg and *that* with the shoulder and there was an ordinance concerning the fat and the inwards. Thus some believers know the details of the sacrifice and we want you, dear friends, to be among this better-instructed class. May you discern the Lord's body and penetrate into the secrets of his soul, and so begin your Christian life with an intelligent and instructed faith. This will secure better running throughout the rest of the road. Still you must look to Jesus only, whether you know little or much. It is not your knowledge, but Jesus himself that must be your one ground of trust.

FOR MEDITATION: A desire to 'see Jesus' (John 12:21) is a good start, but have you gone on to join those who, according to the original Greek, 'shall look *into* him whom they pierced' (John 19:37)?

6 AUGUST (PREACHED 5 AUGUST 1888)

The messages of our Lord's love

'Go your way, tell his disciples and Peter that he goeth before you into Galilee: there shall ye see him, as he said unto you.' Mark 16:7
SUGGESTED FURTHER READING: Matthew 26:30–35

Our Lord remembers his own promises. It was before he died that he said he would go before them into Galilee and, now that he has risen from the dead, he says by the mouth of his angel, 'there shall ye see him, as he said unto you.' The rule of Christ's action is his own word. What he has said he will perform. You and I forget his promises, but he never does. 'As he said unto you' is the remembrance of all that he has spoken. Why does our Lord remember and repeat what he has so graciously spoken? He does so because he spoke with foresight, forethought and care. We make promises and forget them because we did not consider well the matter before we spoke, but if we have thought, calculated, weighed, estimated and come to a deliberate resolve before we speak, then we earnestly remember what we resolved upon. No promise of our Lord Jesus has been spoken in haste, to be repented of afterwards. Infinite wisdom directs infinite love and, when infinite love takes the pen to write a promise, infallible wisdom dictates every syllable. Jesus does not forget, because he spoke the promise with his whole heart. It is not every tongue that represents a heart at all, but, even though true people, we say many things which we mean, but there is no depth of feeling, no potent emotion, no stirring of the heart's centre. Our Lord, when he said, 'You shall be scattered. But after that I am risen, I will go before you into Galilee', spoke with a heavy heart, with many a melting sigh and his whole soul went with the promise which closed the mournful scene. He has purchased what he promised, purchased it with his blood, and therefore he speaks most solemnly and with his whole heart. There is no trifling on Christ's part with one to whom he makes a promise and therefore he never forgets.

FOR MEDITATION: God remembers his promises (Psalm 105:42), so they do not fail (1 Kings 8:56). The Lord Jesus Christ confirms them (Romans 15:8; 2 Corinthians 1:20). But do you respect God's faithfulness to his promises (Hebrews 10:23; 11:11)?

SERMON NO. 2060

7 AUGUST (1887)

Lessons from the Christ of Patmos

'And he had in his right hand seven stars: and out of his mouth went a sharp two-edged sword: and his countenance was as the sun shineth in his strength.' Revelation 1:16
SUGGESTED FURTHER READING: Micah 2:6–3:8

The word is in itself adapted to the divine end, for it is sharp and two-edged; when it is spoken by the Lord, its adaptation is seen. The gospel is very sharp when the Spirit of God lays it home. No doctrine of men has such piercing power. Take care, preacher, that you do not blunt the word or try to cover over its edge, for that would be treason to the Lord who made it to be sharp and cutting. There is much about the true gospel which offends and it should be our desire never to tamper with it, or to tone it down, lest we become enemies to the Lord's truth. Truth which is meant to offend human pride must be stated in its own way, even though seen to produce anger and annoy self-righteousness. Doctrine which is cutting and killing must not be concealed or softened down. 'He that hath my word, let him speak my word faithfully … saith the LORD.' People are disturbed and troubled by the real gospel: under the false gospel they can sleep into destruction. Bring out the sword: it is made to wound; let it exercise its salutary sharpness. The gospel has two edges, so that none may play with it. When they think to run their fingers along the back of it they will find themselves cut to the bone. Whether we regard its threats or its promises, it cuts at sin. Whether we move it up or down, it makes great gashes in that which ought to be wounded and killed. Let us, therefore, know that the power of the church does not lie anywhere but in the word as Jesus himself speaks it. Let us keep to his own pure, unadulterated, unblunted word and let us pray him to send it forth with power out of his own mouth into the hearts and consciences of men.

FOR MEDITATION: God's word operates not only as a lamp (Psalm 119:105), but also as a fire and a hammer (Jeremiah 23:29) as well as a sword (Ephesians 6:17; Hebrews 4:12). Vain attempts have been made to ban it (Jeremiah 11:21; Acts 4:18–21; 5:28–29,40–42), to burn it (Jeremiah 36:20–28,32), to blur it (Ezekiel 20:49; 33:30–33) and to blunt it (Jeremiah 34:8–17; 42:2–7; 43:1–4). It is far less effort simply to believe it (Proverbs 16:20; John 5:24)!

SERMON NO. 1976

8 AUGUST (1889)

'In the garden with him'

'One of the servants of the high priest, being his kinsman whose ear Peter cut off, saith, Did not I see thee in the garden with him?' John 18:26
SUGGESTED FURTHER READING: John 17:6–24

Talking the other evening with a young girl who has, I trust, escaped from the grosser sin into which she might soon have fallen, I said to her: 'There are three things you can do, and those three things I will set before you by an illustration. When you get outside the Tabernacle, there will be a tramcar. Now, go up to the car, put one foot on the car and keep the other foot on the ground, and if you do not come down with a smash I am very much mistaken. Yet many people try to keep in with the world and keep in with Christ, and they will never do it, but will make a terrible fall of it before long. Now, the second thing that you can do is that you can keep standing in the road in the mud and not get into the car at all. You can stop there and let the tramcar go by: that is all fair and straight. If you want to live in the world and be of the world, well, live in the world and be of the world, take what pleasure it can give you and reap the fruit of it at last. But there is a third thing you can do, namely, get right off the road into the car and let the car take you right away where it is going. Now, it is this third thing that I commend to you. Get right into Christ and let the Lord Jesus, by the power of his Holy Spirit, carry you right away from the unclean place where you now stand, bearing you in safety along the tram-lines of holiness till he brings you to the terminus of glory at his own right hand. May the Lord deliver you from halting 'between two opinions', or choosing the wrong opinion; may he now decide you to leap into the gospel chariot and leave all sinful company and doubtful ways that you may own the Lord Jesus and be his true disciple!'

FOR MEDITATION: (*Our Own Hymn Book,* no. 668 v.1—Mary Bowly, 1847)
    'Lord, through the desert drear and wide
    Our erring footsteps need a guide;
    Keep us, oh keep us near Thy side.
    Let us not fall. Let us not fall.'

SERMON NO. 2106

9 AUGUST (1885)

The foundation and its seal: a sermon for the times

'Nevertheless the foundation of God standeth sure, having this seal, The Lord knoweth them that are his. And, Let every one that nameth the name of Christ depart from iniquity.' 2 Timothy 2:19
SUGGESTED FURTHER READING: 1 John 3:1–20

Look at this foundation and observe the instructive inscription. I think this figure best expresses the apostle's intent; he represents the foundation-stone as bearing a writing upon it, like the stone mentioned by the prophet Zechariah, of which we read, 'I will engrave the graving thereof, saith the LORD of hosts, and I will remove the iniquity of that land in one day.' The custom of putting inscriptions upon foundation-stones is ancient and general. In the days of the Pharaohs, the royal cartouche was impressed upon each brick that was placed in buildings raised by royal authority. The structure was thus known to have been erected by a certain Pharaoh. Here we have the royal cartouche, or seal, of the King of kings set upon the foundation of the great palace of the church. The House of Wisdom bears on its forefront and foundation the seal of the Lord. The Jews were accustomed to write texts of Scripture upon the door-posts of their houses; in this also we have an illustration of our text. The Lord has set upon his purpose, his gospel, his truth, the double mark described in the text, the divine election and the divine sanctification. This seal is placed to declare that it belongs to the Lord alone and to set it apart for his personal habitation. The Lord says, 'This is my rest for ever: here will I dwell; for I have desired it.' By his choice and sanctifying grace he has formed a people for himself and they shall show forth his praise. The inscription, is put upon the foundation-stone, that every man may 'take heed how he buildeth thereupon.' We cannot be sure when we build that every stone we place upon the foundation is well and truly laid there: 'The Lord knoweth them that are his.' But we have this mark to guide us: those who truly name 'the name of Christ depart from iniquity.' 'By their fruits ye shall know them.'

FOR MEDITATION: The Lord Jesus Christ sometimes revealed openly his perfect knowledge of those who were his and of those who were not his (John 6:64; 10:14,26–27). We can know this only by self-examination and by observation (1 John 2:4–5; 3:10,14–15; 4:2–6).

SERMON NO. 1854

10 AUGUST (1890)

Christ's testimony received

'He that hath received his testimony hath set to his seal that God is true.'
John 3:33
SUGGESTED FURTHER READING: 1 John 5:6–12

Men know so much that they will not know God. I am struck every day, when reviewing books of the present period, with how wise fools are nowadays. Pardon me; I will put it differently, and say, how foolish the wise are nowadays. I mean the same thing, whichever way I say it. They get a hold of the tail of a dead thing and they shout like men that find great spoil. Here is a great discovery, a discovery of nothing! At one time they find Deuteronomy to be a fraud; now there are two Isaiahs; then the book of Ruth was written far down in the centuries after the exile; Jonah is a myth, Esther is a romance, and so forth. Their criticisms are all false, as others of the same breed soon show. They are always finding some dead cat or other and setting it out on the table, where the children's bread ought to be. What mighty discoveries of mares' nests we have lived to see! Men of this nature will not receive the witness of Jesus: it is a pity that they should: he is honoured by their rejection. You can scarcely read a book nowadays, but you come across a bit of rotten stuff, the fondly-cherished nonsense of some writer who has a taste for that which is far gone in decay. They will not believe God. How can they while they 'receive honour one of another,' as learned critics? It is today as it was in our Lord's time, 'not many wise men after the flesh … are called'. Still have we to ask, 'Where is the wise? where is the scribe? where is the disputer of this world?' Those who glory in fleshly wisdom cannot receive the testimony of the carpenter's Son, a testimony so plain that the poor and illiterate can understand it and enter into eternal life thereby. I hope this will not be the case with any of the more cultured among you. Be willing to take Christ's yoke upon you and learn of him.

FOR MEDITATION: (*Our Own Hymn Book*, no. 531 v.5—Thomas Gibbons, 1769)

>'Oh let these tidings be received
>With universal joy,
>And let the high angelic praise
>Our tuneful powers employ!'

SERMON NO. 2158

11 AUGUST (1889)

Concerning the consolations of God

'Are the consolations of God small with thee? Is there any secret thing with thee?' Job 15:11
SUGGESTED FURTHER READING: Psalm 42:1–11

One of the worst causes of disquietude is unbelief. Have you begun to distrust? Do you really doubt your God? Then I do not wonder that the consolations of God are small with you. Here is the rule of the kingdom: 'According to your faith be it unto you.' If you doubt God, you will get little from him. 'He that wavereth' may not expect to 'receive anything of the Lord.' Strong faith may have what it wills, but when your doubts master your faith, prayer cannot prevail. Few are the dainties from the King's table which come to the dish of mistrust. What do you doubt? Do you question *the Word of God*? Has the Lord said more than the truth will warrant? Do you think so? Will you dare to throw such a handful of mud upon the veracity of God? His truth is one of his crown jewels; would you take it away? Do you distrust *his power*? Do you think he cannot comfort you? Do you imagine that he cannot make you 'ride on the high places of the earth'? Do you think that he cannot put a new song into your mouth and make you rejoice in his name from morning to night? Why should you doubt his power to make you joyful in his house? Do you doubt *the Lord's wisdom*? Do you think the Holy Spirit cannot meet your case and provide comfort suitable for your distress? Surely you cannot have fallen into this base suspicion! Or do you doubt *the Lord's presence*? Do you think that he is too far off to know you and help you? He is everywhere present and he knows the way that you take. Come and trust the Lord.

FOR MEDITATION: (*Our Own Hymn Book*, no. 622 v.3—Anne Steele, 1760)

'But oh! when gloomy doubts prevail,
I fear to call Thee mine;
The springs of comfort seem to fail,
And all my hopes decline.'

SERMON NO. 2099

12 AUGUST (1888)

Crossing the Jordan

'Then Joshua commanded the officers of the people, saying, Pass through the host, and command the people, saying, Prepare you victuals; for within three days ye shall pass over this Jordan.' Joshua 1:10–11
SUGGESTED FURTHER READING: Titus 1:1–14

When he said, 'Prepare you victuals' did he not mean 'Begin to feed on food of that sort upon which you are henceforth to live'? The manna would cease in three days and never fall again. After they crossed the Jordan, they would feed on the corn of the land. Manna was the staple of their wilderness food, but they had eaten other things as well, for they had flocks and herds. They were to prepare, not manna, for that would not keep above a day, but such food as they would subsist upon when they entered upon their estates. Children of God, get good meals of spiritual meat, the kind upon which you will live hereafter. Feed much on the love of God and the glorious truths which are laid up in Christ Jesus. Care nothing for the husks of human thought and carnal eloquence, but take to the solid meat, which is to be your nourishment when you dwell in the presence of God for ever. I wish that professing Christians were more cautious about what they feed on. I am afraid that some, if they hear a sermon, are satisfied, whatever the sort may be. They do not care what the doctrine may be, if a clever man talks prettily and gratifies their ear. Some people can eat sawdust and make a meal of shadows. I could almost wish it were true, that 'if they drink any deadly thing, it shall not hurt them', for they do drink very deadly things when they go to the tavern of modern thought. But I say, feed on Christ, on spiritual food, on the pure truth of God's Word; feed your souls on nothing else. Know the taste of what you eat and let it be as clear and definite as that of butter and honey, that so you may readily 'refuse the evil, and choose the good.'

FOR MEDITATION: (*Our Own Hymn Book,* no. 874 vv.1&3—Samuel Stennett, 1787)
'On Jordan's stormy banks I stand, and cast a wishful eye
To Canaan's fair and happy land, where my possessions lie.
There generous fruits that never fail, on trees immortal grow;
There rocks and hills, and brooks and vales, with milk and honey flow.'

SERMON NO. 2039

13 AUGUST (PREACHED 8 AUGUST 1886)

Confidence and concern

'For the which cause I also suffer these things: nevertheless I am not ashamed: for I know whom I have believed, and am persuaded that he is able to keep that which I have committed unto him against that day. Hold fast the form of sound words, which thou hast heard of me, in faith and love which is in Christ Jesus. That good thing which was committed unto thee keep by the Holy Ghost which dwelleth in us.' 2 Timothy 1:12–14
SUGGESTED FURTHER READING: Jeremiah 9:1–6, 23–24

Observe carefully what Paul had done. He had trusted a person: 'I know whom I have believed'. He had trusted that person with full, clear knowledge of him, so trusted that he did not alter his trust as years rolled by, but as he grew in the knowledge of that person he was also confirmed in his confidence in him: 'I know whom I have believed'. He does not say, 'I know *what* I have believed,' though that would have been true; he does not say, 'I know *when* I believed,' though that would have been correct; nor does he say, 'I know *how much* I have believed,' although he had well weighed his faith. He does not even say, 'I know *in whom* I have believed,' but he goes closer still. He says expressly, 'I know *whom* I have believed', as much as to say, 'I know the person into whose hand I have committed my present condition and my eternal destiny. I know who he is and I therefore, without any hesitation, leave myself in his hands.' Brethren, it is the beginning of spiritual life to believe Jesus Christ. Is not this the one word that we preach to you continually? 'Believe on the Lord Jesus Christ, and thou shalt be saved'. 'He that believeth on the Son hath everlasting life'. 'He that believeth on him is not condemned'. Many are the Scriptural assurances to the same effect. Paul had not ventured upon a fancy, but he had trusted in a well-known friend. He had not done this in ignorance, nor in fanaticism, nor in desperation, but with cool, clear, deliberate judgment, knowing whom he had trusted. Ignorance is a wretched foundation, but sure knowledge is like a rock.

FOR MEDITATION: (*Our Own Hymn Book*, no. 670 v.2—Isaac Watts, 1709)

'Jesus, my God! I know His name,
His name is all my trust;
Nor will He put my soul to shame,
Nor let my hope be lost.'

14 AUGUST (1887)

The blind beggar of the temple, and his wonderful cure

'As long as I am in the world, I am the light of the world. When he had thus spoken, he spat on the ground, and made clay of the spittle, and he anointed the eyes of the blind man with the clay, and said unto him, Go, wash in the Pool of Siloam (which is by interpretation, Sent). He went his way therefore, and washed, and came seeing.' John 9:5–7
SUGGESTED FURTHER READING: Mark 10:46–52

The way of justification by faith is peculiarly open to criticism and is about the last that this wise world would have selected. Yet, eccentric as it may seem for Christ to heal with spittle and dust, it was the best and wisest way for his purpose. Suppose instead he had put his hand into his pocket and had taken out a gold or ivory box, and out of this box he had taken a little crystal bottle. Suppose he had taken out the stopper and then had poured a drop on each of those blind eyes and they had been opened, what would have been the result? Everybody would have said, 'What a wonderful medicine! I wonder what it was! How was it compounded? Who wrote the prescription? Perhaps he found the charm in the writings of Solomon and so he learned to distil the matchless drops.' Thus you see the attention would have been fixed on the means used and the cure would have been ascribed to the medicine rather than to God. Our Saviour used no such rare oils or choice spirits, but simply spat and made clay of the spittle, for he knew that nobody would say, 'The spittle did it,' or 'It was the clay that did it.' No, if our Lord seems to be eccentric in the choice of means, yet is he eminently prudent. The gospel of our Lord Jesus—and there is only one—is the wisdom of God, however singular it may seem in the judgment of the worldly wise. It may be thought strange, but it is the sum of all wisdom and those who try it find it to be so. It would be impossible to improve upon it. Its adaptation to man's case is marvellous; its suitability to its design is matchless; it blesses man, while it gives all glory to God.

FOR MEDITATION: Both this man (John 9:1,8,38) and Bartimaeus (see today's reading) were blind beggars who believed in the Lord Jesus Christ. Likewise our spiritual blindness (2 Corinthians 4:4) can only be removed by begging for God's mercy (Luke 18:13; Romans 10:13) and believing on the Lord Jesus Christ (Acts 16:31; Romans 10:10).

SERMON NO. 1977

15 AUGUST (1886)

Secret drawings graciously explained

'The LORD *hath appeared of old unto me, saying, Yea, I have loved thee with an everlasting love: therefore with lovingkindness have I drawn thee.'* Jeremiah 31:3
SUGGESTED FURTHER READING: John 6:35–45

Sitting down one day, I meditated upon where I was and what I was. I said to myself, 'I have believed in Jesus Christ and I have passed from death unto life. To God be praise!' Then my train of thought ran thus: 'How have I come to be in this condition? Did I make this change in myself? No. Must I praise my own free will? No. Was there originally in me something better which led me to Christ, while my companions have not come?' I dared not say so, and therefore I perceived that the difference was made by the sovereign grace of God. I do not know whereabouts in theology I might have wandered otherwise, but those reflections made me a Calvinist, that is to say, one who traces salvation to the Lord alone. I saw that my salvation was of the Lord from first to last, and I have never had a doubt about the matter since. It is no wish of mine to preach salvation by 'the will of man', or by 'the will of the flesh', but salvation all of grace, from beginning to end, 'According to the eternal purpose which' the Lord 'purposed in Christ Jesus' before the world was. It did not need any intricate reasoning to land me on the rock of free grace doctrine. If the Lord saved me, then he intended to save me: he did not do so by accident or inadvertence. Then, if he once intended to save me, there could be no reason why that intention should begin at any one moment; he must have purposed to save me from all eternity. God has his plan and purpose, and what he actually does must have been known to him and purposed by him from of old. Then I saw, as in a glass, the ways of God towards me, but it was not till the Lord himself had appeared unto me that I had this conception of his ways.

FOR MEDITATION: (*Our Own Hymn Book,* no. 230 v.6—John Kent, 1803)
  'A monument of grace, a sinner saved by blood:
  The streams of love I trace up to the Fountain, God;
  And in His sacred bosom see eternal thoughts of love to me.'

SERMON NO. 1914

16 AUGUST (1885)

A traitor suspected and convicted

'The carnal mind is enmity against God.' Romans 8:7
SUGGESTED FURTHER READING: John 5:36–47

Oh the mournful consequences of living and dying at enmity with God! You cannot succeed in this enmity. You have no power with which to contend against the Lord and to prosper. You need not wish that you could have such power. Why should you want to contend against love, mercy, truth, goodness and righteousness? Oh that the Spirit of all grace would lead you to loathe yourself! You have never committed adultery; you were never a thief; you were never a swearer; but do not compliment yourself upon being free from those crimes: it is sin enough not to love God. It is proof enough of a base heart not to have delighted in the Lord. When I take a friend to see a landscape that enchants me, and he looks at it and mutters, 'I see nothing in it,' I feel sorry for him. When I cause him to hear the delightful strains of Handel's music, and he murmurs, 'There is a deal of noise and I can hear a big drum,' I feel greatly sorry for him that he has no ear for music. So it is when I think of the glories of God and meet with men who do not appreciate them; I feel grieved for them. I would sooner be blind, deaf and dumb and lose all feeling, than lose the sense of the beauty and perfection of God. The capacity to enjoy God and to understand his superlative excellence is the grandest faculty that a being can possess and he that has it not is dead while he lives. He, who does not love the ever-blessed Lord, is a very Nabal, whose heart is like a stone within him. He is a fool written large who knows not God. May the Lord manifest his grace to those of you who are in such a condition and bring you to deplore it and escape from it!

FOR MEDITATION: (*Our Own Hymn Book*, no. 461 v.5—Anne Steele, 1760)

'Oh change these wretched hearts of ours,
And give them life divine!
Then shall our passions and our powers,
Almighty Lord, be Thine.'

SERMON NO. 1878

17 AUGUST (1890)

The hold-fasts of faith

'Who is the father of us all, (as it is written, I have made thee a father of many nations,) before him whom he believed, even God, who quickeneth the dead, and calleth those things which be not as though they were.'
Romans 4:16–17
SUGGESTED FURTHER READING: Genesis 17:15–18:15

Abraham enjoyed the promise. I have often thought of the old man laughing at the thought of the birth of a son to him in his hundredth year. Two people may do the same thing and in the one it may be right, but in the other it may be wrong. Sarah laughed because she thought it absurd and could not believe it, but Abraham laughed because he did believe it and realized it. He knew it would be so and he began to laugh with joy and gladness. Oh for more of such laughing! He believed himself to be the father of many nations and the old man laughed and laughed again; it seemed such a fountain of happiness to him. If you believe, you will laugh too. We have too much crying among us. Oh for a little more filling of the mouth with laughter and the tongue with singing, for 'The LORD hath done great things for us; whereof we are glad'! It is not a fiction; it is a fact. The Lord has given us eternal life in his Son, Jesus Christ our Lord. Let us laugh and laugh again, for an unutterable joy of heart floods our spirit. Bunyan pictures Christiana as saying to Mercy, 'What was the matter that you did laugh in your sleep tonight?' And Mercy said, 'But are you sure I laughed?' When she told her dream, Christiana said, 'Laugh! ay, well you might to see yourself so well.' She laughed because she dreamed she had been welcomed into glory. To faith this is no dream. We have had many dreams of this sort and we know that we are saved by grace, adopted of the Father, united to the Son, indwelt by the Holy Spirit, visions most true; these have made us laugh with an inward, inexpressible delight. The more steadfastly we believe, the more of this rapturous joy we shall experience.

FOR MEDITATION: (*Our Own Hymn Book,* no. 621 v.1—Isaac Watts, 1709)
'Why does your face, ye humble souls,
Those mournful colours wear?
What doubts are these that waste your faith,
And nourish your despair?'

SERMON NO. 2159

18 AUGUST (1889)

Faith essential to pleasing God

'But without faith it is impossible to please him: for he that cometh to God must believe that he is, and that he is a rewarder of them that diligently seek him.' Hebrews 11:6
SUGGESTED FURTHER READING: 2 Peter 3:11–18

The Lord 'is a rewarder of them that diligently seek him.' That is not quite an exact translation: the Greek word means not only seek him, but 'seek him out', that is, seek him till they find him and seek him above all others. It is a very strong word; we hardly know how to transfer its meaning into English, for though it does not say 'diligently,' it implies it. We must seek and seek out, that is, seek till we really find. Those who with their hearts follow after God shall not be losers, if they believe that he will reward them. You have to believe God so as to seek his glory. Even when you do not obtain any present reward for it, you are to say, 'I shall have a reward ultimately, even if I am for a while a loser through his service. If I lose money, respect, friendship or even life from following God, yet still he will be a rewarder and I shall be repaid ten thousand-fold, not of debt, but according to his grace.' He that would please God, must first 'believe that he is,' and then, dedicating himself to God, must be firmly assured that this is the right, wise and prudent thing to do. Be certain that to serve God is in itself gain: it is wealth to be holy; it is happiness to be pleasing to God. It is life to live to God, to know him, to adore him, to commune with him, to become like him. It is glory to make him glorious among the sons of men. For us 'to live is Christ'. This, we are persuaded, is the best pursuit for us; in fact, it is the only one which can satisfy our hearts. God is our shield and our 'exceeding great reward'; in the teeth of everything that happens we hold to this, that to serve God is gain. If God helps us to trust him and therefore to live unto him and seek to be well-pleasing in his sight, we shall succeed in pleasing him.

FOR MEDITATION: (*Our Own Hymn Book,* no. 146 version 1 v.3—Isaac Watts, 1719)
    'Happy the man whose hopes rely
    On Israel's God: He made the sky,
    And earth, and seas, with all their train;
    And none shall find His promise vain.'

SERMON NO. 2100

19 AUGUST (1888)

Sown among thorns

'And some fell among thorns; and the thorns sprung up, and choked them.' 'He also that received seed among the thorns is he that heareth the word; and the care of this world, and the deceitfulness of riches, choke the word, and he becometh unfruitful.' Matthew 13:7,22
SUGGESTED FURTHER READING: Hebrews 12:12–25

A boy in the streets, selling mince pies, kept crying, 'Hot mince pies!' A man bought one of them and found it quite cold. 'Boy,' said he, 'why did you call these pies hot?' 'That's the name they go by, sir,' said the boy. So there are plenty of people that are called Christians, but they are not Christians: that's the name they go by, but all the substance is drained out of them by other matters. You see the shape, the make and some of the talk of a Christian, but the fruit of a Christian is not there. That is the result of the choking by the thorns of care, riches, pleasure and worldliness in general. What life there was in the wheat was very sickly. Let me remind certain people that their spiritual lives are growing weak at this time. Morning prayer this morning, how long did it take? Do not grow red in the face. I will say no more about it. You are not coming out tonight, are you? Half a Sunday is enough worship for you. Would you not like to live in some country place where you did not need to go out to a place of worship even once? Bible reading, how much do you do of that? Family prayer, is that a delight to you? Why, numbers of so-called Christians have given up family religion altogether. How about week-day services? You are not often at a prayer-meeting. No, the distance is too great! Thursday night service? 'Well, you see I might come, but there happens to be a lawn tennis party that night.' Will you come in the winter? 'Yes, I would, but then a friend drops in and we have an evening at bagatelle.' How many there are in this condition! I am not going to judge them, but I remember that an eminent minister used to say, 'When weekday services are forsaken, farewell to the life of godliness.'

FOR MEDITATION: (*Our Own Hymn Book,* no. 643 v.1—Benjamin Beddome, 1818)
    'Strait the gate, the way is narrow, to the realms of endless bliss;
    Sinful men and vain professors, self-deceived, the passage miss;
    Rushing headlong, down they sink the dread abyss.'

SERMON NO. 2040

20 AUGUST (PREACHED 21 AUGUST 1890)

The obedience of faith

'By faith Abraham, when he was called to go out into a place which he should after receive for an inheritance, obeyed; and he went out, not knowing whither he went.' Hebrews 11:8
SUGGESTED FURTHER READING: John 21:20–25

Oh that we were most of all earnest to render personal obedience! It is very easy to offer unto God a sort of 'other people's obedience', to fancy that we are serving God, when we are finding fault with our neighbours and lamenting that they are not so godly as they ought to be. Truly, we cannot help seeing their shortcomings, but we should do well to be less observant of them than we are. Let us turn our magnifying glasses upon ourselves. It is not so much our business to be weeding other people's gardens as to keep our own vineyard. To the Lord each one should cry, 'Lord, what wilt thou have *me* to do?' We, who are his chosen, 'redeemed from among men,' called out from the rest of mankind, ought to feel that if no other ears hear the divine call, our ears must hear it, and if no other heart obeys, our soul rejoices to do so. We are bound with cords to 'the horns of the altar'. The strongest ties of gratitude hold us to the service of Jesus: we must be obedient in life to him who, for our sakes, was 'obedient unto death'. Our service to our Lord is freedom: we will to yield to his will. To delight him is our delight. It is a blessed thing when the inmost nature yearns to obey God, when obedience grows into a habit and becomes the very element in which the spirit breathes. Surely it should be so with every one of the blood-washed children of the Most High and their lives will prove that it is so. Others are bound to obey, but we should attend most to our own personal obligation and set our own houses in order. Our obedience should begin at home and it will find its hands full enough there.

FOR MEDITATION: Christians 'ought to obey God' (Acts 5:29) as his servants (Romans 6:16–17) and as his children (1 Peter 1:14). Obedience is 'better' and God delights in it (1 Samuel 15:22). Do you seek to 'be obedient in all things' (2 Corinthians 2:9)?

SERMON NO. 2195

21 AUGUST (1887)

Trust

'That we should be to the praise of his glory, who first trusted in Christ. In whom ye also trusted, after that ye heard the word of truth, the gospel of your salvation.' Ephesians 1:12–13
SUGGESTED FURTHER READING: 1 Peter 1:18–2:8

Observe, first, that we are bound to trust him from *his very name*. His name is 'Christ,' that is, the 'Anointed.' God has sent him; God has commissioned him; God has equipped him; he is the anointed of God: dare I distrust him? An ambassador from heaven, with the divine warrant at his back, known to speak in the name of the Lord God, how dare I say I have no confidence in him? By the glorious name of Christ I claim for him that you who seek salvation should trust him implicitly and trust him at once. Remember, next, *his glorious person*. He who is set forth as the object of saving trust is none other than the Son of God. In his Godhead and in his humanity, yes, in his undivided person, he claims your trust. Can you not trust him that made heaven and earth, without whom 'was not any thing made that was made'? Can his power fail you? Can his wisdom mislead you? Can his mind change toward you? Can he be unfaithful? The Son of the Highest, can you not trust him? Away with the impertinence of mistrust! Can you doubt the Holy and the True? Dare you doubt the Lamb of God? Be not so foolhardy as thus to defy the incarnate Son of God and treat him as though he could deceive you. Next, trust him, because of *his matchless character*. Have you ever heard of another such as the Christ of God? Among the sons, no one is like him. He is all goodness, the fullness of love and the pattern of tenderness. He is always true and always faithful. By that blessed character which he bears, which I am sure you would not for a moment question, a character which even infidels have been forced to admire, I pray you trust him!

FOR MEDITATION: (*Our Own Hymn Book,* no. 559 v.3—Horatius Bonar, 1857)
   'I rest my soul on Jesus, this weary soul of mine;
   His right hand me embraces, I on His breast recline.
   I love the name of Jesus, Immanuel, Christ the Lord;
   Like fragrance on the breezes, His name abroad is poured.'

SERMON NO. 1978

22 AUGUST (1886)

The ever-living Priest

'And they truly were many priests, because they were not suffered to continue by reason of death: but this man, because he continueth ever, hath an unchangeable priesthood. Wherefore he is able also to save them to the uttermost that come unto God by him, seeing he ever liveth to make intercession for them.' Hebrews 7:23–25
SUGGESTED FURTHER READING: 1 Thessalonians 5:23–28

The Lord Jesus Christ will save us entirely: he will work out the salvation of the whole man, body, soul and spirit. He ever lives to save his people to the utmost, that is to say, all his people and all of every one of his people. Nothing essential to manhood shall be left to perish in the case of those whom he redeems. All that which the first Adam ruined, the second Adam shall restore. The Canaan of manhood from Dan to Beersheba shall be conquered by our Joshua. As yet 'the body is dead because of sin; but the Spirit is life because of righteousness.' But the day comes when the body 'also shall be delivered from the bondage' which sin has brought upon it. Not a bone, nor a piece of a bone, of a redeemed one shall be left in the hands of the enemy. God's deliverances are always complete. When the Lord sent his angel to bring Peter out of prison, he said to the slumbering apostle, 'Cast thy garment about thee, and follow me.' That garment might be only a fisherman's cloak, but it must not be left in Herod's hands. He said also, 'bind on thy sandals', for when the angel of the Lord sets a man free, he will not leave even a pair of old shoes behind him. The redemption of Christ is perfect: it reaches to the uttermost. He seems to say to sin, Satan and death, as the Lord said to Pharaoh, 'there shall not an hoof be left behind'. All that he has redeemed by price he will also redeem by power, and to that end he makes ceaseless intercession before God. 'To the uttermost' from all our doubts, fears, follies and failures, Jesus will bring us by his endless intercession. 'To the uttermost' from every consequence of the fall, personal sin and actual death, Jesus by his intercession will save us. 'To the uttermost'. Oh, think of it!

FOR MEDITATION: (*Our Own Hymn Book,* no. 326 v.5—Anne Steele, 1760)
    'Great Advocate, Almighty Friend, on Him our humble hopes depend:
    Our cause can never, never fail, for Jesus pleads, and must prevail.'

SERMON NO. 1915

23 AUGUST (1885)

The dying thief in a new light

'But the other answering rebuked him, saying, Dost thou not fear God, seeing thou art in the same condemnation? And we indeed justly; for we receive the due reward of our deeds: but this Man hath done nothing amiss. And he said unto Jesus, Lord, remember me when thou comest into thy kingdom.' Luke 23:40–42

SUGGESTED FURTHER READING: Philippians 1:19–26

I remember that Mr Baxter said that he was not in a hurry to be gone to heaven; a friend called upon Dr John Owen, who had been writing about the glory of Christ, and asked him what he thought of going to heaven. That great divine replied, 'I am longing to be there.' 'Why,' said the other, 'I have just spoken to holy Mr Baxter and he says that he would prefer to be here, since he thinks that he can be more useful on earth.' 'Oh!' said Dr Owen, 'my brother Baxter is always full of practical godliness, but for all that I cannot say that I am at all desirous to linger in this mortal state. I would rather be gone.' Each of these men seems to me to have been the half of Paul. Paul was made up of the two, for he was desirous to depart, but he was willing to remain because it was needful for the people. We would put both together and, like Paul, have a strong 'desire to depart, and to be with Christ', and yet be willing to wait if we can do service to our Lord and to his church. Still, I think he has the best of it who is converted and enters heaven the same night. This robber breakfasted with the devil, but dined with Christ on earth and supped with him in Paradise. This was short work, but blessed work. What a host of troubles he escaped! What a world of temptation he missed! What an evil world he quitted! He was just born, like a lamb dropped in the field, and then he was lifted into the Shepherd's bosom straight away. I do not remember the Lord ever saying this to anybody else. I dare say it may have happened that souls have been converted and have gone home at once, but I never heard of anybody that had such an assurance from Christ as this man had.

FOR MEDITATION: (*Our Own Hymn Book,* no. 288 v.2—William Cowper, 1779)
'The dying thief rejoiced to see that fountain in his day;
Oh may I there, though vile as he, wash all my sins away!'

SERMON NO. 1881

24 AUGUST (1890)

Not sufficient, and yet sufficient

'Not that we are sufficient of ourselves to think anything as of ourselves; but our sufficiency is of God; who also hath made us able ministers of the new testament; not of the letter, but of the spirit: for the letter killeth, but the spirit giveth life.' 2 Corinthians 3:5–6
SUGGESTED FURTHER READING (Spurgeon): 2 Corinthians 2:14–17

Trust not your own sufficiency. If we who preach to you, and if those who were far greater than we are, felt bound to say, 'Not that we are sufficient of ourselves to think anything as of ourselves', how little must your sufficiency be! It is very wonderful how fully in Scripture the inability of man is set out. Here we see our inability to think aright: 'Not that we are sufficient of ourselves to think anything as of ourselves'. In another passage we find that a good will is of the Lord. 'Work out your own salvation with fear and trembling. For it is God which worketh in you both to will and to do of his good pleasure.' To will aright is more than to think aright, but we never make so distinct an advance as to will that which is good until we are made willing. When we get so far as that, we pull up all of a sudden and come to a dead halt, finding, with the apostle, 'to will is present with me; but how to perform that which is good I find not'; then are we driven to God for power to turn our willing into acting. In this going to God we are brought to a stand-still again, for we read and feel that 'we know not what we should pray for as we ought'. What can we do, if even in prayer we fail? Suppose we are taught to pray and, helped by the Spirit of God, we begin to work, yet we cannot keep on working without fresh grace, for David, when he had wrought up the people to a very high degree of consecration, thought it needful to pray that the Lord would 'keep this for ever in the imagination of the thoughts of the heart of thy people'. Our Saviour prayed, 'keep them', for we soon go back to the old deadness and lethargy unless he that first made us still keeps us alive.

FOR MEDITATION: 'Who is sufficient' for service (2 Corinthians 2:15–16; 3:5–6), for sacrifice (2 Corinthians 9:6–8), for sickness (2 Corinthians 12:7–9), for singleness (Matthew 19:10–11) or for salvation (Psalm 49:7–9,15)? Only those who can say 'I am self-sufficient in Christ's sufficiency' (Philippians 4:13—The Amplified Bible).

SERMON NO. 2160

25 AUGUST (1887)

Judgments and no repentance: repentance and no salvation

'They repented not to give him glory.' Revelation 16:9
SUGGESTED FURTHER READING: Matthew 26:69–27:5

Judgment may produce a carnal repentance, a repentance that is of the flesh and after the manner of the sinful nature of men. In this repentance the depravity of the heart remains the same in essence, though it takes another form of showing itself. Though the man changes, he is not savingly changed: he becomes another man, but not a new man. The same sin rules in him, but it is called by another name and wears another dress. The stone is carved into a more sightly shape, but it is not turned into flesh. The iron is cast into another image, but it is not transformed into gold. This carnal repentance is caused by fear. Does not every thief repent of robbery when he is convicted and sent to jail? Does not every murderer repent of his crime when he stands under the fatal tree? This is the kind of repentance which the terrors of the Lord will work in men's minds unless they are altogether hardened and under the special dominion of the devil. Travellers in great storms will tremble and, trembling, will confess their guilt and begin to pray, but when the tempest is over, their trembling, confession and praying are all over. They shake because of their sins, but they are not shaken out of their sins. Mariners far out at sea, when the labouring ship threatens to go down to the bottom, will repent, but such repentance is only a few qualms of conscience, because they are in dread of death, judgment and hell. So men that lie upon a bed of sickness, when their bones ache, their hearts melt and the grave yawns beneath their couch, will often repent, yet, if they could be raised up, they would return to their sins as the dog returns to his vomit. This is wretched work. This repentance gives no glory to God, and leads to no saving and lasting deliverance from sin.

FOR MEDITATION: (*Our Own Hymn Book*, no. 570 v.2—Simon Browne, 1720)
    'With heart unshaken I have heard
    Thy dreadful thunders roar:
    When grace in all its charms appeared,
    I only sinned the more.'

SERMON NO. 2054

26 AUGUST (1888)

Jesus known by personal revelation

'He saith unto them, But whom say ye that I am? And Simon Peter answered and said, Thou art the Christ, the Son of the living God. And Jesus answered and said unto him ... flesh and blood hath not revealed it unto thee, but my Father which is in heaven.' Matthew 16:15–17
SUGGESTED FURTHER READING: 1 Timothy 3:14–16

Jesus says, in verse eighteen, 'I will build my church'. It is very significant that our Lord should connect with the church the right idea of himself. In our text we have the test question which must be put to everyone who is to be admitted into the assembly of the Lord: 'whom say ye that I am?' The first question to be put to one who would join the church is, 'What do you think of Jesus?' *'You cannot be right in the rest, unless you think rightly of him.'* If you do not begin aright with Jesus, 'the Christ, the Son of the living God', you will not go on aright and your joining of any visible church will be a mistake which will be injurious both to yourself and the church. Let it be with you first Christ, then the church. There is a certain style of preaching in which the church is the leading idea, meaning, to a great extent, by 'the church,' the priest, as the dispenser of ordinances and the voice of God. But as for us, our chief word is not 'church,' but 'Christ,' and not even the church of Christ, but Christ as very God of very God, the Son of the Highest. First Christ, the root, then the church, the outgrowth; first Christ, the builder, then the church, which is his building. The most important question is not, 'To which part of the church do you belong?' but, 'Do you belong to Christ, who is "the Son of the living God"?' This must be decided by that other question, 'whom say ye that I am?' If you know Christ, if you rest in Christ, if Christ be to you 'the way, the truth, and the life', above all, if Christ be formed 'in you, the hope of glory', your connection with the true church, the church of God's election and redemption, is clear and certain.

FOR MEDITATION: Christ's deity is emphasised by his own claims (John 5:17–18,23; 8:58; 10:30–33; 14:8–9) and by comparing New Testament applications to him with Isaiah's references to Jehovah (e.g. 42:8 & 48:11 with John 17:5,22,24; 44:6 with Revelation 1:17–18; 45:21–23 with Philippians 2:9–11). Some testified to this truth unintentionally (Mark 2:5–7), others gladly (Luke 8:39; John 1:1–3,14; 20:28–29).

SERMON NO. 2041

27 AUGUST (PREACHED 28 AUGUST 1887)

Folly of unbelief

'Then he said unto them, O fools, and slow of heart to believe all that the prophets have spoken.' Luke 24:25
SUGGESTED FURTHER READING: 2 Corinthians 4:1–6

The Lord Jesus says, 'Look unto me, and be ye saved, all the ends of the earth'. The gospel is to be preached to every creature, and every creature that believes it shall be saved: but these people back out of it and begin hammering out reasons for their own destruction. A sadly suicidal business this! Let the devil invent reasons for my not being saved: it is not a business which can bring me any form of good. Nothing can stand against the promise of God: he commands me to believe on his Son Jesus; I do believe and I am saved and shall be saved, despite all the objections which may be raised by carnal reason. Though you find it so hard to *believe Christ*, you have found it very easy to *believe in yourself*. Not long ago you were everybody and now you cannot believe that Christ is everybody. You thought you were very good; you were wonderfully easy in your own mind when you ought to have been afraid. What! Was it easy to believe your poor self and can you not believe the faithful word of a good and gracious Saviour who says that, if you trust him, you shall be saved? Moreover, you are very apt now to *believe Satan* if he comes and says that the Bible is not true, or that Jesus will not accept you, or that you have sinned beyond hope, or that the grace of God cannot save you. Of course, you believe the father of lies and you go mourning and moping, when you might at once go singing and dancing, if you would believe your Saviour. Jesus bids you trust and live, but Satan says it is of no use your trusting; you believe Satan and treat your Lord as if he had intended to deceive you. 'O fools, and slow of heart'!

FOR MEDITATION: (*Our Own Hymn Book*, no. 191 v.5—Isaac Watts, 1709)
  'Oh, for a strong, a lasting faith,
  To credit what the Almighty saith!
  To embrace the message of His Son,
  And call the joys of heaven our own.'

SERMON NO. 1980

28 AUGUST (1890)

Patient Job, and the baffled enemy

'In all this Job sinned not, nor charged God foolishly.' Job 1:22
SUGGESTED FURTHER READING: 1 Peter 4:1–16

If you do not sin while under the stress of heavy trouble, God will be honoured. He is not so much glorified by preserving you from trouble, as by upholding you in trouble. He allows you to be tried that his grace in you may be tested and glorified. When one Winstanley, years ago, built a lighthouse on the Eddystone Rock, he said that he was sure that it would stand any storm that ever blew and he should himself like to be in it in the fiercest tempest that ever drove down the Channel. It came to pass that he was in his own construction one night and there came a tremendous blast, which swept him and his lighthouse clean away, so that he was never heard of again. He courted trial because he believed in his work: God permits trial because he knows that his wisdom and grace have made us able to bear it. The lighthouse which was afterwards built on the Eddystone has had all manner of storms beating upon it, but it has outlived them all, and therefore its builder's name is held in honour. Even thus our God is glorified in every trial of his saints, when their grace enables them to endure with patience. 'There,' says he, 'see what grace can do, what suffering it can endure, what labours it can perform!' Grace is like an athlete performing before the great King and his heavenly court. A 'cloud of witnesses' look down upon the feats of faith and note with joy how it achieves everything which the Lord appoints it to perform. It even enters into contest with the fiend of hell and gives him a signal overthrow, and he that made the athlete and trained him for the contest, is honoured thereby. If you do not sin in your trouble, your endurance of trial will bring glory to God.

FOR MEDITATION: (*Our Own Hymn Book*, no. 744 v.4—William Freeman Lloyd, 1835)
   'Rock of Ages, I'm secure
   With Thy promise full and free,
   Faithful, positive and sure:
   "As thy day, thy strength shall be."'

SERMON NO. 2172

29 AUGUST (1886)

In Christ no condemnation

'There is therefore now no condemnation to them which are in Christ Jesus, who walk not after the flesh, but after the Spirit.' Romans 8:1
SUGGESTED FURTHER READING: Galatians 5:13–26

Judge yourselves in which way you are walking. Are you walking according to the flesh? Do you do whatever you like to do? Do you believe whatever you like to believe? Do you say to yourself, 'I am not going to be limited by Scripture, nor by rules of holiness: these are too old-fashioned and strait-laced for me'? Then you walk after the flesh: you are your own guide: your own wisdom, righteousness and vain desires conduct you whither they will. You are blind, your guide is blind and you will soon fall into the ditch. You think not so, but time will prove my words. Blessed is that man who no longer follows the devices and desires of his own heart and no longer trusts to his own understanding. Blessed is he who bows his mind to the mind of God. My own desire is not to believe what I may imagine, or invent, or think out, but I would believe what the Lord God has taught us in the inspired Scriptures. I submit myself to the guidance of the Spirit of God in connection with the written word. This is safe walking. Combine the two descriptive clauses of my text. On the one hand look to Christ alone and abide in him; then, on the other hand, look for the guidance of the Holy Spirit who is to be in you. By faith we are in Christ and the Holy Spirit is in us. All who can go with me in this are delivered from condemnation, for how shall he be condemned that is in Christ? And how shall he be condemned that has the Holy Spirit within him? 'There is therefore now no condemnation to them which are in Christ Jesus, who walk not after the flesh, but after the Spirit.'

FOR MEDITATION: (*Our Own Hymn Book*, no. 917 v.4—John Mason, 1683)
   'I bless Thy wise and wondrous love,
   Which binds us to be free;
   Which makes us leave our earthly snares,
   That we may come to Thee!'

SERMON NO. 1917

30 AUGUST (1885)

Robinson Crusoe's text

'Call upon me in the day of trouble: I will deliver thee, and thou shalt glorify me.' Psalm 50:15
SUGGESTED FURTHER READING: Jonah 1:1–2:10

One book charmed us all in the days of our youth. Is there a boy alive who has not read it? *Robinson Crusoe* was a wealth of wonders to me: I could have read it over twenty times and never have wearied. I am not ashamed to confess that I can read it even now with ever fresh delight. Robinson and his man Friday, though mere inventions of fiction, are wonderfully real to most of us. A passage in that book comes vividly before my recollection tonight as I read my text, and in it I find something more than an excuse. Robinson Crusoe has been wrecked. He is left in the desert island all alone. His case is a very pitiable one. He goes to his bed and he is smitten with fever. This fever lasts upon him long and he has no one to wait upon him, no one even to bring him a drink of cold water. He is ready to perish. He had been accustomed to sin and had all the vices of a sailor, but his hard case brought him to think. He opens a Bible which he finds in his chest and he lights upon this passage, *'call upon me in the day of trouble: I will deliver thee, and thou shalt glorify me.'* That night he prayed for the first time in his life and ever after there was in him a hope in God, which marked the birth of the heavenly life. Defoe, who composed the story, was, as you know, a Presbyterian minister; though not overdone with spirituality, he knew enough of religion to be able to describe very vividly the experience of a man who is in despair and who finds peace by casting himself upon his God. As a novelist, he had a keen eye for the probable and he could think of no passage more likely to impress a poor broken spirit than this. Instinctively he perceived the mine of comfort which lies within these words.

FOR MEDITATION: (*Our Own Hymn Book*, no. 70 v.1—Charles H. Spurgeon, 1866)
   'Make haste, O God, my soul to bless!
   My help and my deliverer Thou;
   Make haste, for I'm in deep distress,
   My case is urgent; help me *now*.'

SERMON NO. 1876

31 AUGUST (1890)

Self low, but Christ high

'The centurion answered and said, Lord, I am not worthy that thou shouldest come under my roof: but speak the word only, and my servant shall be healed.' Matthew 8:8

SUGGESTED FURTHER READING: James 4:6–5:6

A deep sense of unworthiness is no proof that a man has grossly sinned. It may be viewed in quite the opposite light: if the man had been heinously wicked, his conscience would have lost its sensitiveness and he would not in all probability have felt his unworthiness so keenly. He that has high thoughts of himself is not necessarily a man of clean life; on the other hand he that has very depreciatory thoughts of himself is not thereby proven to be worse than others. He that feels himself unworthy has something about him that God esteems. We are sure of this, for when the Lord seeks a lodging among men, though he might have his choice of palaces, he nevertheless deigns to say, 'I dwell in the high and holy place, with him also that is of a contrite and humble spirit, to revive the spirit of the humble, and to revive the heart of the contrite ones.' Do not judge men by their estimates of themselves, or, if you do, take this as your guide, that he that humbles himself is to be exalted, and he that exalts himself is to be abased. He that is great is little: let him that is little to himself be all the greater with you. God loves not those who boast: 'He hath filled the hungry with good things; and the rich he hath sent empty away.' I commend this sense of unworthiness, because it has a tendency to make a man kind to others. He who thinks himself everybody thinks another man nobody. Pride has no heart and will rather turn a sick servant out of doors than seek a physician for him. If a man is proud, he will say, 'I am a man under authority, having soldiers under me, and I am not to be worried by having sick boys to look after.' Sympathy, tenderness and the valuation of others are strangers in the house of the proud, but they take up their abode with those who think themselves unworthy.

FOR MEDITATION: (*Our Own Hymn Book*, no. 597 v.4—Thomas Raffles, 1812)

'Jesus, save my dying soul; make my broken spirit whole;
Humbled in the dust I lie; Saviour, leave me not to die.'

SERMON NO. 2161

1 SEPTEMBER (1889)

'Pricked in their heart'

'God hath made that same Jesus, whom ye have crucified, both Lord and Christ. Now when they heard this, they were pricked in their heart, and said unto Peter and to the rest of the apostles, Men and brethren, what shall we do?' Acts 2:36–37

SUGGESTED FURTHER READING: Luke 22:54–62

When a man finds out that he has done a fearful wrong to one who loved him, he grows sick at heart and views his own conduct with abhorrence. Remember the story of Llewellyn and his faithful dog. The prince came back from the hunt and missed his infant child, but saw marks of blood everywhere. Suspecting his dog Gelert of having killed the child, he drove his vengeful sword into the faithful hound, which had been bravely defending his child against a huge wolf, which lay there, 'tremendous still in death.' He had slain the faithful creature which had preserved his child. Poor Gelert's dying yell pierced the prince to the heart. If such emotions fitly arise when we discover that we have in error been ungenerous and cruel to a dog, how ought we to feel towards the Lord Jesus, who laid down his life that we, his enemies, might live? I recall an awfully tragic story of an evil couple, who kept an inn of base repute. A young man called one night to lodge. They noticed that he had gold in his purse and murdered him in the night. It was their own son, who had come back to gladden their old age and wished to see whether his parents would remember him. Oh the bitterness of their lamentation when they found that through the lust of gold they had murdered their own son! Take out of such amazing grief its better portion and then add to it a spiritual conviction of the sin of evil-treating the Son of God, the perfect One, the Lover of our souls, and you come near the meaning of being 'pricked in their heart'. Oh to think that we should despise him who loved us and gave himself for us, and should rebel against him that bought us with his own blood while we were his enemies!

FOR MEDITATION: (*Our Own Hymn Book*, no. 279 v.1—Isaac Watts, 1709)

'Alas! and did my Saviour bleed?   Would He devote that sacred head
And did my Sovereign die?   For such a worm as I?'

SERMON NO. 2102

2 SEPTEMBER (1888)

Setting Jesus at nought

'And Herod with his men of war set him at nought.' Luke 23:11
SUGGESTED FURTHER READING: Acts 4:1–31

Sometimes believers show their love and their appreciation of their Master by special acts of homage. Herod, you see, when he made nothing of him, said, 'Here, bring out that glittering white robe of mine and put it on him, that we may heap contempt upon him. He calls himself a King! Let us pay him homage!' They mocked him, they put the robe upon him and then sent him back to Pilate. Now, I want you to imitate Herod in the opposite direction. Let us do our Lord special honour tonight. Let us crown him. As soon as we have opportunity, let us make some special offering of our substance to his cause. Let us set apart a season for adoration and reverent worship. Let us resolve that for his sake we will speak well of his name to somebody to whom we have not yet spoken. It may be that some of you can sing a hymn to Jesus with choice music, or write a glorious verse for his dear sake. Go, take your pen, dip it in your heart and write a fresh tract in honour of his blessed name. Herod 'set him at nought', but let us set him on high in our best manner. Set him at the highest figure that your thought and your imagination can reach. It may be that some brother here could preach about his Lord and yet he has not opened his mouth from timidity. Come, try, my friend. Shake off your bashfulness. It may be that some sister here might teach women, or get together a class of youngsters and glorify Christ by instructing them. I long to undo what Herod did and pay the Well-beloved a recompense for his shame. Oh, how would I honour him!

FOR MEDITATION: (*Our Own Hymn Book*, no. 282 v.5—Isaac Watts, 1709)
   'Were the whole realm of nature mine,
   That were a present far too small;
   Love so amazing, so divine,
   Demands my soul, my life, my all!'

SERMON NO. 2051

3 SEPTEMBER (PREACHED 2 SEPTEMBER 1888)

The maintenance of good works

'This is a faithful saying, and these things I will that thou affirm constantly, that they which have believed in God might be careful to maintain good works. These things are good and profitable unto men.'
Titus 3:8

SUGGESTED FURTHER READING: Luke 10:25–42

'Be careful to maintain good works.' This precept is full in its meaning. In another Scripture you are told to 'Be careful for nothing', but here you are bidden to 'be careful to maintain good works.' We read, 'Casting all your care upon him; for he careth for you', but do not cast off your care 'to maintain good works.' You have a number of cares about you; slip a bridle over their heads and train them to plough in the field of good works. Do not let care be wasted over food, raiment and such temporary matters; these may be left with God, but take sacred cares upon you, the cares of holy and gracious living. Yoke your best thoughts to the care of holiness: 'be careful to maintain good works.' What are good works? The term is greatly inclusive. Of course we number in the list works of charity, works of kindness and benevolence, works of piety, reverence and holiness. Such works as comply with the two tables of commandments are good works. Works of obedience are good works. What you do because God bids you do it, is a good work. Works of love to Jesus, done out of a desire for his glory, these are good works. The common actions of every-day life, when they are well done, with a view not to merit, but out of gratitude, these are good works. 'Be careful to maintain good works' of every sort and kind. You are sure to be working in some way; mind that your works are good works. If you have commenced well, 'be careful to *maintain* good works' and, if you have maintained them, go on to increase them. Remember, you are saved by grace, 'not by works of righteousness', but after you are saved there comes in this precept, 'be careful to maintain good works.'

FOR MEDITATION: The wrong kind of cares can be a great hindrance (Luke 8:14; 10:41; 21:34). Carefulness is better channelled into good works towards the sick (Luke 10:34–35), our families (1 Corinthians 7:32–34), individual Christians (1 Corinthians 12:25–26; Philippians 4:10) and the church (2 Corinthians 8:16; 11:28; Philippians 2:20; 1 Timothy 3:5).

SERMON NO. 2042

4 SEPTEMBER (1887)

God the wonder-worker

'To him who alone doeth great wonders: for his mercy endureth for ever.' Psalm 136:4
SUGGESTED FURTHER READING: Psalm 111:1–10

Many apparent wonders can be explained and, henceforth, the wonder is gone. Certain nations wonder at an eclipse, which to the astronomer is a very simple affair. Now, you cannot explain away election, redemption, regeneration and the pardon of sin: these great wonders of almighty love are all the greater the more you know of them. Many wonders, also, are diminished by familiarity. I remember as a child being taken to see the first train drawn by a steam-engine to our town: I greatly wondered, but I have now ceased to wonder at such an ordinary sight. I remember a viaduct, which to my juvenile mind was stupendous; I have seen it since and it is by no means one of the wonders of the world. The wonders of grace are such, that the more you see them, the more your wonder grows. In these cases it is ignorance which does *not* wonder, but knowledge marvels exceedingly. Those who are most familiar with the Lord think the most of him and of his grace. The wonders of divine grace are so great that they can never be eclipsed by any greater marvels. No one will ever tell us a more marvellous story than the life and death of our Lord for sinful men. In the gift of Jesus Christ the infinite God has outdone all his previous acts. This is the greatest wonder that angels ever heard of; they desire still to look into it. This is the climax of all miracles: 'God so loved the world, that he gave his only begotten Son, that whosoever believeth in him should not perish, but have everlasting life.' When we have, for millions of years, realized what divine mercy means, my conviction is that we shall wonder more at the Lord's grace than we do now. Salvation is an exceeding *great* wonder, like the great mountains or the great sea. The loving-kindness of the Lord is immeasurable.

FOR MEDITATION: (*Our Own Hymn Book*, no. 136 song 2 v.7—Isaac Watts, 1719)
   'He sent His Son with power to save
   From guilt, and darkness, and the grave:
   Wonders of grace to God belong,
   Repeat His mercies in your song.'

SERMON NO. 1981

5 SEPTEMBER (1886)

The abiding of the Spirit the glory of the church

'Be strong, all ye people of the land, saith the LORD, *and work: for I am with you, saith the* LORD *of hosts ... my spirit remaineth among you: fear ye not.'* Haggai 2:4–5

SUGGESTED FURTHER READING: 1 Corinthians 12:1–11

The other day a brother from Wales told me of the great men he remembered: he said that he had never heard such a one as Christmas Evans, who surpassed all men in his fervour. I asked him if he knew another Welsh minister who preached like Christmas Evans. 'No,' he said, 'we have no such man in Wales in our days.' So in England we have neither Wesley nor Whitefield, nor any of their order; yet, as with God is 'the residue of the Spirit', he can fetch out from some chimney-corner another Christmas Evans, or find in our Sunday-school another George Whitefield, who shall declare the gospel with the Holy Spirit sent down from heaven. Let us never fear for the future or despair for the present, since the Spirit of God remains with us. Even if the growing error of the age should silence the last tongue that speaks out the old gospel, let not faith be weakened. I hear the tramp of legions of soldiers of the cross. I hear the clarion voices of hosts of preachers. 'The LORD gave the word: great was the company of those that published it.' Have faith in God through our Lord Jesus Christ! 'When he ascended on high, he led captivity captive, and gave gifts unto men.' He gave apostles, teachers, preachers and evangelists, and he can do it again. Let us fall back upon the eternal God and never be discouraged for an instant. Nor is this all. The Holy Spirit, being with us, can move the whole church to exercise its varied ministries. This is one of the things we want very much, that every member of the church should recognize that he is ordained to service. Everyone in Christ, man or woman, has some testimony to bear, some warning to give, some deed to do in the name of the 'holy child Jesus,' and if the Spirit of God is poured out upon our young men and women, each one will be aroused to energetic service.

FOR MEDITATION: (*Our Own Hymn Book,* no. 957 v.4—Albert Midlane, 1861)

'Revive Thy work, O Lord, exalt Thy precious name;
And, by the Holy Ghost, our love for Thee and Thine inflame.'

SERMON NO. 1918

God our continual resort

'Be thou my strong habitation, whereunto I may continually resort.'
Psalm 71:3
SUGGESTED FURTHER READING: Job 28:1–28

A man's habitation is the place of his intimate knowledge. David knew the Lord even as he knew the caves in which he had sheltered. David could have served as guide to the great hollows of Adullam, and these, in their vastness and sublimity, may be likened to the mysteries of God. There is a weird charm to my mind about caves: I like to visit all that are in my way. One is pleased to pass from one subterranean room to another and mark the secrets which are revealed by the glare of the torches. Here there is a spring of water, there a grand stalactite; here is an ascending staircase leading to another hollow and there you must go down by a ladder to a greater depth. This is a fair allegory of the way in which the Spirit of God leads us into all truth. In God, even in Christ Jesus, 'are hid all the treasures of wisdom and knowledge', and within these hiding-places we find our habitations. David was so much at home with God that he entered by earnest trust into one attribute after another and delighted in them all. He knew the Lord. He could say, 'My meditation of him shall be sweet: I will be glad in the LORD.' He loved to dwell in the rocky strongholds of eternal love, unchanging grace, almighty wisdom, unspotted holiness, unerring purpose and infinite power. O brethren, seek to have the same clear knowledge of the Lord as David had, till you can say that you are at home with God, who is your habitation.

FOR MEDITATION: (*Our Own Hymn Book,* no. 91 song 2 v.1–Henry Francis Lyte, 1834)
'There is a safe and secret place,
Beneath the wings divine,
Reserved for all the heirs of grace,
Oh, be that refuge mine!'

SERMON NO. 1858

7 SEPTEMBER (1890)

And why not me?

'Behold, there came a leper and worshipped him, saying, Lord, if thou wilt, thou canst make me clean. And Jesus put forth his hand, and touched him, saying, I will; be thou clean. And immediately his leprosy was cleansed.' Matthew 8:2–3
SUGGESTED FURTHER READING: Matthew 3:1–12

The leper came alone. He came not through persuading friends. I am afraid that some people join the church because other people press them to do so: this is a mistake. Some will say that they believe in Jesus, because it will give pleasure to earnest friends: this is mischievous. The leper was under no excitement; he was not the fungus of a revival, but the fruit of grace. He did not go into an inquiry-room, see all the rest zealous about Jesus and therefore become subject to a like feeling. No; he came alone, and came deliberately and bowed himself at Jesus' feet. I want any here who are quite unused to religious influences, who have no mother to put her arms around their neck and pray for them, no friends to explain the things of God to them, nevertheless to come to Jesus. You need a Saviour; do you feel that you do? Though not accompanied by others, yet come to Jesus. Come alone and by yourself. Come at once to Christ and cast yourself at his feet. The thoughtful individual believer is often one of the best of converts, for he is most to be relied on. I like much those who are not imitators, but take their own course in coming to Jesus. Some are carried off their legs during a time of religious excitement and think they are converted when they are not. Some profess faith because their brothers, sisters and friends are doing so, but it is not sufficiently an individual matter of heart with them. I set the leper before you as an example of the courage which comes to Jesus by itself, whether others will come or not.

FOR MEDITATION: (*Our Own Hymn Book*, no. 394 v.3—Charles Wesley, 1740)
　'Now, Lord, to whom for help I call,
　Thy miracles repeat;
　With pitying eye behold me fall
　A leper at Thy feet.'

SERMON NO. 2162

8 SEPTEMBER (1889)

The hunger and thirst which are blessed

'Blessed are they which do hunger and thirst after righteousness: for they shall be filled.' Matthew 5:6
SUGGESTED FURTHER READING: Matthew 3:13–4:4

This man is blessed, for in his hunger and thirst he is in accord with the Lord Jesus Christ. When our Lord was here, he hungered after righteousness, longing to do and suffer his Father's will. His disciples, on one occasion, went away to the city to buy meat; he, being left alone, thirsted to bless the poor sinful woman of Samaria, who came to the well to draw water. To her he said, 'Give me to drink', not only to commence the conversation, but because he thirsted to make that woman righteous. He thirsted to convince her of her sin and lead her to saving faith; and when he had done so, his desire was gratified. When his disciples came back, though he had not touched a morsel of bread, or a drop of water, he said, 'I have meat to eat that ye know not of … My meat is to do the will of him that sent me, and to finish his work.' Our Lord, on the cross, said, 'I thirst', and that thirst of his lip and of his mouth was but the index of the deeper thirst of his heart and soul that righteousness might reign by his death. He died that the righteousness of God might be vindicated; he lives that the righteousness of God may be proclaimed; he pleads that the righteousness of God may be brought home to sinners; he reigns that this righteousness may chase out of this world the iniquity which now destroys it. When you 'hunger and thirst after righteousness' in any one of the shapes I have described, you are in a measure partakers with Christ and have fellowship with him in his heart's desire. As he is blessed, so are you, for 'Blessed are they which do hunger and thirst after righteousness'.

FOR MEDITATION: (*Our Own Hymn Book,* no. 653 vv.1&2—Charitie Lees Smith, 1861)
  'Lord I desire to live as one who bears a blood-bought name,
  As one who fears but grieving Thee, and knows no other shame.
  As one by whom Thy walk below should never be forgot;
  As who who fain would keep apart from all Thou lovest not.'

SERMON NO. 2103

9 SEPTEMBER (1888)

The blood of the Lamb, the conquering weapon

'And they overcame him by the blood of the Lamb, and by the word of their testimony; and they loved not their lives unto the death.' Revelation 12:11

SUGGESTED FURTHER READING: Hebrews 2:14–18

By 'the blood of the Lamb' we understand our Lord's death as a substitutionary sacrifice. Let us be very clear here. It is not said that they overcame the arch-enemy by the blood of Jesus, or the blood of Christ, but 'by the blood of *the Lamb*'; the words are expressly chosen because, under the figure of a lamb, we have set before us a sacrifice. The blood of Jesus Christ, shed because of his courage for the truth, or out of pure philanthropy, or out of self-denial, conveys no special gospel to men and has no peculiar power about it. Truly it is an example worthy to beget martyrs, but it is not the way of salvation for guilty men. If you proclaim the death of the Son of God, but do not show that he died 'the just for the unjust, that he might bring us to God,' you have not preached the blood of the Lamb. You must make it known that 'the chastisement of our peace was upon him', and that 'the LORD hath laid on him the iniquity of us all', or you have not declared the meaning of the blood of the Lamb. There is no overcoming sin without a substitutionary sacrifice. The lamb under the old law was brought by the offender to make atonement for his offence and in his place it was slain: this was the type of Christ taking the sinner's place, bearing the sinner's sin and suffering in the sinner's stead, and thus vindicating the justice of God and making it possible for him to 'be just, and the justifier of him which believeth'. I understand this to be the conquering weapon, the death of the Son of God set forth as the propitiation for sin. Sin must be punished: it is punished in Christ's death. Here is the hope of men.

FOR MEDITATION: (*Our Own Hymn Book*, no. 302 v.1—Isaac Watts, 1709)

> 'I sing my Saviour's wondrous death;
> He conquered when He fell:
> "'Tis finished!" said His dying breath,
> And shook the gates of hell.'

SERMON NO. 2043

10 SEPTEMBER (1885)

'Thy rowers have brought thee into great waters'

'Thy rowers have brought thee into great waters.' Ezekiel 27:26
SUGGESTED FURTHER READING: Ezekiel 28:1–19

What crime is more like the pride of Lucifer than the pride of a wretched rebel, who talks about meriting heaven and finding entrance amongst glorified spirits, without washing his robes in the blood of Jesus, under the pretence that they were never foul. Does he imagine that he will be admitted to the courts of the Eternal King, to sing his own praises and thus insult the Lord? While others come there through rich, free and sovereign grace, and, therefore, rapturously adore almighty love, is he to reach the blissful shores to magnify his own excellence? If you have put to sea in the ship of self-righteousness, however strong the rowers who tug those three banks of oars and make the vessel leap through the waves, the day shall come when you will hear a voice across the waters crying, 'Thy rowers have brought thee into great waters: the east wind hath broken thee in the midst of the seas.' The voyage is too great for you: shipwreck is sure. May God give you grace to shun the attempt! Flee from your own works to Christ's work. Place your trust where God has placed his love, namely, in the Lord Jesus. Then shall you have good works indeed, but they shall be the cargo which you carry, not the ship which carries you. They shall then be grounded upon the motive of gratitude and not of selfishness; then shall real virtue be possible to you, virtue based on love to God. When you are delivered from your sin and safe in the righteousness of Christ, then will you say,

> 'Loved of my God, for Him again
> With love intense I burn:
> Chosen of Thee e'er time began,
> I choose Thee in return.'

FOR MEDITATION: All who trust in their own imagined righteousness (Luke 18:9) instead of the Lord Jesus Christ, are lovers of self, not lovers of God (2 Timothy 3:2,4). Paul gladly abandoned his own righteousness to receive God's righteousness (Philippians 3:8–9), but all who cling to self-righteousness place themselves outside the scope of Christ's mission (Luke 5:32). To be self-righteous is to be self-condemned.

SERMON NO. 1933

11 SEPTEMBER (1890)

Fever and its cure

'He ... entered into Simon's house. And Simon's wife's mother was taken with a great fever; ... he rebuked the fever: and it left her.' Luke 4:38–39
SUGGESTED FURTHER READING: 2 Corinthians 12:1–10

Capernaum was in that low, marshy district surrounding the northern part of the Sea of Galilee, near where the Jordan runs into it. There was always a lot of ague about; it had come to Peter's house in its worst form as 'a great fever' and had laid low his mother-in-law, much to the grief of all. However dear you may be to the heart of God and however near you live to him, you will be liable to sorrow. 'Although affliction cometh not forth of the dust, neither doth trouble spring out of the ground; yet man is born unto trouble, as the sparks fly upward.' None of us can hope for entire exemption from affliction. But it so happened that, just when the trial came, Jesus came too. It is beautiful to see the Lord of life close on the track of the fever, ready to deliver his chosen one. When a great affliction comes to a house, a great blessing is coming too. As our tribulations abound, so do our consolations. I have often noticed that when we are very glad, some ill news will calm our excitement. It happened to me this very week: returning from a happy meeting, a telegram met me to announce a sorrowful bereavement. But when we are very sorrowful, the Lord, by his Holy Spirit, causes a sense of peace and rest to steal over and sustain us. How often have I found the divine presence more consciously revealed and more sweetly sustaining in the hour of trouble than at any other season! I would not invite the fever to my house, but if Jesus would come with it, I would not be alarmed at its approach.

FOR MEDITATION: (*Our Own Hymn Book*, no. 746 vv.1&2—Augustus M. Toplady, 1780)
  'When languor and disease invade this trembling house of clay,
  'Tis sweet to look beyond the cage, and long to fly away.
  Sweet to look inward and attend the whispers of His love;
  Sweet to look upward to the place where Jesus pleads above.'
N.B. After a happy orphanage-visit the Spurgeons read of the death of their grandson, Philip, aged 11 months, on holiday at Herne Bay. On 11 September 1890 Spurgeon wrote to console his son Charles and his wife.

SERMON NO. 2174

12 SEPTEMBER (1886)

The very bold prophecy

'I am sought of them that asked not for me; I am found of them that sought me not: I said, Behold me, behold me, unto a nation that was not called by my name.' Isaiah 65:1

SUGGESTED FURTHER READING: John 12:20–46

If anybody were to ask me to state the gospel in a few words I should answer, the Lord says, 'Behold me, behold me'. The way of salvation is, 'Look unto me, and be ye saved, all the ends of the earth'. Christ on the cross cries to the guilty sinner, 'Behold the Lamb of God!' To encourage a trembling soul to behold him with steadfast hope the Lord says twice, 'Behold me, behold me'. Does any sinner exclaim, 'But Lord, I am so filthy'? Do not look at yourself: 'Behold me, for I can cleanse you.' 'But Lord, I am death itself.' Do not look at your own death. 'Behold me, for I am the resurrection and the life.' 'But, Lord, the more I look at myself the more I despair.' 'Then do not look at yourself, but look to me alone. Behold me, and then behold me again and again, and keep on beholding me till your heart finds perfect rest.' Look to Jesus as God is in him revealed as your Saviour and your all. Behold, your King is also your sacrifice. You can be justified through him by whom you shall be judged at the last great day. In this verse our Lord seems delighted to declare that blessed gospel which is the two-edged sword of his grace. Hear it, you sinners! Hear it, and obey it at once! What! Will you not look? Do you deny your Lord a look? Shall God cry, 'Behold me,' and will you hide your faces from him? I trust that some who never knew the gospel before will at this instant 'Behold the Lamb of God'. Look to your bleeding Saviour, your forgiving God. Look and live.

FOR MEDITATION: Read John 1:29–36. John the Baptist had been good at looking and listening (vv.29,32–34,36). His example teaches us to behold the Lord Jesus Christ as the sin-bearer (v.29), as the superior man (v.30), as the Spirit-baptizer (v.33) and as the Son of God (v.34). In the words of Pontius Pilate, 'Behold the man! ... Behold your King!' (John 19:5,14).

SERMON NO. 1919

13 SEPTEMBER (1885)

The cross our glory

'But God forbid that I should glory, save in the cross of our Lord Jesus Christ, by whom the world is crucified unto me, and I unto the world.'
Galatians 6:14
SUGGESTED FURTHER READING: 1 Corinthians 1:18–2:2

Notice that Paul does not here say that he gloried in Christ, though he did so with all his heart, but he declares that he gloried most 'in the cross of our Lord Jesus Christ,' which in the eyes of men was the very lowest and most inglorious part of the history of the Lord Jesus. He could have gloried in *the incarnation:* angels sang of it, wise men came from the Far East to behold it. Did not the new-born King awake the song from heaven of 'Glory to God in the highest'? He might have gloried in *the life of Christ*: was there ever such another, so benevolent and blameless? He might have gloried in *the resurrection of Christ*: it is the world's great hope concerning those that are asleep. He might have gloried in *our Lord's ascension*, for he 'led captivity captive,' and all his followers glory in his victory. He might have gloried in *his second advent*, and I doubt not that he did, for the Lord shall soon 'descend from heaven with a shout, with the voice of the archangel, and with the trump of God', 'to be admired in all them that believe'. Yet the apostle selected beyond all these that centre of the Christian system, that point which is most assailed by its foes, that focus of the world's derision, *the cross* and, putting all else somewhat into the shade, he exclaims, 'God forbid that I should glory, save in the cross of our Lord Jesus Christ'. Learn that the highest glory of our holy religion is the cross. The history of grace begins earlier and goes on later, but in its middle point stands the cross. Of two eternities this is the hinge: of past decrees and future glories this is the pivot.

FOR MEDITATION: (*Our Own Hymn Book*, no. 282 vv.1&2—Isaac Watts, 1709)
   'When I survey the wondrous cross on which the Prince of Glory died,
   My richest gain I count but loss, and pour contempt on all my pride.
   Forbid it, Lord, that I should boast, save in the death of Christ, my God,
   All the vain things that charm me most, I sacrifice them to His blood.'

SERMON NO. 1859

14 SEPTEMBER (PREACHED 13 SEPTEMBER 1885)

But a step

'There is but a step between me and death.' 1 Samuel 20:3
SUGGESTED FURTHER READING (Spurgeon): Psalm 90:1–12

A man who is going to a certain place should think about the place to which he is going and make some preparation for it. If he is a wise man, he will do so. I should like you to attain to such a state that you could feel as Dr Watts did. He said to a friend when he was an old man, 'I go to my bed each night with perfect indifference as to whether I shall wake up in this world or the next.' That is a beautiful state of mind to be in. Or, as the old Scottish minister said when someone asked him, 'Is this disease of yours fatal?' and he replied, 'I do not know and I do not wish to know, for I do not think that it can make much difference to me; for if I go to heaven, I shall be with God and if I stop here, God will be with me.' Is that not a sweet way of putting it? There is not so much difference, after all, between being with God and God's being with us. Old George the Third, who, whatever the faults of his early days, was undoubtedly a godly man in his old age, would have a mausoleum prepared for himself and family; when Mr Wyatt, the architect, went to see him by his own order, he did not know how to speak to the old king about his grave, but George said, 'Friend Wyatt, do not mind speaking about my tomb. I can talk as freely to you about the preparation of a place for me to be buried in, as I could about a drawing-room for me to hold my court in, for I thank God that I am prepared to do my duty if I live and to sleep in Jesus if I die.' There are few, I think, of his rank who could talk so, but every wise man ought to see to it that, as he must die, he is ready for it, ready for the bar of God.

FOR MEDITATION: (*Our Own Hymn Book,* no. 854 v.1—Thomas Kelly, 1804)
   'We've no abiding city here;
   This may distress the worldling's mind,
   But should not cost the saint a tear,
   Who hopes a better rest to find.'

SERMON NO. 1870

15 SEPTEMBER (1889)

The inner side of conversion

'Is Ephraim my dear son? is he a pleasant child? for since I spake against him, I do earnestly remember him still: therefore my bowels are troubled for him; I will surely have mercy upon him, saith the LORD.' Jeremiah 31:20

SUGGESTED FURTHER READING: Philemon 8–20

Let me imagine a scene. A little girl has behaved very badly during the day; mother has threatened her with punishment for her continued ill-conduct. The child, in her bad temper, has run away. The evening comes on; where is Jane? Her brothers and sisters do not know. It is getting late; where can she be? Has anybody seen her? No, she is not hidden away at home; every room has been searched. In alarm, some one is sent to the police-station. Have you seen a little girl? No, they have not seen a little girl. It gets to be ten o'clock at night and the matter is very serious. Eleven strikes like a knell. 'Why don't you go to bed, dear mother?' 'Go to bed! Why, I am her mother!' and she breaks out with, 'My dear child!' Surely a little while ago she might have been called a little good-for-nothing: one might have been glad to miss the worrying little troubler. But now mother cries, 'My dear child!' The clock strikes twelve; the small hours grow into great ages of grief. Father is troubled: he has been up and down the streets and searched everywhere. You meet him and say, 'She was, after all, a very commonplace child and most obnoxious in disposition.' 'You do not know her. She was such a pretty girl! She had her peculiarities, but it makes me angry to hear a word against the dear child.' Mother felt that she never knew before how much she loved that child! What is that? Is the wanderer found? What joy beams from every face! Could you have imagined that one naughty child could have made such a stir and caused such delight? Sinner, this is just what happens about you! Thus does the great God think of his wanderers and rejoice when he sees them returning home. When you cry, 'Father!' he answers with, 'Is he not my dear son? Is he not a pleasant child?' Love takes delight in repenting sinners.

FOR MEDITATION: (*Our Own Hymn Book*, no. 605 v.1—John Morrison, 1781)
> 'Come, let us to the Lord our God with contrite hearts return;
> Our God is gracious, nor will leave the desolate to mourn.'

SERMON NO. 2104

16 SEPTEMBER (1888)

All at it

'Therefore they that were scattered abroad went everywhere preaching the word. The Philip went down to the city of Samaria, and preached Christ unto them.' 'Then Philip opened his mouth, and began at the same scripture, and preached unto him Jesus.' Acts 8:4–5, 35
SUGGESTED FURTHER READING: Ephesians 2:11–22

See Philip. He is a Jew, but he goes to Samaria. 'Philip, what made you go to Samaria? Jews have no dealings with Samaritans.' Brethren, when it comes to preaching Christ we have dealings with everybody, Jews, Turks, infidels, cannibals. The Jew goes to Samaria for Christ and the Samaritans accept the Messiah of the Jews. Then Philip is called down south to journey along a desert way and there he meets an Ethiopian, probably a black man. Ah well! White men were not particularly anxious for the company of Ethiopians, but Philip gets up into his chariot and rides with him. Black and white make a fine mixture when the book of the prophet Isaiah lies between them. What a beautiful picture this would make, Philip and the eunuch riding together reading of the Lord Jesus in the Hebrew prophets! All the paltry differences of sect, politics, nationalities and races go to the winds as soon as we are possessed with a desire to win souls. 'Oh, but they are so dirty!' Let us show them how they can be cleansed. 'But the slum is so foul!' Yet for the love of Jesus we will enter it to carry his saving health among the people. What is more, we shall not only be willing to work for the poor and fallen, but we shall work with them. You, a person of taste and culture, will join hands with the illiterate worker and, while you are half amused at his blunders, you will be charmed by his zeal. You will not despise him, but you may even feel humbled as you see how, with less knowledge than yourself, he often shows more spiritual wisdom and energy. You will take a brotherly pride in such a man. Caste is gone when Christ is come.

FOR MEDITATION: Racial and other human differences do not apply when it comes to seeking God's salvation (Romans 10:11–13) and will not be in force in heaven (Revelation 7:9–10). They are not reasons for separation within the church (Galatians 3:26–28) and should be no hindrance to evangelism (1 Corinthians 9:19–22; Revelation 14:6–7).

SERMON NO. 2044

17 SEPTEMBER (PREACHED 12 SEPTEMBER 1886)

Is it true?

'Nebuchadnezzar spake and said unto them, Is it true, O Shadrach, Meshach, and Abed-nego, do not ye serve my gods, nor worship the golden image which I have set up?' Daniel 3:14

SUGGESTED FURTHER READING: 1 Peter 3:9–17

Be ready to give a reason for 'the hope that is in you with meekness and fear'. Be able to show why you are a believer in God, why you worship the Lord Jesus Christ, why you trust in his atoning sacrifice and why you make him the regulator of your life. Show why you cannot do what others do, why, being a child of God, your nature is changed and you have no wish to do that which you once delighted to do in the days before your conversion. Ask the Lord to help you to go to work with Bible reasons at your fingers' ends, for these are the best of reasons and bear a high authority about them, so that when the question is put to you, 'Is it true?' you may be able to say, 'Yes, it is true and this is why it is true. At such a time God revealed himself to me in his grace and opened my blind eyes to see things in a true light. He renewed my nature when he delivered me from the burden of sin; he made me to be a child of God when I found peace through his name; because of all this I cannot grieve my loving Lord by living in sin. I am not my own, I am bought with a price, and therefore I must do the will of him that redeemed me with his own blood.' I am sure that Shadrach, Meshach and Abed-nego would never have stood out against the imperious monarch as they did, if they had not known their bearings and well understood why it was that Jehovah alone is to be worshipped as God. When the mind is established, the heart is more likely to be firm. Know your duty and the arguments for it, and you are the more likely to be steadfast in the hour of temptation.

FOR MEDITATION: (Philip Bliss, 1838–1876)
   'Dare to be a Daniel!
   Dare to stand alone!
   Dare to have a purpose firm!
   Dare to make it known.'

SERMON NO. 1930

18 SEPTEMBER (1887)

How hearts are softened

'And I will pour upon the house of David, and upon the inhabitants of Jerusalem, the spirit of grace and of supplications: and they shall look upon me whom they have pierced, and they shall mourn for him, as one mourneth for his only son, and shall be in bitterness for him, as one that is in bitterness for his firstborn. In that day shall there be a great mourning in Jerusalem.' Zechariah 12:10–11

SUGGESTED FURTHER READING: Isaiah 61:1–3

Many and great are the advantages connected with softness of spirit. Tenderness of heart is one of the marks of a gracious person. Spiritual sensibility puts life and feeling into all Christian duties. He that prays feelingly, prays indeed; he that praises God with humble gratitude, praises him most acceptably; he that preaches with a loving heart has the essentials of true eloquence. An inward, living tenderness, which trembles at God's word, is of great price in the sight of God. You are in this matter agreed with me: at least, I know that some of you are thoroughly thus minded, for you are longing to be made tender and contrite. Certain of you who are truly softened by divine grace are very prone to accuse yourselves of being stony-hearted. We are poor judges of our own condition and in this matter many make mistakes. Mark this: the man who grieves because he does not grieve is often the man who grieves most. He that feels that he does not feel is probably the most feeling man of us all; I suspect that hardness is almost gone when it is mourned over. He who can feel his insensibility is not insensible. Those who mourn that their heart is a heart of stone, if they were to look calmly at the matter, might perceive that it is not all stone, or else there would not be a mourning because of hardness. But, whether this is so or not, I address myself to all of you whose prayer is for godly sorrow for sin. It is written in the covenant of grace, 'I will take away the stony heart out of your flesh, and I will give you an heart of flesh.' I pray that this may be fulfilled in you even now.

FOR MEDITATION: God's response to a broken heart is not to despise it (Psalm 51:17), but to draw near (Psalm 34:18) and to bring healing (Psalm 147:3). This was part of the purpose for which he sent the Lord Jesus Christ into the world (Isaiah 61:1; Luke 4:18).

SERMON NO. 1983

19 SEPTEMBER (1886)

The unkept vineyard; or, personal work neglected

'They made me the keeper of the vineyards; but mine own vineyard have I not kept.' Song of Solomon 1:6
SUGGESTED FURTHER READING: Proverbs 4:20–27

Just before a general election there is a manifestation of most remarkable men, generally people who know everything and a few things besides, who, if they could only be sent to Parliament, would turn the whole world upside down and put even Pandemonium to rights. They would pay the National Debt within six months and do any other trifle that might occur to them. Very eminent men are these! I have come across impossibly great men. None could be so great as these feel themselves to be. They are an order of very superior persons, reformers or philosophers, who know what nobody else knows, only, happily, they have not patented the secret, but are prepared to tell it out to others and thereby illuminate us all. I suggest to our highly-gifted friends that it is possible to be looking after a great many things and yet to be neglecting your own vineyard. There is a vineyard that a great many neglect and that is their own heart. It is well to have talent; it is well to have influence, but it is better to be right within yourself. It is well for a man to see to his cattle and look well to his flocks and to his herds, but let him not forget to cultivate that little patch of ground that lies in the centre of his being. Let him educate his head and intermeddle with all knowledge, but let him not forget that there is another plot of ground called the heart, the character, which is more important still. Right principles are spiritual gold and he that has them and is ruled by them, is the man who truly lives. He has not life, whatever else he has, who has not his heart cultivated and made right and pure.

FOR MEDITATION: (*Our Own Hymn Book,* no. 454 v.1—Isaac Watts, 1709)
   'Come, Holy Spirit, heavenly Dove,
   With all Thy quickening powers,
   Kindle a flame of sacred love
   In these cold hearts of ours.'

SERMON NO. 1936

20 SEPTEMBER (1885)

Nathanael: or, the man needed for the day

'Behold an Israelite indeed, in whom is no guile!' John 1:47
SUGGESTED FURTHER READING: Luke 8:4–15

The ground mentioned in the parable, which brought forth fruit to the divine sower, is said to be 'honest and good'. By this was not intended any spiritual grace, nor even any moral virtue of high degree, in the condition of the persons who received the gospel, but there was sincerity about the people so described; they were honest, straight, unsophisticated and free from subtlety and cunning. It is in the honest heart that sowing truth takes root. I have known the drunkard saved. I have seen the swearer have his mouth washed, so that he has spoken sweet and goodly words for the rest of his life. I have known the fornicator, adulterer and harlot delivered from the Stygian ditch of abominable lust. I have known men guilty of almost every sin delivered from the power of evil and the living evidence of holy conduct has proved their sincerity beyond all question. But I still say that my memory does not bring before me a single person habitually guilty of the double-shuffle, habitually a liar or a cheat, converted to God at all. The insincere, the canting, the hypocritical, the habitually deceptive—I know not of converts from these classes. There may have been such and I should not wonder if there have been, but I do not happen to have met with them. Most of the converted people I have seen have been straightforward and true after a way. They might curse and swear, they might deny the gospel, they might occasionally lie under strong pressure or from sheer flippancy and they might commit all manner of criminalities, but, as a rule, there they were and you could see them to be what they were. They were bad fellows enough, but they did not dissemble: they sinned most grievously, but they never pretended to be saints. Such were the men that Christ converted.

FOR MEDITATION: (*Our Own Hymn Book*, no. 15 vv.2&3—Charles H. Spurgeon, 1866)
　'Thy gate of pearl stands wide for those who walk upright:
　But those who basely turn aside Thou chasest from Thy sight.
　Oh tame my tongue to peace, and tune my heart to love;
　From all reproaches may I cease, made harmless as a dove.'

SERMON NO. 2068

21 SEPTEMBER (1890)

Entangled in the land

'For Pharaoh will say of the children of Israel, They are entangled in the land, the wilderness hath shut them in.' Exodus 14:3
SUGGESTED FURTHER READING: Psalm 27:1–14

My text is, '*Pharaoh will say* of the children of Israel, They are entangled in the land, the wilderness hath shut them in.' Upon this I make the observation, that this is not true. It is only what Pharaoh said. And so when Satan says, 'They are entangled in the land,' it is not true; it is only one of the sayings of the father of lies. 'They say', says one. Well, what do they say? Let them say it: their saying will not make it true. A troubled one comes to me and complains of a certain charge which has been made, and he adds, as the sharp edge of it all, 'Sir, it is not true.' Well, then, do not fret about it. One cries out, 'They are taking away my character and I feel it keenly because what they say is cruelly false.' Friend, do not feel it at all. You ought to feel it, if what they say is true. Now, what Pharaoh said was not true and his speech did not cause the children of Israel to be really entangled in the land. Pharaoh's tongue speaks his wish, but his wish will not be realized. Our adversaries say that our cause is defeated. Is it? 'Ah!' say they, 'we have shut him up. The man cannot answer us; we have crushed his faith and argued his confidence to death.' Have you? By the grace of God we stand fast in the once-delivered faith, after all your sophistries and boasts. You say that we are entangled, but we are not. 'Show us,' say they, 'the way in which you will get out of the wilderness.' No, that we cannot do, but, if you will wait a while, the Lord will show you *that*, by leading us graciously through the divided sea, and it may be also by drowning you therein, as he did the Egyptians when the waters overwhelmed them. Israel could not guess her way, but Israel could wait till God revealed it.

FOR MEDITATION: (*Our Own Hymn Book*, no. 739 v.2—John Newton, 1779)

'Though many foes beset your road,
And feeble is your arm,
Your life is hid with Christ in God,
Beyond the reach of harm.'

SERMON NO. 2188

22 SEPTEMBER (1889)

Preparation for the coming of the Lord

'And now, little children, abide in him; that, when he shall appear, we may have confidence, and not be ashamed before him at his coming.'
1 John 2:28
SUGGESTED FURTHER READING: John 15:1–8

Our first anxious desire is that our hearers would *come to Christ*. We lay ourselves out to lift him up, 'as Moses lifted up the serpent in the wilderness,' and to bid men look to him and live. There is no salvation except by faith in the Lord Jesus Christ. He says, 'Look unto me, and be ye saved, all the ends of the earth: for I am God, and there is none else.' When men have looked to Jesus, our next anxiety is that they may *be in Christ*, the City of Refuge. We long to speak of them as 'men in Christ Jesus'. My beloved hearers, you must be in living, loving, lasting union with the Son of God, or else you are not in a state of salvation. That which begins with coming to Christ, as the engrafted branch is bound to the vine, continues in your growing into him and receiving of his life. You must be in Christ as the stone is in the building, as the member is in the body. When we have good hope that our hearers have come to Christ and are 'in Christ', a further anxiety springs up in our hearts that they may *'abide' in Christ*. Our longing is that, despite temptations to go away from him, they may always remain at his feet, that, notwithstanding the evil of their nature, they may never betray their Master, but may faithfully hold to him. We would have them mindful of that precept 'As ye have received Christ Jesus the Lord, so walk ye in him'. Oh that they may be 'rooted and built up in him,' and may always be in union with him! Then shall we present them to our Lord in the day of his appearing with exceeding great joy.

FOR MEDITATION: Are you following the C, B, A of the gospel? It is not only the preacher's anxious desire, but also God's express command that we *'come'* to the Lord Jesus Christ (Matthew 11:28; 1 Peter 2:4). Then, having received him, we are to *be* 'in him' (Colossians 2:6–7) and to *'abide'* in him' (John 15:4).

SERMON NO. 2105

23 SEPTEMBER (1888)

Further afield

'Then Paul and Barnabas waxed bold, and said, It was necessary that the word of God should first have been spoken to you: but seeing ye put it from you, and judge yourselves unworthy of everlasting life, lo, we turn to the Gentiles ... And when the Gentiles heard this, they were glad, and glorified the word of the Lord: and as many as were ordained to eternal life believed.' Acts 13:46,48

SUGGESTED FURTHER READING: Mark 12:28–37

I sat yesterday with two tubes in my ears to listen to sounds that came from revolving cylinders of wax. I heard music, though I knew that no instrument was near. It had been caught up months before and now was ringing out as clearly and distinctly in my ears as it could have done had I been present at its first sound. I heard Mr Edison speak: he repeated a childish ditty and, when he had finished, he called upon his friends to repeat it with him and I heard many American voices joining in that repetition. That wax cylinder was present when these sounds were made and now it talked it all out in my ear. Then I heard Mr Edison at work in his laboratory: he was driving nails, working on metal, doing all sorts of things and calling for this and that with that American tone which made one know his nationality. I sat, listened and felt lost in the mystery. But what of all this? What can these instruments convey to us? But to sit and listen to the gospel when your ears are really opened! Then you hear God himself at work; you hear Jesus speak: you hear his voice in suffering and glory; you rise up and say, 'I never thought to have heard such strange things! Where have I been to be so long deaf to this? How could I neglect a gospel in which are locked up such wondrous treasures of wisdom and knowledge, such measureless depths of love and grace?' In the gospel of the Lord Jesus, God speaks into the ear of his child more music than all the harps of heaven can yield. Do not despise it.

FOR MEDITATION: (*Our Own Hymn Book,* no. 910 v.1—Henry Francis Lyte, 1841)
   'Sweet is the task, O Lord, Thy glorious acts to sing,
   To praise Thy name, and hear Thy word, and grateful offerings bring.'

N.B. Thomas Alva Edison had invented the gramophone in 1877.

SERMON NO. 2045

24 SEPTEMBER (PREACHED 26 SEPTEMBER 1886)

Shaven and shorn, but not beyond hope

'Howbeit the hair of his head began to grow again after he was shaven.'
Judges 16:22
SUGGESTED FURTHER READING: 2 Timothy 2:20–26

There are some preachers who are splendid men and yet they are practical failures. You see in them wide knowledge, eloquent language and yet nothing. They can speak so properly that a senate might sit with admiration at their feet, but when they have done, nobody is pricked in the heart, nobody is convinced of sin, nobody is led to behold the beauties of Christ. Yet in their youth these men were soul-winners and were looked upon as champions for Christ. O Samson, how are we to make you strong again? That preacher must begin again to serve God with all his heart. He must give up the idea of being a great man, or a learned man, or an eloquent man. He must give up the idea of charming the *elite* and bringing together the fashionable, and must give himself up to glorify God by the winning of souls. When his hair grows again in that respect, we shall see what Samson can do. He will yet lay hold on the pillars of the Philistine temple and bring them down about the heads of the lords. Give me a man perfectly consecrated and I do not care much what he is. He may be rough, unpolished and even illiterate, but if he be consecrated, the people will feel his power. He may be educated so that he may understand all knowledge and he may speak as eloquently as Cicero, but if he is a consecrated man, his power will be none the less, but perhaps all the greater because of his education. But this one thing is essential: there must be consecration to God and downright earnestness in consequence, or else he will be a shaven Samson. May God give full consecration to each one of us who stand before the people to speak in his name, for in that consecration lies the power of the Holy Spirit to bless us! He cannot and will not bless unconsecrated men. If we do not live to God's glory, God will not use us.

FOR MEDITATION: (*Our Own Hymn Book,* no. 620 v.2—William Cowper, 1779)
  'Where is the blessedness I knew when first I saw the Lord?
  Where is the soul-refreshing view of Jesus and His word?'

SERMON NO. 1939

25 SEPTEMBER (1887)

The child of light walking in darkness

'Who is among you that feareth the LORD, that obeyeth the voice of his servant, that walketh in darkness, and hath no light? let him trust in the name of the LORD, and stay upon his God.' Isaiah 50:10
SUGGESTED FURTHER READING: Lamentations 3:1–24

The person described is one that fears the Lord and obeys the voice of his servant, yet 'walketh in darkness, and hath no light'. To many who know nothing of Christian experience this condition might seem to be a surprising one. Shall the child of light walk in darkness? The normal condition of a child of God is to 'walk in the light, as' God 'is in the light,' and to have fellowship with him; how comes he, then, to have no light? He that believes in the Lord Jesus Christ has passed 'from darkness to light' and he shall never 'come into condemnation'; how, then, does he come into darkness? In the darkness of sin and ignorance we no longer walk, but with the darkness of trouble and perplexity we are sometimes surrounded. The Lord is our light and our salvation, and therefore we do not walk in that darkness wherein the prince of darkness rules supreme, yet at times we are in the gloom of sadness and we see no light of consolation. It is not always so. Many Christian people go on year after year in uninterrupted sunshine and I do not see why we should not all look upon continued joy in the Lord as possible to ourselves. Why should not our peace flow on like an ever-widening river? Those of you who are always bright need not be afraid of your gladness. We are now and then in the dark, but we do not wish others to be so. Spiritual darkness of any sort is to be avoided and not desired; yet, surprising as it may seem to be, it is a fact that some of the best of God's people frequently walk in darkness.

FOR MEDITATION: (*Our Own Hymn Book*, no. 689 v.2—Thomas Kelly, 1815)
   'Though enwrapt in gloomy night,
   We perceive no ray of light;
   Since the Lord Himself is here,
   'Tis not meet that we should fear.'

SERMON NO. 1985

26 SEPTEMBER (1886)

Concerning death

'For I know that thou wilt bring me to death, and to the house appointed for all living.' Job 30:23
SUGGESTED FURTHER READING (Spurgeon): Psalm 39:4–13

You that are youngest and fullest of health and strength, I lovingly invite you not to put away this subject from you. Remember, the youngest may be taken away. Early in the life of my boys I took them to the old churchyard of Wimbledon and bade them measure some of the little graves within that enclosure, and they found several green hillocks which were shorter than themselves. I tried thus to impress upon their young minds the uncertainty of life. I would have every child remember that he is not too young to die. Let others know that they are not too strong to die. The stoutest trees of the forest are often the first to fall beneath the destroyer's axe. Paracelsus, the renowned physician of old time, prepared a medicine of which he said that if a man took it regularly he could never die, except it were of extreme old age; yet Paracelsus himself died a young man. Those who think they have found the secret of immortality will yet learn that they are under a strong delusion. None of us can discover a spot where we are out of bow-shot of the last enemy and therefore it would be idiotic to refuse to think of it. A certain vainglorious French Duke forbade his attendants ever to mention death in his hearing and when his secretary read to him the words, 'The late King of Spain,' he turned upon him with contemptuous indignation and asked him what he meant by it. The poor secretary could only stammer out, 'It is a title which they take.' Yes, indeed, it is a title we shall all take and it will be well to note how it will befit us. The King of terrors comes to kings, nor does he disdain to strip the pauper of his scanty flesh: to you, to me, to all he comes; let us all make ready for his sure approach.

FOR MEDITATION: (*Our Own Hymn Book*, no. 821 v.3—William Williams, 1773)
    'When I tread the verge of Jordan,
    Bid my anxious fears subside;
    Death of deaths, and hell's destruction,
    Land me safe on Canaan's side:
    Songs of praises I will ever give to Thee.'

SERMON NO. 1922

27 SEPTEMBER (1888)

Idols found wanting, but Jehovah found faithful

'Hearken unto me, O house of Jacob, and all the remnant of the house of Israel, which are borne by me from the belly, which are carried from the womb: And even to your old age I am he; and even to hoar hairs will I carry you: I have made, and I will bear; even I will carry, and will deliver you.' Isaiah 46:3–4
SUGGESTED FURTHER READING: Isaiah 40:9–31

As for this '*carrying*' of which the text speaks, assuredly that is no new thing. The Lord carried us in our infancy. Our first spiritual blessing came of our being carried: we were sheep going astray and the Shepherd came after us; when he found us, he carried us upon his shoulders rejoicing and brought us home. After that we were lambs in the fold, and he gathered the lambs in his bosom and carried us. Many a rough place have I encountered in my life's pilgrimage and I have wondered how I should ever get over it, but I have been carried over the rocky way so happily that the passage has made one of the most charming memories of my heart. I begin to like rough places, even as Rutherford fell in love with the cross he had to carry. When the road is smooth, I have to walk, but when it is very rough, I am carried. Therefore, I feel somewhat like the little boy I saw the other night. His father had been carrying him uphill, but when he reached a piece of level road, the boy was a great lump to carry, so his father set him down and let him walk. Then the little gentleman began to pull at his father's coat and I heard him say, 'Carry me, father! Carry me again!' Just so. Any sensible child of God will still say, 'Carry me, Father! Carry me still!' The Father's answer is, 'I have made, and I will bear; even I will carry … you.' Therefore call upon him and ask that, when the road is rough or miry, he will carry you—and he will.

FOR MEDITATION: (*Our Own Hymn Book*, no. 732 v.6—George Keith, 1787)
　'E'en down to old age, all My people shall prove
　My sovereign, eternal, unchangeable love;
　And when hoary hairs shall their temples adorn,
　Like lambs they shall still in My bosom be borne.'

SERMON NO. 2056

28 SEPTEMBER (1890)

Experience and assurance

'Because thou hast been my help, therefore in the shadow of thy wings will I rejoice.' Psalm 63:7
SUGGESTED FURTHER READING: Joshua 23:1–14

An infidel once sneered at a poor woman and said, 'How do you know the Bible is true?' She answered, 'I have experienced the truth of it.' He replied, 'Your experience! That is nothing to me.' 'No,' she said, 'that is very likely, but it is everything to me.' And so it is. My experience may not convince another man, but my experience has rooted, grounded and settled myself. 'But,' says one, 'Surely you are open to conviction?' Yes, I am always open to conviction, but there are some things upon which no man, nor angel, nor devil will ever alter my convictions already formed. There are a few things which we know, I mean things which we have experienced. If we have experienced the truth of them, then we are past all argument to the contrary; we are sure and certain, fixed and rooted. It seems to me that there are two books which a Christian man ought to study: the one is this big Book, the inspired Word of God; the other is the little book of his own life. If the believer lives long enough he will write into that little book all that there is in the great Book, only he will change the tense. When the great Book says, 'I will do this and I will do that,' we shall find in the little book, 'God has done so and so. In my own case the promise has been fulfilled.' The little book will be the echo of the inspired volume, the record of the fact that the Lord has done according to his word of promise. Thus experience becomes a support and a strength to the child of God in times of darkness or controversy. God grant that you may go on writing up your personal memoir and thus confirming the witness of the Spirit! Are not our lives the proof of God's faithfulness? Is not this the sum and substance of them, 'thou hast been my help'?

FOR MEDITATION: (*Our Own Hymn Book,* no. 34 version 1 v.4—Tate and Brady, 1696)
   'Oh make but trial of His love;
   Experience will decide
   How blest are they, and only they
   Who in His truth confide!'

SERMON NO. 2166

29 SEPTEMBER (1889)

The withered fig tree

'As he returned into the city, he hungered. And when he saw a fig tree in the way, he came to it, and found nothing thereon, but leaves only, and said unto it, Let no fruit grow on thee henceforward for ever. And presently the fig tree withered away.' Matthew 21:18–19
SUGGESTED FURTHER READING: Jeremiah 17:5–10

The searcher finds nothing but leaves where fruit might have been expected. Nothing but leaves means nothing but lies. Is that a harsh expression? If I profess faith and have no faith, is not that a lie? If I profess repentance and have not repented, is not that a lie? If I unite with the people of the living God, but have no fear of God in my heart, is not that a lie? If I come to the communion-table and partake of the bread and wine, but never discern the Lord's body, is not that a lie? If I profess to defend the doctrines of grace, but am not assured of the truth of them, is not that a lie? If I have never felt my depravity, never been effectually called, never known my election of God, never rested in the redeeming blood and have never been renewed by the Spirit, is not my defence of the doctrines of grace a lie? If there is nothing but leaves, there is nothing but lies and the Saviour sees that it is so. All the verdure of green leaf to him without fruit is but so much deceit. Profession without grace is the funeral pageantry of a dead soul. Religion without holiness is the light which comes from rotten wood, the phosphorescence of decay: I speak dread words, but how can I speak less dreadfully than I do? If we have a name to live and are dead, what a state we are in! Ours is something worse than corruption: it is the corruption of corruption. To profess religion and live in sin is to sprinkle rose-water upon a dunghill and leave it a dunghill still. To give a spirit an angel's name when it bears the devil's character, is almost to sin against the Holy Spirit. If we remain unconverted, of what use can it be to have our name written among the godly?

FOR MEDITATION: (*Our Own Hymn Book*, no. 652 v.2—John Fawcett, 1782)

'Let deep repentance, faith, and love,
Be joined with godly fear;
And all my conversation prove
My heart to be sincere.'

SERMON NO. 2107

30 SEPTEMBER (1886)

Love's law and life

'If ye love me, keep my commandments.' John 14:15
SUGGESTED FURTHER READING: 1 John 4:19–5:3

If you love Christ, set to work to *find out what his commandments are*. Study the Scriptures upon every point upon which you have the slightest question. This sacred oracle must guide you. Next, *be always true to your convictions* about what Christ's commandments are. Carry them out at all hazards and carry them out at once. It will be wicked to say, 'Hitherto I have obeyed, but I shall stop here.' We are committed to implicit obedience to the whole of the Master's will, involve what it may. Will you not agree to this at the outset? If you love him, you will not demur. *Take note of every commandment as it concerns you*. Let me mention one or two and beg you to obey them as you hear them. 'Go ye into all the world, and preach the gospel to every creature.' Is not this a call to you, my brother, to be a missionary? Do you hear it? Will you not say, 'Here am I; send me'? Another person has come into this house tonight full of enmity: somebody has treated him very badly and he cannot forget it; I pray him to hear the Lord's command: 'Therefore if thou bring thy gift to the altar, and there rememberest that thy brother hath ought against thee; leave there thy gift before the altar, and go thy way; first be reconciled to thy brother, and then come and offer thy gift.' And again: 'Beloved, let us love one another'. If any of you are in debt, obey this commandment: 'Owe no man any thing, but to love one another'. If you neglect the poor and live in a niggardly way, hear this commandment: 'Give to him that asketh thee, and from him that would borrow of thee turn not thou away.' At the back of all comes this, 'If ye love me, keep my commandments.'

FOR MEDITATION: (*Our Own Hymn Book*, no. 792 v.5—Augustus M. Toplady, 1772)
    'Whate'er consists not with Thy love,
    Oh teach me to resign:
    I'm rich to all the intents of bliss,
    If Thou, O God, art mine.'

SERMON NO. 1932

1 OCTOBER (PREACHED 7 OCTOBER 1888)

No compromise

'The servant said unto him, Peradventure the woman will not be willing to follow me unto this land: must I needs bring thy son again unto the land from whence thou camest? And Abraham said unto him, Beware thou that thou bring not my son thither again.' Genesis 24:5-6
SUGGESTED FURTHER READING: Numbers 11:1-20

No good can come of trying to conform to the world. Suppose the servant's policy had been adopted and Isaac had gone down to Nahor's house, what would have been the motive? To spare Rebekah the pain of separating from her friends and the trouble of travelling. If those things could have kept her back, what would she have been worth to Isaac? The test of separation was wholesome and by no means ought to be omitted. She is a poor wife who would not take a journey to reach her husband. And all the converts that the church will ever make by softening down its doctrine and becoming worldly, will not be worth anything. When we get them, the next question will be, 'How can we get rid of them?' They would be of no earthly use to us. It swelled the number of Israelites when they came out of Egypt that a great number of the lower order of Egyptians came out with them. But that mixed multitude became the plague of Israel in the wilderness: 'the mixt multitude ... fell a lusting'. The Israelites were bad enough, but the mixed multitude always led the way in murmuring. Why is there such spiritual death today? Why is false doctrine so rampant in churches? It is because we have ungodly people in the church and in the ministry. Eagerness for numbers has adulterated many churches, making them lax in doctrine and practice and fond of silly amusements. These people despise a prayer-meeting, but rush to see 'living waxworks' in their schoolrooms. God save us from converts made by lowering the standard and tarnishing the spiritual glory of the church!

FOR MEDITATION: (*Our Own Hymn Book,* no. 884 v.5—John Newton, 1779)
   'Saviour, if of Zion's city, I through grace a member am,
   Let the world deride or pity, I will glory in Thy name:
   Fading is the worldling's pleasure, all his boasted pomp and show!
   Solid joys and lasting treasure, none but Zion's children know.'

SERMON NO. 2047

2 OCTOBER (1887)

The child of light walking in light

'If we say that we have fellowship with him, and walk in darkness, we lie, and do not the truth: but if we walk in the light, as he is in the light, we have fellowship one with another, and the blood of Jesus Christ his Son cleanseth us from all sin.' 1 John 1:6–7
SUGGESTED FURTHER READING: Ephesians 5:1–16

Remember how David pronounces him blessed 'in whose spirit there is no guile.' He knew painfully what it was to be full of guile. See him! He has gone astray most grievously. His mind is in the dark. What does David do? There is a foul sin committed: he tries to make himself believe that it is not so very horrible; he labours to hoodwink his conscience. His sin is likely to be seen and he tries to cover it. He brings back Bathsheba's husband. When he declines to go to his house he must be made drunken. The design has failed. David is afraid, but not penitent; on the contrary, he hastens to still greater crime. Uriah is in the wars; there he is wantonly exposed to death and slain in battle. His death is ascribed to the fortune of war. David did not see that it was murder, for he was not walking in the light. He was still in darkness and therefore continued acting a deceitful part with his God and his own conscience. His conduct would not bear the light and so his one idea was to keep out of the light. How changed was all this after Nathan had said to him, 'Thou art the man'! When the light of heavenly conviction had penetrated the night of his soul, he made no more excuses and practiced no more subterfuges. He stood in the light, ashamed and confounded. Amazed at the sight of his sin, he abandoned all idea of covering it and fled at once to the mercy of God crying, 'Have mercy upon me, O God, according to thy lovingkindness'. In the sobbing and sighing of the fifty-first Psalm he lays bare his heart and in plainest terms cries, 'Deliver me from bloodguiltiness, O God, thou God of my salvation'. He is in the light now, for deceit has gone; now God can speak comfortably to him, wash him and make him 'whiter than snow.'

FOR MEDITATION: Our attitude towards the light has corresponding effects upon our behaviour (John 3:19–21). The secret sins of those who rebel against the light (Job 24:13–17) are all known to God (Psalm 90:8), but his blessing rests upon those who walk in the light (Psalm 89:15); 'come ye, and let us walk in the light of the LORD' (Isaiah 2:5).

SERMON NO. 1986

3 OCTOBER (1886)

The annual atonement

'For on that day shall the priest make an atonement for you, to cleanse you, that ye may be clean from all your sins before the LORD.' Leviticus 16:30
SUGGESTED FURTHER READING: Hebrews 9:23–28

It seems that the divine atonement puts away the sin of sin, the essence and heart of sin. Sin has its core, its kernel, its mortal spot. Within a fruit there is a central stone or pip; this may serve as the likeness of sin. Within each iniquity there seems to lie a something more essentially evil than the act itself: this is the kernel of intent, the core of obstinacy, the inner hate of the mind. Whatever may be the sin of the soul or the soul of the sin, atonement has been made for it all. Most sins are a conglomerate of sins. A sin may be compared to a honeycomb: there are as many sins within one sin as there are cells within a piece of comb. Sin is a swarming, hiving, teeming thing. You can never estimate its full vileness, nor perceive all its evil bearings. All sorts of sins may hide away in one sin. It would puzzle all the theologians in the world to tell what sin was absent from Adam's first offence. I could take any point you choose and show that Adam sinned in that direction. All sin was within that first sin. Sin is a multitudinous evil, an aggregate of all manner of filthiness, a chain with a thousand deadly links. A sinner is like a man possessed with a devil who cries, 'My name is Legion: for we are many.' It is one in evil and yet countless in forms. The atonement is more than equal to sin: it takes away all our transgressions in all our sins. It is the fullest purgation that could be imagined. The Lord Jesus has not left upon those for whom he has made atonement a single 'spot, or wrinkle, or any such thing', so far as their justification is concerned. He has not left an iniquity for which they can be condemned before the bar of judgment.

FOR MEDITATION: (*Our Own Hymn Book,* no. 564 v.1—Charles Wesley, 1762; Augustus M. Toplady, 1776)
   'Charged with the complicated load
   Of our enormous debt,
   By faith, I see the Lamb of God
   Expire beneath its weight!'

SERMON NO. 1923

4 OCTOBER (1885)

Departed saints yet living

'Now that the dead are raised, even Moses shewed at the bush, when he calleth the Lord the God of Abraham, and the God of Isaac, and the God of Jacob. For he is not a God of the dead, but of the living: for all live unto him.' Luke 20:37–38

SUGGESTED FURTHER READING: Luke 13:22–30

God is the God of saints, as living distinct lives: Abraham is Abraham, Isaac is Isaac, Jacob is Jacob. The three patriarchs were not all melted into one common Abraham, nor Isaac into one imaginary Isaac, neither was any one so altered as to cease to be himself. Abraham, Isaac and Jacob are all literally living as actual men and the same men as they used to be. Jacob is Jacob, not an echo of Abraham; Isaac is Isaac, not a rehearsal of Jacob. All the saints are existent in their personality, identity, distinction and idiosyncrasy. What is more, the patriarchs are mentioned by their names and so it is clear they are known: they are not three anonymous bodies, but Abraham, Isaac and Jacob. Many ask, 'Shall we know our friends in heaven?' Why not? The saints in heaven are never spoken of in Scripture as moving about anonymously, but their names are spoken of as 'written in the Lamb's book of life.' Why? The apostles knew Moses and Elijah on the Mount, though they had never seen them before. I cannot forget old John Ryland's answer to his wife: 'John,' she said, 'will you know me in heaven?' 'Betty,' he replied, 'I have known you well here and I shall not be a bigger fool in heaven than I am now; therefore I shall certainly know you there.' That seems to be clear enough. We read in the New Testament that many 'shall sit down with Abraham, and Isaac, and Jacob in the kingdom of heaven', not with three unknown individuals in iron masks, or three impersonalities who make a part of the great whole, nor three spirits who are as exactly alike as pins made in a factory, but Abraham, Isaac and Jacob. That is clear enough in the text.

FOR MEDITATION: (*Our Own Hymn Book,* no. 852 v.1—Isaac Watts, 1709)
  'Give me the wings of faith to rise within the veil, and see
  The saints above, how great their joys, how bright their glories be.'

N.B. This sermon was 'suggested by the decease of the Earl of Shaftesbury', aged 84, on 1 October 1885.

SERMON NO. 1863

5 OCTOBER (1890)

Jehovah's valuation of his people

'*I am the* LORD *thy God, the Holy One of Israel, thy Saviour: I gave Egypt for thy ransom, Ethiopia and Seba for thee.*' Isaiah 43:3
SUGGESTED FURTHER READING: 2 Timothy 1:8–14

It may not have struck you before, but what a New Testament combination this is: 'the Holy One ... thy Saviour'! It reminds us of the words 'just, and the justifier of him that believeth'. Here we have one so holy as to be 'separate from sinners' and yet the Saviour of sinners. 'Holy, holy, holy,' is the ascription which is justly due to him and yet he passes by iniquity, transgression, and sin. 'The Holy One of Israel, thy Saviour' is a commingling of attributes which only the cross can explain. Herein is a world of comfort. God's holiness appears to look dark and black upon a sinner, but when he believes in Jesus this attribute of holiness smiles upon him. Is God holy? Then he will never break his promise. If he declares men to be justified through faith in Christ, then depend upon it, they are justified; he will not run back from the compact of his grace. Having exacted at the hand of our great Surety that which vindicates his justice, he makes that justice the guarantee that he will no more be angry with his people. There is a substantial truth in those lines of our hymn:—

>   'Payment God cannot twice demand,
>   First at my bleeding Surety's hand,
>   And then again at mine.'

We can now appeal to the holiness of God and expect that, having accepted a sacrifice on our behalf, he will graciously pass by our sin. His holiness forbids that he should declare the death of his Only-Begotten to be a failure, by punishing those for whom Jesus was an accepted sacrifice. The Lord has made to meet on his beloved Son 'the iniquity of us all'; how, then, shall it be laid at our door?

FOR MEDITATION: (*Our Own Hymn Book,* no. 192 v.3—Isaac Watts, 1709)

>   'Proclaim *Salvation from the Lord,*   His hand has writ the sacred word,
>   *For wretched, dying men:*   With an immortal pen.'

SERMON NO. 2167

Perseverance in holiness

'And I will make an everlasting covenant with them, that I will not turn away from them, to do them good; but I will put my fear in their hearts, that they shall not depart from me.' Jeremiah 32:40
SUGGESTED FURTHER READING: Nehemiah 5:1–15

This is God's great holdfast upon his people, 'I will put my fear in their hearts'. What is this fear of God? It is, first, a *holy awe* and reverence of the great God. Taught of God, we come to see his infinite greatness and the fact that he is everywhere present with us; then, filled with a devout sense of his Godhead, we dare not sin. Since God is near, we cannot offend. The words, 'my fear', also intend *filial fear*. God is our Father and we feel 'the Spirit of adoption, whereby we cry, Abba, Father.' This child-like love kindles in us a fear to grieve him whom we love and therefore we have no desire to depart from him. There moves also in our hearts a deep sense of *grateful obligation*. God is so good to me; how can I sin? He loves me so; how can I vex him? He favours me so greatly from day to day that I cannot do that which is contrary to his will. Did you ever receive a choice and special mercy? It has often fallen to my lot and, when the tears have been in my eyes at the sight of so great a favour, I have felt that, if a temptation came to me, it would come at a time when I had neither heart, nor eye, nor ear for it. Gratitude bars the door against sin. Great love received overthrows great temptation to wander. Our cry is, 'The Lord bathes me in his love, he indulges me with the nearest and dearest fellowship with himself; how then can I do this great wickedness, and sin against God?' Loved of him so specially and united to him by an everlasting covenant, how can we fly in the face of love so wonderful? Surely, we can find no pleasure in offending so gracious a God, but it is our joy to 'do his commandments, hearkening unto the voice of his word.'

FOR MEDITATION: 'The fear of the LORD' will lead us negatively to 'hate evil' (Proverbs 8:13) and to 'depart from evil' (Proverbs 16:6), but also prompt us positively to seek to 'perfect holiness' (2 Corinthians 7:1).

7 OCTOBER (1886)

'Where are the nine?' or, praise neglected

'One of them, when he saw that he was healed, turned back, and with a loud voice glorified God, and fell down on his face at his feet, giving him thanks: and he was a Samaritan. And Jesus answering said, Were there not ten cleansed? but where are the nine? There are not found that returned to give glory to God, save this stranger.' Luke 17:15–18
SUGGESTED FURTHER READING: Philippians 4:4–9

The number of those who pray is greater than the number of those who praise. For these ten men that were lepers all prayed. Poor and feeble as their voices had become through disease, yet they lifted them up in prayer and united in crying: 'Jesus, Master, have mercy on us.' They all joined in the Litany, 'Lord, have mercy upon us! Christ, have mercy upon us!' But when they came to the Te Deum, magnifying and praising God, only one of them took up the note. One would have thought that all who prayed would praise, but it is not so. Cases have been where a whole ship's crew in time of storm has prayed and yet none of that crew have sung the praise of God when the storm has become a calm. Multitudes of our fellow-citizens pray when they are sick and near to dying, but when they grow better, their praises grow sick unto death. The angel of mercy, listening at their door, has heard no canticle of love, no song of thankfulness. It is too sadly true that more pray than praise! I put it in another shape to you who are God's people: most of us pray more than we praise. You pray little enough, I fear, but praise, where is that? At our family altars we always pray, but seldom praise. In our closets we constantly pray, but do we frequently praise? Prayer is not so heavenly an exercise as praise; prayer is for time, but praise is for eternity. Praise deserves the first and highest place. Let us commence the employment which occupies the celestials. Prayer is for a beggar, but he is a poor beggar who does not also give praise when he receives help. Praise ought to follow naturally upon the heels of prayer.

FOR MEDITATION: (*Our Own Hymn Book,* no. 103 version 3 v.1—Henry Francis Lyte, 1834)
'Praise, my soul, the King of heaven; to His feet thy tribute bring!
Ransomed, healed, restored, forgiven, who like me His praise should sing!
Praise Him! praise Him, praise the everlasting King!'

SERMON NO. 1935

8 OCTOBER (PREACHED 11 OCTOBER 1885)

The nobleman's faith

'There was a certain nobleman, whose son was sick at Capernaum. When he heard that Jesus was come out of Judæa into Galilee, he went unto him, and besought him that he would come down, and heal his son: for he was at the point of death ... Jesus saith unto him, Go thy way; thy son liveth. And the man believed the word that Jesus had spoken unto him, and he went his way.' John 4:46–47,50
SUGGESTED FURTHER READING: Mark 9:14–29

Faith in the Lord Jesus Christ, though only a spark, yet influenced this nobleman. It led him to take a considerable journey to find our Lord. From Capernaum he went up the hills to Cana to plead with Jesus. And he went personally. This is the more remarkable because he was a man of rank and position. I do not know whether he was Chuza, Herod's steward. I should not wonder if he was, because we do not hear of any other noble family being on the side of Christ, but we do hear of 'the wife of Chuza Herod's steward,' as amongst those that 'ministered unto him of their substance.' We hear also of Manaen, foster-brother to Herod. It may have been one of these; noblemen were scarce birds in the church then, as indeed they are now. We expect, therefore, to hear of such a person as this again; as we have honourable mention of those two, we are not rash in conjecturing that this nobleman may have been one of them. Now noblemen do not, as a rule, think of taking journeys themselves while they have so many servants at their disposal, but this nobleman came himself to Christ and personally 'besought him that he would come down, and heal his son'. If your faith is weak in some respects, yet strong enough in others to drive you personally to Christ to pray to him, it is faith of an acceptable order. If it leads you to pray to our Lord with all your heart, beseeching him, then your faith is of the right sort. If it leads you to beseech Christ to have mercy upon you, it is the faith which saves the soul. It may be little 'as a grain of mustard seed', but its importunity shows that there is pungency in it; it is true mustard.

FOR MEDITATION: (*Our Own Hymn Book*, no. 603 v.2—William Cowper, 1779)
  'Our faith is feeble, we confess, we faintly trust Thy word;
  But wilt Thou pity us the less? Be that far from Thee, Lord!'

SERMON NO. 1865

9 OCTOBER (1890)

A private enquiry

'What is the thing that the LORD hath said unto thee?' 1 Samuel 3:17
SUGGESTED FURTHER READING: Psalm 119:9–24

'Samuel lay until the morning'. What thoughts passed through his mind on his lone bed! He had been a child when he went to rest last night and now he had suddenly become a man, with a dread secret entrusted to him. A pressing anxiety was on him as to how he should speak to Eli and a battle raged within his heart between a fear of grieving the good old man by the message and the greater fear of grieving God by keeping any of it back. He remained still upon his bed, quietly meditating and turning over what he had heard and thinking of what he should do. I would to God that, after every sermon, all my hearers, young and old, had a quarter of an hour alone! A night of wakeful thought over it would be better still. I am sure that what is wanted with our religious reading is time for private thought. We put into the mill more than it grinds. Some people imagine that, if they read so many chapters of the Bible every day, it will be much to their profit, but it is not so, if the reading is a mere mechanical exercise. It will be far better to read a tenth as much, weigh it and let it take possession of brain and heart. A little food cooked is better for dinner than a great joint raw. A man who wants to see a country must not hurry through it by express train, but he must stop in the towns and villages and see what is to be seen. He will know more about the land and its people, if he walks the highways, climbs the mountains, stays in the homes and visits the workshops, than if he does so many miles in the day and hurries through picture-galleries as if death were pursuing him. Don't hurry through Scripture, but pause for the Lord to speak to you. Oh for more meditation! 'Samuel lay until the morning'. Wise child that!

FOR MEDITATION: The meditation of our hearts will be acceptable in God's sight (Psalm 19:14), if we meditate on his person (Psalm 63:6; 104:34), his word (Joshua 1:8; Psalm 1:2) and his works (Psalm 77:12; 143:5). Then we will have something worthwhile to tell others (Psalm 49:1–3).

SERMON NO. 2184

10 OCTOBER (1886)

A cheering incident at Bethabara

'Therefore they sought again to take him: but he escaped out of their hand, and went away again beyond Jordan into the place where John at first baptized; and there he abode. And many resorted unto him, and said, John did no miracle: but all things that John spake of this man were true. And many believed on him there.' John 10:39–42
SUGGESTED FURTHER READING: Psalm 87:1–7

I suppose it was a lovely quiet spot by the banks of the Jordan, with only a little village or hamlet, named Bethany, close by. The word Bethany was altered by Origen into Bethabara, I suppose for distinction's sake. It really was Bethany, and so our Lord had two Bethanies. It was there, in a rural retreat, that many believed on his name. O hills of Piedmont, when the Vaudois preached the Christ amidst your valleys, it may be said of you 'many believed on him there'! O mosses and hill-sides of Scotland, in the Covenanting times, 'many believed on him there'! Talk not so exceeding proudly, O cathedrals or great tabernacles, for many have believed on Jesus by the highway side, out on the village green or under the spreading oak. Out in the desert of southern France, where men fled for their lives to hear the gospel, many believed on Jesus. In what place cannot Jesus triumph? He needs no Solomon's temple; in its porch he finds critics; but yonder by the willows of the Jordan he finds a people that believe on him. Go forth, heralds of the cross, and preach the gospel everywhere beneath the arch of heaven. At the corners of the street or on the hillside publish the proclamation of the Great King. Let the trees of the wood sing out and the inhabitants of the rock sing. In all ears proclaim the gospel, till by river, sea and plain it shall be said, 'many believed on him there.' Thus have we seen that it is pleasant to note the place where we first believed in Jesus.

FOR MEDITATION: In the book of Acts many came to faith in public gatherings (2:41; 4:4; 8:12; 13:48; 14:1; 18:8). For others the place of conversion was somewhere more private such as a desert road (8:26,37), an official residence (13:12) or a jailer's house (16:31–34). Can you remember where you were when you trusted in the Lord Jesus Christ to become your Saviour? That will be asking too much if you are like those who 'believed not' (17:5; 19:9; 28:24).

SERMON NO. 1924

11 OCTOBER (1888)

A free grace promise

'And it shall come to pass, that whosoever shall call on the name of the LORD *shall be delivered.'* Joel 2:32
SUGGESTED FURTHER READING: 1 Kings 18:17–40

The text contains within it a measure of specific instruction: the prayer must be to the true God: 'whosoever shall call on the name of Jehovah shall be delivered.' There is something distinctive here, for one would call on Baal, another would call on Ashtaroth and a fourth on Moloch, but these would not be saved. The promise is special: 'whosoever shall call on the name of Jehovah shall be delivered.' You know that triune name, 'Father, Son, and Holy Spirit'; call upon it. You know how the name of Jehovah is set forth most conspicuously in the person of the Lord Jesus; call upon him. Call upon the true God. Call upon no idol, call on no Virgin Mary, no saint, dead or living. Call on no image. Call on no impression of your mind! Call upon the living God; call upon him who reveals himself in the Bible; call upon him who manifests himself in the person of his dear Son, for 'whosoever shall call' upon this God 'shall be saved.' You may call upon the idols, but these will not hear you: 'eyes have they, but they see not: they have ears, but they hear not'. You may not call upon men, for they are all sinners like yourselves. Priests cannot help their most zealous admirers; but, 'whosoever shall call on the name of Jehovah shall be delivered.' Mind, then, it is not the mere repetition of a prayer as a sort of charm, or a piece of religious witchcraft, but you must make a direct address to God, an appeal to the Most High to help you in your time of need. In presenting true prayer to the true God you 'shall be delivered.'

FOR MEDITATION: Calling 'on the name of the LORD' began early in history (Genesis 4:26). Among those whom did so were Abraham (Genesis 12:8; 13:4; 21:33), Isaac (Genesis 26:25), an anonymous Psalmist (Psalm 116:4,13,17) and Jeremiah (Lamentations 3:55). Calling 'on the name of the LORD' leads to salvation (Acts 2:21; Romans 10:12–13); failure to do so leads to destruction (Psalm 79:6; Isaiah 64:7; Jeremiah 10:25).

SERMON NO. 2082

12 OCTOBER (1890)

'So it is'

'Lo this, we have searched it, so it is; hear it, and know thou it for thy good.' Job 5:27

SUGGESTED FURTHER READING: Hebrews 2:1–4

If there is salvation in believing in Christ, why are you not saved? You say there is a hell. Why are you going there? You know that there is a heaven. Why are you not preparing for it? You know that there is a Christ, whose wounds bleed salvation; why are you not looking to him? Is it all to be play, this religion of ours, going to meetings, sitting in your seats and listening to the preacher? I would rather be silent than be fiddling to your dancing or going through the service merely to spend a Sabbath in a decorous manner. Sirs, if you are not saved what shall I do? What shall I do? If you are saved, we will meet in heaven and we will praise God for ever, each one of us, and our Lord shall have all the glory. But if you are lost—if you are lost—I cannot come to you, nor can you come to me. Let me do what I can for you before the great gulf divides us. What, what shall I say when I render in my account? Shall I tell the Lord that you were not saved because I was afraid to tell you that there was a hell, and I kept back every threatening doctrine and tried to make things pleasant to you, whether you were saved or not? I could not make that profession, even if it could save your souls, for it would not be in any measure true. 'I have not shunned to declare unto you all the counsel of God', as far as I know it. God is my witness and so are your consciences, that I have longed for your conversion. You that have heard me these years, if you are lost, it will not be for want of pleading with, nor for want of instruction, nor from lack of entreaties. O souls, 'why will ye die'? Why will you keep on procrastinating and crying 'Tomorrow and tomorrow and tomorrow'? Why should it always be tomorrow? There will be no tomorrow of hope for you when once you are lost. Flee now to Christ.

FOR MEDITATION: Stopped ears will prevent us from hearing the truth (Zechariah 7:11–13), dull ears will prevent us from accepting the truth (Matthew 13:15) and itching ears will prevent us from keeping to the truth (2 Timothy 4:3–4), but ears that hear will avoid all these pitfalls and be truly blessed (Matthew 13:16–17).

SERMON NO. 2175

13 OCTOBER (1889)

The eye and the light

'The light of the body is the eye: therefore when thine eye is single, thy whole body also is full of light; but when thine eye is evil, thy body also is full of darkness. Take heed therefore that the light which is in thee be not darkness. If thy whole body therefore be full of light, having no part dark, the whole shall be full of light, as when the bright shining of a candle doth give thee light.' Luke 11:34–36
SUGGESTED FURTHER READING: Micah 7:1–9

Some appear to have a little light in the upper rooms; they have notions in their heads and ideas on their tongues! Alas! The first floor is very dark. From their common conversation the light of God is absent. Enter at the door and you cannot see your way into the passage or up the stairs; the light is up aloft, but not in the dwelling-rooms. Oh for light in the region of the heart and upon the household talk and business conversation! From attic to cellar may the whole house of our humanity be lit up! This is the true work of grace, when the whole man is brought into the light and no part is left to pine in the darkness. Then are we 'the children of light', when we abide in the light, and 'have no fellowship with' darkness. Then is the distinction seen between Israel and Egypt, for while all Egypt sat in a 'darkness which may be felt', in the land of Goshen there was light. Where this light comes it gives *certainty*: we cease to doubt and we know whom we have believed. With this comes *direction*: we see our way and how to walk in it. We pursue a plain path and are no more in a maze. 'This is the way, walk ye in it,' sounds in our ears as the light reveals to us the narrow way which leads to life eternal. This light, when it dwells in the heart, brings *good cheer* with it. Darkness is doleful; light brings delight. Did you never travel by a train which passed through a tunnel, but was destitute of a single lamp? Somebody has struck a match and lit a candle; all eyes have turned towards him. In a small way he was a benefactor: all eyes are glad of light. What a sweet thing is the light of the Holy Spirit to one that has been long in the darkness of ignorance, sorrow and despair!

FOR MEDITATION: (*Our Own Hymn Book*, no. 459 v.2—William Hiley Bathurst, 1831)
  'Light up every dark recess of our heart's ungodliness;
  Show us every devious way, where our steps have gone astray.'

SERMON NO. 2109

14 OCTOBER (1888)

A life-long occupation

'By him therefore let us offer the sacrifice of praise to God continually, that is, the fruit of our lips giving thanks to his name.' Hebrews 13:15
SUGGESTED FURTHER READING: 1 Peter 2:5–10

'We have an *altar*'. What then? If 'We have an altar,' do not allow it to be neglected, deserted, unused. It is not for spiders to spin their webs upon; it is not fit that it should be smothered with the dust of neglect. 'We have an altar'. What then? 'Let us offer the sacrifice of praise to God continually'. Do you not see the force of the argument? Practically obey it. Beside the altar we have a *High Priest*. There is the Lord Jesus Christ, dressed in his robes of glory and beauty, standing within the veil at this moment, ready to present our offerings. Shall he stand there and have nothing to do? What would you think of our great High Priest waiting at the altar, with nothing to present which his redeemed had brought to God? No, 'By him therefore let us offer the sacrifice of praise to God continually'. Bring hither abundantly, people of God, your praises, your prayers, your thank-offerings, and present them to the Ever-blessed! Well may you do so if you will read the connection, for the passage brings before you many things which should compel you to praise God. Behold your Saviour in his passion, offered 'without the gate'! Gaze upon his five bleeding wounds, his sacred head so wounded, his face so full of anguish, his heart bursting with the agony of sin! Can you see that sight and not praise God? Behold redemption accomplished, sin pardoned, salvation purchased, hell vanquished, death abolished and all this achieved by your blessed Lord and Master! Can you see all this and not praise him? His precious blood falling on you and making you clean, bringing you near to God, making you acceptable before the infinite holiness of the Most High! Can you see yourself thus favoured, behold the precious blood which did it and not praise his name?

FOR MEDITATION: (*Our Own Hymn Book*, no. 103 version 2 v.2—Isaac Watts, 1719)
  'Oh, bless the Lord, my soul,
  Nor let His mercies lie
  Forgotten in unthankfulness,
  And without praises die.'

SERMON NO. 2048

15 OCTOBER (PREACHED 12 OCTOBER 1890)

The test of taste

'If so be ye have tasted that the Lord is gracious.' 1 Peter 2:3
SUGGESTED FURTHER READING: Genesis 33:1–11

Let me tell you when we have tasted the graciousness of the Lord. We have done so *after great bitterness*. Our Lord, as George Herbert would say, has put his hand into the bitter box and given us a dose of wormwood and gall. We have drunk the cup in submission and afterwards he has made us taste 'that the Lord is gracious' and then all bitterness has clean gone and our mouth has been as sweet as though wormwood had never entered it. It is wonderful how the delectable grace that is in Christ Jesus drowns the offences of life and makes us say, 'Surely the bitterness of death is passed.' *When a man is ill*, he often loses his taste. The most delicious food is nauseous to him. His 'soul abhorreth all manner of meat'. But such is the flavour of the truth 'that the Lord is gracious', that it is more pleasant to us when we are sick than at any other time. The love of Christ is a delicious refreshment for a sufferer. When our pains multiply and our spirits are depressed, then is a gracious Christ more precious to us than in the day of health and joy. We get fresh sips of sweetness and new tastes of delight when our tribulations abound. *When a man grows old* he sometimes loses his power of taste. Barzillai at fourscore years said to David, 'can thy servant taste what I eat or what I drink?' Age had dulled his palate. But the natural law is not law in the spiritual world, for the older we get the more do we relish the grace of our Lord Jesus Christ. Believers grow more heavenly as they get nearer to heaven or, at least, they should do so. As earth goes, Christ comes. Christ is very choice to us when we are young, but when we are grey-headed he is sweetness itself. We realize our Lord more than ever and we have a keener perception of the grace which he has manifested towards us.

FOR MEDITATION: (*Our Own Hymn Book*, no. 715 v.2—Samuel Medley, 1789)
 'When in my heart His heavenly love
 He sweetly sheds abroad,
 How joyfully He makes me prove
 He is my gracious God!'

SERMON NO. 2168

16 OCTOBER (1887)

'Behold the Lamb of God'

'The next day John seeth Jesus coming unto him, and saith, Behold the Lamb of God, which taketh away the sin of the world.' John 1:29
SUGGESTED FURTHER READING: Revelation 5:1–14

'Behold THE Lamb of God'. In this I think the Baptist comprehended everything that went before. There was *the daily lamb* of which I read to you in the commencement of the service, from Exodus 29. There had been slain before the Lord a lamb every morning and a lamb every evening, all the year round throughout the centuries of Israel's history. Always and ever the continual sacrifice of the lamb was the symbol of Jehovah's dwelling with his people. But John puts his finger down upon a single sacrifice and says, 'Behold *the* Lamb'. All the other daily lambs had only been prefigurations of this. 'Behold the Lamb'. Let me call your attention also to another wonderful lamb, *the Paschal lamb*, slain on the night when Israel went up out of Egypt, when each Hebrew smeared the lintel and side-posts of his door with blood and the sight of that blood sufficed for the deliverance of the family, according to the word of Jehovah, 'when I see the blood, I will pass over you'. These passover lambs were many and sacred to every Jewish mind, but John passes them all over and says, 'Behold *the* Lamb of God'. Do you not think he also had in his mind *the lamb spoken of by Isaiah*, the great evangelical prophet? Had he not in his memory that famous passage, 'he is brought as a lamb to the slaughter'? John the Baptist cries, 'this is he that was spoken of by the prophet'. 'Behold the Lamb of God'. And if John's eyes had been turned to the future as well as to the past, so that he could have looked down the centuries and shared the visions of the seer of Patmos, he would have seen *the lamb in the midst of the throne* and have heard the song unto him that was slain, but after seeing all the visions of the coming glory of the Lamb, he would still have kept his finger pointed towards the blessed Christ of God standing among the people and would have said, 'Behold *the* Lamb'.

FOR MEDITATION: (*Our Own Hymn Book*, no. 331 v.4—Charles Wesley, 1749)
'His only righteousness I show, His saving truth proclaim;
'Tis all my business here below to cry, "Behold the Lamb!"'

SERMON NO. 1987

17 OCTOBER (1886)

Jesus and the children

'And they brought young children to him, that he should touch them: and his disciples rebuked those that brought them. But when Jesus saw it, he was much displeased, and said unto them, Suffer the little children to come unto me, and forbid them not.' Mark 10:13–14

SUGGESTED FURTHER READING: Matthew 18:1–14

The disciples did *wrong to the mothers*; they rebuked them for doing a motherly act, for doing what Jesus loved them to do. They brought their children to Jesus out of respect to him: they valued a blessing from his hands more than gold; they expected that the benediction of God would go with the touch of the great Prophet. They may have hoped that a touch of the hand of Jesus would make their children's lives bright and happy. Though there may have been a measure of weakness in the parents' thought, yet the Saviour could not judge hardly of that which arose out of reverence to his person. He was therefore 'much displeased' to think that those good women, who meant him honour, should be roughly repulsed. There was also *wrong done to the children*. Sweet little ones! What had they done that they should be chided for coming to Jesus? They had not meant to intrude. They would have fallen at his feet in reverent love for the sweet-voiced teacher, who charmed not only men, but children, by his tender words. The little ones meant no ill; why should they be blamed? Besides, there was *wrong done to himself*. It might have made men think that Jesus was stiff, reserved and self-exalted like the Rabbis. If they had thought that he could not condescend to children they would have sadly slandered the repute of his great love. His heart was a great harbour, wherein many little ships might cast anchor. Jesus, the child-man, was never more at home than with children. The 'holy child Jesus' had an affinity for children. Was he to be represented by his own disciples as shutting the door against them? It would do sad injury to his character. Therefore, grieved at the triple evil which wounded the mothers, the children and himself, 'he was much displeased'.

FOR MEDITATION: The Lord Jesus Christ condemned those who blocked the way to heaven (Matthew 23:13). As the only way to God (John 14:6), he quickly overruled any who tried to separate him from those he came to save (Mark 6:35–37; 9:38–39; 10:46–52; Luke 8:49–50; 13:14–16).

SERMON NO. 1925

18 OCTOBER (1885)

The Sunday-school and the Scriptures

'And that from a child thou hast known the holy scriptures which are able to make thee wise unto salvation through faith which is in Christ Jesus.' 2 Timothy 3:15

SUGGESTED FURTHER READING: Philippians 2:19–24

Timothy became above all others a choice companion for Paul, one upon whom Paul looked with love and remembered with joy. Companions for apostles are only to be produced in the school of Holy Scripture. Those who have communed with Moses, David and the prophets, are fit to associate with an apostle. It is something to produce out of a child a comrade for a veteran servant of the living God. Let a man of God get side by side with a youth who knows the Scriptures and he feels, 'This is fit company for me.' Paul, worn with years of persecution, strokes his grey beard and his eyes light up with joy as he looks on that young Timothy. What is there about him more than about any other? Why, only that he knows the Scriptures and they have made him 'wise unto salvation'. There were, no doubt, fine young fellows to be found who gloried in preferring the advanced thought of philosophers to the stereotyped teachings of Holy Scripture, but if they had begun to talk to the apostle upon their new theories, Paul would have dismissed them with words of warning. He knew nothing of them or of their 'other gospel', except that they troubled him and the churches. Without a scriptural training a convert has no grit, no backbone and no soul in him. But when Paul looked on a gracious youth who knew the Scriptures and held fast to them, 'he thanked God, and took courage.' This young man became a minister and an evangelist. He was a preacher of such a sort that we should have been glad to have heard him. God send us many such!

FOR MEDITATION: In Acts 16:1–3 read about Timothy's childhood, character and company. His childhood was notable for his family and his faith (2 Timothy 1:5), his character for his faithfulness (1 Corinthians 4:17) and his company for his fellowship in Paul's work (Acts 19:22; Romans 16:21; 1 Corinthians 16:10; 1 Thessalonians 3:2) and in Paul's writings—in how many of Paul's epistles is Timothy's name linked to his in the first verse?

SERMON NO. 1866

19 OCTOBER (1890)

The man who shall never see death

'If a man keep my saying, he shall never see death. Then said the Jews unto him ... thou sayest, If a man keep my saying, he shall never taste of death.' John 8:51–52
SUGGESTED FURTHER READING: Revelation 21:1–8

Our face is turned away from death. Here am I, poor sinner, convinced of sin and aroused to a fear of wrath. What is before my face? What am I compelled to gaze upon? The Greek is not fully interpreted by the word 'see': it is stronger. According to Westcott, the sight is that of 'a long, steady, exhaustive vision, whereby we become slowly acquainted with the nature of the object to which it is directed.' The awakened sinner is made to look at eternal death, the threatened punishment of sin. He stands gazing upon the result of sin with terror and dismay. Oh the wrath to come! The death that never dies! While unforgiven, I cannot help gazing upon it and foreseeing it as my doom. When the gospel of the Lord Jesus comes to my soul and I keep his saying by faith, I am turned completely round. My back is upon death and my face is towards life eternal. Death is removed, life is received and more life is promised. What do I see within, around and before me? Life in Christ Jesus! He 'is our life'. In my future on earth, what do I see? Final falling from grace? No, for Jesus says, 'I give unto them eternal life'. What do I see far away in eternity? Unending life. 'He that believeth on me hath everlasting life.' Now I begin to realize the meaning of that text, 'I am the resurrection, and the life: he that believeth in me, though he were dead, yet shall he live: and whosoever liveth and believeth in me shall never die.' The man who has received the saying of the Lord Jesus has 'passed from death unto life', 'shall not come into condemnation' and shall never gaze on death. All that lies before the believer is life 'more abundantly,' to the full, eternal. What has become of our death? Our Lord endured it. He died for us.

FOR MEDITATION: (*Our Own Hymn Book*, no. 875 v.1—Isaac Watts, 1709)
  'There is a land of pure delight, where saints immortal reign;
  Infinite day excludes the night, and pleasures banish pain.'
N.B. 'This sermon was preached, in great sorrow, after the sudden death of the senior deacon of the Tabernacle Church, Mr William Olney.'

SERMON NO. 2169

20 OCTOBER (1889)

The mustard seed: a sermon for the Sabbath-school teacher

'Then said he, Unto what is the kingdom of God like? and whereunto shall I resemble it? It is like a grain of mustard seed, which a man took, and cast into his garden; and it grew, and waxed a great tree; and the fowls of the air lodged in the branches of it.' Luke 13:18–19
SUGGESTED FURTHER READING: Romans 1:8–17

Sow the very truth, not your reflections on the truth, not your embellishments of the truth, but the truth itself. This is to be brought into contact with the mind, for the truth is the seed and the human mind is the soil for it to grow in. These remarks of mine are very plain and trite, yet everything depends upon the simple operation described. Nearly everything has been tried in preaching of late, except the plain and clear statement of the glad tidings and of the atoning sacrifice. People have talked about what the church can do and what the gospel can do; we have been informed as to the proofs of the gospel, or the doubts about it, and so forth, but when will they give us the gospel itself? Friends, we must come to the point and teach the gospel, for this is the living and incorruptible seed which abides for ever. It is an easy thing to deliver an address upon mustard seed, to give the children a taste of the pungency of mustard, to tell them how mustard seed would grow, what kind of a tree it would produce and how the birds would sing among its branches. But this is not sowing mustard seed. It is all very fine to talk about the influence of the gospel, the ethics of Christianity, the elevating power of the love of Christ and so on, but what we want is the gospel itself, which exercises that influence. Sow the seed: tell the children the doctrine of the cross, the fact that with the stripes of Jesus we are healed and that by faith in him we are justified. What is wanted is not talk about the gospel, but the gospel itself. We must continually bring the living word of the living God into contact with the hearts of men. Oh for the aid of the Holy Spirit in this! He will help us, for he delights to glorify Jesus.

FOR MEDITATION: Today many preachers seem to be afraid of preaching the gospel itself, but content themselves with preaching *about* the gospel or *about the preaching of* the gospel! But the preacher's charge has always been to 'preach the gospel' (Mark 16:15; Acts 16:10; 1 Corinthians 1:17), not an indirect or second-hand substitute for it.

SERMON NO. 2110

21 OCTOBER (PREACHED 24 OCTOBER 1886)

Love's complaining

'I have somewhat against thee, because thou hast left thy first love. Remember therefore from whence thou art fallen, and repent, and do the first works; or else I will come unto thee quickly, and will remove thy candlestick out of his place, except thou repent.' Revelation 2:4–5
SUGGESTED FURTHER READING: John 21:15–19

This evil was a very serious one; it was love declining: 'thou hast left thy first love.' 'Is *that* serious?' says one. It is the most serious ill of all, for the church is the bride of Christ and for a bride to fail in love is to fail in all things. It is idle for the wife to say that she is obedient and so forth: if love to her husband has evaporated, her wifely duty cannot be fulfilled; she has lost the very life and soul of the marriage state. So this is a most important matter, our love to Christ, because it touches the very heart of that communion with him which is the crown and essence of our spiritual life. As a church we must love Jesus, or else we have lost our reason for existence. A church has no reason for being a church when she has no love within her heart or when that love grows cold. Almost any disease may be hopefully endured except disease of the heart. But when our sickness is a disease of the heart, it is full of danger; it was so in this case: 'thou hast left thy first love.' It is a disease of the heart, a central, fatal disease, unless the great Physician shall interpose to stop its progress and deliver us from it. Oh, in any man, woman or child of God here, let alone in the church as a whole, if there be a leaving of the first love, it is a woeful thing! Lord, have mercy upon us; Christ, have mercy upon us: this should be our solemn litany at once. No peril can be greater than this. Lose love, lose all. Leave our first love, and we have left strength, peace, joy and holiness.

FOR MEDITATION: (*Our Own Hymn Book*, no. 797 v.3—Charles Wesley, 1746)
'God only knows the love of God:
Oh that it now were shed abroad
In this poor stony heart:
For love I sigh: for love I pine:
This only portion, Lord, be mine,
Be mine this better part.'

SERMON NO. 1926

22 OCTOBER (PREACHED 24 OCTOBER 1886)

God's longsuffering: an appeal to the conscience

'And account that the longsuffering of our Lord is salvation.' 2 Peter 3:15
SUGGESTED FURTHER READING: Psalm 107:17–32

I met years ago a soldier who had ridden in the charge of Balaclava. He was one of the few that came back when the saddles were emptied right and left of him. I could not help getting into a corner and saying to him, 'Dear sir, do you not think that God has some design of love to you in sparing you when so many fell? Have you given your heart to him?' I felt that I had a right to say *that*. Perhaps I speak to some of you who were picked off a wreck years ago. Why was that? I hope it was that you might be saved. You have had a fever lately and have scarcely recovered. Why were you saved from that fever when others were cut down? Surely it must mean salvation. At any rate, the God who was so pitiful as to spare you now says to you, 'call upon me in the day of trouble: I will deliver thee, and thou shalt glorify me.' When Master Bunyan was a lad, he was so foolhardy that, when an adder rose against him, he took it in his hand and plucked the sting out of its mouth, but was not harmed. It was his turn to stand sentinel at the siege of Nottingham and, as he was going forth, another man offered to take his place. That man was shot and Master Bunyan thus escaped. We should have had no *Pilgrim's Progress* if it had not been for that. Did not God preserve him on purpose that he might be saved? There are special interpositions of divine providence, by which God spares ungodly men, whom he might have cut down long ago as cumberers of the ground: should we not look upon these as having the intention that the barren tree may be cared for yet another year, in case it may bring forth fruit? Some of you are wonders to yourselves that you are still in the land of the living; account the longsuffering of God to be salvation. See salvation in it. Be encouraged to look to Christ and, looking to him, you shall find salvation, for *'There is life for a look at the Crucified One'*.

FOR MEDITATION: (*Our Own Hymn Book,* no. 529 v.3—Charles Wesley, 1749)
'O God, my inmost soul convert, and deeply on my thoughtful heart
Eternal things impress: give me to feel their solemn weight,
And trembling on the brink of fate, wake me to righteousness.'

SERMON NO. 1997

23 OCTOBER (1887)

The blood of sprinkling and the children

'When your children shall say unto you, What mean ye by this service? ... ye shall say, It is the sacrifice of the LORD's *Passover, who passed over the houses of the children of Israel in Egypt, when he smote the Egyptians, and delivered our houses.'* Exodus 12:26-27
SUGGESTED FURTHER READING: Job 1:1-5

It is well to explain to children the ordinance of the Lord's Supper, for this shows forth the death of Christ in symbol. I regret that children do not oftener see this ordinance. Baptism and the Lord's Supper should be placed in view of the rising generation, that they may then ask us, 'What mean ye by this?' The Lord's Supper is a gospel sermon and turns mainly upon the sacrifice for sin. You may banish the doctrine of the atonement from the pulpit, but it will always live in the church through the Lord's Supper. You cannot explain that broken bread and that cup filled with the fruit of the vine without reference to our Lord's atoning death. You cannot explain 'the communion of the body of Christ' without bringing in the death of Jesus in our place. Let your little ones see the Lord's Supper and be told most clearly what it sets forth. And if not the Lord's Supper (for that is not the thing itself, but only the shadow of the glorious fact), dwell much and often in their presence upon the sufferings and death of our Redeemer. Let them think of Gethsemane, Gabbatha and Golgotha and let them learn to sing of him who laid down his life for us. Tell them who it was that suffered and why. I would have the children sing, *'There is a green hill far away, without a city wall.'* And I would have them learn such lines as these:

> 'He knew how wicked man had been,
> And knew that God must punish sin;
> So, out of pity, Jesus said,
> He'd bear the punishment instead.'

FOR MEDITATION: Israelites were to give their children a general theological education (Deuteronomy 6:6-7; 11:18-19), including detailed instruction on some subjects (Exodus 12:26-27; 13:14-15) and attendance at public services (Deuteronomy 29:10-12; 31:12-13). At the Lord's Supper we can proclaim the Lord's death to children (1 Corinthians 11:26).

SERMON NO. 1988

24 OCTOBER (1889)

Magdalene at the sepulchre: an instructive scene

'And they say unto her, Woman, why weepest thou? She saith unto them, Because they have taken away my Lord, and I know not where they have laid him. And when she had thus said, she turned herself back, and saw Jesus standing, and knew not that it was Jesus.' John 20:13–14

SUGGESTED FURTHER READING: Luke 24:13–27

You have been sitting at your table writing, and a friend has come behind you with noiseless tread, yet on a sudden you have been aware of a presence. Before you had heard or seen you were impressed, what if I say overshadowed? Was it not so with Mary Magdalene and the Saviour? I am not superstitious if I assert that something very similar happens to me when Jesus is near. Many a believer will tell you that he has, at times, when he has been in prayer, hearing the word or meditating, felt as if he could be sure that the Lord stood near him. There could, of course, be no palpable impression upon the flesh, for now, 'after the flesh ... know we him no more', yet his presence has impressed our souls. There are influences of mind on mind which are beyond the recognition of science. The great spirit of our Lord has means of making itself spiritually known to our spirits, means which flesh and blood know nothing of and which lips could not describe. I have discerned the special presence of my Lord with me by a consciousness as sure as that by which I know that I live. Jesus has been as real to me, at my side in this pulpit, as though I had beheld him with my eyes. I appeal to the experience of many of you. Have you not been moved by a mysterious influence, which has overawed, inspired and impressed you beyond description? A divine, majestic, delightful and hallowing presence has been near you and you have turned to look at a something which was so distinct that you would not have been surprised had it been visible to you. Mary did not discover at first that it was the Lord, but she felt his powerful influence and then 'she turned herself back, and saw Jesus'.

FOR MEDITATION: Read again Luke 24:13–27. The couple to whom 'Jesus himself drew near' (v.15) unknowingly proved that God draws near to his people when they sorrow with worries (vv.15–17 c.f. Psalm 34:18), seek his ways (v.18 c.f. Psalm 145:18), speak his works (vv.19–24 c.f. Psalm 73:28) and study his word (vv.25–27 c.f. Psalm 119:148–151).

SERMON NO. 2119

25 OCTOBER (1885)

Jubilate

'Then sang Moses and the children of Israel this song unto the LORD, and spake, saying, I will sing unto the LORD, for he hath triumphed gloriously: the horse and his rider hath he thrown into the sea. The LORD is my strength and song, and he is become my salvation: he is my God, and I will prepare him an habitation.' Exodus 15:1–2
SUGGESTED FURTHER READING: Psalm 22:1–5, 22–26

'*He is my praise*'. The text in the Old Version is, 'I will prepare him an habitation'. This jars a little on my ear; it rather sinks the majesty of the infinite for Israel to think so soon of Jehovah as One for whom she could prepare a habitation. Building a habitation was rather the idea of David in his hour of decline, than of Israel in the day of her astonishment and victory. The Revised Version of the Old Testament, which is infinitely superior to the Revised Version of the New Testament, renders it: 'This is my God: I will praise him.' The fact is, there are two words so nearly alike that it is hard to tell which is correct, 'habitation' or 'praise'. Some of the oldest versions of all have it, 'He is my praise'. I never like meddling with the Old Version, however, so we will take them both and make sure that we do not miss the meaning. Does not the Lord inhabit 'the praises of Israel'? We will prepare him a habitation of praise. As soon as Israel had got clear of the Red Sea, Egypt and Pharaoh, by the power of Jehovah, she said, 'I will praise him'. O God, it shall be the business of thy people henceforth to praise thee! We have no bricks to make, but we will praise thee; we have no whips to fear, but we will praise thee freely; we are not slaves now, but we are bound to thee for ever and we will praise thee. Then the people seem to say, 'We will praise the Lord by regular and abiding worship.' Inasmuch as for worship a place is needed, the thought comes up, 'We will prepare him an habitation'. We will habitually praise our God for this great deliverance. Let us build our God a house of praises; let us lay the deep foundations in love, set up the pillars with gratitude and roof in the whole with joyous hallelujahs.

FOR MEDITATION: (*Our Own Hymn Book*, no. 175 v.5—James Montgomery, 1825)
   'God is our strength and song, and His salvation ours:
   Then be His love in Christ proclaimed with all our ransomed powers.'

SERMON NO. 1867

26 OCTOBER (1890)

The blessing of the High Priest

'And the LORD *spake unto Moses, saying, Speak unto Aaron and unto his sons saying, On this wise ye shall bless the children of Israel, saying unto them, The* LORD *bless thee, and keep thee: the* LORD *make his face shine upon thee, and be gracious unto thee: the* LORD *lift up his countenance upon thee, and give thee peace. And they shall put my name upon the children of Israel; and I will bless them.'* Numbers 6:22–27
SUGGESTED FURTHER READING: Psalm 67:1–7

'The LORD bless thee'. What a blessing the Lord gives! Have we not heard a mother say to her little child, 'Bless you'? What a wealth of meaning she threw into it! But when God says, 'Bless you!' there are infinity and immutability in it. There can be no limit to the goodwill of the infinite God. *Our* gifts are like a handful of pence. God's gifts are so rich that I dare not liken them even to silver or gold. When Jehovah blesses, it is after the manner of his sovereign Almightiness. His benediction sheds joy and glory over our entire manhood. 'The LORD bless thee': what an ocean of blessedness is in it! 'And keep thee': what safe keeping is that! 'The LORD make his face shine upon thee': what a shine is that! 'And be gracious unto thee': what grace is that, 'the grace of the Lord Jesus Christ'! 'The LORD lift up his countenance upon thee': oh to be countenanced of God! What fellowship that means! 'And give thee peace.' What a peace is that which God gives, 'the peace of God, which passeth all understanding'! It behoves us to interpret the words of our text in the largest possible manner and to look upon them as being not only waters up to the knees, but 'waters to swim in'. Here we may cry, 'Oh, the depth!' The Lord blesses his people 'according to the riches of his glory', by Christ Jesus. Do you know what his riches are? Can you measure the estate of God? Can you imagine what 'the riches of his grace' must be? Here you have 'the riches of his glory', yes, and the greatest riches of his glory, by Christ Jesus. The Lord blesses you according to his riches in glory by Christ Jesus, and what can be more? Dwell on that.

FOR MEDITATION: Note how the Lord maintains these blessings in New Testament benedictions which speak of him keeping us (1 Thessalonians 5:23; Jude 24), being gracious unto us (2 Corinthians 13:14) and giving us peace (Romans 15:13,33; 2 Thessalonians 3:16).

SERMON NO. 2170

27 OCTOBER (1889)

Peace: how gained, how broken

'*I will hear what God the* LORD *will speak: for he will speak peace unto his people, and to his saints: but let them not turn again to folly.*' Psalm 85:8

SUGGESTED FURTHER READING: Isaiah 48:17–22

Dear child of God, are you out in the storm just now? Have you no rest? Let me whisper in your ear. Is there not a cause? Somebody on board your vessel has brought this storm upon you. Where is he? He is not among the regular sailors that work the ship; he is neither captain nor mate, but he is a stranger. Down under the hatches is a man named Jonah; is he the cause of the tempest? 'No,' you say, 'he is a good fellow, for he paid his fare.' This makes me feel all the more suspicious. He is the cause of the mischief. You will never get peace until the Jonah of sin is overboard. Cast him into the sea and it will be calm unto you. Many a child of God harbours a traitor and hardly knows that he is doing so, and the Lord is at war with him because of the harboured rebel. When Joab pursued Sheba, the son of Bichri, he came to the city of Abel, where Sheba had taken shelter. A wise woman came to him out of the city and pleaded for the people. Joab explained to her that he warred not with the city, but with the rebel, and he added, 'deliver him only, and I will depart from the city.' Then 'they cut off the head of Sheba … and cast it out to Joab. And he blew a trumpet, and they retired from the city, every man to his tent.' God is besieging you with trials and distresses, turning his batteries against your walls; there is no chance of any peace until the traitorous sin shall be given up to vengeance. I do not know what particular sin it may be, but the head of it must be thrown over the wall: then the warriors of the Lord will go their way. Bring forth the Achan, and 'the accursed thing', and let all Israel stone him with stones. Search and see! Arrest the hidden foe! 'Are the consolations of God small with thee? is there any secret thing with thee?' God help us to institute a solemn search this morning; may we discover the intruder and destroy him!

FOR MEDITATION: For peace to be enjoyed, evil must be driven out (Psalm 34:14; 1 Thessalonians 5:22–23). The mind can harbour other enemies to peace (Romans 8:6; Philippians 4:6–7).

SERMON NO. 2112

28 OCTOBER (1886)

The best bread

'I am that bread of life.' John 6:48
SUGGESTED FURTHER READING: Colossians 2:8–19

Here is a brother who never eats bread, but, instead of eating, he studies the theory of nutrition and he is ready to discuss with anyone the whole system of digestion and assimilation. He has a theory that bread should always be baked in a certain way and he feels bound to discuss and discuss and discuss, till all is mouldy. My dear friend, you may discuss if you like, but I want to eat, and I think that, if you intend to live and not to drop down dead in your discussion, you had better eat a bit yourself and not put discussion into the place of eating. Some of you have been hearing the gospel for years and you have never fed upon Christ yet, but you have a great liking for religious controversy. Why, perhaps, this very afternoon you have been discussing this 'ism' and that 'ism.' Why all this chopping of logic? Why do you not eat, friend? Why do you not eat? What is the use of talking about bread when your fainting body pines for a substantial meal? You are at this time ready to fight anybody about the shape that the portions of bread ought to take when they are cut up for a feast. No, no, I am not going to accept your challenge! I am hungry and want food and to me the form of it does not matter much. Bread is nothing to anybody till he eats it and even our Lord Jesus is nothing to any man until he believes in him, until he receives him, until he takes him into himself. That is the one thing that is wanted and the Lord Jesus Christ silently hints as much when he says, 'I am that bread of life.' When he calls himself bread, he does in effect say, 'Partake of me; eat me; feed upon me.'

FOR MEDITATION: (*Our Own Hymn Book,* no. 488 v.3—Isaac Watts, 1706)
'Eternal Wisdom has prepared
A soul-reviving feast,
And bids your longing appetites
The rich provision taste.'

SERMON NO. 1940

29 OCTOBER (PREACHED 31 OCTOBER 1889)

The planter of the ear must hear

'He that planted the ear, shall he not hear? he that formed the eye, shall he not see?' Psalm 94:9
SUGGESTED FURTHER READING: Psalm 86:1–7

Do you pray, brothers and sisters? I know you do, but do you really believe that God hears you? I cannot help thinking that a great mass of prayers are poured into a vacuum. I cannot shake off the thought that brethren seem often to be praying into the eternal emptinesses, pleading with an infinite nothing. They say the proper words, but they mean little or nothing by them. Does God hear prayer? Do you answer, 'Yes'? Then let us pray as if we truly believed that he did. When we have done praying, let us expect him to answer us. When we go into the bank with our cheques, we hand them in, take up the money and are gone. Do we deal thus at the Bank of Faith? Do we plead the promise? If so, the Lord counts out the money; but do we take it up? I fear we leave it on the counter. The Lord might say, 'Has that man gone? Gone without what he came for? He pleaded my promise and has he gone away content without my reply?' Is it your habit to go to the throne of mercy and ask for the mere sake of asking? Do you grind at a mill for the mere pleasure of grinding? Surely he 'that asketh receiveth' and if he does not, he should enquire the reason why. A little time before prayer, to prepare the petition, would much help towards reality in prayer. A little time after prayer, to consider when and how the blessing is to be used when the Lord sends it, would be a further aid to faith. Sometimes the angels come to our letter-boxes and cannot put in the answers because the boxes are fastened down by unbelief. We are not prepared to receive what God is prepared to give. Let us pray, believing that as surely as God has given us an ear he has an ear himself and will hear our pleadings. 'He that planted the ear, shall he not hear?'

FOR MEDITATION: (*Our Own Hymn Book,* no. 181 v.5—Josiah Conder, 1824)
   'Come, make your wants, your burdens known;
   He will present them at the throne;
   And angel-bands are waiting there,
   His messages of love to bear.'

SERMON NO. 2118

30 OCTOBER (1890)

A sermon for the time present

'In that day it shall be said to Jerusalem, Fear thou not: and to Zion, Let not thine hands be slack. The LORD *thy God in the midst of thee is mighty; he will save, he will rejoice over thee with joy; he will rest in his love, he will joy over thee with singing.'* Zephaniah 3:16–17
SUGGESTED FURTHER READING: Luke 15:11–32

Think of the great Jehovah singing! Can you imagine it? Is it possible to conceive of the Deity breaking into a song, Father, Son and Holy Spirit together singing over the redeemed? God is so happy in the love which he bears to his people that he breaks the eternal silence, and sun and moon and stars with astonishment hear God chanting a hymn of joy. Among Orientals a certain song is sung by the bridegroom when he receives his bride: it is intended to declare his joy in her and in the fact that his marriage has come. Here, by the pen of inspiration, the God of love is pictured as married to his church and so rejoicing in her that he rejoices over her with singing. If God sings, shall not we sing? He did not sing when he made the world. No, he looked upon it and simply said that it was good. The angels sang, 'the sons of God shouted for joy': creation was very wonderful to them, but it was not much to God, who could have made thousands of worlds by his mere will. Creation could not make him sing and I do not even know that Providence ever brought a note of joy from him, for he could arrange a thousand kingdoms of providence with ease. But when it came to redemption, that cost him dear. Here he spent eternal thought and drew up a covenant with infinite wisdom. Here he gave his Only-begotten Son and 'put him to grief' to ransom his beloved ones. When all was done and the Lord saw what became of it in the salvation of his redeemed, then he rejoiced after a divine manner. What must the joy be which recompenses Gethsemane and Calvary! Here we are among the Atlantic waves. The Lord God receives an accession to the infinity of his joy in the thought of his redeemed people. 'He will joy over thee with singing.'

FOR MEDITATION: God can never rejoice in wickedness (Isaiah 9:17), but he does rejoice in his works (Psalm 104:31) and in his people (Isaiah 62:5; 65:19; Jeremiah 32:41). The Lord Jesus Christ rejoiced (Luke 10:21) and longed for his people to share in his joy (John 15:11; 17:13).

SERMON NO. 1990

31 OCTOBER (1886)

Our sympathizing High Priest

'*Who in the days of his flesh, when he had offered up prayers and supplications with strong crying and tears unto him that was able to save him from death, and was heard in that he feared.*' Hebrews 5:7
SUGGESTED FURTHER READING (Spurgeon): Luke 22:39–46

Martyrs have died without the preceding dread which fell upon our Lord, but remember that the help of God which sustained them was taken away from Jesus; consider also that his death was special and differed from that of all others of our race, for in that death there was condensed the penalty due to sin. To the righteous man death is not now a penalty, but a mode of going home: to Jesus it was in the fullest sense the penalty of death for human guilt. He saw before him, as we do not, all the pains and torments of death; he knew what he had to bear and foretasted in the garden the smart involved in being a surety for sinful man. The vials of God's wrath were about to be poured upon him, and Jehovah was heard saying, 'Awake, O sword', as if it had never awoke before: 'Awake, O sword, against my shepherd, and against the man that is my fellow, saith the LORD of hosts'. He saw the abyss into which he must fall. If no dread had come upon him, the very essence of the atoning suffering would have been absent. Fear must take hold upon him, not that of a coward, but that of one terribly oppressed. His soul was 'exceeding sorrowful, even unto death'. So when you tremble after sipping your cup of bitterness, think of Jesus trembling too. When you, in entering into the valley of death's shade, feel yourself greatly disturbed at the prospect before you, think of Jesus who was heard in his fear. Come, you that fear, and find help in one who also feared. Borrow courage from one who out of fear prayed himself into victory. Think of him who cried unto God, 'be not thou far from me, O LORD: O my strength, haste thee to help me.' Trust your souls with him 'Who in the days of his flesh' cried out in anguish, 'My God, my God, why hast thou forsaken me?'

FOR MEDITATION: (*Our Own Hymn Book*, no. 271 v.3—Joseph Hart, 1759)
   'There my God bore all my guilt; this through grace can be believed;
   But the horrors which He felt are too vast to be conceived.
   None can penetrate through thee, doleful, dark Gethsemane!'

SERMON NO. 1927

1 NOVEMBER (1885)

Death and life: the wage and the gift

'For the wages of sin is death; but the gift of God is eternal life through Jesus Christ our Lord.' Romans 6:23
SUGGESTED FURTHER READING: Romans 7:9–25

I may perhaps startle you when I say that 'the wages of sin is death' even in the man who has eternal life. Sin has the same deadly character to one as to the other, only an antidote is found. You, my Christian brother, cannot fall into sin without its being poison to you, as well as to anybody else; in fact, to you it is more evidently poison than to those hardened to it. If you sin, it destroys your joy, your power in prayer, your confidence towards God. If you have spent evenings in frivolity with worldlings, you have felt the deadening influence of their society. What about your prayers at night? You cannot draw nigh unto God. The operation of sin upon your spirit is most injurious to your communion with God. You are like a man who has taken a noxious drug, whose fumes are stupefying the brain and sending the heart into slumber. If you, being a child of God, fall into any of the sins which so easily beset you, I am sure you will never find that those sins quicken your grace or increase your faith, but, on the contrary, they will work you evil, only evil, and that continually. Sin is deadly to any man and every man, whoever he may be, and were it not for the mighty curative operation which the indwelling Spirit of God is always carrying on upon the believer's nature, not one of us would survive the deadly effects of even those sins of infirmity and ignorance into which we fall. I wonder not that Paul cried aloud, 'O wretched man that I am! who shall deliver me from the body of this death?' If a man takes poison and if it does not absolutely kill him, it injures him and thus proves its killing tendency.

FOR MEDITATION: Christians are not immune from being infected by the sins of others (1 Corinthians 15:33–34; Galatians 6:1; 1 Timothy 5:22). How much more damage can be done when sin is allowed to take root again within (Hebrews 3:12–13; James 1:13–15).

SERMON NO. 1868

2 NOVEMBER (1890)

Little faith and great faith

'O thou of little faith, wherefore didst thou doubt?' Matthew 14:31
'O woman, great is thy faith; be it unto thee even as thou wilt.' Matthew 15:28
SUGGESTED FURTHER READING: Matthew 8:5–27

Weak faith is apt to have too high an opinion of its own power. 'Oh,' says one, 'Is it not the error of weak faith to have too low an opinion of its own ability?' No man can have too low an opinion of his own power, because he has no power whatever. The Lord Jesus Christ said, 'without me ye can do nothing' and his witness is true. If we have strong faith, we shall glory in our powerlessness, because the power of Christ rests upon us. If we have weak faith, we shall diminish our trust in Jesus and put instead into our hearts so many measures of confidence in self. In proportion as faith in our Lord is weakened, our idea of ourselves will be strengthened. 'But I thought,' says one, 'that a man who had strong self-reliance was a man of great faith.' He is the man who has no faith at all, for self-reliance and Christ-reliance will not abide in the same heart. Peter has an idea that he can go upon the water to his Master: he is not so sure of the others, but he is clear about himself. James, John, Andrew and the rest of them are in the ship: it does not occur to Peter that any one of these can tread the waves, but he cries, 'Lord, if it be thou, bid *me* come unto thee on the water.' Self-consciousness is no attribute of faith, but a nest for doubt. Had he known himself, he might have said, 'Lord, bid John come to thee on the water; I am unworthy of so high a dignity.' But being weak in faith, he was strong in his own opinion of himself and hurried to the front, as usual, hastened into a pathway quite unfit for his trembling feet to tread and before long found out his error. Weak faith allows high ideas of self. Great faith hides self under its mighty wings.

FOR MEDITATION: (*Our Own Hymn Book*, no. 675 v.1—Philip Doddridge, 1755)
   'Now let the feeble all be strong, and make Jehovah's arm their song,
   His shield is spread o'er every saint, and thus supported, who shall faint?'
N.B. The hymns for this occasion appear only in the sermon notes held by Pastor Alan Stephens, who memorised this sermon for delivery.

SERMON NO. 2173

3 NOVEMBER (1887)

Driving away the vultures from the sacrifice

'And when the fowls came down upon the carcases, Abram drove them away.' Genesis 15:11
SUGGESTED FURTHER READING: 2 John 1–11

We are not ashamed of the words of God himself. And now, henceforth, we do confess that we belong wholly to Christ, from the crown of our head to the sole of our foot, body, soul, spirit, time, talent, thought, substance, all that we are and all that we have. We have been 'bought with a price' and henceforth we put in no claim to ourselves, for we belong absolutely to the Lord that bought us. Now, now the vultures will come! The carrion-crows and kites will from afar behold this sacrifice and they will hasten to the prey. You do not see them tonight, perhaps. No, but the traveller does not see these evil fowls, till all of a sudden the sky seems darkened with them. The horrid, hideous creatures come like lightning for rapidity and they are hungry as death when they arrive on the scene. You that are consecrated to God may expect that, though you do not see them, there are vultures looking down upon the sacrifice and you must be prepared to drive them away. 'What sort of vultures will there be?' says one. Well, there will come doubts as to eternal things. There will be questions about your own wisdom in giving yourself up to God. I hope you have been strangers to such birds of prey, but some of us have not been: doubts as to whether there be a God to serve; doubts as to whether there be a heaven, an eternal future, a blessed reward; doubts as to whether it is well to give up this world for the next, or not. Drive them away, brethren! Drive them away! When the birds come down upon the sacrifice, drive them away, as Moses did when he had all the riches of Egypt offered to him, yet 'endured, as seeing him who is invisible.' This is what you and I must do.

FOR MEDITATION: (*Our Own Hymn Book*, no. 670 v.1—Isaac Watts, 1709)
'I'm not ashamed to own my Lord,
Or to defend His cause;
Maintain the honour of His word,
The glory of His cross.'

SERMON NO. 1993

4 NOVEMBER (PREACHED 3 NOVEMBER 1889)

By the fountain

'Joseph is a fruitful bough, even a fruitful bough by a well; whose branches run over the wall.' Genesis 49:22
'And of Joseph he said, Blessed of the LORD *be his land, for the precious things of heaven, for the dew, and for the deep that coucheth beneath.'* Deuteronomy 33:13
SUGGESTED FURTHER READING: Romans 2:17–29

A good man is in Scripture said to be a godly man. He is a man of God, God's man: he lives for God, with God and on God. If you do not believe in God, love God, or glorify God, neither all the outward forms on earth nor rites that God has given can make up a religion for you that is worth a single penny. You may be orthodox in creed, as I hope you will be, but unless you really grasp and apprehend the things of orthodoxy and so come to the God of truth and the Holy Spirit of truth, you have a set of words and nothing more. A man may possess the catalogue of a library and yet be without a book, and so may you know a list of doctrines and yet be a stranger to truth. You may have in your hand a map of a fine estate and a list of all the treasures in the mansion and yet you may not have a place whereon to set your foot. A knowledge of the technicalities of theology is of small use unless you enjoy the truths to which they refer. You must know the Lord and abide in Christ. Do not say, 'I have joined the church, sir, attend the prayer-meetings and take my share among the workers.' Yes, I know, but true religion is more than this. It is 'repentance toward God'. It is 'faith toward our Lord Jesus Christ'. It is the indwelling of the Holy Spirit. 'Dear sir,' cries one, 'I accept what you say and dispute none of your teaching.' That may be, but this does not content me. If you receive the truth as my teaching, I am sorry. I desire you to receive it as the Word of God. Go to the Bible for yourself. Seek to be taught by the Spirit of God. Ask to have the truth of God written upon your heart by the Holy Spirit.

FOR MEDITATION: (*Our Own Hymn Book,* no. 40 v.1—Isaac Watts, 1719)
  'I waited patient for the Lord,
  He bowed to hear my cry;
  He saw me resting on His word,
  And brought salvation nigh.'

SERMON NO. 2113

5 NOVEMBER (PREACHED 25 AUGUST 1889)

Life and pardon

'And you, being dead in your sins and the uncircumcision of your flesh, hath he quickened together with him, having forgiven you all trespasses.'
Colossians 2:13
SUGGESTED FURTHER READING: Romans 5:12–21

There is no distinction in the condition of natural men before the law. We all fell in Adam. We 'are all gone out of the way' and have all 'become unprofitable'. Any difference which now exists has been made by divine grace, but by nature we are all in the same condemnation and tainted by the same depravity. Where were we when the Lord first looked on us? Answer: we were dead according to the sentence of the law. The Lord had said, 'in the day that thou eatest thereof thou shalt surely die.' Adam did die the moment that he ate of the forbidden fruit and his posterity died in him. What is death natural? It is the separation of the body from the soul, which is its life. What is death spiritual? It is the separation of the soul from God, who is its life. It had been the very life of Adam to be united to God and, when he lost his union of heart with God, his spirit underwent a dreadful death. This death is upon each one of us by nature. Above this comes in the dreadful fact, that 'he that believeth not is condemned already'. The position of every unbeliever is that of one who is dead by law. As far as the liberties, privileges and enjoyments of heavenly things are concerned, he is written among the dead. His name is registered among the condemned. Yet while we are under the sentence of death, the Lord comes to us in almighty grace and quickens us into newness of life, forgiving us 'all trespasses'. Are you trembling because of your condemned condition under the law? Do you recognize the tremendous truth that death is the sure and righteous result of sin? Then to you the lifegiving, pardoning word is sent in the preaching of the everlasting gospel. Oh that you may believe and so escape from condemnation!

FOR MEDITATION: (*Our Own Hymn Book,* no. 405 v.1—Augustus M. Toplady, 1759)
   'O Thou who didst Thy glory leave
   Apostate sinners to retrieve from nature's deadly fall,
   Me Thou hast purchased with a price,
   Nor shall my crimes in judgment rise, for Thou hast borne them all.'

SERMON NO. 2101

6 NOVEMBER (1887)

Song for the free, and hope for the bound

'He brought them out of darkness and the shadow of death, and brake their bands in sunder. Oh that men would praise the LORD for his goodness, and for his wonderful works to the children of men! For he hath broken the gates of brass, and cut the bars of iron in sunder.' Psalm 107:14–16

SUGGESTED FURTHER READING: Psalm 148:1–14

Praise God with all your heart, every one of you, every day. When you have praised God yourselves, entreat others to join with you. The oratorio of God's praise needs a full choir. I remember, years ago, a bill connected with a religious service of a very pretentious character, and on this bill it promised that the Hallelujah Chorus should be sung before the sermon. The friend who led the singing for me at that time came in to me and asked if I could spare him. 'See here,' said he, 'a person has come from the service which has been advertised to say that they have nobody to sing the Hallelujah Chorus. The minister wants me to go down and do it.' I answered, 'Yes; by all means go. If you can sing the Hallelujah Chorus alone, don't throw yourself away on me.' Then we smiled and at last broke out into a laugh; it was too much for our gravity. Surely for a man to think that he can sufficiently praise God alone is much like attempting to sing the Hallelujah Chorus as a solo. The Psalmist therefore utters that great 'Oh!' 'Oh that men would praise the Lord!' I do not think he said 'men,' for the word 'men' is in italics: the translators are accountable for it. He means: Oh that angels, cherubim and seraphim would praise the Lord! Oh that all creatures 'that have breath' would praise the Lord for his goodness! Even that would not be enough, but let the 'mountains and the hills' 'break forth before' him 'into singing, and' let 'all the trees of the field' 'clap their hands.' 'Let the sea roar, and the fullness thereof; the world, and they that dwell therein.' With a great 'Oh!' and a mighty sigh over the holy business, which was far too great for himself, David felt moved to call upon all others to praise the Lord.

FOR MEDITATION: (*Our Own Hymn Book*, no. 136 song 2 v.1—Isaac Watts, 1719)
  'Give to our God immortal praise; mercy and truth are all His ways:
  Wonders of grace to God belong, repeat His mercies in your song.'

SERMON NO. 1992

7 NOVEMBER (1886)

Our ascended Lord

'Who is gone into heaven, and is on the right hand of God; angels and authorities and powers being made subject unto him.' 1 Peter 3:22
SUGGESTED FURTHER READING: Acts 1:1–11

He 'is gone into heaven' despite malicious men. Have you never wondered why they did not attack him when he showed himself openly and led out his disciples to the Mount of Olives? They suborned the soldiers to say that his disciples stole him away while they slept; why did they not seize him? Why is Herod so quiet and Caiaphas so still? Scribes and Pharisees, where are they? Are these lions chained? Our greater Daniel is in their den, but they do not even roar upon him. It is now or never with them: if they could capture him now and stop his way to his eternal triumph, it would be a great victory. It is the last chance for the overthrow of his power. But truly against him did 'not a dog move his tongue'. They were still as a stone while he passed over to take possession of the inheritance. As death could not hinder him, so neither could the malice of men detain him, nor could all the forces of the devil block his way. I see no trace of the arch-enemy after Christ has risen from the dead. O Prince of darkness, you met him in the wilderness at the beginning; why not close with him at the end? Why not assail him by the sea when he stands there with his coals of fire, with 'fish laid thereon, and bread'? Why did you not hasten up to shoot a last arrow at him and summon all your bands to waylay him in mid-air to block his passage to the Golden City? No, the powers of darkness were baffled: in their silence they gnashed their teeth for rage, but they could not even hiss against him. He had so thoroughly cowed and subdued Satan and all his angels in Gethsemane and on the cross, that nothing remained but to triumph over them and lead 'captivity captive'. The leaguered hosts of hell could not summon courage for another encounter: his warfare was accomplished and the road to his Father's capital lay open before him. In peaceful triumph he passed beyond the clouds.

FOR MEDITATION: (*Our Own Hymn Book*, no. 317 v.2—John S. B. Monsell, 1863)
   'Bruised is the serpent's head, hell is vanquished, death is dead
   And to Christ gone up on high, captive is captivity. Alleluia!'

SERMON NO. 1928

Hagar at the fountain

'And she called the name of the LORD that spake unto her, Thou God seest me: for she said, Have I also here looked after him that seeth me? Wherefore the well was called Beer-lahai-roi.' Genesis 16:13–14
SUGGESTED FURTHER READING: John 4:1–30

Hagar's humble worship was expressed by her using an expressive name for the angel of the Lord. She worshipped God heartily and intelligently *according to her knowledge*. She did not use the first word that came to hand, but spoke fitly, thoughtfully and well. She knew that the Lord was the seeing God, for he had seen her, so she worshipped him under that title, 'Thou God seest me'. We cannot worship 'The Unknown God'; such worship lacks eyes and light and is fitter for owls and bats than for man. Yet observe that she worshipped beyond her knowledge *according to her apprehension*, for she said, 'Have I here also looked after him?' as if she knew that she had not fully seen the Lord, but had only looked at him as he retreated from her. Like Moses, in a later day, she only beheld the 'back parts' of God, the skirts of his garments; his face she had not seen. The Hebrew has that force. Hagar felt there was much more of God than she had seen and in that belief she worshipped and adored with lowliest reverence. Her worship was *wonderfully personal*. It is not 'God sees,' but 'Thou God seest me', not, 'Has God looked after his creature?' but 'Have I here also looked after him that seeth me?' True religion is always personal, but it becomes wonderfully so when a man is specially arrested by sovereign grace, for then he adores as if he were the only man in the universe and beholds God as if no other eye throughout all the ages had ever beheld him. It is wonderful to feel alone with the Lord, while the Lord is searching you through and through. Her worship proved deeply true, for it was followed by immediate *practical obedience* to the command of the Lord. Obedience is the best of worship. She returned to her mistress and was subject to her. Oh for grace, if God meets with us, not to wait a single minute in rebellion, but to return at once to subjection to the Lord!

FOR MEDITATION: Consider the ingredients of personal worship—knowledge (John 4:22; Acts 17:22–27), apprehension (Exodus 33:18–34:8) and obedience (John 9:31). 'O come, let us worship and bow down: let us kneel before the LORD our maker' (Psalm 95:6).

SERMON NO. 1869

9 NOVEMBER (PREACHED 20 SEPTEMBER 1885)

'Behold, he prayeth'

'Inquire in the house of Judas for one called Saul, of Tarsus: for, behold, he prayeth.' Acts 9:11
SUGGESTED FURTHER READING (Spurgeon): Luke 18:1–14

It is his first prayer this morning. I see him: the sermon is over and he has reached home. He has gone up to his room; he is afraid somebody will come in and disturb him; he is turning the key. He is kneeling by the side of that bed on which he has slept so often without prayer and cries, 'O God, I do not know what to say, but be merciful to me a sinner and forgive my sins.' I hear the rustling wings of angels as they gather around the sacred spot. They fly upward crying, 'behold, he prayeth.' Years shall pass, young man, and you shall come to middle life and be exposed to sharp temptation; what will you do then? Good spirits watch you, fearing lest you should go astray, and devils watch for your stumbling. You will then remember that day when you first prayed and will say to yourself, 'I will again cry to God, as I have often done.' You go upstairs and say, 'Lord, many days have passed since first I cried to thee and I have not ceased to cry, but now I am in special trouble. I beseech thee, deliver me!' God will help you. The great wheel of providence will revolve for you. Meanwhile, both angels and devils have spied you out: the angels sing and the devils mutter, 'behold, he prayeth.' A few years have passed; the young man has grown old and the time has come when he must die. He has gone up to the same room for the last time and there are those about him who weep and watch. Mark the sweet serenity of the departing soul! He is looking into eternity without fear. He knows whom he has believed and is ready to depart. What is he doing in his expiring moments? 'Behold, he prayeth.' Prayer, which has long been his vital breath and native air, is now

> 'His watchword at the gates of death:
> He enters heaven with prayer.'

FOR MEDITATION: (*Our Own Hymn Book*, no. 977 v.5—James Montgomery, 1819)
> 'Prayer is the contrite sinner's voice, returning from his ways;
> While angels in their songs rejoice, and cry, "Behold he prays!"'

SERMON NO. 1860

10 NOVEMBER (1889)

The drought of nature, the rain of grace, and the lesson therefrom

'Their nobles have sent their little ones to the waters: they came to the pits, and found no water; they returned with their vessels empty; they were ashamed and confounded, and covered their heads. Because the ground is chapt, for there was no rain in the earth, the plowmen were ashamed, they covered their heads.' 'Are there any among the vanities of the Gentiles that can cause rain? or can the heavens give showers? art not thou he, O LORD our God? therefore we will wait upon thee: for thou hast made all these things.' Jeremiah 14:3–4, 22
SUGGESTED FURTHER READING: Psalm 25:1–11

Do I hear somebody say, 'How I would like to pray'? That is the way to come to God, by prayer in the name of Jesus. Do you want a prayer? This chapter is full of petitions and there is a short one which I would point out to you (Jeremiah 14:7), 'O LORD, though our iniquities testify against us, *do thou it*'. 'Lord, I cannot create grace in my own heart any more than I can make rain fall from the sky, but *do thou it*. Lord, I cannot come to thee; come to me; *do thou it*.' Is that not a wonderful prayer? There is more in it than you think: the more you consider it, the bigger you will see it to be. Three monosyllables: 'do thou it!' Then observe the argument: four words all of one syllable, 'for thy name's sake', 'not for my sake, but for Christ's sake, who is the manifestation of thy name. For thine own glory's sake, for thy glory is thy name. Lord, make men see what a sinner thou canst save by saving me! Lord, glorify thy mercy by forgiving me, for if thou wilt save such a poor, unworthy wretch as I am, even heaven itself will ring with thy praises and even in hell they will say, "See what God can do! He saved one who was ripe for the eternal fire and he has placed the rebel among his children."' 'Do thou it for thy name's sake'. Heartily do I commend this prayer to every soul that is seeking the Lord. May the Spirit write it on your hearts!

FOR MEDITATION: (*Our Own Hymn Book*, no. 589 v.5—Charles Wesley, 1742)

'Come, Lord, the drooping sinner cheer,   Appear, in my poor heart appear!
Nor let Thy chariot-wheels delay;   My God, my Saviour, come away!'

SERMON NO. 2115

11 NOVEMBER (PREACHED 23 AUGUST 1888)

Concerning prayer

'Give ear, O LORD, unto my prayer; and attend to the voice of my supplications. In the day of my trouble I will call upon thee: for thou wilt answer me.' Psalm 86:6–7
SUGGESTED FURTHER READING: Romans 8:22–27

Note one thing about this remarkable prayer of David: it is almost entirely devoid of poetry. Men use grand, studied, rapturous and poetical expressions in their praises and they do well. Let God be praised with the noblest thoughts, as well as the most charming music. But when a man comes to prayer and that prayer is out of the depths of sorrow, he has no time or thought for poetry. He goes straight at the matter in hand and pleads with God in downright plainness of speech. You shall notice that in happy prayers, in times of joy, men use similes, metaphors, tropes, symbols and the like, but when it comes to wrestling with God in times of agony, there is no beauty of speech: parable and poetry are laid aside. The man's language is in sackcloth and ashes or, better still, it stands stripped for wrestling, every superfluous word being laid aside. Then the cry is heard, 'I will not let thee go, except thou bless me.' That is not poetry, but it is a great deal better. Throughout this psalm David is a plain-dealer, speaking with God in downright earnest. He has got his grip of the covenant angel and he will not let him go. Men cannot study where to put their feet prettily when they are wrestling: they have to do the best they can to hold their ground and fling their antagonist. In such a prayer-psalm as this, there is no studying of language: it is the pouring out of the heart as the heart boils over, the utterance of the desires as they bubble up from the soul's deeps, with an entire carelessness as to the fashion of the expression. This ought to be a hint to you when you pray. Do not study how to arrange your words when you come before the Lord. Leave the expression to the occasion: 'it shall be given you in that same hour what ye shall speak.'

FOR MEDITATION: (*Our Own Hymn Book,* no. 40 v.5—Isaac Watts, 1719)
 'When I'm afflicted, poor, and low,
 And light and peace depart,
 My God beholds my heavy woe,
 And bears me on His heart.'

SERMON NO. 2053

12 NOVEMBER (1885)

A lesson and a fortune for Christian men of business

'Let your conversation be without covetousness; and be content with such things as ye have: for he hath said, I will never leave thee, nor forsake thee.' Hebrews 13:5
SUGGESTED FURTHER READING: 1 Timothy 6:6–10

People do not know when they are covetous and the man who is most covetous of all is the last person to suspect himself of it. I feel persuaded that it is so. Covetousness breeds an insensibility in the heart, a mortification in the conscience, a blindness in the mind. It is as hard to convict a man of it as to make a deaf ear hear of its own deficiencies. You cannot make a horse-leech see the impropriety of desiring to suck; to all your expostulations it renders the one answer, 'Give, give.' Covetousness goes about in disguise. In *The Holy War* we read that, when Diabolus sent traitors to lurk about the town of Mansoul, he sent among the rest a young fellow named Covetousness, but when he entered into the town of Mansoul, he took the name of Mr Prudent Thrifty and he was engaged at once as a servant, I think it was in the house of Mr Conscience, the Recorder. He seemed such a likely young man, this youth of the name of Prudent Thrifty. Now, mind you, friends, when you are taking a servant, that you do not engage one of the name of Prudent Thrifty, for I have information that he comes of the family of the Greedies and that his true name is 'Covetousness,' though it may be long before you find it out. His near relations are the Screws, the Skinflints and the Grab-alls, but he will not own them, but always mentions his great-uncle, Squire Prudence, and his mother's brother, Professor Economy, of the University of Accumulation. You will need to carry your eyes in your head if you mean to practice the precept, 'Let your conversation be without covetousness; and be content with such things as ye have'.

FOR MEDITATION: Covetousness is dangerous. Pray against it (Psalm 119:36), hate it (Proverbs 28:16), beware of it (Luke 12:15) and avoid any suspicion of it (Ephesians 5:3). Being convicted of covetousness (Romans 7:7) left its mark on the apostle Paul—in his ministry he carefully avoided covetousness both in its open forms (Acts 20:33) and in its disguises (1 Thessalonians 2:5).

SERMON NO. 1880

13 NOVEMBER (UNDATED SERMON)

'David's spoil'

'This is David's spoil.' 1 Samuel 30:20
SUGGESTED FURTHER READING: Mark 12:41–44

There was a poor woman once, whose little fortune could be carried between her finger and her thumb, her fortune I said, for it was all she had. 'Two mites', I am told, was all it came to. She took it, it was her all, and she put it in the treasury, for this was 'David's spoil.' It belonged to the Lord her God and she gave it cheerfully. I do not know whether since the days of the apostles anybody has ever given so much as that woman. I have not. Have you? She gave, not all her savings, but 'all her living.' She had nothing left when she gave her farthing: she loved so much that she consecrated all her living. We sometimes sing,

> 'Yet if I might make some reserve,
> And duty did not call,
> I love my God with zeal so great
> That I should give Him all.'

But do we mean it? If not, why do we sing falsehoods? There was a man who, in God's providence, had been enabled to lay by many thousands. He was a very rich and respected man. I have heard it said that he owned at least half-a-million; at one collection, when he felt especially grateful and generous, he found a well-worn sixpence for the plate, for that was 'David's spoil'! Out of all that he possessed, that sixpence was 'David's spoil'! This was the measure of his gratitude! Judge by this how much he owed or at least how much he desired to pay. For us, who are deep in the Redeemer's debt, who have had much forgiven, who every day are bankrupt debtors to the measureless mercy of infinite love, no paltriness will suffice. We must give something which, if it be not worthy of him, shall at least express the truth and warmth of the gratitude we feel.

FOR MEDITATION: If a Christian you have reasons for giving generously—you have freely received (Matthew 10:8), and been forgiven much (Luke 7:44–47), a blessing is attached (Malachi 3:10; Acts 20:35) and your giving will be reciprocated somehow (Luke 6:38). Anyway you will only be returning to God part of what is his (1 Chronicles 29:14).

SERMON NO. 2017

14 NOVEMBER (1886)

One more cast of the great net

'And it shall come to pass, that whosoever shall call on the name of the LORD *shall be delivered: for in mount Zion and in Jerusalem shall be deliverance, as the* LORD *hath said, and in the remnant whom the* LORD *shall call.'* Joel 2:32

SUGGESTED FURTHER READING: Romans 11:13–27

The Jewish church is a very insignificant portion of the Jewish people. The apostle tells us that 'at this present time also there is a remnant according to the election of grace', and Isaiah says, 'Except the LORD of hosts had left unto us a very small remnant, we should have been as Sodom, and we should have been like unto Gomorrah.' Poor Israel, poor Israel! Most favoured for many an age and yet only a remnant brought to call upon the saving Lord! Many come from distant lands and 'sit down with Abraham, and Isaac, and Jacob, in the kingdom of heaven. But the children of the kingdom shall be cast out into outer darkness', all but a mere remnant. To my mind it is most instructive to notice that even that remnant never called 'on the name of the LORD' until the Lord called upon them; 'the remnant whom the LORD shall call.' We all of us need a miracle of grace to make us perform the simple act of calling upon God. This was manifestly true in the case of Israel, for as a nation it rejected Jesus of Nazareth, and only a few were converted by the power of the Holy Spirit. But whether Jews or Greeks, we are similarly depraved, and unless effectual calling shall call us out of our natural state, the very last thing that we shall ever do will be to come to Jesus and to rest in him. Unhappy condition, to refuse the highest good! Believing Jews are a remnant to this day and only here and there is one called by grace. You say, 'What have we to do with that?' We have much to do with it. Let us pray for our Lord's own countrymen. Let us labour for them. This also let us do: let us learn from their fall.

FOR MEDITATION: Though Paul was the apostle to the Gentiles (Acts 13:47; 22:21; 26:17; Romans 11:13; Galatians 2:8; 1 Timothy 2:7), he is our best guide when it comes to praying for Jews to be saved (Romans 10:1), labouring for Jews to be saved (1 Corinthians 9:20,22) and learning from Jews who refuse to be saved (Romans 11:17–22).

SERMON NO. 1931

15 NOVEMBER (PREACHED 10 AUGUST 1890)

Runaway Jonah, and the convenient ship

'But Jonah rose up to flee unto Tarshish from the presence of the LORD, *and went down to Joppa; and he found a ship going to Tarshish.'* Jonah 1:3
SUGGESTED FURTHER READING: Proverbs 7:1–27

The three holy children would have escaped the fire and Daniel would never have been in the lion's den, if they had been guided by what men call providences. But note other plain instances, such as Joseph. Joseph's mistress is so kind to him and he is in such a splendid position as head of the household; it is hard for him to deny her desire and lose his place. Had not providence put him into his fortunate position? Shall he throw it away? When his mistress tempts him, shall he risk all? Would it not be better to think that providence plainly hinted that he should comply? Joseph was not so base as to reason in that fashion. He knows that adultery cannot be tolerated and so he flees from his mistress and leaves his garment in her hands, rather than remain near her seductions. Look at David, too. He is brought out by Abishai upon the field at night. There lies king Saul, sound asleep and Abishai says to David, 'God hath delivered thine enemy into thine hand this day: now therefore let me smite him, I pray thee, with the spear even to the earth at once, and I will not smite him the second time.' What a providence, was it not? The cruel foe was altogether in David's hands and the executioner was eager to settle all further conflict by one fatal stroke! What could be clearer or simpler? Wonderful providence! Yet David never said a word as to providence, but replied, 'Destroy him not: for who can stretch forth his hand against the LORD's anointed, and be guiltless?' He therefore came away and left the king sleeping as he was. He would not follow opportunities, but would keep to the law of his God. I pray you, do the same, and if ever everything seems to lead up to wrong-doing and many circumstances unite to steer you in that direction, do not yield to them. Your guide in life is not a so-called providence, but an unquestionable precept of the Lord. Do as God bids you and do it at once.

FOR MEDITATION: (*Our Own Hymn Book,* no. 185 v.1—Isaac Watts, 1719)
 'In all my vast concerns with Thee, in vain my soul would try
 To shun Thy presence, Lord, or flee the notice of Thine eye.'

16 NOVEMBER (UNDATED SERMON)

Israel's hope; or, the centre of the target

'Let Israel hope in the LORD: *for with the* LORD *there is mercy, and with him is plenteous redemption.'* Psalm 130:7

SUGGESTED FURTHER READING: Acts 17:22–31

I have too often heard Christian people talk about thanking providence. What is that? Do you mean, 'thank God'? If so, say it boldly! It is God that provides. God arranges, God overrules, God works out his gracious designs. Again, how often do we hear of 'nature' doing this and 'nature' being that and 'nature' producing the other! What do you mean? An infidel, some time ago, was speaking in the open-air, and he orated very eloquently about the elevating influences of nature and what a blessing it was to study nature. A friend in the crowd said to him, 'That is very pretty, but would you have the goodness to tell me what nature is, which does all this?' The orator answered tartly, 'Every fool knows what nature is.' 'Well,' said the questioner, 'then it will be easy to tell us.' 'Nature,' said the speaker, 'Well: nature is nature.' Just so. That is where it ended. And so it is with very many people when they talk about providence or nature. Let us not speak without knowing what we mean, or without declaring our meaning. We do not erect an altar, and inscribe it 'TO THE UNKNOWN GOD.' We know the Lord and are known of him; therefore we would speak of him as our hope, our trust, our joy. We know no providence apart from Jehovah-jireh, the God who foresees and provides. To us there is no fickle chance, but the Lord reigns. Equally to us is there no blind, inexorable fate, but the Most High decrees and works out his wise and sovereign will. Therefore do not let God's Israel talk as if they hoped in luck or fate, but let them 'hope in the LORD' and avow their reliance upon a personal God, who is working for them evermore, for with him 'there is mercy, and with him is plenteous redemption.'

FOR MEDITATION: Deliberately ignoring God as Creator or Provider is asking for trouble, especially when the glory due to him alone is ascribed instead to nature (Romans 1:18–25) or to ourselves (Deuteronomy 8:17–19; Acts 12:21–23).

SERMON NO. 2199

17 NOVEMBER (1889)

The Father's love to his dying Son

'Therefore doth my Father love me, because I lay down my life, that I might take it again.' John 10:17
SUGGESTED FURTHER READING: Ezekiel 34:11–24

The connection of our text enhances our Lord's love. It stands connected with the Good Shepherd. It is he that lays down his life; he gives it for the sheep. Will a man die for sheep? Yes, that may be. But could the Son of God die for such base creatures as we are? We were, of ourselves, by no means so great a treasure to Christ as a sheep is to a man, yet he thought far more of us than shepherds do of their flocks. We were by nature only as so many foxes, or serpents, or creeping things, but the Lord Christ, having set his love upon us, would not rest till he had laid down his life for us. Alas! We were as ungrateful as we were unworthy. We even opposed the efforts of our Saviour. We acted more like goats than sheep, for we butted with our horns against our Shepherd. We were stray sheep and did not return at his call: we did not follow him, but we went farther and farther away. We were lame as to returning; but 'when we were yet without strength, in due time Christ died for the ungodly.' We are sheep, too, that still go astray very grievously. Woe is me that this should be true of me! After having been brought back on his shoulders, after having been pastured by his care, yet still we go astray! We are sheep that were lost; we are sheep that would lose themselves again, if they could, sheep that make a very poor return to him that shepherds us. 'Is this thy kindness to thy friend?' is a question which might often awake sad memories in our hearts. Beloved, let us love our Lord more! Surely we cannot help it, as we perceive our own undeserving and the greatness of his love whereby he laid down his life for us.

FOR MEDITATION: (*Our Own Hymn Book,* no. 379 v.2—John Newton, 1779)
   'He ransomed me from hell with blood;
   And by His power my foes controlled;
   He found me wandering far from God,
   And brought me to His chosen fold.'

SERMON NO. 2117

18 NOVEMBER (PREACHED 5 SEPTEMBER 1889)

The security of believers; or sheep who shall never perish

'My sheep hear my voice, and I know them, and they follow me: and I give unto them eternal life; and they shall never perish, neither shall any man pluck them out of my hand. My Father, which gave them me, is greater than all: and no man is able to pluck them out of my Father's hand. I am my Father are one.' John 10:27–30

SUGGESTED FURTHER READING: Matthew 19:16–30

I could not tell you exactly in English words, but the Greek gives here a kind of personality to the whole company. 'My sheep hear my voice,' that is, the whole of the flock of God. 'I know them,' that is, again, the whole flock of them, altogether. But, 'they follow me' is in the plural number. It is as though it said, 'They, each one, follow me'. We, who are the Lord's chosen, hear *en masse* and the Lord knows the whole church, for, as a whole, it is redeemed by Christ, but we individually follow, each one for himself, through grace. We each one follow him. 'They follow *me*'. I like that singular personal pronoun. It is not written, 'they follow my commandments', though they do. It is not said, 'they follow the route that I have mapped for them', though they do that, but, 'they follow *me*', distinctly. In their individual personality they follow their Lord in his individual personality. They have recognized himself above his words, above his ways and even above his salvation. 'They follow *me*', says he. This is a grand mark of a Christian, not merely a life of morality, a life of integrity, a life of holiness, but a life of all these in connection with Christ. They follow *him*, not holiness, nor morality, nor integrity, apart from Christ, but they follow *their Lord*. A good life is good in any man. We cannot speak evil of virtue, even when we find it in the ordinary moralist, but this is not the complete mark of Christ's sheep. The virtues of Christ's sheep are *in connection with himself*. The Christian is holy and all that, but that is because he follows his perfect Master and keeps close to him. This is one of the peculiar and unfailing marks of the child of God.

FOR MEDITATION: The Christian version of 'follow my leader' commences at a point in time (Matthew 9:9), continues on a daily basis (Luke 9:23) and concludes in eternal glory (Psalm 23:6; Luke 18:28–30). Following the wrong leader involves another course and outcome (2 Peter 2:1–2,12–15).

SERMON NO. 2120

19 NOVEMBER (PREACHED 30 SEPTEMBER 1888)

Consolation from resurrection

'I will ransom them from the power of the grave; I will redeem them from death: O death, I will be thy plagues; O grave, I will be thy destruction: repentance shall be hid from mine eyes.' Hosea 13:14
SUGGESTED FURTHER READING: 1 Corinthians 15:42–57

I notice that certain persons, in their anxiety to suck the meaning out of the word 'everlasting,' so as to avoid everlasting punishment, have questioned the everlasting nature of heaven. They have even gone the length of hinting that they are not quite clear that if believers get to heaven they will always remain there. Nothing is safe from these revolutionists. They would tear away every covenant blessing from the children of God in their zeal to make the punishment of sin a trifle. To do honour to their own intellect, they would sacrifice the eternal blessedness of the blood-washed! But it is not so. Jesus has said, 'because I live, ye shall live also.' As long as Christ lives we must live: as long as Christ is in heaven we must be with him where he is, to behold his glory. So long as God is God his children, partakers of the divine nature, must live for ever and be for ever blessed. Raised from the dead and taken up to Christ's right hand, we shall henceforth fear no second death. When sun and moon grow dim with age and earth's blue skies are rolled up like a worn-out vesture, we shall enjoy an age like the years of God's right hand, like his own eternity. The great I AM shall be the bliss of every soul whom Christ has redeemed from the grave and this shall know no end. To this the Lord sets his seal. Do you want to see the red wax and the divine impression thereon? Look at the close of the text: 'repentance shall be hid from mine eyes.' There Jehovah declares his unalterable will; it must and shall be even so. That his saints shall rise from the dead is the immutable decree of God. In all this let us rejoice.

FOR MEDITATION: (*Our Own Hymn Book*, no. 841 vv.3&4—Isaac Watts, 1709)
'What though our inbred sins require our flesh to see the dust;
Yet as the Lord our Saviour rose, so all His followers must.
There's an inheritance divine reserved against that day:
'Tis uncorrupted, undefiled, and cannot fade away.'

SERMON NO. 2046

20 NOVEMBER (PREACHED 28 SEPTEMBER 1885)

First things first

'Seek ye first the kingdom of God, and his righteousness; and all these things shall be added unto you.' Matthew 6:33
SUGGESTED FURTHER READING: Psalm 45:1–7

By the phrase 'his righteousness', I understand that power in the world which is always working, in some form or other, for that which is good, true and pure. Everything in this world which is holy, honest and of good repute, may count upon the Christian as its friend, for it is a part of God's righteousness. Does drunkenness eat out the very life of our nation? Do you want men of temperance to battle with this evil? The Christian man cries, 'Write down my name.' When the slave had to be freed, the subjects of God's kingdom were to the front in that deed of righteousness, and today, if oppression is to be put down, we dare not refuse our aid. If the people are to be educated and better housed, we hail the proposal with delight. If the horrible sin of the period is to be denounced and punished, we may not shrink from the loathsome conflict. Let each man in his own position labour after purity and, as God shall help us, we may yet sweep these streets of their infamies and deliver our youth from pollution. Every Christian man should say of every struggle for better things, 'I am in it, cost what it may.' Hosts of your professors of religion forget to seek God's righteousness and seem to suppose that their principal business is to save their own souls, poor little souls that they are! Their religion is barely sufficient to fill up the vacuum within their own ribs, where their hearts should be. This selfishness is not the religion of Jesus. The religion of Jesus is unselfish: it enlists a man as a crusader against everything that is unrighteous. We are knights of the red cross and our bloodless battles are against all things that degrade our fellowmen, whether they be causes social, political, or religious. We fight for everything that is good, true and just.

FOR MEDITATION: 'Righteousness exalteth a nation' (Proverbs 14:34), but wickedness all too easily usurps its place (Ecclesiastes 3:16). By God's grace national righteousness can be restored (Isaiah 1:21,26–27), but his people have a part to play in sowing the seeds of righteousness (James 3:13–18).

SERMON NO. 1864

21 NOVEMBER (PROBABLY PREACHED 21 NOVEMBER 1889)

Camp law and camp life

'For the LORD *thy God walketh in the midst of thy camp, to deliver thee, and to give up thine enemies before thee; therefore shall thy camp be holy; that he see no unclean thing in thee, and turn away from thee.'*
Deuteronomy 23:14
SUGGESTED FURTHER READING: Genesis 43:24–31

The Lord would have his people clean in all things. The God of holiness commands and loves purity of all kinds. He says, 'be ye clean, that bear the vessels of the LORD.' Cleanliness of body is sometimes neglected by persons professing godliness; I speak to their shame. It ought not to be possible for grace and dirt to meet in the same person. I must confess I feel a great horror at Christian people who are so dirty that one cannot sit in the same pew with them without nausea. This is the trial of many visitors among poor people who profess religion, that certain of them are not clean in their houses and in their clothes. Filth may be expected in persons of unclean hearts, but those who have been purified in spirit should do their utmost to be pure in flesh, clothes and dwelling. If cleanliness be next to godliness (and I am sure it is), it ought to be observed by those who profess godliness. Does not the same text which says 'having our hearts sprinkled from an evil conscience,' also say, 'and our bodies washed with pure water'? The Christ who redeemed us did not redeem us that we should be covered with filthiness. He has redeemed the body as well as the soul and has made it to be 'the temple of the Holy Ghost'; surely we must cleanse his temple and not allow it to be defiled. I like the idea of those sailors on board ship, who knew that the ship was going down and therefore put on their Sunday's best, that they might die as clean and neat as they could. I would not care to die in filth, or to live in it. A Christian should be clean in all things, in his person, his house, his garments and his habits. For his own sake, but specially for the sake of others, he should carefully observe sanitary laws.

FOR MEDITATION: Outward cleansing can be only skin-deep (Matthew 23:25–28), but should accompany inward cleansing (2 Corinthians 7:1), of which it has been used as a picture (Zechariah 3:3–5; John 13:5–10; 1 Peter 3:21). Godly Joseph took trouble over his outward appearance when he met Pharaoh (Genesis 41:14) and his brothers (Genesis 43:30–31).

SERMON NO. 2177

22 NOVEMBER (1885)

The dream of the barley cake

'When Gideon was come, behold, there was a man that told a dream unto his fellow, and said ... a cake of barley bread tumbled into the host of Midian, and came unto a tent, and smote it that it fell, and overturned it, that the tent lay along. And his fellow answered and said, This is nothing else save the sword of Gideon the son of Joash, a man of Israel: for into his hand hath God delivered Midian.' Judges 7:13–14

SUGGESTED FURTHER READING: 2 Chronicles 18:1–27

A Christian man was afraid to speak about his Lord to one whom he met. It cost him a deal of trouble to screw his courage up to speak to a sceptic, but when he had spoken, he found that the sceptic had all along been afraid that he would be spoken to. It is a pity when we tremble before those who are trembling because of us. By want of faith in God we make our enemies greater than they are. Behold the host of doubters, heretics and revilers, who, at the present time, have come up into the inheritance of Israel, hungry from their deserts of rationalism and atheism! They are eating up all the corn of the land. They cast a doubt upon all the verities of our faith. But we need not fear them, for if we heard their secret counsels, we should perceive that they are afraid of us. Their loud blusterings and constant sneers are the index of real fear. Those who preach the cross of our Lord Jesus are the terror of modern thinkers. In their heart of hearts they dread the preaching of the old-fashioned gospel and they hate what they dread. On their beds they dream of the coming of some evangelist into their neighbourhood. What the name of Richard was to the Saracens, that the name of Moody is to these boastful intellects. They wish they could stop those Calvinistic fellows and evangelical old fogies. So long as the plain gospel is preached in England there will always be hope that these brigands will yet be scattered and the church be rid of their intrusion. Rationalism, Socinianism, Ritualism and Universalism will soon take to their legs, if the clear, decided cry of 'The Sword of the LORD, and of Gideon' is once more heard.

FOR MEDITATION: (*Our Own Hymn Book,* no. 686 v.4—Paul Gerhardt, 1659; tr. by John Wesley, 1739)
  'When He makes bare His arm, what shall His work withstand?
  When He His people's cause defends, who, who shall stay His hand?'

SERMON NO. 1873

23 NOVEMBER (PREACHED 23 AUGUST 1885)

The history of Little-faith

'And immediately Jesus stretched forth his hand, and caught him, and said unto him, O thou of little faith, wherefore didst thou doubt?'
Matthew 14:31
SUGGESTED FURTHER READING: Isaiah 30:15–21

Very early in its life Little-faith has great longings. See it in Peter's case. He is on board ship with his brethren while Jesus is yonder upon the waters; Peter is so earnest to come to his Lord and be with him, that he is ready to plunge into the sea to reach him. Why could he not wait as the others did? His immediate duty was in the ship with his brethren, but his vehement desires carried him above commonplace toiling and rowing. Strong faith exhibits patience where Little-faith is in a hurry. It was well to have longings for Jesus, but it would have been wiser to have waited while the Lord came walking over the sea to the ship. The quiet, self-possessed Christian has deep longings for his Lord, but he has the assured conviction that his Lord will come to him, if he continues faithful to his present duty, and therefore he waits upon the Lord. Little-faith, like Martha, runs to meet Jesus, but Strong-faith, like Mary, sits still in the house. Little-faith is feverish after immediate joy. Little-faith wants to be in heaven tomorrow. Little-faith would convert the world before the sun went down and grows faint because her zeal has not fulfilled her wish. Little-faith must pluck the promises while they are green; she is not content to wait till they become ripe and mellow. Yet I love her longings and would to God that all men had them! However mistaken pressing desires for spiritual joy may be, they are things that do not come into unrenewed hearts. You may thank God for those blessed longings after Christ which some of you feel, which make you cry, 'Oh that I knew where I might find him!' Those who have greater faith know that they have found their Lord; they know that he is as the sun which cannot be hidden; they feel his warmth and rejoice in his light, yet the keen hunger after Christ which goes with Little-faith is an admirable thing and the Lord himself has blessed it.

FOR MEDITATION: (*Our Own Hymn Book*, no. 739 v.4—John Newton, 1779)
   'Though sometimes unperceived by sense, faith sees Him always near,
   A guide, a glory, a defence; then what have you to fear?'

SERMON NO. 1856

24 NOVEMBER (PREACHED 30 AUGUST 1885)

The necessity of growing faith

'We are bound to thank God always for you, brethren, as it is meet, because that your faith groweth exceedingly, and the charity of every one of you all toward each other aboundeth.' 2 Thessalonians 1:3
SUGGESTED FURTHER READING: Romans 4:13–22

The blessing of increased faith is of unspeakable value and praise should be rendered for it. Little-faith will save, but strong faith builds up the church, overcomes the world, wins sinners and glorifies God. Little-faith is slow and feeble and to suit his pace the whole flock travel softly. Little-faith is a wounded soldier and has to be carried in an ambulance by the armies of the Lord, but faith which grows exceedingly lifts the banner aloft, leads the van, meets hand to hand the foes of our Prince and puts them to the rout. If we were invoking blessings upon a church we could scarcely ask for a larger boon than that all the brethren might be 'strong in faith, giving glory to God'. Strong-faith ventures into large endeavours for Christ and missions are projected. Strong-faith carries out the projects of holy zeal and daring ideals are turned into facts. Strong-faith is a shield against the darts of error and is the object of the contempt and hatred of heresy. Strong-faith builds the walls of Zion and casts down the walls of Jericho. Strong-faith smites the Philistines 'hip and thigh' and makes Israel dwell in peace. Oh that the night of Little-faith were over and that the day of glorious faith would come! Soon would our 'young men' 'see visions, and' our 'old men' 'dream dreams', if faith were more among us. 'When the Son of man cometh, shall he find faith in the earth?' At the revival of faith we shall see another Pentecost, with its 'rushing mighty wind' and tongues of flame, but during our lack of faith we still abide in weakness and the enemy will defeat us. O God, we beseech thee, make thy face shine upon us, cause our faith to grow exceedingly and our love to abound yet more and more; then 'times of refreshing shall come from the presence of the Lord'.

FOR MEDITATION: Little faith may produce fear and doubt (Matthew 8:26; 14:31), but great faith is likely to result in persistent prayer (Matthew 15:28), more gospel-opportunities (2 Corinthians 10:15–16) and victory over unfavourable circumstances (James 2:5). May we, like the apostles, say to the Lord, 'Increase our faith' (Luke 17:5).

SERMON NO. 1857

25 NOVEMBER (UNDATED SERMON 1886)

A paradox

'When I am weak, then am I strong.' 2 Corinthians 12:10
SUGGESTED FURTHER READING: Psalm 6:1–10

'When I am weak'. What does that mean? It means when the believer is consciously weak, when he painfully feels and distinctly recognizes that he is weak, then he is strong. In truth, we are always weak, whether we know it or not, but when we not only believe this to be the fact, but see it to be the fact, then it is that we are strong. When it is forced home upon us that we are less than nothing and vanity, when our very soul echoes and re-echoes that word, 'without me ye can do nothing', then it is that we are strong. When a man is thoroughly weak, not only partially, but altogether weak, then is he strong. When apart from the Lord Jesus he is utter weakness and nothing more, then it is that he is strong. Let me persuade you to make a full confession of weakness to the Lord. Say, 'Lord, I cannot do what I ought to do: I cannot do what I want to do: I cannot do what I used to do: I cannot do what other people do: I cannot do what I mean to do: I cannot do what I am sure I shall do: I cannot do what I feel impelled to do, and over this sinful weakness I mourn.' Then add, 'Lord, I long to serve thee perfectly, yet I cannot do it. Unless thou help me, I can do nothing aright. There will be no good in my actions, my words, my feelings, or my desires, unless thou continue to fill me with thine own holy energy. Lord, help me! Lord, help me!' Brother, you are strong while you plead in that fashion. You 'can do all things through Christ which strengtheneth' you and he will strengthen you, now that you are emptied of self. How true it is, 'when I am weak, then am I strong.'

FOR MEDITATION: (*Our Own Hymn Book*, no. 681 v.2—Isaac Watts, 1709)
  'I glory in infirmity,
  That Christ's own power may rest on me.
  When I am weak, then am I strong,
  Grace is my shield, and Christ my song.'

SERMON NO. 2050

26 NOVEMBER (1885)

Our own dear Shepherd

'I am the good Shepherd, and know my sheep, and am known of mine. As the Father knoweth me, even so know I the Father: and I lay down my life for the sheep.' John 10:14–15
SUGGESTED FURTHER READING: 1 Peter 2:18–25

Good shepherd, do you mean to say that you have died for such as these? What! For these sheep? Died for them? What! Die for sheep, shepherd? Surely you have other objects for which to live beside sheep. Have you not other loves, other joys? We know that it would grieve you to see the sheep killed, torn by the wolf, or scattered, but you really have not gone so far in love for them that for the sake of those poor creatures you would lay down your life? 'Ah, yes,' he says, 'I would, I have!' Carry your wondering thoughts to Christ Jesus. What! Son of God, infinitely great and inconceivably glorious Jehovah, wouldst thou lay thy life down for men and women? They are no more in comparison with thee than so many ants and wasps, pitiful and obnoxious creatures. Thou couldst make ten thousand millions of them with a word, or crush them out of existence at one blow of thy hand. They are poor things, make the most you can of them. They have hard hearts and wandering wills and the best of them are no better than they should be. Saviour, didst thou die for such? He looks round and says, 'Yes, I did. I did. I laid down my life for the sheep. I am not ashamed of them and I am not ashamed to say that I died for them.' No, beloved, he is not ashamed of his dying love. He has told it to his brethren up yonder and made it known to all the servants in his Father's house; this has become the song of that house, 'Worthy is the Lamb that was slain'! Shall not we take it up and say, 'for thou wast slain, and hast redeemed us to God by thy blood'? Whatever men may talk about particular redemption, Christ is not ashamed of it. He glories that he laid down his 'life for the sheep.'

FOR MEDITATION: (*Our Own Hymn Book*, no. 402 v.2—Jane E. Leeson, 1842)
    'Loving Shepherd, Thou didst give
    Thine own life that I might live;
    May I love thee day by day,
    Gladly Thy sweet will obey.'

SERMON NO. 1877

27 NOVEMBER (PREACHED 9 SEPTEMBER 1886)

Might have been, or may be

'Some of them said, Could not this man, which opened the eyes of the blind, have caused that even this man should not have died?' John 11:37
SUGGESTED FURTHER READING: Genesis 43:1–15

Perhaps the bitterest griefs that men know come not from facts, but from things which might have been, as they imagine, that is to say, they dig wells of supposition and drink the brackish waters of regret. The sisters of Lazarus did this. Each said, 'Lord, if thou hadst been here, my brother had not died.' In a more unbelieving way the Jews did it, and said, 'Could not this man, which opened the eyes of the blind, have caused that even this man should not have died?' And you say, 'Now, if I had gone to so-and-so, this would not have happened; then the other might have happened and a third thing probably would have occurred; then how different it would have been from what it is now!' You blame yourself for steps which were not only innocent, but wise and right, but now that you see the consequences of them, you begin to imagine that they were not innocent, wise or right, and you fret to think that you took such steps. I have known some go a great deal further than vainly accusing themselves; they have even accused God and say, 'Why was moral evil admitted into the world? Why were men and women constituted as they are? Could not God, who is omnipotent, have so arranged things that there should have been no sin and no sorrow?' What a fine mess we get into once we begin arguing over those points and conjecturing what might have been under other circumstances! These things will not and cannot be; therefore, what is the good of worrying over what is not and cannot be? I will plough, but if there is no field, excuse me. I shall not plough the sea or the mist. I will work on anything practical, but I will not break my heart over fancies.

FOR MEDITATION: (*Our Own Hymn Book,* no. 631 v.1—John Fawcett, 1782)

'O my soul, what means this sadness? Bid thy restless fears be gone:
Wherefore art thou thus cast down? Look to Jesus,
Let thy griefs be turned to gladness, And rejoice in His dear name.'

SERMON NO. 1944

28 NOVEMBER (PREACHED 16 AUGUST 1885)

What is the verdict?

'Beloved, if our heart condemn us not, then have we confidence toward God.' 1 John 3:21

SUGGESTED FURTHER READING: 2 Corinthians 13:5–14

The question to be decided is a very weighty one. What is that question, do you think? I do not think it is the question, 'Am I perfect?' because we can solve that without holding a formal court. The question is not, 'Am I absolutely free from sin?' for, 'if we say that we have no sin, we deceive ourselves, and the truth is not in us.' The question is this: 'Am I sincere in the truth? Is my religion true and am I true in my profession of it?' Next, 'Does love rule in my nature?' All this chapter [1 John 3] deals with love and teaches us that the possession of love is the supreme test of our state. Note the fourteenth verse: 'We know that we have passed from death unto life, because we love the brethren. He that loveth not his brother abideth in death.' The enquiry is, 'Do I love God? Do I love my brother also? Is my spirit that of love? If not, I am not a child of God.' Then the next question is, 'Do I believe in the Lord Jesus Christ?' In the verses which succeed my text this is put as a great test, that we believe in Jesus Christ. Faith is the main question for conscience to decide, together with the following one, 'Do I also keep his commandments? Do I obey God? Do I seek to be holy as Jesus is holy? Or am I living in known sin and tolerating that in myself which does not and cannot please God?' The verse that follows my text puts it, 'we keep his commandments, and do those things that are pleasing in his sight' and the question is, 'Do we not only try to keep the commandments, but do we do so because it is pleasing to God? Is it my master-motive to please God? Do I want to be an Enoch, who "had this testimony, that he pleased God"? Do I keep his commandments and labour to please him?' These are the questions to be tried in the court of conscience, and never was there a weightier issue.

FOR MEDITATION: We cannot do better than ask ourselves the questions the Lord Jesus Christ asked others. Can you identify with those who were able to give him the right answers to his questions about their faith (John 9:35–38; 11:25–27) and their love (John 21:15–17)?

SERMON NO. 1855

29 NOVEMBER (1885)

The preacher's last sermon for the season

'In the last day, that great day of the feast, Jesus stood and cried, saying, if any man thirst, let him come unto me, and drink.' John 7:37
SUGGESTED FURTHER READING: Isaiah 41:17–20

What is this thirst? Thirst is nothing actual or substantive; it is a lack, a want, crying out of its emptiness. It is the absence of a necessary. Sinner, you need not look for any good thing in yourself; the thirst which is sought for is the absence of a good thing. Thirst is a painful need. Have you not needs? Thirst is an emptiness, a vacuum; it is the lack of that which is essential to life. Have you not such a lack? Thirst is conscious need, conscious to a painful degree; have you not this? This sense of need is your thirst. The need naturally begets a pain. When our system needs drink, a merciful providence creates a pang so that we are driven to take notice that a requisite of life must be immediately supplied. Thirst rings the alarm-bell and the mind and body set to work to supply the urgent demand. It would be a dreadful thing if the system needed water and yet did not thirst, for we might be fatally injured before we knew that any harm was happening to us. The pain of thirst is a salutary warning that something very important is wanted. Now, soul, if you are suffering from fear or despondency, if you endure heaviness of heart and disquietude of spirit, if you have a longing, a sighing, a pining after something better and holier, then you are thirsty. If you have this thirst in any measure or degree, you are bidden to come to Christ and drink. If you have not as yet a burning thirst, nor a fever, but if you have any sort of thirst, you may come and drink. If you do in any measure long for mercy and renewal, you are included in this invitation, 'If any man thirst, let him come unto me, and drink.'

FOR MEDITATION: (*Our Own Hymn Book,* no. 492 v.3—Joseph Hart, 1759)
   'Let not conscience make you linger nor of fitness fondly dream:
   All the *fitness* He requireth, is to feel your need of Him:
   This He gives you; 'tis the Spirit's rising beam.'
N.B. This is the latest date in the year on which Spurgeon preached at the Metropolitan Tabernacle during the last seven years of his ministry.

SERMON NO. 1875

30 NOVEMBER (PREACHED 11 SEPTEMBER 1887)

Love at its utmost

'As the Father hath loved me, so have I loved you: continue ye in my love.' John 15:9

SUGGESTED FURTHER READING: Romans 8:35–39

Meditate upon the love of Christ to you. It is a love ancient and venerable, tried and proved. He loved you when you were not; he loved you when you were, but were not what you should be. He has loved you into spiritual being; he has loved you so as to keep you in that being. He loved you so as to suffer and die, and he loves you so as to permit you 'to suffer for his sake'. He has loved you so well as to bear with your ill manners, your shortcomings, your transgressions, your coldness, your backsliding, your lack of prayer, your hardness of heart, your little love to your brethren and all the other sins of which I will not now accuse you, for it is a time of love. He has loved you right on without pausing or slackening. Some of you have known his love these twenty, thirty, forty, fifty years, yes, some of you even more than that. It is no new thing with us to sing, 'Jesus loves me.' All this while he has never failed us once, nor done us an ill turn. The kindest husband that ever lived may sometimes be faulty, but this husband of our souls overflows with divine affection every day and all the day. We could not find fault or flaw in his love, if we were to try. Doubtless, in the future we shall have to make continued trial of his love, but we are sure it will endure every test. We may have rough ways to traverse, but he will tread them with us and we shall lean upon our Beloved. We may be very sick and faint, but he has borne our sicknesses and will sympathize with us. He has said, and we believe it, 'I will never leave thee, nor forsake thee.' His promise is 'Certainly I will be with thee' and 'even to your old age I am he; and even to hoar hairs will I carry you'. The longer we live the more abundant evidence shall we receive of that love of Christ, which at this moment is assuredly ours.

FOR MEDITATION: (*Our Own Hymn Book*, no. 792 v.2—Augustus M. Toplady, 1772)
   'The sense of Thy expiring love
   Into my soul convey:
   Thyself bestow; for Thee alone
   I absolutely pray.'

SERMON NO. 1982

1 DECEMBER (UNDATED SERMON)

The hairs of your head numbered

'But the very hairs of your head are all numbered.' Matthew 10:30
SUGGESTED FURTHER READING: Psalm 139:13–18

Learned men will not talk about the hairs of your head; all their discourse is upon the nebulae, stars, geological periods, organic remains, evolution, the solidarity of the race and I know not what besides. They will not stoop to common-place things, but must say something great, sublime, dazzling, brilliant, full of fireworks. The Master is as far removed from all this as the heavens are from the gaudiest canopy that ever adorned a mortal's throne. He talks in homely language because he is at home; he speaks the language of the heart because he is all heart and wants to reach the hearts of those to whom he speaks. I commend the text to you for that reason and for many others besides. 'The very hairs of your head are all numbered.' These words seem to have in them four things at least and we may take four views of their meaning: the first is *foreordination*: 'the very hairs of your head have been all numbered.' You will find that to be a more accurate version of the text than that which is before us. The verb is not in the present, but in the perfect tense. The very hairs of your head have been all numbered before worlds were made. Secondly, I see in the text *knowledge*. This is very clear: God so knows his people that the very hairs of their head are all numbered by him. Thirdly, there is here *valuation*: he sets such a high estimate upon his own servants that of them it is said, 'the very hairs of your head are all numbered.' You are so precious that the least portion of you is precious; the King keeps a register of every part of you. Lastly, here is most evidently *preservation*. The Saviour has been telling them not to fear those that can 'kill the body, but are not able to kill the soul'. He speaks of God's preserving them. In another place he told his disciples, 'there shall not an hair of your head perish', and he intends the same sense in this case; there shall be a perfect preservation of his people.

FOR MEDITATION: We cannot begin to number the stars of the sky (Genesis 15:5), the sand of the sea (Genesis 32:12; Hosea 1:10) or those saved from their sin (Revelation 7:9–10), but it is the same all-knowing God, who numbers the stars (Psalm 147:4), who also numbers your days (Job 14:5) and 'the very hairs of your head'.

SERMON NO. 2005

2 DECEMBER (UNDATED SERMON)

A testimony to free and sovereign grace

'But the salvation of the righteous is of the LORD.*'* Psalm 37:39
SUGGESTED FURTHER READING: John 10:22–30

When God saves he saves eternally. Some one said to me the other day, 'I do not quite know whether that doctrine of final perseverance is true or not.' So I said to him, 'What kind of life does Jesus Christ give his sheep?' He answered correctly, 'he said, "I give unto them eternal life".' 'Does that not settle it? If he has given them eternal life, they have eternal life.' 'But,' he said, 'might they not die?' I answered, 'Is it not clear that those who die have not eternal life? If they had *eternal* life, how could they die? Does eternal life mean six months' life?' 'No.' 'Does it only mean six hundred years' life?' 'No. It must mean nothing less than life which has no end.' Death is out of the question. I must live if I am one of those of whom the Great Shepherd says, 'I give unto them eternal life'. If you cannot quite see the truth from that expression, what follows? Will the sheep of Christ ever perish? Here is his answer: 'they shall never perish'. What language could better describe their security? But another question is raised: may it not mean that, if they get away from the Lord Jesus, they shall perish? Then comes the next sentence: 'neither shall any man pluck them out of my hand.' Does that not answer it? But perhaps the Saviour might fail! We think not: but listen again: 'My Father, which gave them me, is greater than all; and no man is able to pluck them out of my Father's hand.' There are four great reasons why believers are and must be saved; nothing can shake the force of any one of them. If words mean anything, those who are in Christ are safe. The Lord God Almighty has given unto them eternal life, they shall never perish, neither shall any pluck them out of Christ's hand and over that first hand of Jesus is the Father's hand to make assurance doubly sure.

FOR MEDITATION: (*Our Own Hymn Book,* no. 37 song 1 vv.3&4—Henry Francis Lyte, 1834)
  'The Lord is wise, the Lord is just, the Lord is good and true,
  And they who on His promise trust will find it bear them through.
  His word will stay their sinking hearts; their feet shall never slide:
  The heavens dissolve, the earth departs, they safe in God abide.'

SERMON NO. 1953

3 DECEMBER (UNDATED SERMON)

To the saddest of the sad

'And Moses spake so unto the children of Israel: but they hearkened not unto Moses for anguish of spirit, and for cruel bondage.' Exodus 6:9
SUGGESTED FURTHER READING (Spurgeon): Exodus 4:31–5:23

In the process of salvation it often happens that after people have come to hear the gospel and have, in some measure, become attentive to its invitations, they have for a season been much more miserable than they were before. Have you never noticed, in taking a medicine, how often you are made to feel more sick before you are made well? It is often so in the workings of the great remedy of divine grace: it reveals to us our disease that we may the more heartily accept the heavenly medicine. Yes, and in special cases there may be evils within the spiritual system which must be thrown out in the flesh, to be made visible and so to become the subjects of repentance and abhorrence. The man who judges with shortness and straitness of judgment, demands a remedy that will cure his soul of all evils on the spot and, if it does not evidently and immediately do this, he cries, 'Away with it.' I find that the Hebrew word translated 'anguish' here signifies 'shortness'. Your marginal Bibles have 'straitness'. So they could not believe because of the shortness of their judgment: they measured God by inches. They limited the great and infinite God to minutes and days and so, as they found themselves at first getting into a worse case than before, they said to Moses, deliberately, 'Let us alone, that we may serve the Egyptians'. They did as good as say, 'You have done us no good; indeed you have increased our miseries and we cannot believe in you or accept your message as really from God, seeing it has caused us a terrible increase of our sufferings.' Grace may truly and effectually come to a heart and for a while cause no joy, no peace, but the reverse.

FOR MEDITATION: (*Our Own Hymn Book*, no. 502 vv.3&4—William Freeman Lloyd, 1835)
> 'Do you fear your own unfitness, burdened as you are with sin?
> 'Tis the Holy Spirit's witness; Christ invites you—enter in.
> Do your sins and your distresses 'gainst this sacred record plead?
> Know that Christ most kindly blesses those who feel the most their need.'

SERMON NO. 2026

4 DECEMBER (UNDATED SERMON)

Rejoice evermore

'*Rejoice evermore.*' 1 Thessalonians 5:16
SUGGESTED FURTHER READING: 1 Peter 1:3–9

If ever you fail to rejoice, permit me to exhort you to arouse each one of the graces of the Spirit to its most active exercise. Begin with the first of them: *faith*. Believe; and as you believe this and that out of the ten thousand blessings which God has promised, joy will spring up in your soul. Have you exercised faith? Then lead out the sister grace of *hope*. Begin hoping for the resurrection, hoping for the second coming, hoping for the glory which is then to be revealed. What sources of joy are these! When you have indulged hope, then go on to *love* and let this fairest of the heavenly sisters point you to the way of joy. Go on to love God more and more, to love his people and to love poor sinners; as you love, you will not fail to rejoice, for joy is born of love! Love has on her left hand sorrow for the griefs of those she loves, but at her right hand a holy joy in the very fact of loving her fellows, for he that loves does a joyful thing. If you cannot get joy either out of hope, or faith, or love, then go on to *patience*. I believe that one of the sweetest joys under heaven comes out of the severest suffering when patience is brought into play. 'Sweet,' says Toplady, 'to lie passive in thy hand, and know no will but thine.' And it is so sweet, so inexpressibly sweet, that, to my experience, the joy that comes of perfect patience is, under certain aspects, the divinest of all the joys that Christians know this side of heaven. The abyss of agony has a pearl in it which is not to be found upon the mountain of delight. Put patience to her perfect work, and she will bring you the power to 'Rejoice evermore.'

FOR MEDITATION: (*Our Own Hymn Book*, no. 764 v.4—George Burden Bubier, 1856)
'Oh, this is life! Oh, this is joy,
My God, to find Thee so;
Thy face to see, Thy voice to hear,
And all Thy love to know.'

SERMON NO. 1900

5 DECEMBER (UNDATED SERMON)

A mingled strain

'Purge me with hyssop, and I shall be clean: wash me, and I shall be whiter than snow.' Psalm 51:7
SUGGESTED FURTHER READING: 1 Corinthians 11:23–32

In what state of heart should we come to the communion-table? It is no light matter: in what manner shall we come before the Lord in so sacred an ordinance? By the very nature of the sacred supper we are taught that there should be a mixture of emotions. The bitter and the sweet, the joyful and the sorrowful, are here intermingled. The sacrifice of Christ for sin, is it more a subject of sorrow or of joy? Can we look to the cross without mourning for sin? Can we look at it without rejoicing in pardon bought with blood? Is not the most suitable state of heart for coming to the communion-table just this: mourning for our transgression and joy because of the great salvation? There is a double character about this holy rite: it is a festival of life and yet it is a memorial of death. Here is a cup; it is filled with wine; this surely indicates gladness. Listen to me; that wine is the symbol of blood! This as surely indicates sorrow. In my hand is bread, bread to be eaten, bread which strengthens man's heart; shall we not eat bread with thankfulness? But that bread is broken to represent a body afflicted with pain and anguish: there must be mourning on account of that agony. At the Paschal supper, the lamb of the Lord's Passover had a special sweetness in it, yet the commandment expressly ran 'with bitter herbs they shall eat it.' So is it at this table. Here we with joy commemorate 'the Lamb of God, which taketh away the sin of the world', but with deep sorrow we recall the sin which, though taken away, causes us in the recollection of it to repent with great bitterness of heart.

FOR MEDITATION: 'What mean ye by this service?' (Exodus 12:26). Refresh your memory from 1 Corinthians 11. Where is the Lord's Supper received (vv.18,20,33)? What does the Lord's Supper represent (vv.24–26)? Why is the Lord's Supper retained (vv.24–25)? Whom does the Lord's Supper remember (vv.24–25)? When is the Lord's Supper repeated (v.26)? How is the Lord's Supper respected (vv.27–30)?

SERMON NO. 1937

6 DECEMBER (UNDATED SERMON)

To those who feel unfit for the communion

'*A multitude ... had not cleansed themselves, yet did they eat the passover otherwise than it was written. But Hezekiah prayed for them, saying, The good* LORD *pardon every one that prepareth his heart to seek God ... though he be not cleansed according to the purification of the sanctuary. And the* LORD *hearkened to Hezekiah, and healed the people.*'
2 Chronicles 30:18–20
SUGGESTED FURTHER READING: Acts 2:41–47

If Hezekiah and his people won the blessing and 'praised the LORD day by day, singing with loud instruments unto the LORD', we may look for the same joy and holy exultation. They 'kept the feast of unleavened bread seven days with *great gladness*'. If there is any place where we are bound to be glad, it is at the Lord's Supper. This is no funeral feast, no memorial of one who lies rotting in the grave. Here we remember that Jesus died, but also hear those prophetic words, 'till he come.' He lives and shall come with all the glory and majesty of heaven to claim the kingdoms as his own and to judge the nations in equity. Therefore have we joy as we come to the table. It is a memorial of a death by which the life of myriads was purchased, the memorial of a great struggle which ended in the most glorious of victories. 'It is finished' is the banner which waves over us. Such a victory is a joy for ever; let it be gladly commemorated. Here we celebrate the feast of pardoning love delighting itself in being enabled justly to spare the guilty. Here is the feast of redeemed bondsmen, the jubilee of emancipation from everlasting slavery. We come as those that are alive from the dead to feast with him who was slain, but has risen again and become our life and joy. Bring 'an instrument of ten strings' and the psaltery; let every string be awakened to ecstasy on behalf of Jesus, to set forth in worthy notes his passion and triumph.

FOR MEDITATION: (*Our Own Hymn Book*, no. 457 v.1—Isaac Watts, 1709)
  'Come, dearest Lord, descend and dwell
  By faith and love in every breast;
  Then shall we know, and taste, and feel
  The joys that cannot be expressed.'

SERMON NO. 2131

7 DECEMBER (UNDATED SERMON)

Exhortation—'set your heart'

'Now set your heart and your soul to seek the LORD your God.'
1 Chronicles 22:19
SUGGESTED FURTHER READING: 2 Chronicles 30:13–22

David had gathered these noblemen around his bed to urge them to build a temple, but he was a spiritual man and knew that temple-building was not everything, although he valued it highly. He knew that there was something better than outward service and said to these men, 'Now set your heart and your soul to seek the LORD your God'. By all manner of means attend the house of God, though you are not a Christian, but do go with the desire that God will bless the word and make you a Christian. While you diligently attend to the outward ordinances of God's house, do not trust in them, but 'seek the LORD your God' himself. Baptism is the duty of every believer, but it is not the duty of anybody except a believer: do not put the sign in the place of the thing signified. Do not trust in baptism. Why, if you were not only immersed, but immersed in a thousand seas, this would not help you to salvation! You 'must be born again.' You must seek the Lord. There is no salvation in an outward ceremony. If any of you come to the Lord's table, do not come with any view of getting grace by coming or finding salvation in the eating of a morsel of bread and the taking of a sip of wine. The elements upon the table cannot help you. The communion will be injurious to you, if you are not a true believer. Examine yourself whether you 'be in the faith' and so eat of that bread, but do not dare to eat of it unless in your very heart you have first known the Lord and are feeding upon him. I put this to every person who is not yet converted. Do not rest in hymn-singing, church-going, chapel-going, bending your knee in private prayer, or in anything else that comes of yourself. Your salvation lies outside of yourself, in Christ Jesus. Fly away to Jesus!

FOR MEDITATION: (*Our Own Hymn Book,* no. 606 v.6—William Hammond, 1745)
   'Thou has promised to forgive
   All who in Thy Son believe;
   Lord, I know Thou canst not lie;
   Give me Christ, or else I die.'

SERMON NO. 1884

8 DECEMBER (UNDATED SERMON)

Peter after his restoration

'When thou art converted, strengthen thy brethren.' Luke 22:32
SUGGESTED FURTHER READING: Hebrews 4:14–5:4

The restored believer should strengthen his brethren, because it will be such a benefit to himself. He will derive great personal benefit from endeavouring to cherish and assist the weak ones in the family of God. Brother, do this continually and heartily, for thus you will be made to see your own weakness. You will see it in those whom you succour. As you see how they doubt, or grow cold, or become lukewarm, you will say to yourself, 'These are men of like passions with myself. I see which way I shall drift unless the grace of God sustains me.' It will lead you to throw out another anchor and get a fresh hold, as you see how they yield to the tide. One man is wonderfully like another man, only that other men are better than we are, and when we are trying to strengthen them, we are not to look upon ourselves as superior beings, but rather as inferior beings and say, 'He fell yesterday; I may fall today, and if I do not fall today, I may tomorrow.' All the weaknesses and follies you see in others, believe that they are in yourself and that will tend to humble you. I think that a true minister is often excited to better work by what he sees of weakness in his people, because he says to himself, 'Am I feeding this flock well?' Perhaps he thinks to himself, 'If I had properly tended them, they would not have shown all these weaknesses', and then he will begin to blame his own ministry and look to his own heart; that is a good thing for us all. We very seldom, I think, blame ourselves too much and it is a benefit to us to see our own failings in others.

FOR MEDITATION: The manner in which the Jewish high priest could treat other sinners (Hebrews 5:1–2) is a good pattern for those who belong to the priesthood of all believers (Revelation 1:5–6). The Christian is called upon 'to bear the infirmities of the weak' (Romans 15:1) and to 'support the weak' (1 Thessalonians 5:14).

SERMON NO. 2035

9 DECEMBER (UNDATED SERMON)

The suffering Saviour's sympathy

'For in that he himself hath suffered being tempted, he is able to succour them that are tempted.' Hebrews 2:18
SUGGESTED FURTHER READING: Matthew 4:1–11

I want you that are tempted to draw the following inferences from the suffering and temptation of the Lord Jesus: first, that *temptation to sin is no sin*. It is no sin to be tempted, for in him was no sin and yet he was tempted. He 'suffered being tempted', but there was no sin in that, because there was no sin in himself. You may be horribly tempted and yet no blame whatever may attach to you, for it is no fault of yours that you are tempted. You need not repent of that which has no sin in it. If you yield to the temptation, therein is sin, but the mere fact that you are tempted, however horrible the temptation, is no sin of yours. And, in the next place, *temptation does not show any displeasure on God's part*. He permitted his Only-begotten Son to be tempted: he was always the Son of his love, and yet he was tried. 'This is my beloved Son,' said he at his baptism, yet the next hour that Son was led 'of the Spirit into the wilderness to be tempted of the devil.' It does not even show displeasure on God's part that he permits you to be tempted; on the contrary, it may be consistent with the clearest manifestations of divine favour. And again, *temptation really implies no doubt of your being a son of God,* for *the* Son of God was tempted, even the unquestioned Son of the Highest. The prime model and paragon of sonship, Christ himself, was tempted. Then why not you? Temptation is a mark of sonship rather than any reflection thereupon. Note, next, that *temptation need not lead to any evil consequences in any case*. It did not in your Lord's case lead up to sin. The Lord Jesus was as innocent in temptation and after temptation as before it, and so may we be through his grace. It is written by the beloved John concerning the man that is born of God, that he 'keepeth himself, and that wicked one toucheth him not.'

FOR MEDITATION: (*Our Own Hymn Book,* no. 328 v.2—Isaac Watts, 1709)
   'Touched with a sympathy within, He knows our feeble frame;
   He knows what sore temptations mean, For He has felt the same.'

SERMON NO. 1974

10 DECEMBER (UNDATED SERMON)

The Lord's own view of his church and people

'A garden inclosed is my sister, my spouse; a spring shut up, a fountain sealed.' Song of Solomon 4:12
SUGGESTED FURTHER READING: 2 Corinthians 6:14–7:1

Great attempts have been made of late to make the church receive the world and, wherever it has succeeded, it has come to this result: the world has swallowed up the church. It must be so. The greater is sure to swamp the less. They say, 'Do not let us draw any hard and fast lines. A great many good people attend our services who may not be quite decided, but still their opinion should be consulted, and their vote should be taken upon the choice of a minister, and there should be entertainments and amusements in which they can assist.' The theory seems to be, that it is well to have a broad gangway from the church to the world: if this is carried out, the result will be that the nominal church will use that gangway to go over to the world, but it will not be used in the other direction. It is thought by some that it would perhaps be better to have no distinct church at all. If the world will not come up to the church, let the church go down to the world; that seems to be the theory. Let the Israelites dwell with the Canaanites and become one happy family. Such a blending does not appear to have been anticipated by our Lord in the chapter which was read just now: I mean the fifteenth of John. Read verses eighteen and nineteen: 'If the world hate you, ye know that it hated me before it hated you. If ye were of the world, the world would love his own: but because ye are not of the world, but I have chosen you out of the world, therefore the world hateth you.' Did he ever say, 'Try to make an alliance with the world and in all things be conformed to its ways'? Nothing could have been further from our Lord's mind. Oh that we could see more of holy separation, more dissent from ungodliness, more nonconformity to the world!

FOR MEDITATION: The world is in no doubt about its attitude towards Christians (John 15:18–19), but many Christians and churches seem to be unsure about their attitude towards the world (James 4:4) and stand in desperate need of clear teaching on the subject (1 John 2:15–17).

SERMON NO. 1957

11 DECEMBER (UNDATED SERMON)

The heart: a gift for God

'My son, give me thine heart.' Proverbs 23:26
SUGGESTED FURTHER READING: Matthew 6:19–24

I knew a man who lost his heart. His wife had not got it, his children had not got it and he did not seem as if he had got it himself. 'That is odd,' you say. Well, he used to starve himself. He scarcely had enough to eat. His clothes were threadbare. He starved all who were round him. He did not seem to have a heart. A poor woman owed him a little rent. Out she went into the street. He had no heart. A person had fallen back a little in the payment of money that he had lent him. The debtor's little children were crying for bread. The man did not care who cried for hunger or what became of the children. He would have his money. He had lost his heart. I never could make out where it was till I went to his house one day and saw a huge chest. I think they called it an iron safe: it stood behind the door of an inner room; when he unlocked it with a heavy key, and the bolts were shot and the inside was opened, there was a musty, fussy thing within it, as dry and dead as the kernel of a walnut seven years old. It was his heart. If you have locked up your heart in an iron safe, get it out as quickly as you can. It is a horrible thing to pack up a heart in five-pound notes or bury it under heaps of silver and gold. Hearts are never healthy when covered up with hard metal. 'Your gold and silver is cankered' if your heart is bound up with them. I knew a young lady whose heart I could never see. I could not make out why she was so flighty, giddy, frothy, till I discovered that she had kept her heart in a wardrobe. A poor prison for an immortal soul, is it not? Fetch it out before the moth eats it as wool. When our garments become the idols of our hearts, we are so foolish that we can hardly be said to have hearts at all. Even such foolish hearts as these it is well to get out of the wardrobe and give to Christ. Where is your heart?

FOR MEDITATION: (*Our Own Hymn Book*, no. 797 v.1—Charles Wesley, 1746)
'O love divine, how sweet Thou art!
When shall I find my willing heart all taken up by Thee!
I thirst, I faint, I die to prove the greatness of redeeming love,
The love of Christ to me!'

SERMON NO. 1995

12 DECEMBER (UNDATED SERMON)

The trial of your faith

'The trial of your faith.' 1 Peter 1:7
SUGGESTED FURTHER READING: James 1:1–17

I believe that the Lord frequently tries us by the blessings which he sends us. This is a fact which is too much overlooked. When a man is permitted to grow rich, what a trial of faith is hidden away in that condition! It is one of the severest of providential tests! Where I have known one man fail through poverty, I have known fifty men fail through riches. When our friends get on in the world and have a long stretch of prosperity, they should invite their brethren to offer special prayer for them, that they may be preserved, for the thick clay is heavy stuff to walk upon, and when the feet slip into it and it adheres to you, it makes travelling to heaven a very difficult thing. When we do not cling to wealth, it will not harm us, but there is a deal of bird-lime in money. You that have no riches may yet find a test in your daily mercies: your domestic comfort, that loving wife, those dear children may all tempt you to walk by sight instead of by faith. Yes, and continued health, the absence of all depression of spirit, and the long abiding of friends and relatives, may all make you self-contented and keep you away from your God. It is a great trial of faith to have much for sight to rest upon. To be in the dark, altogether in the dark, is a grand thing for faith, for then you are sure that what you see is not seen of the flesh, but is in very deed a vision of spiritual faith. To be under a cloud is a trial, truly, but not one-half so much a trial as it is to have continually the light of this world. We are so apt to mistake the light of carnal comfort for the light of God, that it is well to see how we fare without it.

FOR MEDITATION: A wrong response to the trial of faith posed by God's bountiful provision can be a snare to a nation (Deuteronomy 8:11–20), to a church (Revelation 3:14–17) and to an individual (2 Chronicles 32:22–31). For the right and safe response see Psalm 103:1–5 & 116:12–14.

SERMON NO. 2055

13 DECEMBER (UNDATED SERMON)

Holding fast our profession

'Let us hold fast the profession of our faith without wavering; (for he is faithful that promised).' Hebrews 10:23
SUGGESTED FURTHER READING: Titus 1:15–2:10

Only when you are out-and-out for Jesus can you be in a right condition. Anything short of this is full of evil. Since Satan tempts you to hide your faith, feel that he seeks your harm and, therefore, come out all the more decidedly. Beloved friends, may God help us never to do anything contrary to the confession of our faith. I have heard of such a thing as a Christian man making a confession of his faith by paying sixpence in the pound in the Bankruptcy Court. They say that he is making a good thing out of his failure. He is making his own damnation sure if he is robbing his creditors and yet professing to be a Christian. Here is a man making a confession of his faith. He is a very good Christian man in his own esteem, but he also knows a good glass of wine and is most fluent when he is getting far into the bottle. Have drunkards any hope of eternal life? Look at yonder professor; he is going across to the public-house to stand at the counter and drink with those who blaspheme. That is his way of confessing his faith, I suppose. It is not mine. Have I not seen Christian women become noisily angry and say harsh things to their servants? That is showing your Christianity, is it? I do not want to be sarcastic, but I want you not to tempt me to be so. If you love the Lord, live as if you loved him. Let us all try to do so and let us watch that we never undo with our hands what we say with our tongues. I heard in Lancashire of some people who preached with their feet. It is the best way of preaching in the world. By your walk and conversation you will preach twice as well as by your talk. Your tongue is too soft a thing to influence dull minds; you must influence such by your lives.

FOR MEDITATION: (*Our Own Hymn Book,* no. 668 v.3—Mary Bowly, 1847)
    'Lord, we are blind, and halt, and lame,
    We have no strong-hold but Thy name;
    Great is our fear to bring it shame,
    Let us not fall. Let us not fall.'

14 DECEMBER (UNDATED SERMON)

The tender enquiry of a friend

'How long wilt thou cut thyself?' Jeremiah 47:5
SUGGESTED FURTHER READING: Psalm 38:1–22

David's great sin was put away so that he did not die, but he was never the same David as before. The Lord's people seem to have shunned him for a time while the adversary found occasion to blaspheme. I think they had, in a measure, turned away from him in horror at his great sin. They began to stand in doubt of him. They had loved him as their champion in his earlier days, when he led the van of the armies of the Lord of hosts and when as a youth he returned from the battle bringing the head of Goliath. They had looked up to him when he was in the wilderness because of his integrity. Though hunted like a partridge by the ungodly party, yet he was the hope of Israel and the joy of all the saints. With what delight did they gather round him at Hebron and Jerusalem when he was crowned their king! They felt that God had blessed his people in giving them such a leader. But when it was whispered that he had defiled his neighbour's wife, then the godly shuddered. They knew what blasphemy and rebuke would come of it and they kept out of his way. They must have been deeply grateful when they found him truly penitent. When he was crying to God for mercy, probably some of them would know it and perhaps step in to cheer him. But still David was scarcely David again, either to the people of God or to himself. The Lord out of very love to him chastened him sorely and pursued him with plague upon plague. His family became his dishonour and his sorrow. He went with broken bones to the grave, 'a man of sorrows, and acquainted with grief'. How grievously he had injured himself! How long he had to cut himself with anguish for that one sin? His life, surely, from the time when he fell with Bath-sheba, was penitential sorrow rather than confident delight and though the Lord left him not, but brought him to much maturity of grace out of his brokenness of heart, yet, still, as often as he went to his couch, the memory of his great transgression would cut and wound his heart.

FOR MEDITATION: (*Our Own Hymn Book*, no. 537 v.5—Cecil Frances Alexander, 1858)
   'Lift up Thy bleeding hand, O Lord; unseal that cleansing tide;
   We have no shelter from our sin, but in Thy wounded side.'

SERMON NO. 2025

15 DECEMBER (UNDATED SERMON)

Fallen angels a lesson to fallen men

'God spared not the angels that sinned, but cast them down to hell, and delivered them into chains of darkness, to be reserved unto judgment.'
2 Peter 2:4
SUGGESTED FURTHER READING: Jude 1–7, 20–23

However great Lucifer was, he degenerated into Satan: the Son of the Morning became Apollyon the Destroyer. However excellent the fallen angels may once have been, they are now potent only for mischief; their wisdom has curdled into cunning; their strength has soured into a vicious force. So no man may say, 'I am a clear thinker; I shall never become an infidel,' or, 'I am gifted in prayer; I shall never become a blasphemer.' You know not what you may become. There is a great difference between gift and grace in prayer: gift will breed pride and pride will ensure destruction; only grace can preserve unto eternal glory. There is also a great difference between office and person; a man may not say, 'I am a minister: I shall be kept faithful in the church of God.' We have seen leaders turn aside and need not marvel, for if angels fall, what man may think that he can stand? To trust our office is to rest upon a broken reed. The grace of God can keep the weakest of us, but apart from that heavenly power how dare any man hope to be preserved to the end? Self-confidence is the beginning of declension. He who reckons he is past temptation is already entangled in its net. We must never presume. Angels fell: why not men? Angels occupy a high position near God's throne: 'Are they not all ministering spirits?' We have evidence in Scripture that they are called on grand occasions to discharge high commissions for the King of kings. Yet even these courtiers, household messengers of the palace of heaven, domestics of glory, went astray, fell and turned into devils. Let no man dream that because he occupies an office in the church his salvation is secure: an apostle fell.

FOR MEDITATION: (*Our Own Hymn Book,* no. 668 v.2—Mary Bowly, 1847)
  'We have no fear that Thou shouldst lose
  One whom eternal love could choose;
  But we would ne'er this grace abuse.
  Let us not fall. Let us not fall.'

SERMON NO. 1820

16 DECEMBER (UNDATED SERMON)

The unchanging God cheering Jacob in the change of dwelling-place

'God ... said, Jacob, Jacob ... I am God, the God of thy father: fear not to go down into Egypt; for I will there make of thee a great nation: I will go down with thee into Egypt.' Genesis 46:2–4

SUGGESTED FURTHER READING: Genesis 31:1–21

No doubt Jacob felt that the change would involve himself and his family in new temptations. They had behaved badly among the simple pastoral people: what would they do amidst the vices of Egypt? I often feel great diffidence in advising people to make changes, especially in leaving the country to go to the city. Change has its perils. You begin to know your temptations and are somewhat prepared to withstand them, but know not what may happen in another sphere with other surroundings and influences. I would rather carry my old burden; it begins to fit my back, which has grown somewhat used to it. But a new burden might be more heavy, try me in fresh places and cause fresh wounds. I am not anxious to make changes, for I have read the words of Solomon the wise: 'As a bird that wandereth from her nest, so is a man that wandereth from his place.' When God commands a man to follow an untried path, he may go rightly and wisely, even as the young swallows fly in their appointed time, though they have never traversed the continents before. But he who wanders out of sheer wantonness, may find that he has gone from bad to worse and wish himself back again to what he despised. If Jacob trembled at making so great a change, it was not without reason. All the family's habits would be rudely shaken and a new mode of life forced upon them. He could not have guessed that there would be a Goshen for the shepherds and must have dreaded leaving a quiet pastoral life for the refinements of Egyptian society and the blandishments of Egyptian idolatry.

FOR MEDITATION: (*Our Own Hymn Book*, no. 732 v.2—George Keith, 1787)
> 'In every condition—in sickness, in health,
> In poverty's vale, or abounding in wealth;
> At home and abroad, on the land, on the sea,
> As thy days may demand shall thy strength ever be.'

SERMON NO. 2116

17 DECEMBER (UNDATED SERMON)

Man, whose breath is in his nostrils

'Cease ye from man, whose breath is in his nostrils: for wherein is he to be accounted of?' Isaiah 2:22
SUGGESTED FURTHER READING: Psalm 146:1–10

Cease to idolize any man by giving him undue honour. There is an honour to be paid to all, for the apostle says, 'Honour all men.' A measure of courtesy and respect is to be paid to every person and especially to those whose offices demand it; therefore is it written, 'Honour the king.' Some by their character deserve much respect from their fellow men and I trust we shall never refuse 'honour to whom honour' is due, but there is a limit to this or we shall become sycophants, slaves and, what is worse, idolaters. It grieves one to see how certain people dare not even think, much less speak, till they have asked how other people think. In some congregations there are weak people who do not know whether they have liked the sermon till they have asked a certain venerable critic to whom they act as echoes. The bulk of people are like a flock of sheep: there is a gap and, if one sheep goes through, all will follow. If the ringleader happens to be an infidel or a new-theology man, so much the worse; if he happens to be orthodox, it is much better in some ways, but then it is a pity that people should follow the truth in so thoughtless a manner. Public opinion is a poor substitute for conscience and is no substitute at all for righteousness and truth. Because the general opinion bids you bow down before this man or that, will you do so? Will you forget God, conscience, right and truth and ask another man to tell you when you may breathe? God's people should scorn such grovelling. 'If the Son ... shall make you free, ye shall be free indeed.' Jesus loves his soldiers to own his supremacy, but once owning him as Lord, he would have them feel that no man or set of men shall draw them away from his word, either in doctrine or precept. Worship is for God only: render it to him, and 'Cease ye from man, whose breath is in his nostrils'.

FOR MEDITATION: (*Our Own Hymn Book,* no. 688 v.4—John Ryland, 1777)

'No good in creatures can be found   I must have all things, and abound,
But may be found in Thee;   While God is God to me.'

SERMON NO. 1984

18 DECEMBER (UNDATED SERMON)

Washed to greater foulness

'If I wash myself with snow water, and make my hands never so clean; yet shalt thou plunge me in the ditch, and mine own clothes shall abhor me.' Job 9:30–31

SUGGESTED FURTHER READING: 2 Kings 5:1–14

> 'Not all the outward forms on earth,
> Nor rites that God has given,
> Nor will of man, nor blood, nor birth,
> Can raise a soul to heaven.'

If I 'make my hands never so clean', is an expression peculiarly racy in the original. The Hebrew word has an allusion to soap or nitre. Such was the ordinary and obvious method anyone would take to whiten his hands when they were grimy. Tradition tells that certain stains of blood cleave to the floor. The idea is that human blood, shed in murder, can never be scrubbed or scraped off the boards. Thus is it most certainly with the dye of sin. 'In thy skirts is found the blood of the souls', is the terrible language of Jeremiah 2:34. When you think that baptism can begin, that confirmation can further and that other sacraments can complete your purification, you are mere dupes of your own folly. 'If I wash myself with snow water, and make my hands never so clean; yet shalt thou plunge me in the ditch, and mine own clothes shall abhor me.' There it stands; it is the testimony of one man, yet it is true; the Almighty attests it and all human experience affirms it. These worthless experiments to cleanse yourselves would be ended once for all if you would have regard to the great truth of the gospel: 'without shedding of blood is no remission.' 'The blood of Jesus Christ his Son cleanseth us from all sin.' God alone can remove sin and he does so by the blood of Jesus. But as sure as ever quickened souls try to get purity in the wrong way, God will thrust them down into the ditch. This is a terrible predicament.

FOR MEDITATION: (*Our Own Hymn Book*, no. 556 v.3—Charles Wesley, 1739)
> 'At last I own it cannot be that I should fit myself for Thee:
> Here, then, to Thee I all resign; Thine is the work, and only Thine.'

SERMON NO. 1908

19 DECEMBER (UNDATED SERMON)

Cleansing: a covenant blessing

'Then will I sprinkle clean water upon you, and ye shall be clean: from all your filthiness, and from all your idols, will I cleanse you.' Ezekiel 36:25
SUGGESTED FURTHER READING: 1 John 1:5–10

'From all your filthiness … will I cleanse you.' What a vast 'all' that is! 'All your filthiness'. All the filthiness of your birth-sin; all the filthiness of your natural temperament, constitution and disposition. 'From all your filthiness … will I cleanse you.' All the filthiness that came out of you in your childhood, that was developed in you in your youth, that still has vexed your manhood and perhaps even now dishonours your old age. From all your actual filthiness, as well as from all your original filthiness, 'will I cleanse you.' From all your secret filthiness, from all your public filthiness, from everything that was wrong in the family, from everything that was wrong in the business, from everything that was wrong in your own heart, 'from all your filthiness … will I cleanse you.' From all your pride. What a filthy thing that is! From all your unbelief. What an abominable thing that is! From all your tainted imaginations, from all your lustings, from all your wrong words, from all your covetousness, from all your murmuring, from all your anger, from all your malice, from all your envy, from all your distrust, 'from all your filthiness … will I cleanse you.' Read the Ten Commandments, then stop at each and say, 'Lord, thou hast said, From all your filthiness will I cleanse you. Cleanse me in both ways: take away the evil of the sin and take away my tendency to the sin.'

> 'Let the water and the blood,
> From Thy riven side which flowed,
> Be of sin the double cure,
> Cleanse me from its guilt and power.'

That seems so full of richness: 'from all your filthiness … will I cleanse you.' Do not believe that any filthiness need stay upon you in practice.

FOR MEDITATION: For initial cleansing we must own our filthiness (Proverbs 30:12); for continued cleansing we must disown our filthiness (2 Corinthians 7:1; Ephesians 5:4; Colossians 3:8; James 1:21).

SERMON NO. 1921

20 DECEMBER (UNDATED SERMON)

Witnesses against you

'I set a great assembly against them.' Nehemiah 5:7
SUGGESTED FURTHER READING (Spurgeon): Isaiah 1:1–20

God is against you. 'The face of the LORD is against them that do evil, to cut off the remembrance of them from the earth.' He would have you saved. He has sworn with an oath, 'As I live, saith the Lord GOD, I have no pleasure in the death of the wicked; but that the wicked turn from his way and live'. But if you will not turn, you must burn. If you will not repent, you must perish. God has said it and he will not lie. Justice demands it and 'the Judge of all the earth' must be just. And, to crown all, *Jesus Christ, the Son of God, is against you* if you resolve to be the enemy of God. He loves sinners: he died for sinners: he is ever willing to receive them, but as long as they remain impenitent and unbelieving, he cannot love their sin and cannot love them, viewing them in the light of wilful, persistent rebels. And when he comes in the latter days, you know what will happen to those that loved not Christ: they will be *Anathema Maranatha,* cursed at his coming. He himself will say it and it appals me to have to remind you of the fact; he himself, whose gentle lips were like lilies dropping sweet-smelling myrrh, tender as a woman's, he himself, when he comes, will say, 'Depart from me, ye cursed, into everlasting fire, prepared for the devil and his angels'. You will find no friend in Christ in that last tremendous day. He will break you in pieces 'with a rod of iron', as potters' vessels are broken into shivers. So, then, I set this great assembly against you: saints on earth and saints in heaven, the angels, God and Christ himself against you. Who is there for you? Who is there on your side, enemies of God? It is as dreadful to think of those who are for you as of those who are against you, for those who are for you and on your side are the ungodly like yourselves, the lost in hell, who are now what you must be unless you escape, and the devil and his angels, themselves punished for their sins. A grim assembly, surely, those that are for you!

FOR MEDITATION: If God can 'have a few things against' those he has saved (Revelation 2:4,14,20), he has everything against those who oppose him as Father (Romans 8:7; Jude 15), Son (Acts 4:26–27) and Holy Spirit (Mark 3:29). Do you still have Almighty God's wrath (Romans 1:18), judgment (Romans 2:2) and face (1 Peter 3:12) against you?

SERMON NO. 2123

21 DECEMBER (UNDATED SERMON)

God fighting sin

'But they rebelled, and vexed his holy Spirit: therefore he was turned to be their enemy, and he fought against them.' Isaiah 63:10
SUGGESTED FURTHER READING: Hebrews 12:25–29

What is to be done with the man who will not have mercy when it is set before him? If a convicted criminal is invited to confess and receive pardon and he will not do it, what remains but to carry out the sentence? Both justice and injured mercy require that it should be so. When a man gets into the next world, who dies refusing Christ and rejecting divine mercy, he will fight against God there and, according to his ability, he will be a greater sinner there than here. Shall God give him pleasure? Shall the Lord make such a rebel happy? Shall he stand by and say, 'I will reward the rebel. He has vexed my Spirit, but I will ennoble and reward him'? Shall 'the Judge of all the earth' act so? If you will turn to this Book, you will not find between these two covers a solitary ray of hope for a man who dies without God and without Christ. I defy any man who believes this Book to be inspired, to find anything in its sacred page but blank despair for the man who will not in this life accept the mercy of God in Christ Jesus. My Lord and Master said, 'He that believeth and is baptized shall be saved; but he that believeth not shall be damned.' That is his word; there it stands and there it will stand for ever. It will never be reversed. It is the final sentence, 'Depart from me, ye cursed, into everlasting fire, prepared for the devil and his angels'. I charge you, by the living God, do not provoke him to this. Rush not upon the edge of Jehovah's sword. At once look to Jesus crucified, Jesus crucified for the guilty, Jesus who came into the world, took our nature, and bare our sin and shame. He cries from the cross, 'Look unto me, and be ye saved, all the ends of the earth'.

FOR MEDITATION: (*Our Own Hymn Book,* no. 570 v.4—Compiled from Simon Browne, 1720)
   'Confounded, Lord, I wrap my face,
   And hang my guilty head;
   Ashamed of all my wicked ways,
   The hateful life I've led.'

SERMON NO. 2179

22 DECEMBER (UNDATED SERMON)

Public testimony: a debt to God and man

'Then they said one to another, We do not well: this day is a day of good tidings, and we hold our peace: if we tarry till the morning light, some mischief will come upon us: now therefore come, that we may go and tell the king's household.' 2 Kings 7:9
SUGGESTED FURTHER READING: Ezekiel 3:16–21

Had those lepers held their tongues, they would actually have been doing evil. If they had kept their secret for twenty-four hours, many hundreds might have died of starvation within the walls of Samaria: had they so perished, would not the lepers have been guilty of their blood? Do you not agree with that? May not neglect be as truly murder as a stab or a shot? If, in your street, a man shall perish through not knowing the Saviour and you never made an effort to instruct him, how will you be guiltless at the last great day? If there be any within your reach who sink down to perdition for lack of the knowledge of Christ and you could have given them that knowledge, will your skirts be free from blood in the day when the great inquest shall be held and God shall make inquisition for the blood of Christ? I put it to the consciences of many silent Christians, who have never yet made known to others what God has made known to them: how can you be clear from guilt in this matter? Do not say, 'Am I my brother's keeper?' for I shall have to give you a horrible answer if you do. I shall have to say, 'No, Cain, you are not your brother's keeper, but you are your brother's killer.' If by your effort you have not sought his good, by your neglect you have destroyed him. If I could swim and saw you in a stream, but merely looked at you and greatly regretted that you should be so foolish as to tumble in, and never stretched out a hand to rescue you, your death would lie at my door; I am sure it is so with those who talk about enjoying religion, yet keep it all to themselves and never rescue the perishing. Stern truths these! Let them go home where they ought to go home and may God the Holy Spirit bless them!

FOR MEDITATION: God's word is supposed to silence those who oppose it (Romans 3:19; Titus 2:7–8), not those who love it (1 Peter 3:15–16). There is 'a time to keep silence' (Ecclesiastes 3:7), but in the matter of our testimony that time is not yet (Psalm 115:17–18). The first Christmas ushered in a day of 'good tidings' for all people (Luke 2:10–11).

SERMON NO. 1996

23 DECEMBER (PREACHED 21 SEPTEMBER 1890)

The serpent's sentence

'And the LORD *God said unto the serpent ... I will put enmity between thee and the woman, and between thy seed and her seed; it shall bruise thy head, and thou shalt bruise his heel.'* Genesis 3:14–15
SUGGESTED FURTHER READING: Revelation 12:1–12

Why has God left devils without hope, yet has sent his Son to redeem mankind? Is not divine sovereignty manifested here? We can give no answer to the question, 'What is man, that' God thus visits him with distinguishing grace? save this: 'I will have mercy on whom I will have mercy, and I will have compassion on whom I will have compassion.' Intending no forgiveness to this evil spirit, the Lord put no questions to him. His interrogation of our first parents was a sign of mercy. When God chides a man's conscience, it is with the view of blessing him. Do I speak to any man whose sense of sin is aroused, who is accused by the Word of God, who feels the Spirit of God working within him as a spirit of bondage? You may be hopeful because it is so. If God had meant to destroy you, he would have left you alone, even as he left the serpent without a word of expostulation, and he would have passed sentence upon you speedily. The very rebukes of God are tokens of his favour towards men. With the serpent, that is, with the evil spirit, God had no upbraidings, but dealt at once by way of doom. He pronounced a sentence upon the serpent, which, while it was terrible to him, is most encouraging to us; so far as our first parents understood it, it must have been a sun of light to their dark, depressed souls. For many a year this was the lone star of believing hearts, this gospel of the serpent's doom. Satan was their enemy; he had done them wrong. He was also God's enemy, but God would fight against him and call them into his battle. He would raise up One who would suffer, but win the victory, One who is the seed of the woman. By him Satan's head would be bruised and in that very fact, the race of man would be unspeakably blessed.

FOR MEDITATION: (*Our Own Hymn Book,* no. 477 v.4—Isaac Watts, 1709)
   'Must angels sink for ever down,
   And burn in quenchless fire,
   While God forsakes His shining throne
   To raise us wretches higher?'

SERMON NO. 2165

24 DECEMBER (PREACHED 14 SEPTEMBER 1890)

Immanuel—the light of life

'The people that walked in darkness have seen a great light: they that dwell in the land of the shadow of death, upon them hath the light shined.' Isaiah 9:2

SUGGESTED FURTHER READING: Matthew 1:18–25

The sign of coming light is Jesus. 'Therefore the Lord himself shall give you a sign; Behold, a virgin shall conceive, and bear a son, and shall call his name Immanuel.' In Judah's trouble, the virgin-born was God's token that he would deliver and that speedily, for in less time than it would take such a child to reach years of knowledge, both of Judah's royal adversaries would be gone. The sign was good for Ahaz, but is far better for us. Behold the incarnate Son of God born of Mary at Bethlehem; what can this intend for us but grace? If the Lord had meant to destroy us, he would not have assumed our nature. If he had not been moved with mighty love to a guilty race, he would never have taken upon himself their flesh and blood. It is a miracle of miracles that the Infinite should become an infant, that he, who is pure spirit and fills all things, should be wrapped in swaddling bands and cradled in a manger. 'He took not on him the nature of angels', though that would have been a tremendous stoop from Deity, but he descended lower still, for 'he took on him the seed of Abraham.' He was made in all things 'like unto his brethren,' though he counted 'it not robbery to be equal with God'. It is not in the power of human lips to speak out all the comfort which this one sign contains. If any troubled soul will look believingly at God in human flesh, he must take heart of hope. If he looks believingly, his comfort will come speedily. The birth of Jesus is the proof of the good will of God to men: I am unable to conceive of proof more sure. He would not have come here to be born among men, to live among them, to suffer and to die for them, if he had been slow to pardon, or unwilling to save.

FOR MEDITATION: (*Our Own Hymn Book,* no. 256 v.4—Charles Wesley, 1739)

> 'Mild He lays His glory by;
> Born that men no more might die;
> Born to raise the sons of earth;
> Born, to give them second birth.'

SERMON NO. 2163

25 DECEMBER (PREACHED 27 SEPTEMBER 1885)

The true tabernacle, and its glory of grace and peace

'And the Word was made flesh, and dwelt among us, (and we beheld his glory, the glory as of the only begotten of the Father,) full of grace and truth.' 'For the law was given by Moses, but grace and truth came by Jesus Christ.' John 1:14, 17

SUGGESTED FURTHER READING: Luke 2:1–20

Jesus Christ is the Son of God; he is his only begotten Son. Others are begotten of God, but no other was ever begotten of God as Christ was; consequently, when he came into this world, the glory that was about him was a 'glory as of the only begotten'. A very singular, very special and incommunicable glory abides in the person of our Lord. Part of this was the glory of his grace. Now, in the Old Testament, in Exodus 34:6, you notice that the glory of God lay in his being 'The LORD God, merciful and gracious, longsuffering, and abundant in goodness and truth.' The glory 'of the only begotten of the Father' must lie in the same things as the glory of the Father, namely, in longsuffering, goodness and truth. In Christ there is a wonderful display of the gentleness, patience, pity, mercy and love of God. Not merely did he teach the grace of God and invite us to the grace of God, but in himself he displayed the grace of God. This is to be seen in his incarnation. It is a wonderful instance of divine grace that the Word should be made flesh, dwell among us and reveal his glory to us. Apart from anything that springs out of the incarnation of Christ, that incarnation itself is a wondrous act of grace. There must be hope for men now that man is next akin to God through Jesus Christ. The angels were not mistaken when they not only sang, 'Glory to God in the highest,' but also, 'on earth peace, good will toward men', because in Bethlehem the Son of God was born of a virgin. God in our nature must mean God with gracious thoughts towards us. If the Lord had meant to destroy the race, he never would have espoused it and taken it into union with himself. There is fullness of grace in the fact of the Word made flesh tabernacling among us.

FOR MEDITATION: (*Our Own Hymn Book*, no. 256 v.6—Charles Wesley, 1739)
   'Glory to the new-born King! Let us all the anthem sing,
   "Peace on earth, and mercy mild; God and sinners reconciled."'

SERMON NO. 1862

26 DECEMBER (UNDATED SERMON)

Jesus: 'all blessing and all blest'

'Men shall be blessed in him: all nations shall call him blessed.' Psalm 72:17

SUGGESTED FURTHER READING: Luke 6:17–23

To bless and be blessed is the noblest sort of fame, yet how few have thought it worth seeking! Many a name in the roll of fame has been written there with a finger dipped in blood. It would seem as if men loved those most who have killed the most. They call those greatest who have been the greatest cut-throats. They make their greatest illuminations over massacres of their fellows, calling them victories. To be set aloft upon a column, represented by a public statue or to have poets ringing out your name, it seems necessary to grasp the sword and to hack and slay your fellow-men. O misery, that wholesale murder should be the shortest method of becoming illustrious! One name will last when all others have died out; that name is connected only with blessing. Jesus Christ came into the world to bless men. Men find in him a blessing wide as the world. While here he blessed and cursed not. By speech, act, glance and thought he was an incarnate blessing. All that came to him, unless they wilfully rejected him, obtained blessings at his hands. The home of his infancy, the friends of his youth, the comrades of his manhood, he blessed unsparingly. To bless men he laboured, parted with everything, became poor and at last died. Those outstretched hands upon the cross are spread wide in benediction and are fastened there as if they would remain outstretched till the whole world is blessed. Our Lord's resurrection from the dead brings blessings to mankind. Redemption from the grave and life eternal he has won for us. He waited on earth a while until he ascended, blessing men as he went up. His last attitude below the skies was that of pronouncing a blessing upon his disciples. He has gone into the glory, but he has not ceased to bless our race.

FOR MEDITATION: (*Our Own Hymn Book*, no. 72 song 1 v.4—Isaac Watts, 1719)

    'Blessings abound where'er He reigns;
    The prisoner leaps to lose his chains;
    The weary find eternal rest;
    And all the sons of want are blessed.'

SERMON NO. 2187

27 DECEMBER (PREACHED 19 SEPTEMBER 1886)

Believers as blessed as the blessed virgin

'As he spake these things, a certain woman ... said unto him, Blessed is the womb that bare thee ... But he said, Yea rather, blessed are they that hear the word of God, and keep it.' Luke 11:27–28
SUGGESTED FURTHER READING (Spurgeon): Luke 1:26–56

This earnest woman did not mean to praise Christ's mother. I do not know that she had even seen Mary, or that she would have entered into her mind, apart from her matchless Son. It is often the way in the East: if they want to insult a man, they speak vilely of his mother; if they wish to honour him, they praise his mother to the skies; yet they may have neither dislike nor esteem for the mother; they only reach the son through her. It was while Jesus was preaching that this cry was raised: 'it came to pass, as he spake these things'. It was because he spoke so well, that this woman could not withhold her word of praise. After her fashion as an Eastern woman, she praised the Lord Jesus by extolling his mother. But lest such an expression, commendable enough in itself, should in after years lend any kind of countenance to that Mariolatry which our Saviour foresaw, Jesus said, 'Yes, she is blessed doubtless; but still more blessed are they that hear the word of God, and keep it.' Our Divine Saviour, with all the love of his manhood towards his mother, acted towards her in such a way as for ever to forbid any degree of religious worship being rendered to her. He gave no countenance to the superstitious titles of 'Our Lady,' 'Mother of God' and so on, but, on the contrary, taught that the nearest fleshly relationship to himself was nothing compared with spiritual union to him. Remember how it is written: 'Then one said unto him, Behold, thy mother and thy brethren stand without, desiring to speak with thee. But he answered and said unto him that told him, Who is my mother? and who are my brethren? And he stretched forth his hand towards his disciples, and said, Behold my mother and my brethren! For whosoever shall do the will of my Father which is in heaven, the same is my brother, and sister, and mother.'

FOR MEDITATION: Before the Saviour's birth Mary was already blessed through hearing and believing God's word (Luke 1:38,45). Afterwards she habitually kept things in her heart (Luke 2:19,51). We should do what she told the servants at Cana (John 2:5).

SERMON NO. 1920

28 DECEMBER (UNDATED SERMON)

'He cometh with clouds'

'Behold, he cometh with clouds; and every eye shall see him, and they also which pierced him: and all kindreds of the earth shall wail because of him. Even so, Amen.' Revelation 1:7

SUGGESTED FURTHER READING: Mark 13:24-37

I think I see John. He is 'in the Spirit', but suddenly he seems startled into a keener and more solemn attention. His mind is more awake than usual, though he was ever a man of bright eyes that saw afar. We always liken him to the eagle for the height of his flight and the keenness of his vision, yet suddenly even he seems startled with a more astounding vision. He cries out, 'Behold'! He has caught sight of his Lord. He says not, 'He will come by-and-by,' but, 'I can see him; he is now coming.' He has evidently realized the second advent. He has so conceived of the second coming of the Lord that it has become a matter of fact to him, a matter to be spoken of and even written down. 'Behold, he cometh'. Have you and I ever realized the coming of Christ so fully as this? Perhaps we believe that he will come. I should hope that we all do that. If we believe that the Lord Jesus has come the first time, we believe also that he will come 'the second time'; but are these equally assured truths to us? Perhaps we have vividly realized the first appearing: from Bethlehem to Golgotha and from Calvary to Olivet we have traced the Lord, understanding that blessed cry, 'Behold the Lamb of God, which taketh away the sin of the world.' Yes, 'the Word was made flesh, and dwelt among us, (and we beheld his glory, the glory as of the only begotten of the Father,) full of grace and truth.' But have we with equal firmness grasped the thought that he comes again without a sin-offering 'unto salvation'? Do we now say to each other, as we meet in happy fellowship, 'Yes, our Lord is coming'? It should be to us not only a prophecy assuredly believed among us, but a scene pictured in our souls and anticipated in our hearts.

FOR MEDITATION: (*Our Own Hymn Book*, no. 360 v.1—Joseph Tritton, 1856)
  'Behold He comes! the glorious King
  Whom once a cross upbore;
  Let saints redeemed His praises sing,
  And angel hosts adore.'

SERMON NO. 1989

29 DECEMBER (UNDATED SERMON)

Hope for your future

'I will settle you after your old estates, and will do better unto you than at your beginnings.' Ezekiel 36:11

SUGGESTED FURTHER READING: Joel 2:11–25

Have you ever noticed that when nations fall they seldom rise again? Babylon and Nineveh become mountains of rubbish. If the Medo-Persian kingdom falls, the throne is never revived. If Greece and ancient Rome cease from their eminence, we see no more of them than their ruins. But God's people are not numbered amongst the nations, so that when Israel falls she revives again. Though for many centuries the ancient people have been scattered and peeled, derided and despised, yet every Israelite may put down his foot with joyous tread, and say, 'No, Israel, you shall never perish!' Even in her ashes live her past fires and the days shall come when Israel shall own her Messiah and her God will fulfil the promise of the text, 'I will settle you after your old estates, and will do better unto you than at your beginnings; and ye shall know that I am the LORD.' I believe that to be the first sense of the passage; but since all the blessings of the covenant, which belong to the seed 'according to the flesh', do spiritually belong to all those who are in that covenant 'according to the spirit', we shall take this word as spoken to all believers. If a hypocrite falls, he falls like Lucifer, never to hope again. He is a meteor, that flashes across the sky and disappears, a wandering star, for 'whom is reserved the blackness of darkness for ever.' Let Judas fall from his apostleship and there is no restoring 'the son of perdition'. But how different is the case of God's own, when they fall! Alas, that they should do so! Yet of them it is said, 'Rejoice not against me, O mine enemy: when I fall, I shall arise'. Peter at a look from his Master 'wept bitterly' and lived to say, 'thou knowest that I love thee.' There is hope of a tree, if it be cut down, that it will sprout again, for there is life in it, and where there is life there is hope.

FOR MEDITATION: As a sheep David trusted the Lord, his Shepherd, to restore his soul (Psalm 23:3); as a sinner he looked to the Lord, his Saviour, to restore his joy (Psalm 51:12). Does the close of the year need to be a time of restoration for you?

SERMON NO. 2125

30 DECEMBER (UNDATED SERMON)

Retrospect—'the LORD hath blessed'

'Forasmuch as the LORD hath blessed me hitherto.' Joshua 17:14
SUGGESTED FURTHER READING: Genesis 49:22–28

I believe that every flower in a garden, which is tended by a wise gardener, could tell of some particular care that the gardener takes of it. He does for the dahlia what he does not for the sunflower; something is wanted by the rose that is not required by the lily and the geranium calls for an attention which is not given to the honeysuckle. Each flower wins from the gardener a special culture. The vine has a dressing all its own and the apple-tree a pruning peculiar to itself. There is a blessing for the house of Manasseh and a blessing for the house of Ephraim, and so is there a special benediction for each child of God. All the names of the tribes were written on the breastplate, but there was a different colour in the jewel allotted to each tribe, and I believe that there is a speciality of grace about every child of God. There is not only an election from the world, but an election out of the elect. Twelve were taken from the disciples; three were taken out of the twelve; one greatly beloved was taken out of the three. Uniformity of love does not prevent diversity of operations. As a crystal is made up of many crystals, so is grace composed of many graces. In one ray of the light of grace there are seven colours. Each saint may tell his fellow something that he does not know and in heaven it will be a part of the riches of glory to hold commerce in those specialities which each one has for himself alone. I shall not be you, neither will you be me, neither shall the two of us be like another two, or the four of us like any other four, though all of us shall be like our Lord when 'we shall see him as he is.' I want you each to feel at this hour, 'the LORD hath blessed *me* hitherto'.

FOR MEDITATION: (*Our Own Hymn Book,* no. 720 v.8—Isaac Watts, 1709)
'The men of grace have found
Glory begun below;
Celestial fruits on earthly ground
From faith and hope may grow.'

SERMON NO. 1882

31 DECEMBER (UNDATED SERMON)

Prospect—'he will keep'

'Holy Father, keep through thine own name those whom thou hast given me, that they may be one, as we are. While I was with them in the world, I kept them in thy name: those that thou gavest me I have kept, and none of them is lost, but the son of perdition; that the scripture might be fulfilled.' John 17:11-12
SUGGESTED FURTHER READING: Jude 24-25

I delight to see the traces of the Trinity in every act of grace. From the first transactions of covenant love, even to the ingathering of the whole election of grace and the introduction of the chosen into glory, we hear the sound of that voice which of old said, 'Let us make man'. The three divine Persons work together in absolute union for the production of one grand result. 'Glory be unto the Father, and to the Son, and to the Holy Ghost; as it was in the beginning, is now, and ever shall be, world without end! Amen.' Observe that our text is all about keeping. Three or four times over we have some tense or other of the word '*keep*'. 'Holy Father, keep ... those whom thou hast given me'. 'While I was with them in the world, I kept them'. Greatly do we need keeping. You have been redeemed, but you must still be kept. You have been regenerated, but you must be kept. You are pure in heart and hands, but you must be kept. You are quickened with the divine life, you have aspirations after the holiest things, your love to Christ is intense, but you must be kept. You have had a deep experience and you know the temptations of the enemy, but still you must be kept. The sunlight of heaven rests upon your honoured brow; you are near the gates of glory, but you must be kept. The same hand that bought you must keep you and the same Father, who 'hath begotten' you 'again unto a lively hope', must keep you to his eternal 'kingdom and glory.' All glory be 'unto him that is able to keep' us 'from falling'! Let all unite in the song 'Who are kept by the power of God'.

FOR MEDITATION: (*Our Own Hymn Book*, no. 668 v.4—Mary Bowly, 1847)
    'Lord, evermore Thy face we seek:
    Tempted we are. And poor, and weak;
    Keep us with lowly hearts, and meek.
    Let us not fall. Let us not fall.'

SERMON NO. 1883

Subject Index

Summary of Subject Index

Section 1   **The Godhead**
　　　　　　　　The Trinity
　　　　　　　　God the Father
　　　　　　　　God the Son: His Person
　　　　　　　　God the Son: His work
　　　　　　　　God the Holy Spirit
　　　　　　　　The Law of God
　　　　　　　　The Word of God
　　　　　　　　Angels, God's servants

Section 2   **Man in his natural sinful state**

Section 3   **The Gospel**
　　　　　　　　Salvation—of God
　　　　　　　　Proclamation
　　　　　　　　Responses & Effects

Section 4   **The Church**

Section 5   **The Christian Life**
　　　　　　　　Blessings from God
　　　　　　　　Duties & Fruitfulness
　　　　　　　　Spiritual warfare

Section 6   **Life in society**

Section 7   **Biographical**

Section 8   **Times & Seasons**

Section 9   **Death & the future state**

Subject Index

Section 1 **The Godhead**

The Trinity
Nearness	17 Jul

God the Father
Fatherhood	19 Jul; 15 Sep
Justice	29 Feb
Light	12 Apr
Love	29 Feb; 13,15 Jun
Omniscience	4 Aug
Presence	2 Jan
Providence	22 Oct; 16 Nov
Revelation	29 Jan; 13 Apr
Righteousness	16 Jul
Singing	30 Oct
Thoughts	28 May
Whole-heartedness	29 Jul

God the Son—His Person 21,26 Aug
Bridegroom	6 May
Captain	7 Jun
Delights	30 Apr
Graciousness	15 Oct
Greatness	1 Feb
Homeliness	1 Dec
Joy	28 Apr
Kingship	19 Jun
Lamb of God	23 Mar; 9 Jul; 16 Oct
Love	30 Nov
Lowliness	25 Jun
Nearness	24 Oct
Pattern	17 Jun
Preciousness	30 Mar
Promises	6 Aug

375

Subject Index

	Righteousness	8 Sep
	Saviour	13 Feb
	Self-restraint	27 Mar
	Shepherd	17,26 Nov
	Subordination	11 May
	The Way	25 Mar
	Weeping	23 Jun
	God the Son—His work	10 Mar; 13 Sep; 26 Dec
	Birth	24–25 Dec
	Sufferings & Death	3 Apr
	Resurrection	1,6,10,21,25 Apr
	Ascension	7 Nov
	Intercession, mediation & Priesthood	25 Feb; 6 Jul
	Second coming	30 Jan; 15 May; 28 Dec
	God the Holy Spirit	10 Mar; 29 Aug; 5 Sep
	Filling	26 May
	Gifts	27 Apr
	Teaching	24 May
	The Law of God	20 Jan (preaching); 5 Jun
	The Word of God	22 Jan; 11 Mar; 7,19 Apr; 5,18 May; 3 Jun; 5 Jul
	Angels, God's servants	8 Jul
	Fallen angels	15 Dec
Section 2	**Man in his natural sinful state**	
	Blindness	4 May
	Covetousness	12 Nov
	Deadness	5 Nov
	Enmity with God	16 Aug

Subject Index

	Evolution	18 Jun
	External righteousness	1 May
	False peace	3 Aug
	Formality	2 Jun; 4 Nov
	Modern thought	18 Jan; 18 Jun; 10 Aug
	Rejection of God	6 Mar
	Robbing God	27 Jul
	Ruin	4 Mar
	Scepticism	22 Nov
	Scoffing	17 Jan
	Self-cleansing	18 Dec
	Self-righteousness	10 Sep
	Sincerity	20 Sep
	Sins	25 Jul
	Vain remedies	8 Apr
	Weakness of character	5 Mar
Section 3	**The Gospel**	
	Salvation—of God	14–15 Aug
	Anger removed	14 Jan
	Cleansing	19 Dec
	Complete salvation	22 Aug
	Conversion	15 Jan; 2 Feb
	Covenant	14 Feb
	Deliverance	4,8 Mar
	Direction	27 Jun
	Drawing	7 May
	Election	1 Jul
	Eternal gift	14 May
	Eternal life	4 Feb
	Forgiveness	6 Feb; 20 Jun
	Grace	4 Sep
	Redemption	17 Mar
	Righteousness	20 May; 21 Jul

377

Subject Index

Sanctification	12 Feb; 29 Mar
Softening	18 Sep
Substitutionary atonement & Justification	11–13 Jan; 2,15 Mar; 16 Apr; 2,27 May; 12 Jun; 18 Jul; 9 Sep; 3,5,31 Oct; 26 Nov
Sure salvation	20 Mar
The Way	1 Aug

Proclamation

Foundation-laying	7 Jul
Literature	21 May
Locations	10 Oct
Persuasion	26 Jun
Preaching	12 Mar; 29 Apr; 8 Jul; 7 Aug; 20 Oct
Testimony	24 Mar; 15 Apr; 6 Jun; 17 Sep; 22 Dec
Watchmen	8 Feb

Responses & Effects

	22 Sep
Apostasy	15 Dec
Calling on God	1 Mar; 11 Oct; 10 Nov
Coming to God	19 May; 30 Jun
Conviction	20 Feb; 1 Sep
Criticism	29 May
Faith	17 Feb; 3 Mar; 13,15,31 May; 20 Jul; 8 Oct; 23–24 Nov
Feeding on Christ	28 Oct
Following the crowd	9 Mar
Imitation faith	22 Feb; 7 Sep
Knowing Christ	13 Aug
Living a lie	29 Sep
Looking (in)to Christ	14 Jul; 5 Aug; 12 Sep
Misery	3 Dec

Subject Index

	Neglect	12 Oct
	New life	2 Apr
	Receiving	26 Mar
	Remembering	11 Jun
	Repentance	19 Feb; 3 Mar; 25 Aug
	Self-examination	28 Nov
	Squinting	14 Jul
	Stillness	15 Jul
	Thirst	29 Nov
	Unbelief	9 Jun; 27 Aug
Section 4	**The Church**	
	Amusements	18 Apr
	Baptism	26 Apr; 3 Jul
	Children	17,23 Oct
	Compromise	1 Oct
	Externals	7 Dec
	Giving	13 Nov
	Holding the faith	5 Feb
	Jewish nation	23 Mar; 14 Nov; 29 Dec
	Lord's Supper	2–3 Jul; 23 Oct; 5–6 Dec
	Mariolatry	27 Dec
	Martyrs	10 Jan
	Ministry—consecration	19 Mar; 24 Sep
	Ministry—hearing	18 Mar; 28 Jun; 12 Aug; 23 Sep
	Ministry—meditation	21 Jan
	Ministry—responsibilities	19 Jan
	Ministry—training	18 Oct
	Mission & Outreach	1 Jul; 16 Sep
	Revival	7 Feb; 24 Jul
	Statistics	5 Apr

379

Subject Index

Section 5   **The Christian life**

Blessings from God   26 Oct; 1,30 Dec
Appropriation   12 May
Blessedness   30 Jul
Carrying   27 Sep
Chastisement   28 Jul
Comfort in affliction   12 Apr; 14 Jun; 30 Aug; 11 Sep; 15 Oct
Communion   6–7 Jan
Covenant bond   9 May
Experience   28 Sep
Friendship   8 May
Heaven on earth   3 Feb
Knowing God   6 Sep
Light   13 Oct
Ownership   9 Aug
Preservation   31 Dec
Promises   23 May
Provision   24 Feb
Rest   16 Jun
Restoration   4 Jun; 29 Dec
Revelation   22 Apr
Reward   18 Aug
Security   2 Dec
Strength in weakness   3 Jan; 25 Nov
Training   4 Apr

Duties & Fruitfulness
Assurance   20 Apr
Blessing God   5 Jan
Cleanliness   21 Nov
Consecration   3 Nov
Cross-bearing   2 Aug
Fear of God   6 Oct

Subject Index

Following Christ	18 Nov
Forbearance	17 May
Forgiveness	17 May
Girding the mind	11 Jul
Glorifying God	28 Aug
Good works	3 Sep
Gratitude	10 May
Growth	13 May
Holiness	11 Feb
Homage	22 Mar
Honouring Christ	2 Sep
Humility	31 Aug
Imitation	24 Jun
Keeping the heart	19 Sep
Laughter	17 Aug
Living for Christ	28 Jan
Looking to God	3 Apr
Meditation	21 Jan; 9 Oct
Obedience	20 Aug; 30 Sep
Order	29 Jun
Patience	31 Jan
Peace	4 Jan; 31 Mar
Praise	30 May; 7,14,25 Oct; 6 Nov
Prayer	8,23–25 Jan; 10,21 Feb; 29 Oct; 9,11 Nov
Putting on Christ	23 Feb
Rejoicing	25 May; 4 Dec
Sanctification	7 Mar
Service	16 Jan; 11 May; 7 Jun; 5 Sep
Steadfastness	17 Apr
Stewardship	24 Apr
Sympathy	14 Apr; 8 Jun
Trust	21 Aug
Understanding	15 Feb
Worship	8 Nov

Subject Index

Spiritual Warfare

Backsliding	22 Jul; 14 Dec
Balancing truths	9 Feb
Change, fear of	16 Dec
Conjecture	27 Nov
Darkness & light	25 Sep; 2 Oct
Dead works	21 Jun
Deceit	2 Oct
Dependence on man	17 Dec
Discouraging others	26 Jul
Distrust	11 Aug
Doubts	3 Nov
False allegations	21 Sep
Fearfulness	22 May
Fearlessness	27 Feb
Half-obedience	26 Feb
Harboured sin	27 Oct
Hardness of heart	28 Mar
Inconsistency	22 Jun; 13 Dec
Insufficiency	24 Aug
Loss of love	21 Oct
Nominalism	13 Mar; 19 Aug
Persecution	9–10 Jan; 17 Jun
Pride	31 Aug
Prosperity	12 Dec
'Providence'	15 Nov
Self, fear of	1 Jun
Self-reliance	2 Nov
Sin's deceitfulness	16 Feb
Sin's effects	1 Nov
Trials & Temptations	19 Apr; 9 Dec
1. The Devil	16 Feb; 23 Dec
2. The World (worldliness)	8 Aug; 10–11 Dec
3. The Flesh	29 Aug
Weaknesses	8 Dec

Subject Index

	Weariness of God	11 Apr
	Worrying	16 May
Section 6	**Life in Society**	
	Citizenship	9 Jan
	House-hunting	23 Apr
	National righteousness	20 Nov
	National sin	10 Jun
	Parenting	26 Jan; 10 Jul
	Politicians	19 Sep
	Races	16 Sep
	Unconverted relatives	19 May
	Work	27 Jan
Section 7	**Biographical**	
	Baxter, Richard	23 Aug
	Bunyan, John	22 Oct; 12 Nov (Holy War)
	Covenanters	31 Jul
	Defoe, Daniel	30 Aug
	Edison, Thomas	23 Sep
	Edwards, Jonathan	25 Jan; 1 Jul
	Evans, Christmas	5 Sep
	Foxe (Book of Martyrs)	10 Jan
	Gadsby, William	12 Mar
	George III	14 Sep
	Gordon, General	23 May
	Hogarth, William	29 Jun
	Llewellyn, Prince	1 Sep
	Luther, Martin	18 Feb
	Müller, George	19 Mar
	Nicholas (Czar)	2 May
	Owen, John	23 Aug
	Saphir, Adolph	12 Apr
	Spurgeon, C.H.	21 May; 15 Aug; 11,26 Sep; 6 Nov

Subject Index

	Thorpe, John	3 Jun
	Watts, Isaac	14 Sep
	Wesley, John	7 Feb
	Whitefield, George	7 Feb; 3 Jun; 1 Jul
	Wilkinson, John	23 Mar
	Winstanley, Henry	28 Aug
Section 8	**Times & Seasons**	
	Start of year	1–3 Jan
	The seasons	14 Mar; 21 Apr
	Christmas	23–25 Dec
Section 9	**Death & the future state**	
	Death	5 Jun; 14,26 Sep
	Eternal death	19 Oct
	Glory	21 Mar
	Heaven	9 Apr; 23 Aug; 4 Oct
	Judgment	16 Mar; 4 Jul; 20–21 Dec
	Perfection	13 Jul
	Resurrection	19 Nov
	Sin's destruction	23 Jul

Scripture Index

Index of original texts and suggested further readings
(Spurgeon's complete texts are identified below by an asterisk*).

Genesis
3:1–24	4 Mar
3:14–15*	23 Dec
4:6–7*	9 Jan
6:5–22	1 Jun
8:22*	14 Mar
11:31*	26 Feb
12:5*	26 Feb
13:1–18	23 Apr
15:11*	3 Nov
16:13–14*	8 Nov
17:15–18:15	17 Aug
18:22–33	25 Jan
19:15–29	25 Jan
24:5–8*	1 Oct
28:10–22	6 Jan
31:1–21	16 Dec
32:12*	23 May
33:1–11	15 Oct
43:1–15	27 Nov
43:24–31	21 Nov
46:1–4*	16 Dec
48:15–16*	10 Jul
49:22*	4 Nov
49:22–28	30 Dec

Exodus
4:31–5:23	3 Dec
6:9*	3 Dec
12:1–28	23 Mar
12:21–27*	23 Oct
14:3*	21 Sep
15:1–2*	25 Oct
20:18–20*	28 Jul
25:10–22	5 Jul
28:36–38*	6 Jul
34:29–35*	4 May

Leviticus
2:13*	11 Feb
16:30*	3 Oct
22:21*	20 Jan

Numbers
6:22–27*	26 Oct
11:1–20	1 Oct
26:63–65*	5 Apr
32:23*	26 Jul

Deuteronomy
3:21–28	5 Jun
9:6–29	21 Feb
23:14*	21 Nov
30:11–14*	12 Jun
32:2*	21 Jan
33:13*	4 Nov
33:24–25*	3 Jan
34:5*	5 Jun

Joshua
1:2–3*	12 May

1:10–11*	12 Aug
17:14*	30 Dec
17:18*	12 Jul
23:1–14	28 Sep
24:14–31	7 Jun

Judges
7:13–14*	22 Nov
16:22*	24 Sep

Ruth
—

1 Samuel
3:10–14	26 Jan
3:17*	9 Oct
20:3*	14 Sep
30:20*	13 Nov
30:21–25*	7 Jun

2 Samuel
6:20–22*	1 Jul

1 Kings
5:17*	7 Jul
9:2–3*	10 Feb
18:17–40	11 Oct

2 Kings
4:3*	25 Jan
5:1–14	18 Dec
7:3–7*	6 Jun
7:9*	22 Dec

1 Chronicles
22:19*	7 Dec

385

Scripture Index

2 Chronicles		5:11*	25 May	68:18*	27 Apr
18:1–27	22 Nov	6:1–10	25 Nov	71:1–24	30 May
24:1–27	9 Mar	12:6*	5 May	71:3*	6 Sep
30:13–22	7 Dec	16:1–11	2 Jan	71:16*	16 Jul
30:17–20*	6 Dec	19:7–14	7 Apr	72:17*	26 Dec
33:1–13	29 Jan	19:11*	16 Mar	73:1–28	9 Feb
34:29–33	31 Jul	22:1–5,22–26	25 Oct	77:9*	31 May
		23:1–6	16 Jun	85:1–13	7 Feb
Ezra	–	25:1–11	10 Nov	85:8*	27 Oct
		25:10*	31 Jul	86:1–7	29 Oct
Nehemiah		27:1–14	21 Sep	86:6–7*	11 Nov
1:1–11	24 Jan	29:11*	3 Aug	87:1–7	10 Oct
4:1–15	26 Jul	31:15*	16 May	90:1–12	14 Sep
5:1–15	6 Oct	32:1–11	20 Jun	94:9*	29 Oct
5:7*	20 Dec	32:8–9*	15 Feb	98:1–9	25 May
		33:1–12	29 Jul	100:1–5	16 Jan
Esther	–	34:1–10	6 Jun	103:1*	5 Jan
		34:6*	8 Mar	103:1–22	1 Jan
Job		35:22–28	16 Jul	104:1–35	5 Jan
1:1–5	23 Oct	37:18–29	3 Jan	106:7*	10 May
1:22*	28 Aug	37:39*	2 Dec	106:44–45*	14 Feb
2:1–13	14 Apr	38:1–22	14 Dec	107:1–9	27 Jun
5:27*	12 Oct	39:4–13	26 Sep	107:14–16*	6 Nov
7:12*	7 May	40:6–8*	30 Apr	107:17–32	22 Oct
9:30–31*	18 Dec	40:7*	2 May	109:1–7	10 Feb
15:11*	11 Aug	42:1–11	11 Aug	110:1–7	1 Feb
22:26*	3 May	45:1–7	20 Nov	111:1–10	4 Sep
23:10*	4 Aug	46:1–3*	27 Feb	116:1–19	10 May
28:1–28	6 Sep	48:8*	18 Mar	119:1–11	28 Mar
29:11–16	8 Jun	50:15*	30 Aug	119:9–24	9 Oct
30:23*	26 Sep	51:1–19	20 Feb	119:49*	23 Jan
42:5–6*	19 Feb	51:7*	5 Dec	119:97–104	21 Jan
		63:1–11	3 Apr	119:131–133*	29 Jun
Psalms		63:7*	28 Sep	119:145–152	17 Jul
4:4–5*	15 Jul	67:1–7	26 Oct	119:165*	22 Jan

Scripture Index

130:7*	16 Nov	6:1–13	10 Jun	63:1*	13 Feb
136:4*	4 Sep	9:1–2*	24 Dec	63:10*	21 Dec
139:1–12	4 Aug	12:1–6	14 Jan	65:1*	12 Sep
139:13–18	1 Dec	21:6–12	8 Feb	66:10*	18 Apr
145:1–2*	30 May	25:1–12	31 Mar		
146:1–10	17 Dec	26:3*	4 Jan	**Jeremiah**	
148:1–14	6 Nov	30:15–21	23 Nov	6:16–21	18 Jun
149:2*	19 Jun	33:24*	20 Jun	9:1–6,23–24	13 Aug
		35:8*	1 Aug	11:18–12:6	22 May
Proverbs		40:1–5	1 Aug	14:3–4,22*	10 Nov
4:1–19	10 Jul	40:9–31	27 Sep	17:5–10	29 Sep
4:20–27	19 Sep	41:8*	8 May	23:21–32	3 Jun
4:25*	14 Jul	41:17–20	29 Nov	29:1–14	4 Jun
6:12–19	25 Jul	42:4*	30 Jan	29:11*	28 May
7:1–27	15 Nov	43:1–4*	11 Apr	31:3*	15 Jun
8:22–31	30 Apr	43:3*	5 Oct	31:3*	15 Aug
14:10*	14 Apr	43:22–24*	11 Apr	31:18–20*	15 Sep
15:19*	27 Jan	44:21–23*	11 Apr	31:34*	29 Jan
23:17–18*	22 Jun	46:1–4*	27 Sep	32:26–27*	22 Apr
23:19*	18 Jun	48:17–22	27 Oct	32:40*	6 Oct
23:19–24:7	26 May	49:10*	3 Feb	32:41*	29 Jul
23:26*	11 Dec	50:10*	25 Sep	33:17–26	14 Mar
24:30–32*	26 Jan	52:7–12	19 Mar	38:5*	5 Mar
30:2*	13 Apr	53:1–12	12 Jan	47:5*	14 Dec
		53:10*	10 Jan		
Ecclesiastes	–	53:12*	11 Jan	**Lamentations**	
		54:4–10	15 Jun	3:1–24	25 Sep
Song of Solomon		54:9*	14 Jan	3:25–33	15 Jul
1:6*	19 Sep	55:3*	30 Jun		
4:12*	10 Dec	55:6–11	28 May	**Ezekiel**	
		55:7–9*	6 Feb	3:16–21	22 Dec
Isaiah		61:1–3	18 Sep	11:16*	6 Jan
1:1–20	20 Dec	61:10–62:5	20 May	14:12–20	14 Jun
1:20*	11 Mar	62:6–7*	8 Feb	20:34–38*	9 May
2:22*	17 Dec	62:11–12*	13 Feb	27:26*	10 Sep

Scripture Index

28:1–19	10 Sep	**Micah**		5:17–30	20 Jan
33:1–9	24 Mar	2:6–3:8	7 Aug	6:7–13	8 Jan
34:11–24	17 Nov	2:7*	13 Mar	6:19–24	11 Dec
36:11*	29 Dec	2:12–13*	20 Mar	6:25–34	16 May
36:25*	19 Dec	6:1–8	11 Apr	6:33*	20 Nov
36:27*	12 Apr	7:1–9	13 Oct	8:2–3*	7 Sep
47:8*	23 Jul	7:7*	24 Jan	8:5–27	2 Nov
48:35*	2 Jan	7:18–20	6 Feb	8:8*	31 Aug
				8:14–15*	23 Apr
Daniel		**Nahum**	–	8:16–17*	12 Jan
3:14*	17 Sep			10:30*	1 Dec
7:9–14	19 Jun	**Habakkuk**	–	11:25–30	25 Jun
				13:1–23	28 Jun
Hosea		**Zephaniah**		13:7,22*	19 Aug
1:7*	24 Jul	3:16–18*	30 Oct	14:31*	2 Nov
6:4–5*	9 Mar			14:31*	23 Nov
13:14*	19 Nov	**Haggai**		15:27*	9 Feb
14:1–3*	1 Mar	2:4–5*	5 Sep	15:28*	2 Nov
				16:13–17*	26 Aug
Joel		**Zechariah**		18:1–14	17 Oct
2:11–25	29 Dec	9:9*	25 Jun	18:12–13*	28 Apr
2:25*	4 Jun	12:10–11*	18 Sep	19:16–30	18 Nov
2:32*	11 Oct			21:9*	22 Mar
2:32*	14 Nov	**Malachi**		21:17–20*	29 Sep
		1:1*	19 Jan	22:10*	6 May
Amos		3:8*	27 Jul	22:11–13*	20 May
6:1–6	18 Apr			23:23–28	1 May
		Matthew		25:14–30	24 Apr
Obadiah		1:18–25	24 Dec	26:10*	28 Jan
17*	19 Mar	3:1–12	7 Sep	26:20–29	2 Jul
		3:13–4:4	8 Sep	26:28*	3 Jul
Jonah		4:1–11	9 Dec	26:30–35	6 Aug
1:1–2:10	30 Aug	4:19*	18 Jan	26:53–54*	27 Mar
1:3*	15 Nov	5:1–12	30 Jul	26:69–27:5	25 Aug
		5:6*	8 Sep	27:43*	17 Jun

Scripture Index

27:45*	16 Apr	4:38–39*	11 Sep	22:32*	8 Dec
27:46*	2 Mar	5:17*	29 May	22:39–46	31 Oct
27:50–51*	25 Mar	5:17–26	13 Feb	22:47–53	27 Mar
27:50–53*	2 Apr	6:17–23	26 Dec	22:54–62	1 Sep
		7:11–17*	15 Jan	22:60–62*	22 Jul
Mark		7:18–23	14 Jul	23:11*	2 Sep
1:1–15	3 Mar	7:42–43*	16 Jan	23:39–49	16 Apr
1:40–42*	12 Feb	7:50*	17 Jan	23:40–42*	23 Aug
2:1–12	29 May	8:4–15	20 Sep	23:42–43*	9 Apr
3:5*	28 Mar	8:43–44*	8 Apr	24:13–27	24 Oct
4:35–41	7 May	8:47*	15 Apr	24:25*	27 Aug
4:40*	22 May	10:25–42	3 Sep	24:25–47	3 Apr
6:45–51	7 May	11:1–4	1 Mar	24:36–44*	10 Apr
7:20–23*	25 Jul	11:21*	3 Aug		
8:4*	7 Feb	11:27–28*	27 Dec	**John**	
9:14–29	8 Oct	11:33–36*	13 Oct	1:9–13	8 Apr
9:42–50	11 Feb	12:1–12	15 Apr	1:14,17*	25 Dec
10:13–16*	17 Oct	12:13–31	4 Feb	1:29*	16 Oct
10:32–45	2 May	12:35–44	11 Jul	1:43–51	22 Apr
10:46–52	14 Aug	13:18–19*	20 Oct	1:47*	20 Sep
12:6–9*	6 Mar	13:22–30	4 Oct	1:50*	17 Feb
12:28–37	23 Sep	14:20*	19 May	2:11*	20 Jul
12:41–44	13 Nov	15:1–7	28 Apr	3:8*	2 Feb
13:24–37	28 Dec	15:11–32	30 Oct	3:13–18	20 Jul
15:21*	2 Aug	17:15–19*	7 Oct	3:16*	11 Jun
15:21–39	2 Mar	17:20–37	30 Jan	3:33*	10 Aug
16:1–14	10 Apr	18:1–14	9 Nov	4:1–30	8 Nov
16:7*	6 Aug	18:8*	15 May	4:31–38*	21 May
		18:13*	20 Feb	4:46–53*	8 Oct
Luke		19:11–27	6 Mar	5:36–47	16 Aug
1:26–56	27 Dec	19:12–13*	24 Apr	6:35–45	15 Aug
1:67–75	14 Feb	19:41–48	23 Jun	6:48*	28 Oct
1:77–79*	27 Jun	20:37–38*	4 Oct	7:37*	29 Nov
2:1–20	25 Dec	22:19*	2 Jul	8:30–32*	22 Feb
4:1–19	19 Apr	22:31–38	27 Mar	8:51–53*	19 Oct

389

Scripture Index

9:5–7*	14 Aug	20:10–16*	24 Oct	**Romans**		
9:35*	20 Apr	21:12*	24 Feb	1:1–8	25 Apr
10:14–15*	26 Nov	21:15–19	21 Oct	1:8–17	20 Oct
10:17*	17 Nov	21:20–25	20 Aug	1:16–25	13 Apr
10:22–30	2 Dec			2:16*	4 Jul
10:27–30*	18 Nov	**Acts**		2:17–29	4 Nov
10:39–42*	10 Oct	1:1–11	7 Nov	3:19–26	29 Feb
11:1–36	7 Jan	2:22–42	3 Jul	4:13–22	24 Nov
11:35*	23 Jun	2:36–37*	1 Sep	4:16–17*	17 Aug
11:37*	27 Nov	2:41–47	6 Dec	5:1–11	4 Jan
12:1–8	27 Jul	3:1–4:4	24 Jul	5:5*	13 Jun
12:12–19	22 Mar	3:15*	6 Apr	5:12–21	5 Nov
12:20–46	12 Sep	4:1–31	2 Sep	5:20*	4 Mar
12:37–41*	10 Jun	5:19–20*	8 Jul	6:1–11	2 Apr
12:47–13:20	11 May	7:1–5	26 Feb	6:4*	29 Mar
13:23–26*	7 Jan	7:17–38	24 Jun	6:12–17	4 Apr
14:1–6	25 Mar	8:4–5,35*	16 Sep	6:16–23	9 May
14:15*	30 Sep	9:10*	26 Apr	6:23*	1 Nov
14:17*	10 Mar	9:11*	9 Nov	7:9–25	1 Nov
14:24–26*	24 May	10:1–33	8 Jul	8:1*	29 Aug
15:1–8	22 Sep	10:34–48	10 Mar	8:7*	16 Aug
15:7*	8 Jan	12:1–24	10 Jan	8:9–13	21 Apr
15:9*	30 Nov	13:26–41	6 Apr	8:14–23	19 Jul
15:9–17	8 May	13:46–48*	23 Sep	8:22–27	11 Nov
15:18–27	17 Jun	17:1–12	18 May	8:28–34	14 May
16:1–15	2 Feb	17:22–31	16 Nov	8:35–39	30 Nov
16:33*	31 Mar	17:27*	17 Jul	9:30–33*	1 May
17:6–24	8 Aug	18:1–17	26 Jun	10:1–3*	18 Feb
17:11–12*	31 Dec	18:27*	23 Mar	10:1–17	31 May
17:17*	7 Mar	20:21*	3 Mar	10:9*	25 Apr
17:18*	11 May	22:1–16	26 Apr	10:11*	18 May
17:24*	21 Mar	25:18–19*	1 Apr	11:13–27	14 Nov
18:26*	8 Aug	27:13–44	27 Feb	12:1–8	29 Jun
19:1–16	5 Mar	28:23*	26 Jun	13:14*	23 Feb
19:31–37*	3 Apr			15:30–33*	21 Feb

Scripture Index

16:17–20	17 Jan	3:20*	25 Feb	**Colossians**	
		3:23–29	23 Feb	1:21–29	2 Aug
1 Corinthians		4:1–7	17 Mar	2:8–19	28 Oct
1:18–2:2	13 Sep	5:13–26	29 Aug	2:13*	5 Nov
2:6–16	24 May	6:1–10	22 Jul	2:20–3:4	3 Feb
2:12*	14 May	6:14*	13 Sep	3:12–17	22 Jan
3:10–17	7 Jul			3:13*	17 May
7:10–16	19 May	**Ephesians**		3:18–4:1	28 Jan
11:23–32	5 Dec	1:1–23	12 May		
12:1–11	5 Sep	1:7*	13 Jan	**1 Thessalonians**	
14:33–40	5 May	1:12–13*	21 Aug	1:1–10	18 Jul
15:1–11	15 Mar	2:1–7	15 Jan	1:8*	24 Mar
15:12–24	1 Apr	2:11–22	16 Sep	2:1–8	12 Mar
15:42–57	19 Nov	3:14–21	13 Jun	2:13–14*	26 Mar
		4:1–6	17 May	2:17–3:10	21 May
2 Corinthians		4:7–13	27 Apr	4:1–12	7 Mar
2:14–17	24 Aug	4:17–24	12 Feb	5:1–11	3 Aug
3:5–6*	24 Aug	5:1–16	2 Oct	5:16*	4 Dec
3:7–18	4 May	5:18*	26 May	5:23–28	22 Aug
4:1–6	27 Aug	5:21–33	21 Jul		
4:4*	12 Mar	6:10–20	12 Jul	**2 Thessalonians**	
5:16–21	27 May	6:17*	19 Apr	1:1–4	13 May
5:20–21*	18 Jul			1:3*	24 Nov
6:14–7:1	10 Dec	**Philippians**		2:13–3:5	17 Apr
7:2–16	19 Feb	1:3–7*	13 Jul	3:5*	31 Jan
11:1–15	16 Feb	1:19–26	23 Aug	3:6–13	27 Jan
12:1–10	11 Sep	2:19–24	18 Oct		
12:10*	25 Nov	3:7–11	5 Aug	**1 Timothy**	
12:14–21	5 Apr	3:10*	21 Apr	2:1–6	25 Feb
13:5–14	28 Nov	3:12–4:1	13 Jul	3:14–16	26 Aug
		3:20–21*	17 Apr	4:6–16	19 Jan
Galatians		4:1*	17 Apr	6:6–10	12 Nov
1:11*	29 Apr	4:4–9	7 Oct	6:12,19*	4 Feb
2:15–3:14	18 Feb	4:10–20	24 Feb		
3:10–14*	27 May				

391

Scripture Index

2 Timothy
1:8–14　　　　5 Oct
1:12–14*　　 13 Aug
2:1–10　　　　1 Jul
2:9*　　　　　7 Apr
2:19*　　　　 9 Aug
2:20–26　　　20 Sep
3:1–17　　　　22 Feb
3:5*　　　　　2 Jun
3:15*　　　　 18 Oct
4:1–8　　　　 5 Feb
4:9–18　　　　8 Mar

Titus
1:1–14　　　　12 Aug
1:15–2:10　　 13 Dec
2:11–14*　　　4 Apr
2:11–3:7　　　13 Jan
3:3–8*　　　　3 Sep

Philemon
8–20　　　　　15 Sep

Hebrews
1:1–14　　　　30 Mar
2:1–4　　　　 12 Oct
2:5–13　　　　21 Mar
2:14–18　　　 9 Sep
2:18*　　　　 9 Dec
3:7–19　　　　9 Jun
3:13*　　　　 16 Feb
4:2*　　　　　9 Jun
4:3*　　　　　16 Jun
4:12*　　　　 3 Jun
4:14–5:4　　　8 Dec
4:15*
5:7–10*
5:11–6:12
6:13–20
7:4*
7:23–25*
7:23–8:12
9:11–22
9:12*
9:13–14*
9:23–28
9:26–28*
10:1–18
10:5–7*
10:19–20*
10:19–39
10:23*
11:1–6
11:6*
11:7*
11:8*
11:8–22
11:24–26*
12:1–2*
12:3–11
12:12–25
12:24–25*
12:24–25*
12:25–29
13:5*
13:5–15
13:15*

James
1:1–17

8 Jun
31 Oct
21 Jun
20 Mar
1 Feb
22 Aug
6 Jul
28 Feb
17 Mar
21 Jun
3 Oct
15 Mar
12 Jun
30 Apr
25 Mar
15 May
13 Dec
17 Feb
18 Aug
1 Jun
20 Aug
23 May
24 Jun
5 Aug
28 Jul
19 Aug
28 Feb
29 Feb
21 Dec
12 Nov
11 Mar
14 Oct

12 Dec

1:12*　　　　 30 Jul
1:16–25　　　 26 Mar
1:21–22*　　 28 Jun
1:23–25*　　　5 Jul
2:1–9　　　　 29 Apr
2:23*　　　　 8 May
3:1–13　　　　15 Feb
4:6–5:6　　　 31 Aug
5:7–11　　　　31 Jan
5:11*　　　　 14 Jun

1 Peter
1:3–9　　　　 4 Dec
1:7*　　　　　12 Dec
1:10–17　　　 22 Jun
1:13*　　　　 11 Jul
1:18–2:8　　　21 Aug
2:3*　　　　　15 Oct
2:5–10　　　　14 Oct
2:7*　　　　　30 Mar
2:11–17　　　 9 Jan
2:18–25　　　 26 Nov
3:9–17　　　　17 Sep
3:18–4:2　　　29 Mar
3:22*　　　　 7 Nov
4:1–16　　　　28 Aug

2 Peter
1:1–15　　　　11 Jun
2:1–3　　　　 18 Jan
2:4*　　　　　15 Dec
3:1–10　　　　16 Mar
3:11–18　　　 18 Aug
3:15*　　　　 22 Oct

Scripture Index

1 John		2 John		5:1–14	16 Oct
1:1–5	12 Apr	1–11	3 Nov	5:6–7*	9 Jul
1:5–10	19 Dec			7:1–17	9 Apr
1:6–7*	2 Oct	3 John		7:16–17*	3 Feb
2:1–17	20 Apr			12:1–12	23 Dec
2:28*	22 Sep	Jude		12:11*	9 Sep
3:1*	19 Jul	1–7,20–23	15 Dec	14:1–12	9 Jul
3:1–20	9 Aug	8–19	2 Jun	16:9*	25 Aug
3:21*	28 Nov	24–25	31 Dec	19:6–9	6 May
4:1–6	18 Mar			19:7–8*	21 Jul
4:7–12	11 Jan	Revelation		20:11–15	4 Jul
4:19–5:3	30 Sep	1:7*	28 Dec	21:1–8	19 Oct
5:6–12	10 Aug	1:16*	7 Aug	21:5*	1 Jan
5:13*	13 May	2:4–5*	21 Oct	22:1–15	23 Jul
5:13–15	23 Jan	2:12–13*	5 Feb	22:16–21	30 Jun
		3:1–6	13 Mar		

Where Spurgeon Preached

1. Location of numbers (in order of appearance)

The Metropolitan Tabernacle, Newington (364)

1816, 1818, 1820, 1835–6, 1838–50, 1852–63, 1865–70, 1873–1940, 1942, 1944–99, 2001–60, 2062–4, 2067–70, 2072–2184, 2186–2208

The Mansion House (Egyptian Hall) (1)

1864 (Monday 28/9/1885—see 20/11)

Unplaced (at an assembly of ministers) (1)

2185 (Friday 25/4/1890—see 29/4)

2. Time of numbers

The time of most sermons is given on the title page; that of the undated sermons is in most cases indicated by internal references. Most of the sermons were preached on **the Lord's Day in the morning**; the exceptions are as follows:—**Sunday evening (30)**—1850, 1870, 1874, 1876, 1878, 1881, 1889, 1930, 1934, 1936, 1938–9, 1991, 1997, 2038, 2051, 2059–60, 2068, 2081, 2111, 2122, 2126, 2138, 2152, 2171, 2175, 2178, 2180, 2188

Monday afternoon (1)—1864

Thursday evening (43)—1816, 1861, 1877, 1880, 1916, 1932–3, 1935, 1940, 1944, 1953, 1979, 1993–4, 1998, 2005, 2010, 2035, 2049–50, 2053–4, 2056–8, 2062, 2064, 2067, 2082, 2085, 2106, 2118–21, 2164, 2172, 2174, 2177, 2181, 2184, 2195, 2206

Undated evenings, probably Sunday or Thursday (28)—1882, 1897, 1899, 1906, 1921, 1929, 1937, 1969, 1974, 1989, 1996, 1999, 2021, 2026, 2028, 2052, 2063, 2114, 2116, 2123–4, 2131, 2176, 2179, 2182–3, 2186, 2199

Undated & untimed (probably Sunday or Thursday evenings) (22)—1820, 1879, 1883–4, 1900, 1908, 1942, 1948, 1957, 1984, 1995, 2001, 2017, 2025, 2027, 2055, 2069–70, 2125, 2127, 2187, 2207

Friday morning (1)—2185

3. Sermons preached on behalf of societies etc.

London Hospitals—1845 (14/6/1885), [1907 (27/6/1886), 1968 (19/6/1887), 2091 (23/6/1889), 2148 (8/6/1890)]

London Banks' Christian Union—1864 (28/9/1885—see 20/11)

British & Foreign Sailors' Society—**2206** (7/5/1891)

4. Dating of undated sermons

1997: A footnote to **2492**, preached on 7 November 1886, indicates that **1997** (dated Autumn 1886) was the sermon mentioned as having been preached in the evening two weeks previously, thus dating it to Sunday evening 24 October 1886.

2021: This undated evening sermon is identified in a footnote to the exposition attached to **2375**, preached on 24 June 1888, as another sermon on Nathanael preached 'a short time ago'. It was published about the end of April 1888 and probably relates to one of the unrepresented dates in that month.

2177: This undated sermon, published after the death of William Olney in October 1890, is said to have been preached on a Thursday evening before Spurgeon left for his winter's rest. Internal references indicate that William Olney was present and that Spurgeon had known the congregation for 36 years. He first preached at New Park Street Chapel in December 1853 and the various factors would seem to date **2177** to Thursday 21 November 1889 just before his winter holiday at Mentone. A letter attached to **2117** and dated Mentone, Nov. 28 1889 announced his safe arrival. However, G.H. Pike, *The life and work of Charles Haddon Spurgeon*, vol. 6 p. 312 states 'On November 17 he preached for the last time before going to his winter retreat'.

N.B. One sermon is incorrectly dated— **2010**, said to have been preached on 17 May 1887, which would have been a Tuesday, not a Thursday as stated. It may have been on 17 March 1887.

5. Details of omitted short sermons

1941 (To a few friends at Mentone, at the breaking of bread, on Lord's Day afternoon, 2 January 1887)—'Grace for communion' (Song of Solomon 4:16)

1943 (To a few friends at Mentone, at the breaking of bread, on Lord's Day afternoon, 9 January 1887)—'Love joying in love' (Song of Solomon 5:1)

6. Contents of volumes used in this compilation

Vol. 31 nos. 1816, 1818, 1820, 1835–1836, 1838–1850, 1852–1870, 1873–1876

Vol. 32 nos. 1877–1937

Where Spurgeon Preached

Vol. 33 nos. 1938–1940, 1942, 1944–1999

Vol. 34 nos. 2001–2060

Vol. 35 nos. 2062–2064, 2067–2070, 2072–2120

Vol. 36 nos. 2121–2181

Vol. 37 nos. 2182–2208

Analysis of sermons

New Park Street and Metropolitan Tabernacle Pulpit

1. LOCATION OF SPURGEON'S SERMONS (omitting written numbers)

(a) Main London locations

Newington—The Metropolitan Tabernacle (3033 sermons)
369, 373–5, 379, 382–4, 391–454, 456–536, 538–568, 570–7, 579–623, 625–58, 661–80, 682–97, 699–714, 716–41, 747–55, 757, 759–66, 769–810, 812–40, 842–1357, 1359–1508, 1510–7, 1519–32, 1534–95, 1597–1696, 1698–1733, 1738–9, 1741–9, 1751–3, 1755–6, 1758–61, 1763–77, 1779–84, 1786–91, 1793–1863, 1865–1940, 1942, 1944–2184, 2186–2208 (last sermon)
2209–2391, 2393–2442, 2444–2553, 2555–7, 2559–61, 2564–6, 2568–71, 2573–5, 2577–80, 2582–4, 2586–8, 2590–3, 2595–6, 2600–1, 2603–6, 2608–10, 2612–4, 2617–20, 2622–4, 2626–8, 2630–3, 2635–8, 2640–1, 2643–6, 2648–50, 2652–5, 2657–9, 2661–3, 2665–7, 2669–72, 2674–6, 2678–80, 2682–5, 2687–9, 2691–4, 2696–9, 2701–2, 2704–6, 2708–10, 2712–4, 2716–9, 2721–3, 2725–7, 2729–32, 2734–6, 2738–40, 2742–5, 2747–9, 2751–3, 2755–8, 2760–2, 2764–5, 2767–71, 2773–5, 2777–9, 2781–4, 2786–8, 2790–3, 2795–7, 2799–2801, 2803–6, 2808–10, 2812–4, 2816–35, 2837–74, 2876–95, 2897–3005, 3007–32, 3034–5, 3037–41, 3043–7, 3049–53, 3055–9, 3061–5, 3067–76, 3078–80, 3082–6, 3088–92, 3094, 3096–9, 3101–4, 3106–7, 3109–13, 3115–9, 3121, 3123–5, 3127–32, 3134–8, 3140–74, 3176–96, 3198–3241, 3243–54, 3256–66, 3268–94, 3296–3318, 3320–44, 3346–9, 3351–60, 3362–9, 3371–3563 (final issue)

Southwark—New Park Street Chapel (181 sermons)
1–6, 10, 28–38, 41–83, 86–7, 89, 91, 93, 95, 97, 99–101, 103, 117, 121, 125, 147, 157, 174, 178, 180, 217, 220, 226, 232, 239, 244, 254, 262, 282, 284, 310, 319–25, 337, 362, 364
2392, 2443, 2554, 2558, 2562–3, 2567, 2572, 2576, 2581, 2585, 2589, 2594, 2602, 2607, 2611, 2615–6, 2621, 2629, 2634, 2639, 2642, 2647, 2651, 2656, 2660, 2664, 2668, 2673, 2677, 2681, 2686, 2690, 2695, 2700, 2703, 2707, 2711, 2715, 2720, 2724, 2728, 2733, 2737, 2741, 2746, 2750, 2754, 2759, 2763, 2766, 2772, 2776, 2780, 2785, 2789, 2794, 2798, 2802, 2807, 2811, 2815, 2875, 2896,

397

Analysis of sermons

2908, 2915, 3036, 3042, 3048, 3054, 3060, 3066, 3077, 3081, 3087, 3093, 3100, 3105, 3108, 3114, 3120, 3126, 3242

Strand—Exeter Hall (103 sermons)
7–9, 11–27, 84–5, 88, 90, 92, 96, 98, 102, 108, 219, 221, 290–309, 311, 313, 315–8, 326–30, 333–6, 338–41, 343–61, 363, 365–8, 1596, 1734–7, 1740, 1750, 1754, 1762, 1778, 1792

Walworth—Surrey Gardens Music Hall (156 sermons)
104–7, 109–16, 118–20, 122–4, 126–46, 148–53, 156, 158–73, 175–7, 179, 181–91, 193–7, 200–16, 218, 222–5, 227–31, 233–8, 240–3, 245–53, 255–61, 263–7, 271–81, 283, 285–9

(b) Other locations

Amersham—Baptist Chapel (1 sermon)
2836

Bayswater—Cornwall Road Chapel (4 sermons)
537, 578, 660, 698

Bayswater—Westbourne Grove Chapel (1 sermon)
681

Bishopsgate St.—Friends' Meeting House (1 sermon)
3095

Blackfriars Road—Baptist Chapel, Church St. (1 sermon)
3139

Blackfriars Road—Surrey Chapel (5 sermons)
312, 455, 756, 767–8

Bloomsbury Chapel (2 sermons)
192, 841

Analysis of sermons

Bow—East London Tabernacle (1 sermon)
3361

Bromley—Baptist Chapel (1 sermon)
3006

Camden Road Chapel (1 sermon)
758

Epsom—The Grand Stand, Epsom Race Course (2 sermons)
198–9

Hackney—A Field, King Edward's Road (1 sermon)
39–40 (double number)

Islington—The Agricultural Hall (5 sermons)
742–6

Islington—Union Chapel (1 sermon)
1785

Kingsland—Maberley Chapel (1 sermon)
94

Lambeth—Upton Chapel (4 sermons)
569, 624, 3122, 3197

Mansion House—The Egyptian Hall (1 sermon)
1864

Mentone, Southern France (10 sermons)
1518, 1757, 1941, 1943, 3175, 3255, 3267, 3295, 3319, 3345

Mildmay Park (1 sermon)
3370

Analysis of sermons

Moorfields—The Tabernacle (1 sermon)
314

Notting Hill—The Free Tabernacle (1 sermon)
715

Shoreditch Tabernacle (1 sermon)
1533

Shouldham Street Chapel (1 sermon)
2625

Southwark—Maze Pond Chapel (1 sermon)
3033

Southwark—Unicorn Yard Chapel (1 sermon)
3133

Stoke Newington—Devonshire Square Chapel (1 sermon)
3350

Sydenham—The Crystal Palace (1 sermon)
154–5 (double number)

Tottenham Court Road Chapel (1 sermon)
342

Tottenham Court Road—Whitefield's Tabernacle (1 sermon)
2598

Upper Tooting—Trinity Road Chapel (1 sermon)
1697

Westminster Bridge Road—Christ Church (3 sermons)
1358, 2597, 2599

# Analysis of sermons

Westminster Chapel (1 sermon)
811

No location given (3 sermons)
659, 1634(b), 2185

2. SERMONS PREACHED ON BEHALF OF SOCIETIES

Aged Pilgrim's Friend Society, The (1 sermon)
99

Baptist British and Irish Missionary Society, The (1 sermon)
929

Baptist Fund for the Relief of Poor Ministers, The (1 sermon)
65

Baptist Irish Society, The (1 sermon)
629

Baptist Missionary Society, The (7 sermons)
76, 190, 383, 1471, 1596, 1655, 1778

Baptist Young Men's Missionary Association, The (3 sermons)
806, 876, 977

British and Foreign Bible Society, The (1 sermon)
3303

British and Foreign Sailors' Society, The (3 sermons)
2206, 3291, 3321

British Society for the Propagation of the Gospel amongst the Jews, The (2 sermons)
582, 3243

Analysis of sermons

Centenary of Sabbath Schools, The (1 sermon)
1545

Christian Blind Relief Society, The (1 sermon)
3139

Gospel Ministers' Relief Society, The (1 sermon)
3133

London Banks' Prayer Union, The (1 sermon)
1864

London Hospitals (14 sermons)
(see below)

London Missionary Society, The (3 sermons)
314, 811, 1358

Luther commemorations (2 sermons)
1749, 1750

Metropolitan Benefit Societies' Asylum, The (1 sermon)
94

Mildmay Park Conference, The (1 sermon)
3370

Pastors' College Conferences (4 sermons)
2213, 2879, 3211, 3350

Prayer Meeting for Sabbath Schools (1 sermon)
3237(b)

Religious Tract Society, The (2 sermons)
312, 1233

Analysis of sermons

Sunday School Union, The (3 sermons)
192, 1383, 1785

Note: Sermons preached by Spurgeon at annual meetings of **The Baptist Union of Great Britain and Ireland** are not represented in *The Metropolitan Tabernacle Pulpit.* For his engagements in other parts of the country he regularly re-used the texts and subject-matter upon which he had been recently preaching in his London ministry. According to W. Y. Fullerton (*The Sword and the Trowel,* June 1898, p.292) the sermon on 1 Corinthians 1:23, delivered to The Baptist Union in Leeds on 9 October 1878, was a repeat of a sermon preached to his college students on 4 October 1878. That this was often the case in respect of gatherings of **The Baptist Union** would appear to be indicated by the following instances when he preached on the same text:

Date	Sermon	Text	Same text at Baptist Union	
BM* 1866	no. 3147	Psalm 102:16	Bradford	12/10/1865
7/10/1866	no. 716	Ephesians 5:14	Liverpool	17?/10/1866
18/9/1870	no. 952	Acts 10:36	Cambridge	19+/9/1870
5/10/1879	no. 1498	Numbers 14:11	Glasgow	8/10/1879
23/10/1881	no. 1625	John 15:5	Portsmouth	26/10/1881
1/10/1882	no. 1682	James 4:2–3	Liverpool	6/10/1882

The last of these was Spurgeon's final address to The Baptist Union.
* = *The Baptist Messenger*

3. DATES OF REGULAR SPECIAL SUNDAY SERVICES 1876–1890
a.m. = **Hospital Sunday** (collection taken on behalf of **London Hospitals**)
p.m. = seats vacated by members (building opened to 'strangers')

	a.m.	p.m.
1876	18 Jun: 1300	16 Jul: 1315
		22 Oct: 1322
1877		13 May: 1355
	17 Jun: 1360	19 Aug: 1389
		11 Nov: 2856
1878		12 May: 1414
	30 Jun: 1422	11 Aug: 1466

Analysis of sermons

1879	15 Jun: 1479	10 Aug: 1489
1880		09 May: 2000
	13 Jun: 1542	
1881	Unknown	12 Jun: 1691
		11 Sep: 1620
1882	11 Jun: 1664	11 Jun: 1717
1883		11 Mar: 2575
	10 Jun: 1725	10 Jun: 1746
1884	15 Jun: 1786	
1885	14 Jun: 1845	
1886	27 Jun: 1907	
1887	19 Jun: 1968	
1888	Unknown (Spurgeon sick for 1st half of June)	
1889	23 Jun: 2091	
1890	08 Jun: 2148	

Undated p.m. Seats vacated—1579 (pub. in **1881**)
Undated/untimed **Hospital Sunday**?—1995 (pub. in **1887**)

4. ANNUAL ANAYLSIS OF NUMBERED SERMONS

(a) New Park Street period

Year	Sun a.m.	p.m.	Mon	Tue	Wed	Thu	Fri	???	Error	TOTAL
1854	5	1	–	–	–	–	–	2	–	8
1855	46	12	2	2	1	2	–	–	–	65
1856	43	17	1	1	–	3	–	1	–	66
1857	51	13	–	1	2	2	–	2	–	71
1858	49	8	–	1	1	7	2	–	–	68
1858–9	–	–	–	–	–	1	–	–	–	1
1859	51	8	–	–	–	10	–	–	–	69
1859–60	–	1	–	–	–	–	–	–	–	1
1860	46	14	–	–	1	2	–	–	–	63
1860–1	–	2	–	–	–	–	–	–	–	2
1861	11	5	–	–	–	–	–	–	–	16
Unknown	3	1	–	–	–	–	–	8	–	12
TOTALS	**305**	**82**	**3**	**5**	**5**	**27**	**2**	**13**	**–**	**442**

Analysis of sermons

(b) Metropolitan Tabernacle period

Year	Sun a.m.	p.m.	Mon	Tue	Wed	Thu	Fri	???	Error	TOTAL
1861	36	11	1	–	–	2	2	–	1	53
1861–2	–	5	–	–	–	1	–	–	–	6
1862	51	18	–	–	1	1	–	4	–	75
1863	49	19	–	1	–	4	–	10	–	83
1864	47	12	–	1	–	5	–	9	1	75
1865	45	9	–	–	1	1	–	4	–	60
1866	48	29	–	2	–	22	–	2	–	103
1867	43	13	–	1	–	18	–	–	–	75
1868	48	17	–	–	1	13	–	–	3	82
1868–9	–	–	–	–	–	–	–	1	–	1
1869	44	12	–	1	–	12	–	1	1	71
1870	49	26	–	–	–	15	–	–	1	91
1871	37	17	–	–	–	5	–	4	1	64
1872	44	18	–	–	–	15	–	1	–	78
1873	48	26	–	–	–	15	–	4	–	93
1874	44	24	–	–	–	15	–	1	–	84
1875	34	29	–	–	–	17	–	1	–	81
1876	45	39	–	–	–	23	1	–	–	108
1877	40	29	–	1	1	12	1	1	–	85
1878	33	20	–	–	–	9	–	–	1	63
1879	31	24	–	–	–	10	–	1	–	66
1880	36	23	–	1	–	11	–	5	–	76
1881	38	25	–	–	1	21	–	1	–	86
1882	41	39	–	–	–	23	–	1	–	104
1883	42	36	–	–	–	30	–	–	–	108
1884	38	30	–	–	2	24	–	4	1	99
1885	33	27	1	–	–	18	–	–	–	79
1886	37	29	–	–	–	22	–	–	–	88
1887	39	34	1	–	–	25	–	–	1	100
1888	37	31	–	–	–	26	–	1	–	95
1889	39	33	–	–	–	26	–	–	1	99
1890	40	32	–	–	1	28	1	–	–	102
1891	16	12	–	–	–	10	1	–	–	39

Analysis of sermons

Unknown	1	6	–	–	–	18	–	497	–	522
Written	–	–	–	–	–	–	–	10	–	10
TOTALS	**1253**	**754**	**3**	**8**	**8**	**497**	**6**	**563**	**12**	**3104**
BOTH	**1558**	**836**	**6**	**13**	**13**	**524**	**8**	**576**	**12**	**3546**

N.B. The *New Park Street* and *Metropolitan Tabernacle Pulpits* consist of 3563 weekly numbers, but the total number of Spurgeon's sermons contained within them is only 3546 for the following reasons:—

(a) *The New Park Street Pulpit* includes 9 long sermons which take up double numbers plus 5 numbers reporting special meetings.

(b) *The Metropolitan Tabernacle Pulpit* includes 14 numbers containing reports of special meetings and sermons by other preachers marking the opening of the Metropolitan Tabernacle in 1861. However, there are also 11 numbers containing two sermons, 9 of which each include a short sermon written during Spurgeon's long absence at the start of 1879.

1. CHRISTMAS

1854	24 Dec	2392	The birth of Christ (Isaiah 7:14–15)
		2915	A visit to Bethlehem (Luke 2:15)
1855	23 Dec	57	The incarnation and birth of Christ (Micah 5:2)
1856	21 Dec	109	Going home—a Christmas sermon (Mark 5:19)
1857	20 Dec	168	The first Christmas carol (Luke 2:14)
1859	25 Dec	291	A Christmas question (Isaiah 9:6)
1860	23 Dec	352	A merry Christmas (Job 1:4–5)
1861	22 Dec	430	The two advents of Christ (Hebrews 9:27–28)
1862	21 Dec	485	No room for Christ in the inn (Luke 2:7)
1863	20 Dec	545	The holy child, Jesus (Acts 4:30)
1864	25 Dec	606	Mary's song (Luke 1:46–47)
1865	24 Dec	666	Holy work for Christmas (Luke 2:17–20)
1866	23 Dec	727	God incarnate, the end of fear (Luke 2:10)
1867	22 Dec	786	The great mystery of godliness (1 Timothy 3:16)
1868	20 Dec	846	Good cheer for Christmas (Isaiah 25:6)
1869	26 Dec	907	Christ—the fall and rise of many (Luke 2:34)
1870	25 Dec	967	The sages, the star, and the Saviour (Matthew 2:2)
1871	24 Dec	1026	Joy born at Bethlehem (Luke 2:10–12)
1872	19 Dec	1086	Jesus, the king of truth (John 18:37)
	22 Dec	1087	The hexapla of mystery (1 Timothy 3:16)
1875	26 Dec	1270	'God with us' (Matthew 1:23)
1876	24 Dec	1330	The great birthday (Luke 2:10)
1881	25 Dec	2340	The best Christmas fare (Psalm 119:103)
1882	24 Dec	1698	The star and the wise men (Matthew 2:1–2,9–10)
1884	21 Dec	1815	The great birthday and our coming of age (Galatians 4:3–6)

2. END & START OF YEAR (* = motto text provided by 'a venerable clergyman of the Church of England')

1855	7 Jan	1	The immutability of God (Malachi 3:6)
	30 Dec	58	Canaan on Earth (Deuteronomy 11:10–12)
		2602	Good news for the aged (Matthew 20:6)
	31 Dec	59	Watch-night service (Lamentations 2:19)
1856	28 Dec	110	Heavenly worship (Revelation 14:1–3)
1857	27 Dec	169	What have I done? (Jeremiah 8:6)

Spurgeon's seasonal sermons

1858	3 Jan	170	The immutability of Christ (Hebrews 13:8)
		2660	Suffering without the camp (Hebrews 13:12)
	26 Dec	230	The vanguard and rearguard of the church (Isaiah 52:12)
1859	2 Jan	231	Faith in perfection (Psalm 138:8*)
1860	1 Jan	292	A New Year's benediction (1 Peter 5:10*)
1861	6 Jan	354	A sermon for the week of prayer (Colossians 4:2*)
1862	5 Jan	427	A Psalm for the New Year (2 Peter 3:18)
	28 Dec	486	The sinner's end (Psalm 73:17–18)
		496	The new song (Psalm 98:1)
1863	1 Jan	3283	The voices of our days (Job 32:7)
	4 Jan	487	A tempted Saviour—our best succour (Hebrews 2:18*)
	27 Dec	546	Alpha and Omega (Revelation 22:13)
	31 Dec	—	To-day (Hebrews 3:7) [In *The Sword and the Trowel* Jan 1911]
1864	3 Jan	547	Suffering and reigning with Jesus (2 Timothy 2:12*)
	25 Dec	3072	An observation of the preacher (Ecclesiastes 7:8)
	27 Dec?	2497	A new leaf for the New Year (Genesis 42:21)
1865	1 Jan	607	True unity promoted (Ephesians 4:3*)
		3073	Thrice happy day! (Haggai 2:19)
	31 Dec	667	Last things (Proverbs 5:11)
1866	7 Jan	668	Unity in Christ (John 17:20–21*)
1867	6 Jan	728	Good cheer for the New Year (Deuteronomy 11:12)
	26 Dec	3371	Two choice benedictions (Numbers 6:23–27; 2 Corinthians 13:14)
	29 Dec	787	A song, a solace, a sermon and a summons (Psalm 136)
1868	5 Jan	788	Creation's groans and the saint's sighs (Romans 8:22–23*)
		3275	A kind of firstfruits (James 1:18)
	27 Dec	847	Joyful transformations (Isaiah 42:16)
		857	Timely reflections (Romans 13:11)
	31 Dec OR	3323	The believer's glad prospects (Song of Solomon 2:17)
1869	3 Jan		
		848	Jesus Christ immutable (Hebrews 13:8*)
	26 Dec	2445	The last sermon for the year (Luke 16:2)

Spurgeon's seasonal sermons

1870	2 Jan	908	Assured security in Christ (2 Timothy 1:12)
1871	1 Jan	968	Life in Christ (John 14:19*)
		2342	A New Year's retrospect and prospect (Psalm 10:17)
1872	4 Jan	3545	Our glorious leader (Luke 19:28)
1873	5 Jan	3130	'In remembrance' (1 Corinthians 11:24–25)
	28 Dec	3230	The last message for the year (John 6:37)
1874	1 Jan	3231	A New Year's wish (Philippians 4:19)
	4 Jan	3127	A promise and precedent (John 16:14)
	27 Dec	1209	A grateful summary of twenty volumes (Ephesians 3:8)
		1217	Rightly dividing the word of truth (2 Timothy 2:15)
1875	3 Jan	1215	Solemn pleadings for revival (Isaiah 41:1)
		2935	Christ's joy and ours (John 15:11)
1876	31 Dec	1331	The two comes (Revelation 22:17)
		2863	Great forgiveness for great sin (Ephesians 1:7)
1877	30 Dec	1391	A golden prayer (John 12:28)
1878	6 Jan	1392	A catechism for the proud (1 Corinthians 4:7)
1879	'Jan'	1451	This year also (Luke 13:8) [From the sick-chamber]
1882	1 Jan	1637	The beginning of months (Exodus 12:1–2)
		2617	Shining Christians (Isaiah 60:1)
	31 Dec	1699	Supposing him to be the gardener (John 20:15)
1883	16 Dec	1757	The New Year's guest (Matthew 25:35; John 1:12)
1884	28 Dec	2549	Luminous words (1 Peter 4:1–3)
1885	1 Jan	1816	Sermon for New Year's Day (Revelation 21:5)
????	????	2289	The right key-note for the New Year (Psalm 115:18)

3. PALM SUNDAY

1891	22 Mar	2196	Hosanna! (Matthew 21:9)

4. GOOD FRIDAY

1861	29 Mar	373	Christ set forth as a propitiation (Romans 3:24–25)
		374	The interest of Christ and his people in each other (Song of Solomon 2:16)

5. EASTER SUNDAY

1855	8 Apr	18	The tomb of Jesus (Matthew 28:6)

Spurgeon's seasonal sermons

1857	12 Apr	127	Spiritual resurrection (Ephesians 2:1)
1862	20 Apr	445	Resurrection—Christ the first fruits (1 Corinthians 15:20)
1863	5 Apr	503	Death and life in Christ (Romans 6:8–11)
1865	16 Apr	625	Jesus appearing to Mary Magdalene (Mark 16:9)
1868	12 Apr	805	Resurrection with Christ (Ephesians 2:4–5)
1869	28 Mar	863	The stone rolled away (Matthew 28:2)
1870	17 Apr	3224	'Repentance and remission' (Luke 24:47)
1873	13 Apr	1106	'The Lord is risen indeed' (Luke 24:5–6)
1880	28 Mar	1530	Following the risen Christ (Colossians 3:1–2)
		2712	Bonds which could not hold (Acts 2:24)
1882	9 Apr	1653	The resurrection of our Lord Jesus (2 Timothy 2:8)
1884	13 Apr	1775	'My Lord and my God' (John 20:28)
1886	25 Apr	1898	Mouth and heart (Romans 10:9)
1887	10 Apr	1958	The first appearance of the risen Lord to the eleven (Luke 24:36–44)
		2408	Christ the cure for troubled hearts (Luke 24:38)
1888	1 Apr	2016	Jesus affirmed to be alive (Acts 25:18–19)
1889	21 Apr	2080	The power of his resurrection (Philippians 3:10)
1890	6 Apr	2139	The Prince of life (Acts 3:15)
1891	29 Mar	2197	Christ's resurrection and our newness of life (Romans 6:4)

6. THE CENSUS

| 1861 | 14 Apr | 382 | The last census (Psalm 87:6) |
| 1891 | 5 Apr | 2198 | The census of Israel (Numbers 26:63–65) |

7. ASCENSION DAY—[No known instances]

8. WHIT SUNDAY—PENTECOST

1863	24 May	511	Pentecost (Acts 2:1–4)
1867	9 Jun	754	The saint and the Spirit (John 14:17)
1882	28 May	1662	The indwelling and outflowing of the Holy Spirit (John 7:38–39; 16:7)
1884	1 Jun	1783	Pentecost (Acts 2:1)
1885	24 May	1842	The private tutor (John 14:24–26)

| 1886 | 13 Jun | 1904 | The personal Pentecost and the glorious hope (Romans 5:5) |

9. HARVEST-TIME

1854	20 Aug	2896	Harvest time (1 Samuel 12:17)
1855	9 Sep	43	The death of the Christian (Job 5:26)
1856	????	2585	Spiritual gleaning (Ruth 2:15) [In the Autumn]
1858	25 Jul	206	Everybody's sermon (Hosea 12:10)
1862	10 Aug	464	A sermon for gleaners (Ruth 2:15–16)
	24 Aug	466	The loaded wagon (Amos 2:13)
1863	2 Aug	522	Mealtime in the cornfields (Ruth 2:14)
	27 Sep	532	Thanksgiving and prayer (Psalm 65:11)
1865	30 Jul	642	Withholding corn (Proverbs 11:26)
	????	3058	The joy of harvest (Isaiah 9:3)
1866	29 Jul	706	Fields white for harvest (John 4:35)
1867	23 Jun	757	In the hayfield (Psalm 104:14)
1868	16 Aug	825	The sieve (Amos 9:9)
1869	11 Jul	880	The former and the latter rain (Jeremiah 5:24)
1870	14 Aug	945	Ripe fruit (Micah 7:1)
1872	18 Aug	1066	A call to revival (Song of Solomon 7:11–13)
1873	17 Aug	1127	Harvest men wanted (Matthew 9:37–10:1)
1874	16 Aug	3109	Sowing and reaping (Galatians 6:7)
1876	17 Sep	2910	The harvest and the vintage (Revelation 14:14–20)
1881	25 Aug	1626	The principal wheat (Isaiah 28:25)
1890	6 Jul	2265	Harvest joy (Isaiah 9:3)
????	????	1025	A visit to the harvest field (James 5:7–8)
????	????	3315	Joy in harvest (Isaiah 9:3)

Original sources of posthumously published sermons

ORIGINAL SOURCES OF 393 (MOSTLY UNDATED) SERMONS PUBLISHED AFTER SPURGEON'S DEATH (sometimes with new or modified titles):

(a) Previously in *The Pulpit Library* Vols. 1 & 2 **(19 sermons)**
1856: 2875, 2896, 2908, 3108, 3114, 3120, 3133, 3139
1858: 3036, 3042, 3048, 3054, 3060, 3066, 3077, 3081, 3087, 3093, 3100

(b) Previously in *The Baptist Messenger* **(261 sermons)**
1855: 2554, 3105, 3126
1856: 2558, 2562, 2563, 2567, 2572, 2576, 2581, 2585, 2589, 2594, 2602
1857: 2443, 2598, 2607, 2611, 2615, 2616, 2621, 2625, 2629, 2634, 2639, 2642, 2647, 2651
1858: 2656, 2660, 2664, 2668, 2673, 2677, 2681, 2686, 2690, 2695, 2700, 2703, 2707
1859: 2711, 2715, 2720, 2724, 2728, 2733, 2737, 2741, 2746, 2750, 2754
1860: 2759, 2763, 2766, 2772, 2776, 2780, 2785, 2789
1861: 2794, 2798, 2802, 2807, 2811, 2815, 2819, 2823, 2828, 2833, 2841, 2872
1862: 2868, 2880, 2885, 2889, 2894, 2898, 2902, 2911, 2920, 2924, 2929, 2988
1863: 2934, 2938, 2943, 2947, 2952, 2955, 2960, 2963, 2967, 2972, 2974
1864: 2979, 2984, 2992, 2997, 3001, 3005, 3009, 3013, 3018, 3023, 3026
1865: 3030, 3038, 3044, 3050, 3056, 3058, 3062, 3072, 3073, 3079, 3085, 3091
1866: 2444, 3097, 3103, 3110, 3116, 3122, 3131, 3137, 3147, 3151, 3163, 3167
1867: 2450, 3141, 3172, 3179, 3185, 3191, 3197, 3203, 3209, 3215, 3233, 3239
1868: 3245, 3251, 3257, 3263, 3269, 3275, 3281, 3287, 3293, 3299, 3305, 3311
1869: 3317, 3323, 3326, 3338, 3343, 3347, 3352, 3360, 3365, 3368, 3374, 3379
1870: 2448, 3332, 3334, 3385, 3389, 3391, 3395, 3397, 3399, 3404
1871: 3402, 3403, 3406, 3410, 3414, 3418, 3422, 3424, 3426, 3432, 3441, 3445

Original sources of posthumously published sermons

1872: 3408, 3412, 3416, 3420, 3428, 3430, 3433, 3435, 3438, 3440, 3447, 3448
1873: 3450, 3453, 3455, 3457, 3459, 3461, 3462, 3467, 3469, 3470, 3472, 3480
1874: 3474, 3477, 3482, 3485, 3487, 3491, 3494, 3495, 3497, 3500, 3502, 3505
1875: 3508, 3510, 3511, 3514, 3516, 3519, 3520, 3522, 3523, 3524, 3526, 3528
1876: 3529, 3530, 3534, 3537, 3538, 3541, 3542, 3546, 3547, 3552, 3553, 3559
1877: 3532, 3533, 3536, 3543, 3549, 3550, 3555, 3556, 3560, 3561
1878: 3562, 3563
1884: 3446

(c) Previously in *The Sword and the Trowel* **(66 sermons)**
1866: 2970
1867: 2982
1869: 2976, 2999, 3014, 3028
1870: 2990, 2995, 3007, 3021, 3034
1871: 3040, 3046, 3052, 3064, 3070
1872: 3075, 3083, 3089, 3101, 3129
1873: 3107, 3112, 3118, 3124, 3135
1874: 3143, 3149, 3155, 3156
1875: 3161, 3165, 3168
1876: 3174, 3181, 3187, 3193, 3199
1877: 3205, 3211, 3217, 3231, 3237(a), 3237(b)
1878: 3243, 3283
1879: 3249
1880: 3255, 3261, 3267
1881: 3153, 3273
1882: 3279
1883: 3289, 3295, 3301, 3307, 3313, 3319
1884: 3330, 3340
1885: 3345
1887: 3350, 3479

Original sources of posthumously published sermons

1890: 2645
1891: 3175

(d) Previously in books of Sunday and Thursday evening sermons (almost all of the other sermons in these books appeared first in *The Baptist Messenger*)

In *Types and emblems* (2 sermons)
1873: 2913, 3297

In *Trumpet calls to Christian energy* (2 sermons)
1875: 2850, 2854

In *The present truth* (2 sermons)
1883: 2799, 2914

In *Storm signals* (1 sermon)
1885: 2859

(e) Previously in *Spurgeon's Shilling Series*
In *Christ's glorious achievements* (1 sermon)
1877: 3309

In *Seven wonders of grace* (6 sermons)
1877: 3354, 3359, 3363, 3367, 3372, 3377

In *The Mourner's Comforter* (4 sermons)
1878: 3325, 3336, 3341, 3349

In *Be of good cheer* (7 sermons)
1881: 3016, 3020, 3128, 3145, 3153, 3277, 3285

(f) Previously in *Farm Sermons* (7 sermons)
1882: 2977, 3024, 3315, 3381, 3383, 3388, 3393

(g) Previously in *Grace Triumphant* (15 sermons)

Original sources of posthumously published sermons

1904: 3170, 3177, 3183, 3189, 3195, 3201, 3207, 3213, 3219, 3235, 3241, 3247, 3253, 3259, 3265

Other as yet undated sermons published posthumously
2289–2293, 2295–2299, 2861, 3033, 3321, 3328, 3342

Dating of undated sermons (addenda)

(see *365 Days with Spurgeon vol. 5*)

1515: According to T. Hancocks in *The Sword and the Trowel*, February 1900, pp. 75–77, this Thursday evening sermon 'was preached on the night following the medical decision that "Son Tom" could not possibly continue to reside in England, but must return to the sunny Antipodes.' This probably dates it to 18 September 1879.

1583: A description by W. J. Harris in *The Sword and the Trowel*, December 1900, pp.628–9, identifies this sermon on Exodus 33:14 as that preached on the evening of the last Thursday (25th) of September 1879.

2581: Spurgeon had seen the Queen's plate on the morning of the Thursday on which he preached this '1856' sermon, so dated because it appeared in the 1856 *Baptist Messenger*. In **71**, preached on 23 March 1856, he mentioned having seen it at Windsor. By means of a reference in **2651**, preached on Sunday evening 23 September 1855, a visit to Windsor Castle can be dated to the previous Thursday 20 September 1855.

3181: This sermon, which originally appeared in *The Sword and the Trowel*, March 1876, is identified as having been preached on a Thursday evening in January 1876 by Pastor Henry Knee in *The Sword and the Trowel*, August 1900, pp.422–5. The only Thursday in the month for which there is no allocated sermon is 13 January 1876.